Blackstone's Statutes

Criminal Justice & Sentencing

Blackstone's Statutes on
Criminal Justice & Sentencing

....

First Edition

Edited by

Barry Mitchell

Reader in Criminal Justice at the University of Coventry

and

Salim Farrar

Lecturer in Law at the University of Manchester

OXFORD
UNIVERSITY PRESS

OXFORD
UNIVERSITY PRESS

Great Clarendon Street, Oxford OX2 6DP

Oxford University Press is a department of the University of Oxford.
It furthers the University's objective of excellence in research, scholarship,
and education by publishing worldwide in

Oxford New York

Auckland Bangkok Buenos Aires Cape Town Chennai
Dar es Salaam Delhi Hong Kong Istanbul Karachi Kolkata
Kuala Lumpur Madrid Melbourne Mexico City Mumbai Nairobi
São Paulo Shanghai Taipei Tokyo Toronto

Oxford is a registered trade mark of Oxford University Press
in the UK and in certain other countries

Published in the United States
by Oxford University Press Inc., New York

A Blackstone Press book

This selection © Barry Mitchell and Salim Farrar 2002

British Library Cataloguing in Publication Data
Data available

Crown Copyright material is reproduced with the permission of
the Controller of HMSO and the Queen's Printer for Scotland

ISBN 0–19–925485–0

1 3 5 7 9 10 8 6 4 2

Typeset in ITC Stone Serif and ITC Stone Sans
by RefineCatch Limited, Bungay, Suffolk
Printed in Great Britain by
Antony Rowe Ltd., Chippenham

CONTENTS

EDITORS' PREFACE

There are numerous undergraduate and postgraduate courses in law and other disciplines such as criminology which include various aspects of criminal justice and sentencing. In the general sense at least, sentencing is an integral part of the criminal justice process, and it is arguable therefore that there is no need to identify sentencing separately. We have done so however simply because not all courses include it—some do not go beyond the point of conviction—and we obviously want to make it clear that this book encompasses important statutory provisions which apply across the whole gamut of the criminal justice system.

As most of us appreciate (if only through the media), there has been a constant stream of legislation, especially during the last fifteen years or so, which has affected all dimensions of criminal justice. Although this has precipitated a considerable number of statutory instruments, working guidelines and practice directions, this book confines itself to relevant statutory provisions (including the Codes of Practice under the Police and Criminal Evidence Act 1984). In an attempt to consolidate what had become an increasingly unmanageable mass of provisions on sentencing contained in several statutes, Parliament enacted the Powers of Criminal Courts (Sentencing) Act 2000. As is evident from the Contents pages at the start of this book, this has simplified the situation, but amendments have already been made to it (which we have incorporated) by, for example, the Criminal Justice and Court Services Act 2000. Furthermore, there are some sections of the Powers of Criminal Courts (Sentencing) Act 2000 which contain important changes to the law but which have not yet been brought into force. For example, sections 87 and 88 will replace section 67 of the Criminal Justice Act 1967 on time spent in custody on remand, and section 61 of the PCC(S)A 2000 will abolish detention in a young offender institution and thereby lower the eligibility for imprisonment from 21 to 18 years of age. At the time of writing, no dates have been fixed for implementing these changes but they have been included in italic type. Other amendments to the PCC(S)A 2000 include the introduction of exclusion orders, a new type of community order, but it is unknown when this amendment will be brought into effect and the relevant provisions have been omitted from this book.

One area in which Parliament has recently been active is surveillance and electronic searches. The statutes relating to these issues are the Police Act 1997 and the Regulation of Investigatory Powers Act 2000, but the subject is very complex and one which we feel merits separate consideration elsewhere.

There were various formats available to us for structuring the book. We suspect that most people will want to use it by reference to a particular topic—arrest and detention, bail, disclosure, etc.—and we have set the book out on that basis.

We should like to record our thanks to colleagues at Oxford University Press, especially to Barbara Laing and John Grandidge, for their support, assistance and patience. As ever, though, any errors remain our responsibility.

Barry Mitchell and Salim Farrar
August 2002

PART I

Criminal Justice

(a) ACCESS TO JUSTICE

Right to legal representation

European Convention of Human Rights

Article 6   **Right to a fair trial**

3. Everyone charged with a criminal offence has the following minimum rights:

. . .

   (b) to have adequate time and facilities for the preparation of his defence;

   (c) to defend himself in person or through legal assistance of his own choosing or, if he has not sufficient means to pay for legal assistance, to be given it free when the interests of justice so require.

Access to Justice Act 1999

12   **Criminal Defence Service**

(1) The Commission shall establish, maintain and develop a service known as the Criminal Defence Service for the purpose of securing that individuals involved in criminal investigations or criminal proceedings have access to such advice, assistance and representation as the interests of justice require.

(2) In this Part "criminal proceedings" means—

   (a) proceedings before any court for dealing with an individual accused of an offence,

   (b) proceedings before any court for dealing with an individual convicted of an offence (including proceedings in respect of a sentence or order),

   (c) proceedings for dealing with an individual under section 9 of, or paragraph 6 of Schedule 1 to, the Extradition Act 1989,

   (d) proceedings for binding an individual over to keep the peace or to be of good behaviour under section 115 of the Magistrates' Courts Act 1980 and for dealing with an individual who fails to comply with an order under that section,

   (e) proceedings on an appeal brought by an individual under section 44A of the Criminal Appeal Act 1968,

   (f) proceedings for contempt committed, or alleged to have been committed, by an individual in the face of a court, and

   (g) such other proceedings concerning an individual, before any such court or other body, as may be prescribed.

(3) The Commission shall fund services as part of the Criminal Defence Service in accordance with sections 13 to 15.

(4) The Commission may accredit, or authorise others to accredit, persons or bodies providing services which may be funded by the Commission as part of the Criminal Defence Service; and any system of accreditation shall include provision for the monitoring of the services provided by accredited persons and bodies and for the withdrawal of accreditation from any providing services of unsatisfactory quality.

(5) The Commission may charge—
    (a) for accreditation,
    (b) for monitoring the services provided by accredited persons and bodies, and
    (c) for authorising accreditation by others;
and persons or bodies authorised to accredit may charge for accreditation, and for such monitoring, in accordance with the terms of their authorisation.

(6) The Lord Chancellor may by order require the Commission to discharge the functions in subsections (4) and (5) in accordance with the order.

13 Advice and assistance

(1) The Commission shall fund such advice and assistance as it considers appropriate—
    (a) for individuals who are arrested and held in custody at a police station or other premises, and
    (b) in prescribed circumstances, for individuals who—
        (i) are not within paragraph (a) but are involved in investigations which may lead to criminal proceedings,
        (ii) are before a court or other body in such proceedings, or
        (iii) have been the subject of such proceedings;
and the assistance which the Commission may consider appropriate includes assistance in the form of advocacy.

(2) The Commission may comply with the duty imposed by subsection (1) by—
    (a) entering into contracts with persons or bodies for the provision of advice or assistance by them,
    (b) making payments to persons or bodies in respect of the provision of advice or assistance by them,
    (c) making grants or loans to persons or bodies to enable them to provide, or facilitate the provision of, advice or assistance,
    (d) establishing and maintaining bodies to provide, or facilitate the provision of, advice or assistance,
    (e) making grants to individuals to enable them to obtain advice or assistance,
    (f) employing persons to provide advice or assistance, or
    (g) doing anything else which it considers appropriate for funding advice and assistance.

(3) The Lord Chancellor may by order require the Commission to discharge the function in subsection (2) in accordance with the order.

(4) The Commission may fund advice and assistance by different means—
    (a) in different areas in England and Wales, and
    (b) in relation to different descriptions of cases.

14 Representation

(1) Schedule 3 (which makes provision about the grant of a right to representation in criminal proceedings) has effect; and the Commission shall fund representation to which an individual has been granted a right in accordance with that Schedule.

(2) Subject to the following provisions, the Commission may comply with the duty imposed by subsection (1) by—
    (a) entering into contracts with persons or bodies for the provision of representation by them,

(b) making payments to persons or bodies in respect of the provision of representation by them,

(c) making grants or loans to persons or bodies to enable them to provide, or facilitate the provision of, representation,

(d) establishing and maintaining bodies to provide, or facilitate the provision of, representation,

(e) making grants to individuals to enable them to obtain representation,

(f) employing persons to provide representation, or

(g) doing anything else which it considers appropriate for funding representation.

(3) The Lord Chancellor—

(a) shall by order make provision about the payments which may be made by the Commission in respect of any representation provided by non-contracted private practitioners, and

(b) may by order make any other provision requiring the Commission to discharge the function in subsection (2) in accordance with the order.

(4) For the purposes of subsection (3)(a) representation is provided by a non-contracted private practitioner if it is provided, otherwise than pursuant to a contract entered into by the Commission, by a person or body which is neither—

(a) a person or body in receipt of grants or loans made by the Commission as part of the Criminal Defence Service, nor

(b) the Commission itself or a body established or maintained by the Commission.

(5) The provision which the Lord Chancellor is required to make by order under subsection (3)(a) includes provision for reviews of, or appeals against, determinations required for the purposes of the order.

(6) The Commission may fund representation by different means—

(a) in different areas in England and Wales, and

(b) in relation to different descriptions of cases.

15 Selection of representative

(1) An individual who has been granted a right to representation in accordance with Schedule 3 may select any representative or representatives willing to act for him; and, where he does so, the Commission is to comply with the duty imposed by section 14(1) by funding representation by the selected representative or representatives.

(2) Regulations may provide that in prescribed circumstances—

(a) the right conferred by subsection (1) is not to apply in cases of prescribed descriptions,

(b) an individual who has been provided with advice or assistance funded by the Commission under section 13 by a person whom he chose to provide it for him is to be taken to have selected that person as his representative pursuant to that right,

(c) that right is not to include a right to select a representative of a prescribed description,

(d) that right is to select only a representative of a prescribed description,

(e) that right is to select not more than a prescribed number of representatives to act at any one time, and

(f) that right is not to include a right to select a representative in place of a representative previously selected.

(3) Regulations under subsection (2)(b) may prescribe circumstances in which an individual is to be taken to have chosen a person to provide advice or assistance for him.

(4) Regulations under subsection (2) may not provide that only a person employed by the Commission, or by a body established and maintained by the Commission, may be selected.

(5) Regulations may provide that in prescribed circumstances the Commission is not required to fund, or to continue to fund, representation for an individual by a particular representative (but such provision shall not prejudice any right of the individual to select another representative).

(6) The circumstances which may be prescribed by regulations under subsection (2) or (5) include that a determination has been made by a prescribed body or person.

16   Code of conduct

(1) The Commission shall prepare a code of conduct to be observed by employees of the Commission, and employees of any body established and maintained by the Commission, in the provision of services as part of the Criminal Defence Service.

(2) The code shall include—

    (a) duties to avoid discrimination,

    (b) duties to protect the interests of the individuals for whom services are provided,

    (c) duties to the court,

    (d) duties to avoid conflicts of interest, and

    (e) duties of confidentiality,

and duties on employees who are members of a professional body to comply with the rules of the body.

(3) The Commission may from time to time prepare a revised version of the code.

(4) Before preparing or revising the code the Commission shall consult the Law Society and the General Council of the Bar and such other bodies or persons as it considers appropriate.

(5) After preparing the code or a revised version of the code the Commission shall send a copy to the Lord Chancellor.

(6) If he approves it he shall lay it before each House of Parliament.

(7) The Commission shall publish—

    (a) the code as first approved by the Lord Chancellor, and

    (b) where he approves a revised version, either the revisions or the revised code as appropriate.

(8) The code, and any revised version of the code, shall not come into force until it has been approved by a resolution of each House of Parliament.

17   Terms of provision of funded services

(1) An individual for whom services are funded by the Commission as part of the Criminal Defence Service shall not be required to make any payment in respect of the services except where subsection (2) applies.

(2) Where representation for an individual in respect of criminal proceedings in any court other than a magistrates' court is funded by the Commission as part of the Criminal Defence Service, the court may, subject to regulations under subsection (3), make an order requiring him to pay some or all of the cost of any representation so funded for him (in proceedings in that or any other court).

(3) Regulations may make provision about—

    (a) the descriptions of individuals against whom an order under subsection (2) may be made,

    (b) the circumstances in which such an order may be made and the principles to be applied in deciding whether to make such an order and the amount to be paid,

    (c) the determination of the cost of representation for the purposes of the making of such an order,

    (d) the furnishing of information and evidence to the court or the Commission for the purpose of enabling the court to decide whether to make such an order and (if so) the amount to be paid,

(e) prohibiting individuals who are required to furnish information or evidence from dealing with property until they have furnished the information or evidence or until a decision whether to make an order, or the amount to be paid, has been made,

(f) the person or body to which, and manner in which, payments required by such an order must be made and what that person or body is to do with them, and

(g) the enforcement of such an order (including provision for the imposition of charges in respect of unpaid amounts).

18 Funding

(1) The Lord Chancellor shall pay to the Commission such sums as are required to meet the costs of any advice, assistance and representation funded by the Commission as part of the Criminal Defence Service.

(2) The Lord Chancellor may—

(a) determine the manner in which and times at which the sums referred to in subsection (1) shall be paid to the Commission, and

(b) impose conditions on the payment of the sums.

(3) In funding services as part of the Criminal Defence Service the Commission shall aim to obtain the best possible value for money.

(b) POLICE POWERS AND ISSUES DURING INVESTIGATION

Rights to liberty, security and privacy

European Convention on Human Rights

Article 5 Right to liberty and security

1. Everyone has the right to liberty and security of person. No one shall be deprived of his liberty save in the following cases and in accordance with a procedure prescribed by law:

(a) the lawful detention of a person after conviction by a competent court;

(b) the lawful arrest or detention of a person for non-compliance with the lawful order of a court or in order to secure the fulfilment of any obligation prescribed by law;

(c) the lawful arrest or detention of a person effected for the purpose of bringing him before the competent legal authority on reasonable suspicion of having committed an offence or when it is reasonably considered necessary to prevent his committing an offence or fleeing after having done so;

(d) the detention of a minor by lawful order for the purpose of educational supervision or his lawful detention for the purpose of bringing him before the competent legal authority;

(e) the lawful detention of persons for the prevention of the spreading of infectious diseases, of persons of unsound mind, alcoholics or drug addicts or vagrants;

(f) the lawful arrest or detention of a person to prevent his effecting an unauthorised entry into the country or of a person against whom action is being taken with a view to deportation or extradition.

2. Everyone who is arrested shall be informed promptly, in a language which he understands, of the reasons for his arrest and of any charge against him.

3. Everyone arrested or detained in accordance with the provisions of paragraph 1.c of this article shall be brought promptly before a judge or other officer authorised by law to exercise judicial power and shall be entitled to trial within a reasonable time or to release pending trial. Release may be conditioned by guarantees to appear for trial.

4. Everyone who is deprived of his liberty by arrest or detention shall be entitled to take proceedings by which the lawfulness of his detention shall be decided speedily by a court and his release ordered if the detention is not lawful.

5. Everyone who has been the victim of arrest or detention in contravention of the provisions of this article shall have an enforceable right to compensation.

Article 8

1. Everyone has the right to respect for his private and family life, his home and his correspondence.

2. There shall be no interference by a public authority with the exercise of this right except such as is in accordance with the law and is necessary in a democratic society in the interests of national security, public safety or the economic well-being of the country, for the prevention of disorder or crime, for the protection of health or morals, or for the protection of the rights and freedoms of others.

Stop and search

Police and Criminal Evidence Act 1984

1   Power of constable to stop and search persons, vehicles etc.

(1) A constable may exercise any power conferred by this section—

 (a) in any place to which at the time when he proposes to exercise the power the public or any section of the public has access, on payment or otherwise, as of right or by virtue of express or implied permission; or

 (b) in any other place to which people have ready access at the time when he proposes to exercise the power but which is not a dwelling.

(2) Subject to subsection (3) to (5) below, a constable—

 (a) may search—

  (i)   any person or vehicle;

  (ii) anything which is in or on a vehicle,

  for stolen or prohibited articles or any article to which subsection (8A) below applies; and

 (b) may detain a person or vehicle for the purpose of such a search.

(3) This section does not give a constable power to search a person or vehicle or anything in or on a vehicle unless he has reasonable grounds for suspecting that he will find stolen or prohibited articles or any article to which subsection (8A) below applies.

(4) If a person is in a garden or yard occupied with and used for the purposes of a dwelling or on other land so occupied and used, a constable may not search him in the exercise of the power conferred by this section unless the constable has reasonable grounds for believing—

 (a) that he does not reside in the dwelling; and

 (b) that he is not in the place in question with the express or implied permission of a person who resides in the dwelling.

(5) If a vehicle is in a garden or yard occupied with and used for the purposes of a dwelling or on other land so occupied and used, a constable may not search the vehicle or anything in or on it in the exercise of the power conferred by this section unless he has reasonable grounds for believing—

> (a) that the person in charge of the vehicle does not reside in the dwelling; and
>
> (b) that the vehicle is not in the place in question with the express or implied permission of a person who resides in the dwelling.

(6) If in the course of such a search a constable discovers an article which he has reasonable grounds for suspecting to be a stolen or prohibited article or any article to which subsection (8A) below applies, he may seize it.

(7) An article is prohibited for the purposes of this Part of this Act if it is—

> (a) an offensive weapon; or
>
> (b) an article—
>> (i) made or adapted for use in the course of or in connection with an offence to which this sub-paragraph applies; or
>>
>> (ii) intended by the person having it with him for such use by him or by some other person.

(8) The offences to which subsection (7)(b)(i) above applies are—

> (a) burglary;
>
> (b) theft;
>
> (c) offences under section 12 of the Theft Act 1968 (taking motor vehicle or other conveyance without authority); and
>
> (d) offences under section 15 of that Act (obtaining property by deception).

(8A) This subsection applies to any article in relation to which a person has committed, or is committing or is going to commit an offence under section 139 of the Criminal Justice Act 1988.

(9) In this Part of this Act "offensive weapon" means any article—

> (a) made or adapted for use for causing injury to persons; or
>
> (b) intended by the person having it with him for such use by him or by some other person.

2   Provisions relating to search under section 1 and other powers

(1) A constable who detains a person or vehicle in the exercise—

> (a) of the power conferred by section 1 above; or
>
> (b) of any other power—
>> (i) to search a person without first arresting him;
>>
>> or
>>
>> (ii) to search a vehicle without making an arrest,

need not conduct a search if it appears to him subsequently—

> (i) that no search is required; or
>
> (ii) that a search is impracticable.

(2) If a constable contemplates a search, other than a search of an unattended vehicle, in the exercise—

> (a) of the power conferred by section 1 above; or
>
> (b) of any other power, except the power conferred by section 6 below and the power conferred by section 27(2) of the Aviation Security Act 1982—
>> (i) to search a person without first arresting him;
>>
>> or
>>
>> (ii) to search a vehicle without making an arrest,

it shall be his duty, subject to subsection (4) below, to take reasonable steps before he commences the search to bring to the attention of the appropriate person—

(i)   if the constable is not in uniform, documentary evidence that he is a constable; and

(ii) whether he is in uniform or not, the matters specified in subsection (3) below;

and the constable shall not commence the search until he has performed that duty.

(3) The matters referred to in subsection (2)(ii) above are—

(a) the constable's name and the name of the police station to which he is attached;

(b) the object of the proposed search;

(c) the constable's grounds for proposing to make it; and

(d) the effect of section 3(7) or (8) below, as may be appropriate.

(4) A constable need not bring the effect of section 3(7) or (8) below to the attention of the appropriate person if it appears to the constable that it will not be practicable to make the record in section 3(1) below.

(5) In this section "the appropriate person" means—

(a) if the constable proposes to search a person, that person; and

(b) if he proposes to search a vehicle, or anything in or on a vehicle, the person in charge of the vehicle.

(6) On completing a search of an unattended vehicle or anything in or on such a vehicle in the exercise of any such power as is mentioned in subsection (2) above a constable shall leave a notice—

(a) stating that he has searched it;

(b) giving the name of the police station to which he is attached;

(c) stating that an application for compensation for any damage caused by the search may be made to that police station; and

(d) stating the effect of section 3(8) below.

(7) The constable shall leave the notice inside the vehicle unless it is not reasonably practicable to do so without damaging the vehicle.

(8) The time for which a person or vehicle may be detained for the purposes of such a search is such time as is reasonably required to permit a search to be carried out either at the place where the person or vehicle was first detained or nearby.

(9) Neither the power conferred by section 1 above nor any other power to detain and search a person without first arresting him or to detain and search a vehicle without making an arrest is to be construed—

(a) as authorising a constable to require a person to remove any of his clothing in public other than an outer coat, jacket or gloves; or

(b) as authorising a constable not in uniform to stop a vehicle.

(10) This section and section 1 above apply to vessels, aircraft and hovercraft as they apply to vehicles.

3   Duty to make records concerning searches

(1) Where a constable has carried out a search in the exercise of any such power as is mentioned in section 2(1) above, other than a search—

(a) under section 6 below; or

(b) under section 27(2) of the Aviation Security Act 1982, he shall make a record of it in writing unless it is not practicable to do so.

(2) If—

(a) a constable is required by subsection (1) above to make a record of a search; but

(b) it is not practicable to make the record on the spot, he shall make it as soon as practicable after the completion of the search.

(3) The record of a search of a person shall include a note of his name, if the constable knows it, but a constable may not detain a person to find out his name.

(4) If a constable does not know the name of a person whom he has searched, the record of the search shall include a note otherwise describing that person.

(5) The record of a search of a vehicle shall include a note describing the vehicle.

(6) The record of a search of a person or a vehicle—

    (a) shall state—

        (i) the object of the search;

        (ii) the grounds for making it;

        (iii) the date and time when it was made;

        (iv) the place where it was made;

        (v) whether anything, and if so what, was found;

        (vi) whether any, and if so what, injury to a person or damage to property appears to the constable to have resulted from the search; and

    (b) shall identify the constable making it.

(7) If a constable who conducted a search of a person made a record of it, the person who was searched shall be entitled to a copy of the record if he asks for one before the end of the period specified in subsection (9) below.

(8) If—

    (a) the owner of a vehicle which has been searched or the person who was in charge of the vehicle at the time when it was searched asks for a copy of the record of the search before the end of the period specified in subsection (9) below; and

    (b) the constable who conducted the search made a record of it,

the person who made the request shall be entitled to a copy.

(9) The period mentioned in subsections (7) and (8) above is the period of 12 months beginning with the date on which the search was made.

(10) The requirements imposed by this section with regard to records of searches of vehicles shall apply also to records of searches of vessels, aircraft and hovercraft.

CODES OF PRACTICE, CODE A

1 General

1.1   This code of practice must be readily available at all police stations for consultation by police officers, detained persons and members of the public.

1.2   The notes for guidance included are not provisions of this code, but are guidance to police officers and others about its application and interpretation. Provisions in the annexes to the code are provisions of this code.

1.3   This code governs the exercise by police officers of statutory powers to search a person without first arresting him or to search a vehicle without making an arrest. The main stop and search powers to which this code applies at the time the code was prepared are set out in *Annex A*, but that list should not be regarded as definitive.

1.4   This code does not apply to the following powers of stop and search:

    (i) Aviation Security Act 1982, s 27(2);

    (ii) Police and Criminal Evidence Act 1984, s 56(1) (which relates specifically to powers of constables employed by statutory undertakers on the premises of the statutory undertakers).

1.5   This code applies to stops and searches under powers:

    (a) requiring reasonable grounds for suspicion that articles unlawfully obtained or possessed are being carried;

    (b) authorised under section 60 of the Criminal Justice and Public Order Act 1994, (as amended by section 8 of the Knives Act 1997) based upon a reasonable belief that incidents involving serious violence may take place within a locality;

    (c) authorised under section 13A of the Prevention of Terrorism (Temporary Provisions) Act 1989, (as amended by section 81 of the Criminal Justice and Public Order Act 1994 and section 1 of the Prevention of Terrorism (Additional Powers) Act 1996);

(d) authorised under section 13B of the Prevention of Terrorism (Temporary Provisions) Act 1989, (as inserted by section 1 of the Prevention of Terrorism (Additional Powers) Act 1996);

(e) exercised under paragraph 4(2) of Schedule 5 to the Prevention of Terrorism (Temporary Provisions) Act 1989.

[See *Note 1A*]

(a) Powers requiring reasonable suspicion

1.6   Whether a reasonable ground for suspicion exists will depend on the circumstances in each case, but there must be some objective basis for it. An officer will need to consider the nature of the article suspected of being carried in the context of other factors such as the time and the place, and the behaviour of the person concerned or those with him. Reasonable suspicion may exist, for example, where information has been received such as a description of an article being carried or of a suspected offender; a person is seen acting covertly or warily or attempting to hide something; or a person is carrying a certain type of article at an unusual time or in a place where a number of burglaries or thefts are known to have taken place recently. But the decision to stop and search must be based on all the facts which bear on the likelihood that an article of a certain kind will be found.

1.6A   For example, reasonable suspicion may be based upon reliable information or intelligence which indicates that members of a particular group or gang, or their associates, habitually carry knives unlawfully or weapons or controlled drugs.

1.7   Subject to the provision in paragraph 1.7AA below, reasonable suspicion can never be supported on the basis of personal factors alone. For example, a person's colour, age, hairstyle or manner of dress, or the fact that he is known to have a previous conviction for possession of an unlawful article, cannot be used alone or in combination with each other as the sole basis on which to search that person. Nor may it be founded on the basis of stereotyped images of certain persons or groups as more likely to be committing offences.

1.7AA   However, where there is reliable information or intelligence that members of a group or gang who habitually carry knives unlawfully or weapons or controlled drugs, and wear a distinctive item of clothing or other means of identification to indicate membership of it, the members may be identified by means of that distinctive item of clothing or other means of identification. [See *Note 1H*]

1.7A   Where a police officer has reasonable grounds to suspect that a person is in innocent possession of a stolen or prohibited article or other item for which he is empowered to search, the power of stop and search exists notwithstanding that there would be no power of arrest. However every effort should be made to secure the person's co-operation in the production of the article before resorting to the use of force.

(b) Authorisation under section 60 of the Criminal Justice and Public Order Act 1994, as amended by section 8 of the Knives Act 1997.

1.8   Authority to exercise the powers of stop and search under section 60 of the Criminal Justice and Public Order Act 1994, as amended by section 8 of the Knives Act 1997, may be given where it is reasonably believed that incidents involving serious violence may take place in a locality, and it is expedient to use these powers to prevent their occurrence. Authorisation should normally be given by an officer of the rank of inspector or above, in writing, specifying the locality in which the powers may be exercised and the period of time for which they are in force. The period authorised shall be no longer than appears reasonably necessary to prevent, or try to prevent incidents of serious violence, or to deal with the problem of carrying dangerous instruments or offensive weapons and it may not exceed 24 hours. If an inspector gives an authorisation, he must, as soon as practicable, inform an officer of or above the rank of superintendent. An officer of or above the rank of superintendent may direct that the period shall be extended for a further 24 hours if violence or the carrying of dangerous instruments or offensive weapons has occurred or is suspected to have occurred and the continued use of the powers is considered necessary to prevent further violence. That direction must also be given in writing at the time or as soon as practicable afterwards. [See *Notes 1A, 1F and 1G*]

(c) Authorisation under section 13A of the Prevention of Terrorism (Temporary Provisions) Act 1989.

1.9   An authorisation given under section 13A of the Prevention of Terrorism (Temporary Provisions) Act 1989 gives a constable in uniform the power to stop and search any vehicle, its driver and any passengers for articles which could be used for terrorist purposes. A constable may exercise the power whether or not he has any grounds for suspecting the presence of such articles.

1.10   Authority for the use of the power may be given where it appears expedient to do so to prevent acts of terrorism. The authorisation must:

    (i) be given by an officer of the rank of assistant chief constable (or equivalent or above);

    (ii) be in writing (it may be given orally at first but should be confirmed in writing by the officer who gave it as soon as reasonably practicable);

    (iii) be signed, dated and timed by the officer giving the authorisation;

    (iv) state the geographical area in which the power may be used (i.e. whether it applies to the whole or only a specific part of his force area); and

    (v) specify the time and date that the authorisation starts and ends (up to a maximum of 28 days from the time the authorisation was given).

1.11   Further use of the power requires a new authorisation. [See *Notes 1F, 1G and 1I*]

(d) Authorisation under section 13B of the Prevention of Terrorism (Temporary Provisions) Act 1989.

1.12   An authorisation given under section 13B of the Prevention of Terrorism (Temporary Provisions) Act 1989 gives a constable in uniform the power to stop a pedestrian and search him, or anything carried by him, for articles which could be used for terrorist purposes. A constable may exercise the power whether or not he has any grounds for suspecting the presence of such articles.

1.13   Authority for the use of the power may be given where it appears expedient to do so to prevent acts of terrorism. The authorisation must be given in exactly the same way as explained in paragraph 1.10 (and may in fact be combined with a section 13A authorisation). However, the officer giving an authorisation under section 13B must cause the Secretary of State to be informed, as soon as reasonably practicable, that such an authorisation has been given. The authorisation may take effect before the Secretary of State has decided whether to confirm it. But it ceases to have effect if it is not confirmed by the Secretary of State within 48 hours of its having been given.

1.14   Following notification of the authorisation, the Secretary of State may:

    (i) cancel the authorisation with immediate effect or with effect from such other time as he may direct;

    (ii) confirm it but for a shorter period than that specified in the authorisation (which may not be more than 28 days); or

    (iii) confirm the authorisation as given.

1.15   Further use of the power requires a new authorisation.

1.16   The selection of persons stopped under sections 13A and 13B of the Prevention of Terrorism (Temporary Provision) Act 1989 should reflect an objective assessment of the threat posed by the various terrorist groups active in Great Britain. The powers should not be used to stop and search for reasons unconnected with terrorism. Officers should take particular care not to discriminate against members of ethnic minorities in the exercise of these powers. There may be circumstances, however, where it is appropriate for officers to take account of a person's ethnic origin in selecting persons to be stopped in response to a specific terrorist threat (for example, some international terrorist groups are associated with particular ethnic identities). [See *Notes 1F, 1G and 1I*]

Notes for guidance

   1A   Section 60 is amended by section 25 of the Crime and Disorder Act 1998 to provide a power to demand the removal of face coverings where an authority referred to in paragraph 1.8 above is given. The officer exercising the power must reasonably believe that someone is wearing the face covering wholly or mainly for the purpose of concealing identity. There is also a power to seize face coverings where the officer believes that a person intends to wear them for this purpose. There is not a power to stop and search for face coverings. An officer may seize any face covering which he comes across when exercising a power of search for something else, or which he sees being carried, and which he reasonably believes it intended to be used for concealing anyone's identity.

   1AA   It is important to ensure that powers of stop and search are used responsibly by those who exercise them and those who authorise their use. An officer should bear in mind that he may be required to justify the authorisation or use of the powers to a senior officer and in court, and that misuse of the powers is likely to be harmful to the police effort in the long term and can lead to mistrust of the police by the community. Regardless of the power exercised, all police officers should be careful to ensure that the selection and treatment of those questioned or searched is based upon objective factors and not upon personal prejudice. It is also particularly important to ensure that any person searched is treated courteously and considerately. Where there may be religious sensitivities about asking someone to remove a face covering using the powers in section 25 of the Crime and Disorder Act 1998, for example in the case of a Muslim woman wearing a face covering for religious purposes, the officer should permit the item to be removed out of public view. Where practicable, the item should be removed in the presence of an officer of the same sex as the person and out of sight of anyone of the opposite sex. In all cases, the officer must reasonably believe that the person is wearing the item in question wholly or mainly to conceal his or her identity.

   1B   This code does not affect the ability of an officer to speak to or question a person in the ordinary course of his duties (and in the absence of reasonable suspicion) without detaining him or exercising any element of compulsion. It is not the purpose of the code to prohibit such encounters between the police and the community with the co-operation of the person concerned and neither does it affect the principle that all citizens have a duty to help police officers to prevent crime and discover offenders.

   1C   [Not Used]

   1D   Nothing in this code affects

   a.   *the routine searching of persons entering sports grounds or other premises with their consent, or as a condition of entry; or*

   b.   *the ability of an officer to search a person in the street with his consent where no search power exists. In these circumstances an officer should always make it clear that he is seeking the consent of the person concerned to the search being carried out by telling the person that he need not consent and that without his consent he will not be searched.*

   1E   If an officer acts in an improper manner this will invalidate a voluntary search. Juveniles, people suffering from a mental handicap or mental disorder and others who appear not to be capable of giving an informed consent should not be subject to a voluntary search.

   1F   It is for the authorising officer to determine the period of time during which the powers mentioned in paragraph 1.5(b), (c) and (d) may be exercised. The officer should set the minimum period he considers necessary to deal with the risk of violence or terrorism. A direction to extend the period authorised under the powers mentioned in paragraph 1.5(b) may be given only once. Thereafter further use of the powers requires a new authorisation. There is no provision to extend an authorisation of the powers mentioned in paragraph 1.5(c) and (d); further use of the powers requires a new authorisation.

   1G   It is for the authorising officer to determine the geographical area in which the use of the powers are to be authorised. In doing so he may wish to take into account factors such as the nature and venue of the anticipated incident, the numbers of people who may be in the immediate area of any possible incident, their access to surrounding areas and the anticipated level of violence. The officer should not set a geographical area which is wider than that he believes necessary for the purpose of preventing anticipated violence or terrorism. It is particularly important to ensure that constables exercising such powers are fully aware of where they may be used. If the area specified is smaller than the whole force area, the officer giving the authorisation should specify either the streets which form the boundary of the area or a divisional boundary within the force area. If the power is to be used in response to a threat or incident that straddles police force areas, an officer from each of the forces concerned will need to give an authorisation.

1H   Other means of identification might include jewellery, insignias, tattoos or other features which are known to identify members of the particular gang or group.

1I   An officer who has authorised the use of powers under section 13B of the Prevention of Terrorism (Temporary Provisions) Act 1989 must take immediate steps to send a copy of the authorisation to the National Joint Unit, Metropolitan Police Special Branch, who will forward it to the Secretary of State. The Secretary of State should be informed of the reasons for the authorisation. The National Joint Unit will inform the force concerned, within 48 hours of the authorisation being made, whether the Secretary of State has confirmed or cancelled or altered the authorisation. The National Joint Unit should also be sent a copy of all section 13A authorisations for national monitoring purposes.

2   Action before a search is carried out

(a) Searches requiring reasonable suspicion

2.1   Where an officer has the reasonable grounds for suspicion necessary to exercise a power of stop and search he may detain the person concerned for the purposes of and with a view to searching him. There is no power to stop or detain a person against his will in order to find grounds for a search.

2.2   Before carrying out a search the officer may question the person about his behaviour or his presence in circumstances which gave rise to the suspicion, since he may have a satisfactory explanation which will make a search unnecessary. If, as a result of any questioning preparatory to a search, or other circumstances which come to the attention of the officer, there cease to be reasonable grounds for suspecting that an article is being carried of a kind for which there is a power of stop and search, no search may take place. [See Note 2A]

2.3   The reasonable grounds for suspicion which are necessary for the exercise of the initial power to detain may be confirmed or eliminated as a result of the questioning of a person detained for the purposes of a search (or such questioning may reveal reasonable grounds to suspect the possession of a different kind of unlawful article from that originally suspected); but the reasonable grounds for suspicion without which any search or detention for the purposes of a search is unlawful cannot be retrospectively provided by such questioning during his detention or by his refusal to answer any question put to him.

(b) All searches

2.4   Before any search of a detained person or attended vehicle takes place the officer must take reasonable steps to give the person to be searched or in charge of the vehicle the following information:
   (i)   his name (except in the case of enquiries linked to the investigation of terrorism, in which case he shall give his warrant or other identification number) and the name of the police station to which he is attached;
   (ii) the object of the search; and
   (iii) his grounds or authorisation for undertaking it.

2.5   If the officer is not in uniform he must show his warrant card. In doing so in the case of enquiries linked to the investigation of terrorism, the officer need not reveal his name. Stops and searches under the powers mentioned in paragraphs 1.5(b) and (c) and (d) may be undertaken only by a constable in uniform.

2.6   Unless it appears to the officer that it will not be practicable to make a record of the search, he must also inform the person to be searched (or the owner or person in charge of a vehicle that is to be searched, as the case may be) that he is entitled to a copy of the record of the search if he asks for it within a year. If the person wishes to have a copy and is not given one on the spot, he shall be advised to which police station he should apply.

2.7   If the person to be searched, or in charge of a vehicle to be searched, does not appear to understand what is being said, or there is any doubt about his ability to understand English, the officer must take reasonable steps to bring the information in paragraphs 2.4 and 2.6 to his attention. If the person is deaf or cannot understand English and has someone with him then the officer must try to establish whether that person can interpret or otherwise help him to give the required information.

Note for Guidance

2A   In some circumstances preparatory questioning may be unnecessary, but in general a brief conversation or exchange will be desirable, not only as a means of avoiding unsuccessful searches, but to explain the grounds for the stop/search, to gain co-operation and reduce any tension there might be surrounding the stop/search. Where a person is lawfully detained for the purpose of a search, but no search in the event takes place, the detention will not thereby have been rendered unlawful.

3   Conduct of the search

3.1   Every reasonable effort must be made to reduce to the minimum the embarrassment that a person being searched may experience.

3.2   The co-operation of the person to be searched shall be sought in every case, even if he initially objects to the search. A forcible search may be made only if it has been established that the person is unwilling to co-operate (e.g. by opening a bag) or resists. Although force may only be used as a last resort, reasonable force may be used if necessary to conduct a search or to detain a person or vehicle for the purposes of a search.

3.3   The length of time for which a person or vehicle may be detained will depend on the circumstances, but must in all circumstances, be reasonable and not extend beyond the time taken for the search. Where the exercise of the power requires reasonable suspicion, the thoroughness and extent of a search must depend on what is suspected of being carried, and by whom. If the suspicion relates to a particular article which is seen to be slipped into a person's pocket, then, in the absence of other grounds for suspicion or an opportunity for the article to be moved elsewhere, the search must be confined to that pocket. In the case of a small article which can readily be concealed, such as a drug, and which might be concealed anywhere on the person, a more extensive search may be necessary. In the case of searches mentioned in paragraph 1.5(b), (c), (d) and (e), which do not require reasonable grounds for suspicion, the officer may make any reasonable search to find what he is empowered to search for. [See *Note 3B*]

3.4   The search must be conducted at or nearby the place where the person or vehicle was first detained.

3.5   Searches in public must be restricted to superficial examination of outer clothing. There is no power to require a person to remove any clothing in public other than an outer coat, jacket or gloves (other than under sections 13A and 13B of the Prevention of Terrorism (Temporary Provisions) Act 1989, which grant a constable in addition to the power to require a person to remove in public any headgear and footwear, or under section 60 of the Criminal Justice and Public Order Act 1994 as amended by the Crime and Disorder Act 1998, which grants a constable power to require the removal of any item worn to conceal identity). Where on reasonable grounds it is considered necessary to conduct a more thorough search (e.g. by requiring a person to take off a T-shirt), this shall be done out of public view for example, in a police van or police station if there is one nearby. Any search involving the removal of more than an outer coat, jacket, gloves, headgear or footwear, or any other item concealing identity, may only be made by an officer of the same sex as the person searched and may not be made in the presence of anyone of the opposite sex unless the person being searched specifically requests it. [*See Note 3A and 3C*]

No search involving exposure of intimate parts of the body may take place in a police van. All searches involving exposure of intimate parts of the body shall be conducted in accordance with paragraph 11 of Annex A to Code C. The other provisions of Code C do not apply to persons at police stations for the puposes of searches under stop and search powers.

3.5A   The powers under sections 13A and 13B of the Prevention of Terrorism (Temporary Provisions) Act 1989 allow a constable to search only for articles which could be used for terrorist purposes. The powers must not be used for any other purpose (for example to search for drugs in the absence of reasonable grounds for suspicion). However, this would not prevent a search being carried out under other powers if, in course of exercising powers under sections 13A or 13B, the police officer formed reasonable grounds for suspicion.

Notes for guidance

3A   A search in the street itself should be regarded as being in public for the purposes of paragraph 3.5 above, even though it may be empty at the time a search begins. Although there is no power to require a person to do so, there is nothing to prevent an officer from asking a person to voluntarily remove more than an outer coat, jacket or gloves (and headgear or footwear under section 13A and 13B of the Prevention of Terrorism (Temporary Provisions) Act 1989) in public.

3B   As a search of a person in public should be superficial examination of outer clothing, such searches should be completed as soon as possible.

3C   Where there may be religious sensitivities about asking someone to remove headgear using a power under section 13A or 13B of the Prevention of Terrorism (Temporary Provisions) Act 1989, the police officer should offer to carry out the search out of public view (for example, in a police van or police station if there is one nearby).

Criminal Justice and Public Order Act 1994 (as amended)

60   Powers to stop and search in anticipation of violence

(1) If a police officer of or above the rank of inspector reasonably believes—

   (a) that incidents involving serious violence may take place in any locality in his police area, and that it is expedient to give an authorisation under this section to prevent their occurrence, or

   (b) that persons are carrying dangerous instruments or offensive weapons in any locality in his police area without good reason,

he may give an authorisation that the powers conferred by this section are to be exercisable at any place within that locality for a specified period not exceeding 24 hours.

(2) Repealed.

(3) If it appears to an officer of or above the rank of superintendent that it is expedient to do so, having regard to offences which have, or are reasonably suspected to have, been committed in connection with any activity falling within the authorisation, he may direct that the authorisation shall continue in being for a further 24 hours.

(3A) If an inspector gives an authorisation under subsection (1) he must, as soon as it is practicable to do so, cause an officer of or above the rank of superintendent to be informed.

(4) This section confers on any constable in uniform power—

   (a) to stop any pedestrian and search him or anything carried by him for offensive weapons or dangerous instruments;

(b) to stop any vehicle and search the vehicle, its driver and any passenger for offensive weapons or dangerous instruments.

(5) A constable may, in the exercise of the powers conferred by subsection (4) above stop any person or vehicle and make any search he thinks fit whether or not he has any grounds for suspecting that the person or vehicle is carrying weapons or articles of that kind.

(6) If in the course of a search under this section a constable discovers a dangerous instrument or an article which he has reasonable grounds for suspecting to be an offensive weapon, he may seize it.

(7) This section applies (with the necessary modifications) to ships, aircraft and hovercraft as it applies to vehicles.

(8) A person who fails (a) to stop, or to stop the vehicle; or (b) to remove an item worn by him, when required to do so by a constable in the exercise of his powers under this section shall be liable on summary conviction to imprisonment for a term not exceeding one month or to a fine not exceeding level 3 on the standard scale or both.

(9) Any authorisation under this section shall be in writing signed by the officer giving it and shall specify the grounds on which it is given and the locality in which and the period during which the powers conferred by this section are exercisable and a direction under subsection (3) above shall also be given in writing or, where that is not practicable, recorded in writing as soon as it is practicable to do so.

(9A) The preceding provisions of this section, so far as they relate to an authorisation by a member of the British Transport Police Force (including one who for the time being has the same powers and privileges as a member of a police force for a police area), shall have effect as if the references to a locality in his police area were references to any locality in or in the vicinity of any policed premises, or to the whole or any part of any such premises.

(10) Where a vehicle is stopped by a constable under this section, the driver shall be entitled to obtain a written statement that the vehicle was stopped under the powers conferred by this section if he applies for such a statement not later than the end of the period of twelve months from the day on which the vehicle was stopped as respects a pedestrian who is stopped and searched under this section.

(10A) A person who is searched by a constable under this section shall be entitled to obtain a written statement that he was searched under the powers conferred by this section if he applies for such a statement not later than the end of the period of twelve months from the day on which he was searched.

(11) In this section—

"British Transport Police Force" means the constables appointed under section 53 of the British Transport Commission Act 1949;

"dangerous instruments" means instruments which have a blade or are sharply pointed;

"offensive weapon" has the meaning given by section 1(9) of the Police and Criminal Evidence Act 1984 or, in relation to Scotland, section 47(4) of the Criminal Law (Consolidation) (Scotland) Act 1995; and "policed premises" , in relation to England and Wales, has the meaning given by section 53(3) of the British Transport Commission Act 1949 and, in relation to Scotland, means those places where members of the British Transport Police Force have the powers, protection and privileges of a constable under section 53(4)(a) of that Act (as it relates to Scotland);

"vehicle" includes a caravan as defined in section 29(1) of the Caravan Sites and Control of Development Act 1960.

(11A) For the purposes of this section, a person carries a dangerous instrument or an offensive weapon if he has it in his possession.

(12) The powers conferred by this section are in addition to and not in derogation of, any power otherwise conferred.

The power to take intimate and non-intimate body samples

Police and Criminal Evidence Act 1984 (as amended)

61   Fingerprinting

(1) Except as provided by this section no person's fingerprints may be taken without the appropriate consent.

(2) Consent to the taking of a person's fingerprints must be in writing if it is given at a time when he is at a police station.

(3) The fingerprints of a person detained at a police station may be taken without the appropriate consent—

  (a) if an officer of at least the rank of inspector authorises them to be taken; or
  (b) if—
    (i) he has been charged with a recordable offence or informed that he will be reported for such an offence; and
    (ii) he has not had his fingerprints taken in the course of the investigation of the offence by the police.

(4) An officer may only give an authorisation under subsection (3)(a) above if he has reasonable grounds—

  (a) for suspecting the involvement of the person whose fingerprints are to be taken in a criminal offence; and
  (b) for believing that his fingerprints will tend to confirm or disprove his involvement [or will facilitate the ascertainment of his identity (within the meaning of section 54A) or both].

(6) Any person's fingerprints may be taken without the appropriate consent if—

  (a) he has been convicted of a recordable offence;
  (b) he has been given a caution in respect of a recordable offence which, at the time of the caution, he has admitted; or
  (c) he has been warned or reprimanded under section 65 of the Crime and Disorder Act 1998 (c. 37) for a recordable offence.

(7) In a case where by virtue of subsection (3) or (6) above a person's fingerprints are taken without the appropriate consent—

  (a) he shall be told the reason before his fingerprints are taken; and
  (b) the reason shall be recorded as soon as is practicable after the fingerprints are taken.

(7A) If a person's fingerprints are taken at a police station, whether with or without the appropriate consent—

  (a) before the fingerprints are taken, an officer shall inform him that they may be the subject of a speculative search; and
  (b) the fact that the person has been informed of this possibility shall be recorded as soon as is practicable after the fingerprints have been taken.

(8) If he is detained at a police station when the fingerprints are taken, the reason for taking them and, in the case falling within subsection (7A) above, the fact referred to in paragraph (b) of that subsection shall be recorded on his custody record.

(9) Nothing in this section—

  (a) affects any power conferred by paragraph 18(2) of Schedule 2 to the Immigration Act 1971; or
  (b) applies to a person arrested or detained under the terrorism provisions.

62   Intimate samples

(1) [Subject to section 63B below] an intimate sample may be taken from a person in police detention only—

(a) if a police officer of at least the rank of superintendent authorises it to be taken; and

(b) if the appropriate consent is given.

(1A) An intimate sample may be taken from a person who is not in police detention but from whom, in the course of the investigation of an offence, two or more non-intimate samples suitable for the same means of analysis have been taken which have proved insufficient—

(a) if a police officer of at least the rank of inspector authorises it to be taken; and

(b) if the appropriate consent is given.

(2) An officer may only give an authorisation under subsection (1) or (1A) above if he has reasonable grounds—

(a) for suspecting the involvement of the person from whom the sample is to be taken in a recordable offence; and

(b) for believing that the sample will tend to confirm or disprove his involvement.

(3) An officer may given an authorisation under subsection (1) or (1A) above orally or in writing but, if he gives it orally, he shall confirm it in writing as soon as is practicable.

(4) The appropriate consent must be given in writing.

(5) Where—

(a) an authorisation has been given; and

(b) it is proposed that an intimate sample shall be taken in pursuance of the authorisation,

an officer shall inform the person from whom the sample is to be taken—

(i) of the giving of the authorisation; and

(ii) of the grounds for giving it.

(6) The duty imposed by subsection (5)(ii) above includes a duty to state the nature of the offence in which it is suspected that the person from whom the sample is to be taken has been involved.

(7) If an intimate sample is taken from a person—

(a) the authorisation by virtue of which it was taken;

(b) the grounds for giving the authorisation; and

(c) the fact that the appropriate consent was given,

shall be recorded as soon as is practicable after the sample is taken.

(7A) If an intimate sample is taken from a person at a police station—

(a) before the sample is taken, an officer shall inform him that it may be the subject of a speculative search; and

(b) the fact that the person has been informed of this possibility shall be recorded as soon as practicable after the sample has been taken.

(8) If an intimate sample is taken from a person detained at a police station, the matters required to be recorded by subsection (7) or (7A) above shall be recorded in his custody record.

(9) An intimate sample, other than a sample of urine or a dental impression, may only be taken from a person by a registered medical practitioner or a registered nurse and a dental impression may only be taken by a registered dentist.

(10) Where the appropriate consent to the taking of an intimate sample from a person was refused without good cause, in any proceedings against that person for an offence—

(a) the court, in determining—

(i) whether to commit that person for trial; or

(ii) whether there is a case to answer; and

(aa) a judge, in deciding whether to grant an application made by the accused under—

(i) section 6 of the Criminal Justice Act 1987 (application for dismissal of charge of serious fraud in respect of which notice of transfer has been given under section 4 of that Act); or

(ii) paragraph 5 of Schedule 6 to the Criminal Justice Act 1991 (application for dismissal of charge of violent or sexual offence involving child in respect of which notice of transfer has been given under section 53 of that Act; and

(b) the court or jury, in determining whether that person is guilty of the offence charged, may draw such inferences from the refusal as appear proper.

(11) Nothing in this section affects sections 5 to 12 of the Road Traffic Act 1972.

(12) Nothing in this section applies to a person arrested or detained under the terrorism provisions; and subsection (1A) shall not apply where the non- intimate samples mentioned in that subsection were taken under paragraph 10 of Schedule 8 to the Terrorism Act 2000.

63   Other samples

(1) Except as provided by this section, a non-intimate sample may not be taken from a person without the appropriate consent.

(2) Consent to the taking of a non-intimate sample must be given in writing.

(3) A non-intimate sample may be taken from a person without the appropriate consent if—

(a) he is in police detention or is being held in custody by the police on the authority of a court; and

(b) an officer of at least the rank of inspector authorises it to be taken without the appropriate consent.

(3A) A non-intimate sample may be taken from a person (whether or not he fails within subsection (3)(a) above) without the appropriate consent if—

(a) he has been charged with a recordable offence or informed that he will be reported for such an offence; and

(b) either he has not had a non-intimate sample taken from him in the course of the investigation of the offence by the police or he has had a non-intimate sample taken from him but either it was not suitable for the same means of analysis or, though so suitable, the sample proved insufficient.

(3B) A non-intimate sample may be taken from a person without the appropriate consent if he has been convicted of a recordable offence.

(3C) A non-intimate sample may also be taken from a person without the appropriate consent if he is a person to whom section 2 of the Criminal Evidence (Amendment) Act 1997 applies (persons detained following acquittal on grounds of insanity or finding of unfitness to plead).

(4) An officer may only give an authorisation under subsection (3) above if he has reasonable grounds—

(a) for suspecting the involvement of the person from whom the sample is to be taken in a recordable offence; and

(b) for believing that the sample will tend to confirm or disprove his involvement.

(5) An officer may give an authorisation under subsection (3) above orally or in writing but, if he gives it orally, he shall confirm it in writing as soon as is practicable.

(6) Where—

(a) an authorisation has been given; and

(b) it is proposed that a non-intimate sample shall be taken in pursuance of the authorisation,

an officer shall inform the person from whom the sample is to be taken—

(i) of the giving of the authorisation; and

(ii) of the grounds for giving it.

(7) The duty imposed by subsection (6)(ii) above includes a duty to state the nature of the offence in which it is suspected that the person from whom the sample is to be taken has been involved.

(8) If a non-intimate sample is taken from a person by virtue of subsection (3) above—
    (*a*) the authorisation by virtue of which it was taken; and
    (*b*) the grounds for giving the authorisation,
shall be recorded as soon as is practicable after the sample is taken.

(8A) In a case where by virtue of subsection (3A), (3B) or (3C) above a sample is taken from a person without the appropriate consent—
    (a) he shall be told the reason before the sample is taken; and
    (b) the reason shall be recorded as soon as practicable after the sample is taken.

(8B) If a non-intimate sample is taken from a person at a police station, whether with or without the appropriate consent—
    (a) before the sample is taken, an officer shall inform him that it may be the subject of a speculative search; and
    (b) the fact that the person has been informed of this possibility shall be recorded as soon as practicable after the sample has been taken.

(9) If a non-intimate sample is taken from a person detained at a police station, the matters required to be recorded by subsection (8) or (8A) above shall be recorded in his custody record.

(10) Nothing in this section applies to a person arrested or detained under the terrorism provisions.

63A   Fingerprints and samples: supplementary provisions

(1) Where a person has been arrested on suspicion of being involved in a recordable offence or has been charged with such an offence or has been informed that he will be reported for such an offence, fingerprints or samples or the information derived from samples taken under any power conferred by this Part of this Act from the person may be checked against—
    (a) other fingerprints or samples to which the person seeking to check has access and which are held by or on behalf of any one or more relevant law-enforcement authorities or which are held in connection with or as a result of an investigation of an offence;
    (b) information derived from other samples if the information is contained in records to which the person seeking to check has access and which are held as mentioned in paragraph (a) above.

(1A) In subsection (1) above "relevant law-enforcement authority" means—
    (a) a police force;
    (b) the National Criminal Intelligence Service;
    (c) the National Crime Squad;
    (d) a public authority (not falling within paragraphs (a) to (c)) with functions in any part of the British Islands which consist of or include the investigation of crimes or the charging of offenders;
    (e) any person with functions in any country or territory outside the United Kingdom which—
      (i) correspond to those of a police force; or
      (ii) otherwise consist of or include the investigation of conduct contrary to the law of that country or territory, or the apprehension of persons guilty of such conduct;
    (f) any person with functions under any international agreement which consist of or include the investigation of conduct which is—
      (i) unlawful under the law of one or more places,
      (ii) prohibited by such an agreement, or
      (iii) contrary to international law,
or the apprehension of persons guilty of such conduct.

(1B) The reference in subsection (1A) above to a police force is a reference to any of the following—

    (a) any police force maintained under section 2 of the Police Act 1996 (c. 16) (police forces in England and Wales outside London);

    (b) the metropolitan police force;

    (c) the City of London police force;

    (d) any police force maintained under or by virtue of section 1 of the Police (Scotland) Act 1967 (c. 77);

    (e) the Police Service of Northern Ireland;

    (f) the Police Service of Northern Ireland Reserve;

    (g) the Ministry of Defence Police;

    (h) the Royal Navy Regulating Branch;

    (i) the Royal Military Police;

    (j) the Royal Air Force Police;

    (k) the Royal Marines Police;

    (l) the British Transport Police;

    (m) the States of Jersey Police Force;

    (n) the salaried police force of the Island of Guernsey;

    (o) the Isle of Man Constabulary.

(1C) Where—

    (a) fingerprints or samples have been taken from any person in connection with the investigation of an offence but otherwise than in circumstances to which subsection (1) above applies, and

    (b) that person has given his consent in writing to the use in a speculative search of the fingerprints or of the samples and of information derived from them, the fingerprints or, as the case may be, those samples and that information may be checked against any of the fingerprints, samples or information mentioned in paragraph (a) or (b) of that subsection.

(1D) A consent given for the purposes of subsection (IC) above shall not be capable of being withdrawn.

(2) Where a sample of hair other than pubic hair is to be taken the sample may be taken either by cutting hairs or by plucking hairs with their roots so long as no more are plucked than the person taking the sample reasonably considers to be necessary for a sufficient sample.

(3) Where any power to take a sample is exercisable in relation to a person the sample may be taken in a prison or other institution to which the Prison Act 1952 applies.

(3A) Where—

    (a) the power to take a non-intimate sample under section 63(3B) above is exercisable in relation to any person who is detained under Part III of the Mental Health Act 1983 in pursuance of—

        (i) a hospital order or interim hospital order made following his conviction for the recordable offence in question, or

        (ii) a transfer direction given at a time when he was detained in pursuance of any sentence or order imposed following that conviction, or

    (b) the power to take a non-intimate sample under section 63(3C) above is exercisable in relation to any person,

the sample may be taken in the hospital in which he is detained under that Part of that Act. Expressions used in this subsection and in the Mental Health Act 1983 have the same meaning as in that Act.

(3B) Where the power to take a non-intimate sample under section 63(3B) above is exercisable in relation to a person detained in pursuance of directions of the Secretary of State under section 92 of the Powers of Criminal Courts (Sentencing) Act 2000 the sample may be taken at the place where he is so detained.

(4) Any constable may, within the allowed period, require a person who is neither in police detention nor held in custody by the police on the authority of a court to attend a police station in order to have a sample taken where—

    (a) the person has been charged with a recordable offence or informed that he will be reported for such an offence and either he has not had a sample taken from him in the course of the investigation of the offence by the police or he has had a sample so taken from him but either it was not suitable for the same means of analysis or, though so suitable, the sample proved insufficient; or

    (b) the person has been convicted of a recordable offence and either he has not had a sample taken from him since the conviction or he has had a sample taken from him (before or after his conviction) but either it was not suitable for the same means of analysis or, though so suitable, the sample proved insufficient.

(5) The period allowed for requiring a person to attend a police station for the purpose specified in subsection (4) above is—

    (a) in the case of a person falling within paragraph (a), one month beginning with the date of the charge or of his being informed as mentioned in that paragraph or one month beginning with the date on which the appropriate officer is informed of the fact that the sample is not suitable for the same means of analysis or has proved insufficient, as the case may be;

    (b) in the case of a person falling within paragraph (b), one month beginning with the date of the conviction or one month beginning with the date on which the appropriate officer is informed of the fact that the sample is not suitable for the same means of analysis or has proved insufficient, as the case may be.

(6) A requirement under subsection (4) above—

    (a) shall give the person at least 7 days within which he must so attend; and

    (b) may direct him to attend at a specified time of day or between specified times of day.

(7) Any constable may arrest without a warrant a person who has failed to comply with a requirement under subsection (4) above.

(8) In this section "the appropriate officer" is—

    (a) in the case of a person falling within subsection (4)(a), the officer investigating the offence with which that person has been charged or as to which he was informed that he would be reported;

    (b) in the case of a person falling within subsection (4)(b), the officer in charge of the police station from which the investigation of the offence of which he was convicted was conducted.

63B   Testing for presence of Class A drugs

(1) A sample of urine or a non-intimate sample may be taken from a person in police detention for the purpose of ascertaining whether he has any specified Class A drug in his body if the following conditions are met.

(2) The first condition is—

    (a) that the person concerned has been charged with a trigger offence; or

    (b) that the person concerned has been charged with an offence and a police officer of at least the rank of inspector, who has reasonable grounds for suspecting that the misuse by that person of any specified Class A drug caused or contributed to the offence, has authorised the sample to be taken.

(3) The second condition is that the person concerned has attained the age of 18.

(4) The third condition is that a police officer has requested the person concerned to give the sample.

(5) Before requesting the person concerned to give a sample, an officer must—

(a) warn him that if, when so requested, he fails without good cause to do so he may be liable to prosecution, and

(b) in a case within subsection (2)(b) above, inform him of the giving of the authorisation and of the grounds in question.

(6) A sample may be taken under this section only by a person prescribed by regulations made by the Secretary of State by statutory instrument.

No regulations shall be made under this subsection unless a draft has been laid before, and approved by resolution of, each House of Parliament.

(7) Information obtained from a sample taken under this section may be disclosed—

(a) for the purpose of informing any decision about granting bail in criminal proceedings (within the meaning of the Bail Act 1976) to the person concerned:

(b) where the person concerned is in police detention or is remanded in or committed to custody by an order of a court or has been granted such bail, for the purpose of informing any decision about his supervision;

(c) where the person concerned is convicted of an offence, for the purpose of informing any decision about the appropriate sentence to be passed by a court and any decision about his supervision or release;

(d) for the purpose of ensuring that appropriate advice and treatment is made available to the person concerned.

(8) A person who fails without good cause to give any sample which may be taken from him under this section shall be guilty of an offence.

63C Testing for presence of Class A drugs: supplementary

(1) A person guilty of an offence under section 63B above shall be liable on summary conviction to imprisonment for a term not exceeding three months, or to a fine not exceeding level 4 on the standard scale, or to both.

(2) A police officer may give an authorisation under section 63B above orally or in writing but, if he gives it orally, he shall confirm it in writing as soon as is practicable.

(3) If a sample is taken under section 63B above by virtue of an authorisation, the authorisation and the grounds for the suspicion shall be recorded as soon as is practicable after the sample is taken.

(4) If the sample is taken from a person detained at a police station, the matters required to be recorded by subsection (3) above shall be recorded in his custody record.

(5) Subsections (11) and (12) of section 62 above apply for the purposes of section 63B above as they do for the purposes of that section; and section 63B above does not prejudice the generality of sections 62 and 63 above.

(6) In section 63B above—

"Class A drug" and "misuse" have the same meanings as in the Misuse of Drugs Act 1971;

"specified" (in relation to a Class A drug) and "trigger offence" have the same meanings as in Part III of the Criminal Justice and Court Services Act 2000.

64 Destruction of fingerprints and samples

(1A) Where—

(a) fingerprints or samples are taken from a person in connection with the investigation of an offence, and

(b) subsection (3) below does not require them to be destroyed,

the fingerprints or samples may be retained after they have fulfilled the purposes for which they were taken but shall not be used by any person except for purposes related to the prevention or detection of crime, the investigation of an offence or the conduct of a prosecution.

(1B) In subsection (1A) above—

(a)   the reference to using a fingerprint includes a reference to allowing any check to be made against it under section 63A(1) or (1C) above and to disclosing it to any person;

(b)   the reference to using a sample includes a reference to allowing any check to be made under section 63A(1) or (1C) above against it or against information derived from it and to disclosing it or any such information to any person;

(c)   the reference to crime includes a reference to any conduct which—

(i)   constitutes one or more criminal offences (whether under the law of a part of the United Kingdom or of a country or territory outside the United Kingdom); or

(ii)   is, or corresponds to, any conduct which, if it all took place in any one part of the United Kingdom, would constitute one or more criminal offences; and

(d)   the references to an investigation and to a prosecution include references, respectively, to any investigation outside the United Kingdom of any crime or suspected crime and to a prosecution brought in respect of any crime in a country or territory outside the United Kingdom.

(3) If—

(a)   fingerprints or samples are taken from a person in connection with the investigation of an offence; and

(b)   that person is not suspected of having committed the offence,

they must, except as provided in the following provisions of this section, be destroyed as soon as they have fulfilled the purpose for which they were taken.

(3AA) Samples and fingerprints are not required to be destroyed under subsection (3) above if—

(a)   they were taken for the purposes of the investigation of an offence of which a person has been convicted; and

(b)   a sample or, as the case may be, fingerprint was also taken from the convicted person for the purposes of that investigation.

(3AB) Subject to subsection (3AC) below, where a person is entitled under subsection (3) above to the destruction of any fingerprint or sample taken from him (or would be but for subsection (3AA) above), neither the fingerprint nor the sample, nor any information derived from the sample, shall be used—

(a)   in evidence against the person who is or would be entitled to the destruction of that fingerprint or sample; or

(b)   for the purposes of the investigation of any offence;

and subsection (1B) above applies for the purposes of this subsection as it applies for the purposes of subsection (1A) above.

(3AC) Where a person from whom a fingerprint or sample has been taken consents in writing to its retention—

(a)   that sample need not be destroyed under subsection (3) above;

(b)   subsection (3AB) above shall not restrict the use that may be made of the fingerprint or sample or, in the case of a sample, of any information derived from it; and

(c)   that consent shall be treated as comprising a consent for the purposes of section 63A(1C) above;

and a consent given for the purpose of this subsection shall not be capable of being withdrawn.

(3AD) For the purposes of subsection (3AC) above it shall be immaterial whether the consent is given at, before or after the time when the entitlement to the destruction of the fingerprint or sample arises.

(5) If fingerprints are destroyed—
  (a) any copies of the fingerprints shall also be destroyed; and
  (b) any chief officer of police controlling access to computer data relating to the fingerprints shall make access to the data impossible, as soon as it is practicable to do so.

(6) A person who asks to be allowed to witness the destruction of his fingerprints or copies of them shall have a right to witness it.

(6A) If—
  (a) subsection (5)(b) above falls to be complied with; and
  (b) the person to whose fingerprints the data relate asks for a certificate that it has been complied with,

such a certificate shall be issued to him, not later than the end of the period of three months beginning with the day on which he asks for it, by the responsible chief officer of police or a person authorised by him or on his behalf for the purposes of this section.

(6B) In this section—

"the responsible chief officer of police" means the chief officer of police in whose police area the computer data were put on to the computer.

(7) Nothing in this section—
  (a) affects any power conferred by paragraph 18(2) of Schedule 2 to the Immigration Act 1971 or section 20 of the Immigration and Asylum Act 1999 (c. 33) (disclosure of police information to the Secretary of State for use for immigration purposes); or
  (b) applies to a person arrested or detained under the terrorism provisions.

64A   Photographing of suspects etc

(1) A person who is detained at a police station may be photographed—
  (a) with the appropriate consent; or
  (b) if the appropriate consent is withheld or it is not practicable to obtain it, without it.

(2) A person proposing to take a photograph of any person under this section—
  (a) may, for the purpose of doing so, require the removal of any item or substance worn on or over the whole or any part of the head or face of the person to be photographed; and
  (b) if the requirement is not complied with, may remove the item or substance himself.

(3) Where a photograph may be taken under this section, the only persons entitled to take the photograph are—
  (a) constables; and
  (b) persons who (without being constables) are designated for the purposes of this section by the chief officer of police for the police area in which the police station in question is situated;

and section 117 (use of force) applies to the exercise by a person falling within paragraph (b) of the powers conferred by the preceding provisions of this section as it applies to the exercise of those powers by a constable.

(4) A photograph taken under this section—
  (a) may be used by, or disclosed to, any person for any purpose related to the prevention or detection of crime, the investigation of an offence or the conduct of a prosecution; and
  (b) after being so used or disclosed, may be retained but may not be used or disclosed except for a purpose so related.

(5) In subsection (4)—
  (a) the reference to crime includes a reference to any conduct which—

      (i) constitutes one or more criminal offences (whether under the law of a part of the United Kingdom or of a country or territory outside the United Kingdom); or

     (ii) is, or corresponds to, any conduct which, if it all took place in any one part of the United Kingdom, would constitute one or more criminal offences; and

   (b) the references to an investigation and to a prosecution include references, respectively, to any investigation outside the United Kingdom of any crime or suspected crime and to a prosecution brought in respect of any crime in a country or territory outside the United Kingdom.

(6) References in this section to taking a photograph include references to using any process by means of which a visual image may be produced; and references to photographing a person shall be construed accordingly.

65 Part V—supplementary

(1) In this Part of this Act—

"appropriate consent" means—

   (a) in relation to a person who has attained the age of 17 years, the consent of that person;

   (b) in relation to a person who has not attained that age but has attained the age of 14 years, the consent of that person and his parent or guardian; and

   (c) in relation to a person who has not attained the age of 14 years, the consent of his parent or guardian;

"authorising policeman" shall be construed in accordance with subsection (2) and (3) below;

"drug trafficking" and "drug trafficking offence" have the same meaning as in the Drug Trafficking Act 1994

"fingerprints" includes palm prints;

"intimate sample" means—

   (a) a sample of blood, semen or any other tissue fluid, urine or pubic hair;

   (b) a dental impression;

   (c) a swab taken from a person's body orifice other than the mouth;

"intimate search" means a search which consists of the physical examination of a person's body orifices other than the mouth;

"legal adviser" means—

   (a) a person who has a general qualification within the meaning of section 71 of the Courts and Legal Services Act 1990,

   (b) an advocate or solicitor in Scotland;

   (c) a member of the Bar of Northern Ireland or a solicitor of the Supreme Court of Northern Ireland; or

   (d) a person having in any Commonwealth country or territory outside the United Kingdom rights and duties similar to those of a barrister or solicitor in England and subject to punishment or disability for a breach of professional rules;

"non-intimate sample" means—

   (a) a sample of hair other than pubic hair;

   (b) a sample taken from a nail on from under a nail;

   (c) a swab taken from any part of a person's body including the mouth but not any other body orifice;

   (d) saliva;

   (e) a footprint or a similar impression of any part of a person's body other than a part of his hand;

"registered dentist" has the same meaning as in the Dentists Act 1984;

"serious service offence" means an offence under any of the service discipline Acts which cannot be dealt with summarily or which appears to a service policeman to be serious;

"service discipline Acts" means the Army Act 1955, the Air Force Act 1955 and the Naval Discipline Act 1957;

"service medical authority" means the Royal Army Medical Corps, the Royal Army Dental Corps, Queen Alexandra's Royal Army Nursing Corps, the Royal Air Force Medical Branch, the Royal Air Force Dental Branch, Princess Mary's Royal Air Force Nursing Service, the Royal Naval Medical Branch, the Royal Naval Dental Branch or Queen Alexandra's Royal Naval Nursing Service;

"service policeman" means a member of the Royal Naval Regulating Branch, the Royal Marines Police, the Royal Military Police, the Royal Air Force Police or the staff of the Royal Air Force Provost Marshal.

"speculative search", in relation to a person's fingerprints or samples, means such a check against other fingerprints or samples or against information derived from other samples as is referred to in section 63A(1) above;

"sufficient" and "insufficient", in relation to a sample, means sufficient or insufficient (in point of quantity or quality) for the purpose of enabling information to be produced by the means of analysis used or to be used in relation to the sample;

"the terrorism provisions" means section 41 of the Terrorism Act 2000, and any provision of Schedule 7 to that Act conferring a power of detention; and

"terrorism" has the meaning given in section 1 of that Act.

references in this Part to any person's proceeds of drug trafficking are to be construed in accordance with the Drug Trafficking Act 1994

(2) Subject to subsection (3) below, no person shall act as an authorising policeman unless he is a service policeman of or above the rank of Lieutenant (Royal Navy), Captain (Army) or Flight Lieutenant (Royal Air Force).

(3) In any case where it is not practicable to comply with the provisions of subsection (2) above, any service policeman may act as an authorising policeman so long as he is senior in rank to the service policeman seeking authorisation.

(4) Except for the purposes of the provisions in section 55 above (intimate searches), in any case where it is not practicable for a service policeman to seek the authorisation of an authorising policeman, a service policeman may act as if such an authorisation had been given if he has reasonable grounds for believing or suspecting the matters which an authorising policeman is required to have reasonable grounds for believing or suspecting.

Criminal Evidence (Amendment) Act 1997

Extension of power to take non-intimate body samples without consent

1 Persons imprisoned or detained by virtue of pre-existing conviction for sexual offence etc

(1) This section has effect for removing, in relation to persons to whom this section applies, the restriction on the operation of section 63(3B) of the Police and Criminal Evidence Act 1984 (power to take non-intimate samples without the appropriate consent from persons convicted of recordable offences)—

  (a) which is imposed by the subsection (10) inserted in section 63 by section 55(6) of the Criminal Justice and Public Order Act 1994, and

  (b) by virtue of which section 63(3B) does not apply to persons convicted before 10th April 1995.

(2) —

(3) This section applies to a person who was convicted of a recordable offence before 10th April 1995 if—

    (a) that offence was one of the offences listed in Schedule 1 to this Act (which lists certain sexual, violent and other offences), and

    (b) at the relevant time he is serving a sentence of imprisonment in respect of that offence.

(4) This section also applies to a person who was convicted of a recordable offence before 10th April 1995 if—

    (a) that offence was one of the offences listed in Schedule 1 to this Act, and

    (b) at the relevant time he is detained under Part III of the Mental Health Act 1983 in pursuance of—

        (i) a hospital order or interim hospital order made following that conviction, or

        (ii) a transfer direction given at a time when he was serving a sentence of imprisonment in respect of that offence.

Expressions used in this subsection and in the Mental Health Act 1983 have the same meaning as in that Act.

(5) Where a person convicted of a recordable offence before 10th April 1995 was, following his conviction for that and any other offence or offences, sentenced to two or more terms of imprisonment (whether taking effect consecutively or concurrently), he shall be treated for the purposes of this section as serving a sentence of imprisonment in respect of that offence at any time when serving any of those terms.

(6) For the purposes of this section, references to a person serving a sentence of imprisonment include references—

    (a) to his being detained in any institution to which the Prison Act 1952 applies in pursuance of any other sentence or order for detention imposed by a court in criminal proceedings, or

    (b) to his being detained (otherwise than in any such institution) in pursuance of directions of the Secretary of State under section 92 of the Powers of Criminal Courts (Sentencing) Act 2000,

and any reference to a term of imprisonment shall be construed accordingly.

2 Persons detained following acquittal on grounds of insanity or finding of unfitness to plead

(1) This section has effect for enabling non-intimate samples to be taken from persons under section 63 of the 1984 Act without the appropriate consent where they are persons to whom this section applies.

(2) —

(3) This section applies to a person if—

    (a) at the relevant time he is detained under Part III of the Mental Health Act 1983 in pursuance of an order made under—

        (i) section 5(2)(a) of the Criminal Procedure (Insanity) Act 1964 or section 6 or 14 of the Criminal Appeal Act 1968 (findings of insanity or unfitness to plead), or

        (ii) section 37(3) of the Mental Health Act 1983 (power of magistrates' court to make hospital order without convicting accused); and

    (b) that order was made on or after the date of the passing of this Act in respect of a recordable offence.

(4) This section also applies to a person if—

    (a) at the relevant time he is detained under Part III of the Mental Health Act 1983 in pursuance of an order made under—

      (i) any of the provisions mentioned in subsection (3)(a), or

     (ii) section 5(1) of the Criminal Procedure (Insanity) Act 1964 as originally enacted; and

   (b) that order was made before the date of the passing of this Act in respect of any offence listed in Schedule 1 to this Act.

(5) Subsection (4)(a)(i) does not apply to any order made under section 14(2) of the Criminal Appeal Act 1968 as originally enacted.

(6) For the purposes of this section an order falling within subsection (3) or (4) shall be treated as having been made in respect of an offence of a particular description—

   (a) if, where the order was made following—

      (i) a finding of not guilty by reason of insanity, or

     (ii) a finding that the person in question was under a disability and did the act or made the omission charged against him, or

    (iii) a finding for the purposes of section 37(3) of the Mental Health Act 1983 that the person in question did the act or made the omission charged against him, or

    (iv) (in the case of an order made under section 5(1) of the Criminal Procedure (Insanity) Act 1964 as originally enacted) a finding that he was under a disability,

that finding was recorded in respect of an offence of that description; or

   (b) if, where the order was made following the Court of Appeal forming such opinion as is mentioned in section 6(1) or 14(1) of the Criminal Appeal Act 1968, that opinion was formed on an appeal brought in respect of an offence of that description.

(7) In this section any reference to an Act "as originally enacted" is a reference to that Act as it had effect without any of the amendments made by the Criminal Procedure (Insanity and Unfitness to Plead) Act 1991.

Arrest

Police and Criminal Evidence Act 1984

24   Arrest without warrant for arrestable offences

(1) The powers of summary arrest conferred by the following subsections shall apply—

   (a) to offences for which the sentence is fixed by law;

   (b) to offences for which a person of 21 years of age or over (not previously convicted) may be sentenced to imprisonment for a term of five years (or might be so sentenced but for the restrictions imposed by section 33 of the Magistrates' Courts Act 1980); and

   (c) to the offences to which subsection (2) below applies, and in this Act "arrestable offence" means any such offence.

(2) The offences to which this subsection applies are—

   (a) offences for which a person may be arrested under the customs and excise Acts, as defined in section 1(1) of the Customs and Excise Management Act 1979;

   (b) offences under the Official Secrets Acts 1911 and 1920 that are not arrestable offences by virtue of the term of imprisonment for which a person may be sentenced in respect of them;

 (bb) offences under any provision of the Official Secrets Act 1989 except section 8(1), (4) or (5);

(c) offences under section 14 (indecent assault on a woman), 22 (causing prostitution of women) or 23 (procuration of girl under 21) of the Sexual Offences Act 1956;

(ca) an offence under section 46 of the Criminal Justice and Police Act 2001;

(d) offences under section 12(1) (taking motor vehicle or other conveyance without authority etc.) or 25(1) (going equipped for stealing, etc.) of the Theft Act 1968; and

(e) any offence under the Football (Offences) Act 1991.

(f) an offence under section 2 of the Obscene Publications Act 1959 (publication of obscene matter);

(g) an offence under section 1 of the Protection of Children Act 1978 (indecent photographs and pseudo-photographs of children);

(ga) an offence under section 1 of the Sexual Offences Act 1985 (c. 44) (kerb-crawling);

(gb) an offence under subsection (4) of section 170 of the Road Traffic Act 1988 (c. 52) (failure to stop and report an accident) in respect of an accident to which that section applies by virtue of subsection (1)(a) of that section (accidents causing personal injury);

(h) an offence under section 166 of the Criminal Justice and Public Order Act 1994 (sale of tickets by unauthorised persons);

(i) an offence under section 19 of the Public Order Act 1986 (publishing, etc. material intended or likely to stir up racial hatred);

(j) an offence under section 167 of the Criminal Justice and Public Order Act 1994 (touting for hire car services);

(k) an offence under section 1(1) of the Prevention of Crime Act 1953 (prohibition of the carrying of offensive weapons without lawful authority or reasonable excuse);

(l) an offence under section 139(1) of the Criminal Justice Act 1988 (offence of having article with blade or point in public place);

(m) an offence under section 139A(1) or (2) of the Criminal Justice Act 1988 (offence of having article with blade or point (or offensive weapon) on school premises);

(n) an offence under section 2 of the Protection from Harassment Act 1997 (harassment);

(o) an offence under section 60AA(7) of the Criminal Justice and Public Order Act 1994 (failing to comply with requirement to remove mask etc.);

(p) an offence falling within section 32(1)(a) of the Crime and Disorder Act 1998 (racially or religiously aggravated);

(q) an offence under section 14J or 21C of the Football Spectators Act 1989 (failure to comply with requirements imposed by or under a banning order or a notice under section 21B);

(qa) an offence under section 12(4) of the Criminal Justice and Police Act 2001;

(s) an offence under section 1(1) or (2) or 6 of the Wildlife and Countryside Act 1981 (taking, possessing, selling etc. of wild birds) in respect of a bird included in Schedule 1 to that Act or any part of, or anything derived from, such a bird;

(t) an offence under any of the following provisions of the Wildlife and Countryside Act 1981—
    (i) section 1(5) (disturbance of wild birds),
    (ii) section 9 or 13(1)(a) or (2) (taking, possessing, selling etc. of wild animals or plants),
    (iii) section 14 (introduction of new species etc.).

(u) an offence under section 21C(1) or 21D(1) of the Aviation Security Act 1982 (c. 36) (unauthorised presence in restricted zone or on aircraft);

(v) an offence under section 39(1) of the Civil Aviation Act 1982 (c. 16) (trespass on aerodrome).

(3) Without prejudice to section 2 of the Criminal Attempts Act 1981, the powers of summary arrest conferred by the following subsections shall also apply to the offences of—

(a) conspiring to commit any of the offences mentioned in subsection (2) above;

(b) attempting to commit any such offence;

(c) inciting, aiding, abetting, counselling or procuring the commission of any such offence;

and such offences are also arrestable offences for the purposes of this Act.

(4) Any person may arrest without a warrant—

(a) anyone who is in the act of committing an arrestable offence;

(b) anyone whom he has reasonable grounds for suspecting to be committing such an offence.

(5) Where an arrestable offence has been committed, any person may arrest without a warrant—

(a) anyone who is guilty of the offence;

(b) anyone whom he has reasonable grounds for suspecting to be guilty of it.

(6) Where a constable has reasonable grounds for suspecting that an arrestable offence has been committed, he may arrest without a warrant anyone whom he has reasonable grounds for suspecting to be guilty of the offence.

(7) A constable may arrest without a warrant—

(a) anyone who is about to commit an arrestable offence;

(b) anyone whom he has reasonable grounds for suspecting to be about to commit an arrestable offence.

25 General arrest conditions

(1) Where a constable has reasonable grounds for suspecting that any offence which is not an arrestable offence has been committed or attempted, or is being committed or attempted, he may arrest the relevant person if it appears to him that service of a summons is impracticable or inappropriate because any of the general arrest conditions is satisfied.

(2) In this section "the relevant person" means any person whom the constable has reasonable grounds to suspect of having committed or having attempted to commit the offence or of being in the course of committing or attempting to commit it.

(3) The general arrest conditions are—

(a) that the name of the relevant person is unknown to, and cannot be readily ascertained by, the constable;

(b) that the constable has reasonable grounds for doubting whether a name furnished by the relevant person as his name is his real name;

(c) that—

(i) the relevant person has failed to furnish a satisfactory address for service; or

(ii) the constable has reasonable grounds for doubting whether an address furnished by the relevant person is a satisfactory address for service;

(d) that the constable has reasonable grounds for believing that arrest is necessary to prevent the relevant person—

(i) causing physical injury to himself or any other person;

(ii) suffering physical injury;

(iii) causing loss of or damage to property;

(iv) committing an offence against public decency; or

(v) causing an unlawful obstruction of the highway;

(e) that the constable has reasonable grounds for believing that arrest is necessary to protect a child or other vulnerable person from the relevant person.

(4) For the purposes of subsection (3) above an address is a satisfactory address for service if it appears to the constable—

    (a) that the relevant person will be at it for a sufficiently long period for it to be possible to serve him with a summons; or

    (b) that some other person specified by the relevant person will accept service of a summons for the relevant person at it.

(5) Nothing in subsection (3)(d) above authorises the arrest of a person under sub-paragraph (iv) of that paragraph except where members of the public going about their normal business cannot reasonably be expected to avoid the person to be arrested.

(6) This section shall not prejudice any power of arrest conferred apart from this section.

27 Fingerprinting of certain offenders

(1) If a person—

    (a) has been convicted of a recordable offence;

    (b) has not at any time been in police detention for the offence; and

    (c) has not had his fingerprints taken—

        (i) in the course of the investigation of the offence by the police; or

        (ii) since the conviction,

any constable may at any time not later than one month after the date of the conviction require him to attend a police station in order that his fingerprints may be taken.

(2) A requirement under subsection (1) above—

    (a) shall give the person a period of at least 7 days within which he must so attend; and

    (b) may direct him to so attend at a specified time of day or between specified times of day.

(3) Any constable may arrest without warrant a person who has failed to comply with a requirement under subsection (1) above.

(4) The Secretary of State may by regulations make provision for recording in national police records convictions for such offences as are specified in the regulations.

(4A) In subsection (4) above "conviction" includes—

    (a) a caution within the meaning of Part V of the Police Act 1997; and

    (b) a reprimand or warning given under section 65 of the Crime and Disorder Act 1998.

(5) Regulations under this section shall be made by statutory instrument and shall be subject to annulment in pursuance of a resolution of either House of Parliament.

28 Information to be given on arrest

(1) Subject to subsection (5) below, where a person is arrested, otherwise than by being informed that he is under arrest the arrest is not lawful unless the person arrested is informed that he is under arrest as soon as is practicable after his arrest.

(2) Where a person is arrested by a constable, subsection (1) above applies regardless of whether the fact of the arrest is obvious.

(3) Subject to subsection (5) below, no arrest is lawful unless the person arrested is informed of the ground for the arrest at the time of, or as soon as is practicable after, the arrest.

(4) Where a person is arrested by a constable, subsection (3) above applies regardless of whether the ground for the arrest is obvious.

(5) Nothing in this section is to be taken to require a person to be informed—

    (a) that he is under arrest; or

    (b) of the ground for the arrest,

if it was not reasonably practicable for him to be so informed by reason of his having escaped from arrest before the information could be given.

56   Right to have someone informed when arrested

(1) Where a person has been arrested and is being held in custody in a police station or other premises, he shall be entitled, if he so requests, to have one friend or relative or other person who is known to him or who is likely to take an interest in his welfare told, as soon as is practicable except to the extent that delay is permitted by this section, that he has been arrested and is being detained there.

(2) Delay is only permitted—
- (a) in the case of a person who is in police detention for a serious arrestable offence; and
- (b) if an officer of at least the rank of superintendent authorises it.

(3) In any case the person in custody must be permitted to exercise the right conferred by subsection (1) above within 36 hours from the relevant time, as defined in section 41(2) above.

(4) An officer may give an authorisation under subsection (2) above orally or in writing but, if he gives it orally, he shall confirm it in writing as soon as is practicable.

(5) Subject to subsection (5A) below an officer may only authorise delay where he has reasonable grounds for believing that telling the named person of the arrest—
- (a) will lead to interference with or harm to evidence connected with a serious arrestable offence or interfernce with or physical injury to other persons; or
- (b) will lead to the alerting of other persons suspected of having committed such an offence but not yet arrested for it; or
- (c) will hinder the recovery of any property obtained as a result of such an offence.

(5A) An officer may also authorise delay where the serious arrestable offence is a drug trafficking offence or an offence to which Part VI of the Criminal Justice Act 1988 applies (offences in respect of which confiscation orders under that Part may be made) and the officer has reasonable grounds for believing—
- (a) where the offence is a drug trafficking offence, that the detained person has benefited from drug trafficking and that the recovery of the value of that person's proceeds of drug trafficking will be hindered by telling the named person of the arrest; and
- (b) where the offence is one to which Part VI of the Criminal Justice Act 1988 applies, that the detained person has benefited from the offence and that the recovery of the value of the property obtained by that person from or in connection with the offence or of the pecuniary advantage derived by him from or in connection with it will be hindered by telling the named person of the arrest.

(6) If a delay is authorised—
- (a) the detained person shall be told the reason for it; and
- (b) the reason shall be noted on his custody record.

(7) The duties imposed by subsection (6) above shall be performed as soon as is practicable.

(8) The rights conferred by this section on a person detained at a police station or other premises are exercisable whenever he is transferred from one place to another; and this section applies to each subsequent occasion on which they are exercisable as it applies to the first such occasion.

(9) There may be no further delay in permitting the exercise of the right conferred by subsection (1) above once the reason for authorising delay ceases to subsist.

(10) Nothing in this section applies to a person arrested or detained under the terrorism provisions.

SCHEDULE 2

PRESERVED POWERS OF ARREST

1892 c.43.	Section 17(2) of the Military Lands Act 1892.
1911 c.27.	Section 12(1) of the Protection of Animals Act 1911.
1920 c.55.	Section 2 of the Emergency Powers Act 1920.
1936 c.6.	Section 7(3) of the Public Order Act 1936.
1952 c.52.	Section 49 of the Prison Act 1952.
1952 c.67.	Section 13 of the Visiting Forces Act 1952.
1955 c.18.	Section 186 and 190B of the Army Act 1955.
1955 c.19.	Section 186 and 190B of the Air Force Act 1955.
1957 c.53.	Section 104 and 105 of the Naval Discipline Act 1957.
1959 c.37.	Section 1(3) of the Street Offences Act 1959.
1969 c.54.	Section 28(2) and 32 of the Children and Young Persons Act 1969.
1971 c.77.	Section 24(2) of the Immigration Act 1971 and paragraphs 17, 24 and 33 of Schedule 2 and paragraph 7 of Schedule 3 to that Act.
1972 c.20.	Sections 5(5), 7 and 100 of the Road Traffic Act 1972.
1976 c.63.	Section 7 of the Bail Act 1976.
1977 c.45.	Sections 6(6), 7(11), 8(4), 9(7) and 10(5) of the Criminal Law Act 1977.
1980 c.5.	Section 16 of the Child Care Act 1980.
1980 c.9.	Schedule 5 to the Reserve Forces Act 1980.
1981 c.22.	Sections 60(5) and 61(1) of the Animal Health Act 1981.
1983 c.20.	Sections 18, 35(10), 36(8), 38(7), 136(1) and 138 of the Mental Health Act 1983.
1984 c.8.	Sections 12 and 13 of the Prevention of Terrorism (Temporary Provisions) Act 1984.
1984 c.47.	Section 5(5) of the Repatriation of Prisoners Act 1984.

CODES OF PRACTICE, CODE C

3 Initial action

(a) Detained persons: normal procedure

3.1   When a person is brought to a police station under arrest or is arrested at the police station having attended there voluntarily, the custody officer must tell him clearly of the following rights and of the fact that they are continuing rights which may be exercised at any stage during the period in custody.

- (i) the right to have someone informed of his arrest in accordance with section 5 below;
- (ii) the right to consult privately with a solicitor and the fact that independent legal advice is available free of charge; and
- (iii) the right to consult these codes of practice.
  [See *Note 3E*]

(c) Persons attending a police station voluntarily

3.15   Any person attending a police station voluntarily for the purpose of assisting with an investigation may leave at will unless placed under arrest. If it is decided that he should not be allowed to leave then he must be informed at once that he is under arrest and brought before the custody officer, who is responsible for ensuring that he is notified of his rights in the same way as other detained persons. If he is not placed under arrest but is cautioned in accordance with section 10 below, the officer who gives the caution must at the same time inform him that he is not under arrest, that he is not obliged to remain at the police station but if he remains at the police station he may obtain free and independent legal advice if he wishes. The officer shall point out that the right to legal advice includes the right to speak with a solicitor on the telephone and ask him if he wishes to do so.

Notes for guidance

3E   The right to consult the codes of practice under paragraph 3.1 above does not entitle the person concerned to delay unreasonably and necessary investigative or administrative action while he does so. Procedures requiring the provision of breath, blood or urine specimens under the terms of the Road Traffic Act 1988 need not be delayed.

Detention

Police and Criminal Evidence Act 1984

37   Duties of custody officer after charge

(1) Where—
- (a) a person is arrested for an offence—
  - (i) without a warrant; or
  - (ii) under a warrant not endorsed for bail, the custody officer at each police station where he is detained after his arrest shall determine whether he has before him sufficient evidence to charge that person with the offence for which he was arrested and may detain him at the police station for such period as is necessary to enable him to do so.

(2) If the custody officer determines that he does not have such evidence before him, the person arrested shall be released either on bail or without bail, unless the custody officer has reasonable grounds for believing that his detention without being charged is necessary to secure or preserve evidence relating to an offence for which he is under arrest or to obtain such evidence by questioning him.

(3) If the custody officer has reasonable grounds for so believing, he may authorise the person arrested to be kept in police detention.

(4) Where a custody officer authorises a person who has not been charged to be kept in police detention, he shall, as soon as is practicable, make a written record of the grounds for the detention.

(5) Subject to subsection (6) below, the written record shall be made in the presence of the person arrested who shall at that time be informed by the custody officer of the grounds for his detention.

(6) Subsection (5) above shall not apply where the person arrested is, at the time when the written record is made—
- (a) incapable of understanding what is said to him;
- (b) violent or likely to become violent; or
- (c) in urgent need of medical attention.

(7) Subject to section 41(7) below, if the custody officer determines that he has before him sufficient evidence to charge the person arrested with the offence for which he was arrested, the person arrested—
- (a) shall be charged; or
- (b) shall be released without charge, either on bail or without bail.

(8) Where—
- (a) a person is released under subsection (7)(b) above; and
- (b) at the time of his release a decision whether he should be prosecuted for the offence for which he was arrested has not been taken,

it shall be the duty of the custody officer so to inform him.

(9) If the person arrested is not in a fit state to be dealt with under subsection (7) above, he may be kept in police detention until he is.

(10) The duty imposed on the custody officer under subsection (1) above shall be carried out by him as soon as practicable after the person arrested arrives at the police station or, in the case of a person arrested at the police station, as soon as practicable after the arrest.

(15) In this Part of this Act—

"arrested juvenile" means a person arrested with or without a warrant who appears to be under the age of 17 and is not excluded from this Part of this Act by section 52 below;

"endorsed for bail" means endorsed with a direction for bail in accordance with section 117(2) of the Magistrates' Courts Act 1980.

38 Duties of custody officer after charge

(1) Where a person arrested for an offence otherwise than under a warrant endorsed for bail is charged with an offence, the custody officer shall, subject to section 25 of the Criminal Justice and Public Order Act 1994, order his release from police detention, either on bail or without bail, unless—

   (a) if the person arrested is not an arrested juvenile—
      (i) his name or address cannot be ascertained or the custody officer has reasonable grounds for doubting whether a name or address furnished by him as his name or address is his real name or address;
      (ii) the custody officer has reasonable grounds for believing that the person arrested will fail to appear in court to answer to bail;
      (iii) in the case of a person arrested for an imprisonable offence, the custody officer has reasonable grounds for believing that the detention of the person arrested is necessary to prevent him from committing an offence;
      (iiia) in the case of a person who has attained the age of 18, the custody officer has reasonable grounds for believing that the detention of the person is necessary to enable a sample to be taken from him under section 63B below,
      (iv) in the case of a person arrested for an offence which is not an imprisonable offence, the custody officer has reasonable grounds for believing that the detention of the person arrested is necessary to prevent him from causing physical injury to any other person or from causing loss of or damage to property;
      (v) the custody officer has reasonable grounds for believing that the detention of the person arrested is necessary to prevent him from interfering with the administration of justice or with the investigation of offences or of a particular offence; or
      (vi) the custody officer has reasonable grounds for believing that the detention of the person arrested is necessary for his own protection;
   (b) if he is an arrested juvenile—
      (i) any of the requirements of paragraph (a) above is satisfied; or
      (ii) the custody officer has reasonable grounds for believing that he ought to be detained in his own interests.

(2) If the release of a person arrested is not required by subsection (1) above, the custody officer may authorise him to be kept in police detention [but may not authorise a person to be kept in police detention by virtue of subsection (1)(a)(iiia) after the end of the period of six hours beginning when he was charged with the offence].

(2A) The custody officer, in taking the decisions required by subsection (1)(a) and (b) above (except (a)(i) and (vi) and (b)(ii)), shall have regard to the same considerations as those which a court is required to have regard to in taking the corresponding decisions under paragraph 2 of Part I of Schedule 1 to the Bail Act 1976.

(3) Where a custody officer authorises a person who has been charged to be kept in police detention, he shall, as soon as practicable, make a written record of the grounds for the detention.

(4) Subject to subsection (5) below, the written record shall be made in the presence of the person charged who shall at that time be informed by the custody officer of the grounds for his detention.

(5) Subsection (4) above shall not apply where the person charged is, at the time when the written record is made—

    (a) incapable of understanding what is said to him;

    (b) violent or likely to become violent; or

    (c) in urgent need of medical attention.

(6) Where a custody officer authorises an arrested juvenile to be kept in police detention under subsection (1) above, the custody officer shall, unless he certifies—

    (a) that, by reason of such circumstances as are specified in the certificate, it is impracticable for him to do so; or

    (b) in the case of an arrested juvenile who has attained the age of 12 years, that no secure accommodation is available and that keeping him in other local authority accommodation would not be adequate to protect the public from serious harm from him, secure that the arrested juvenile is moved to local authority accommodation.

(6A) In this section—

"local authority accommodation" means accommodation provided by or on behalf of a local authority (within the meaning of the Children Act 1989);

"secure accommodation" means accommodation provided for the purpose of restricting liberty;

"sexual offence" and "violent offence" have the same meanings as in the Powers of Criminal Courts (Sentencing) Act 2000;

and any reference, in relation to an arrested juvenile charged with a violent or sexual offence, to protecting the public from serious harm from him shall be construed as a reference to protecting members of the public from death or serious personal injury, whether physical or psychological, occasioned by further such offences committed by him.

(6B) Where an arrested juvenile is moved to local authority accommodation under subsection (6) above, it shall be lawful for any person acting on behalf of the authority to detain him.

(7) A certificate made under subsection (6) above in respect of an arrested juvenile shall be produced to the court before which he is first brought thereafter.

(7A) In this section "imprisonable offence" has the same meaning as in Schedule 1 to the Bail Act 1976.

(8) In this Part of this Act "local authority" has the same meaning as in the Children and Young Persons Act 1969.

39   Responsibilities in relation to persons detained

(1) Subject to subsections (2) and (4) below, it shall be the duty of the custody officer at a police station to ensure—

    (a) that all persons in police detention at that station are treated in accordance with this Act and any code of practice issued under it and relating to the treatment of persons in police detention; and

    (b) that all matters relating to such persons which are required by this Act or by such codes of practice to be recorded are recorded in the custody records relating to such persons.

(2) If the custody officer, in accordance with any code of practice issued under this Act, transfers or permits the transfer of a person in police detention—

    (a) to the custody of a police officer investigating an offence for which that person is in police detention; or

    (b) to the custody of an officer who has charge of that person outside the police station,

the custody officer shall cease in relation to that person to be subject to the duty imposed on him by subsection (1)(a) above; and it shall be the duty of the officer to whom the transfer is made to ensure that he is treated in accordance with the provisions of this Act and of any such codes of practice as are mentioned in subsection (1) above.

(3) If the person detained is subsequently returned to the custody of the custody officer, it shall be the duty of the officer investigating the offence to report to the custody officer as to the manner in which this section and the codes of practice have been complied with while that person was in his custody.

(4) If an arrested juvenile is transferred to the care of a local authority in pursuance of arrangements made under section 38(6) above, the custody officer shall cease in relation to that person to be subject to the duty imposed on him by subsection (1) above.

(5) [Repealed]

(6) Where—

    (a) an officer of higher rank than the custody officer gives directions relating to a person in police detention; and

    (b) the directions are at variance—

        (i) with any decision made or action taken by the custody officer in the performance of a duty imposed on him under this Part of this Act; or

        (ii) with any decision or action which would but for the directions have been made or taken by him in the performance of such a duty,

the custody officer shall refer the matter at once to an officer of the rank of superintendent or above who is responsible for the police station for which the custody officer is acting as custody officer.

40   Review of police detention

(1) Reviews of the detention of each person in police detention in connection with the investigation of an offence shall be carried out periodically in accordance with the following provisions of this section—

    (a) in the case of a person who has been arrested and charged, by the custody officer; and

    (b) in the case of a person who has been arrested but not charged, by an officer of at least the rank of inspector who has not been directly involved in the investigation.

(2) The officer to whom it falls to carry out a review is referred to in this section as a "review officer".

(3) Subject to subsection (4) below—

    (a) the first review shall be not later than six hours after the detention was first authorised;

    (b) the second review shall be not later than nine hours after the first;

    (c) subsequent reviews shall be at intervals of not more than nine hours.

(4) A review may be postponed—

    (a) if, having regard to all the circumstances prevailing at the latest time for it specified in subsection (3) above, it is not practicable to carry out the review at that time;

    (b) without prejudice to the generality of paragraph (a) above—

        (i) if at that time the person in detention is being questioned by a police officer and the review officer is satisfied that an interruption of the questioning for the purpose of carrying out the review would prejudice the investigation in connection with which he is being questioned; or

   (ii) if at that time no review officer is readily available.

(5) If a review is postponed under subsection (4) above it shall be carried out as soon as practicable after the latest time specified for it in subsection (3) above.

(6) If a review is carried out after postponement under subsection (4) above, the fact that it was so carried out shall not affect any requirement of this section as to the time at which any subsequent review is to be carried out.

(7) The review officer shall record the reasons for any postponement of a review in the custody record.

(8) Subject to subsection (9) below, where the person whose detention is under review has not been charged before the time of the review, section 37(1) to (6) above shall have effect in relation to him, but with the substitution—

   (a) of references to the person whose detention is under review for references to the person arrested; and

   (b) of references to the review officer for references to the custody officer.

(9) Where a person has been kept in police detention by virtue of section 37(9) above, section 37(1) to (6) shall not have effect in relation to him but it shall be the duty of the review officer to determine whether he is yet in a fit state.

(10) Where the person whose detention is under review has been charged before the time of the review, section 38(1) to (6) above shall have effect in relation to him, but with the substitution of references to the person whose detention is under review for references to the person arrested.

(11) Where—

   (a) an officer of higher rank than the review officer gives directions relating to a person in police detention; and

   (b) the directions are at variance—

      (i) with any decision made or action taken by the review officer in the performance of a duty imposed on him under this Part of this Act; or

      (ii) with any decision or action which would but for the directions have been made or taken by him in the performance of such a duty,

the review officer shall refer the matter at once to an officer of the rank of superintendent or above who is responsible for the police station for which the review officer is acting as review officer in connection with the detention.

(12) Before determining whether to authorise a person's continued detention the review officer shall give—

   (a) that person (unless he is asleep); or

   (b) any solicitor representing him who is available at the time of the review,

an opportunity to make representations to him about the detention.

(13) Subject to subsection (14) below, the person whose detention is under review or his solicitor may make representations under subsection (12) above either orally or in writing.

(14) The review officer may refuse to hear oral representations from the person whose detention is under review if he considers that he is unfit to make such representations by reason of his condition or behaviour.

41 Limits on period of detention without charge

(1) Subject to the following provisions of this section and to section 42 and 43 below, a person shall not be kept in police detention for more than 24 hours without being charged.

(2) The time from which the period of detention of a person is to be calculated (in this Act referred to as "the relevant time")—

(a) in the case of a person to whom this paragraph applies, shall be—

    (i)   the time at which that person arrives at the relevant police station; or

    (ii) the time 24 hours after the time of that person's arrest,

whichever is the earlier;

(b) in the case of a person arrested outside England and Wales, shall be—

    (i)   the time at which that person arrives at the first police station to which he is taken in the police area in England or Wales in which the offence for which he was arrested is being investigated; or

    (ii) the time 24 hours after the time of that person's entry into England and Wales, whichever is the earlier;

(c) in the case of a person who—

    (i)   attends voluntarily at a police station; or

    (ii) accompanies a constable to a police station without having been arrested, and is arrested at the police station, the time of his arrest;

(d) in any other case, except where subsection (5) below applies, shall be the time at which the person arrested arrives at the first police station to which he is taken after his arrest.

(3) Subsection (2)(a) above applies to a person if—

(a) his arrest is sought in one police area in England and Wales;

(b) he is arrested in another police area; and

(c) he is not questioned in the area in which he is arrested in order to obtain evidence in relation to an offence for which he is arrested;

and in sub-paragraph (i) of that paragraph "the relevant police station" means the first police station to which he is taken in the police area in which his arrest was sought.

(4) Subsection (2) above shall have effect in relation to a person arrested under section 31 above as if every reference in it to his arrest or his being arrested were a reference to his arrest or his being arrested for the offence for which he was originally arrested.

(5) If—

(a) a person is in police detention in a police area in England and Wales ("the first area"); and

(b) his arrest for an offence is sought in some other police area in England and Wales ("the second area"); and

(c) he is taken to the second area for the purposes of investigating that offence, without being questioned in the first area in order to obtain evidence in relation to it,

the relevant time shall be—

    (i)   the time 24 hours after he leaves the place where he is detained in the first area; or

    (ii) the time at which he arrives at the first police station to which he is taken in the second area,

whichever is the earlier.

(6) When a person who is in police detention is removed to hospital because he is in need of medical treatment, any time during which he is being questioned in hospital or on the way there or back by a police officer for the purpose of obtaining evidence relating to an offence shall be included in any period which falls to be calculated for the purposes of this Part of this Act, but any other time while he is in hospital or on his way there or back shall not be so included.

(7) Subject to subsection (8) below, a person who at the expiry of 24 hours after the relevant time is in police detention and has not been charged shall be released at that time either on bail or without bail.

(8) Subsection (7) above does not apply to a person whose detention for more than 24 hours after the relevant time has been authorised or is otherwise permitted in accordance with section 42 or 43 below.

(9) A person released under subsection (7) above shall not be re-arrested without a

warrant for the offence for which he was previously arrested unless new evidence justifying a further arrest has come to light since his release [; but this subsection does not prevent an arrest under section 46A below].

42   Authorisation of continued detention

(1) Where a police officer of the rank of superintendent or above who is responsible for the police station at which a person is detained has reasonable grounds for believing that—

    (a) the detention of that person without charge is necessary to secure or preserve evidence relating to an offence for which he is under arrest or to obtain such evidence by questioning him;

    (b) an offence for which he is under arrest is a serious arrestable offence; and

    (c) the investigation is being conducted diligently and expeditiously,

he may authorise the keeping of that person in police detention for a period expiring at or before 36 hours after the relevant time.

(2) Where an officer such as is mentioned in subsection (1) above has authorised the keeping of a person in police detention for a period expiring less than 36 hours after the relevant time, such an officer may authorise the keeping of that person in police detention for a further period expiring not more than 36 hours after that time if the conditions specified in subsection (1) above are still satisfied when he gives the authorisation.

(3) If it is proposed to transfer a person in police detention to another police area, the officer determining whether or not to authorise keeping him in detention under subsection (1) above shall have regard to the distance and the time the journey would take.

(4) No authorisation under subsection (1) above shall be given in respect of any person—

    (*a*) more than 24 hours after the relevant time; or

    (*b*) before the second review of his detention under section 40 above has been carried out.

(5) Where an officer authorises the keeping of a person in police detention under subsection (1) above, it shall be his duty—

    (a) to inform that person of the grounds for his continued detention; and

    (b) to record the grounds in that person's custody record.

(6) Before determining whether to authorise the keeping of a person in detention under subsection (1) or (2) above, an officer shall give—

    (a) that person; or

    (b) any solicitor representing him who is available at the time when it falls to the officer to determine whether to give the authorisation,

an opportunity to make representations to him about the detention.

(7) Subject to subsection (8) below, the person in detention or his solicitor may make representations under subsection (6) above either orally or in writing.

(8) The officer to whom it falls to determine whether to give the authorisation may refuse to hear oral representations from the person in detention if he considers that he is unfit to make such representations by reason of his condition or behaviour.

(9) Where—

    (a) an officer authorises the keeping of a person in detention under subsection (1) above; and

    (b) at the time of the authorisation he has not yet exercised a right conferred on him by section 56 or 58 below,

the officer—

    (i) shall inform him of that right;

    (ii) shall decide whether he should be permitted to exercise it;

    (iii) shall record the decision in his custody record; and

    (iv) if the decision is to refuse to permit the exercise of the right, shall also record the grounds for the decision in that record.

(10) Where an officer has authorised the keeping of a person who has not been charged in detention under subsection (1) or (2) above, he shall be released from detention, either on bail or without bail, not later than 36 hours after the relevant time, unless—

(a) he has been charged with an offence; or

(b) his continued detention is authorised or otherwise permitted in accordance with section 43 below.

(11) A person released under subsection (10) above shall not be re-arrested without a warrant for the offence for which he was previously arrested unless new evidence justifying a further arrest has come to light since his release [; but this subsection does not prevent an arrest under section 46A below].

43   Warrants of further detention

(1) Where, on an application on oath made by a constable and supported by an information, a magistrates' court is satisfied that there are reasonable grounds for believing that the further detention of the person to whom the application relates is justified, it may issue a warrant of further detention authorising the keeping of that person in police detention.

(2) A court may not hear an application for a warrant of further detention unless the person to whom the application relates—

(a) has been furnished with a copy of the information; and

(b) has been brought before the court for the hearing.

(3) The person to whom the application relates shall be entitled to be legally represented at the hearing and, if he is not so represented but wishes to be so represented—

(a) the court shall adjourn the hearing to enable him to obtain representation; and

(b) he may be kept in police detention during the adjournment.

(4) A person's further detention is only justified for the purposes of this section or section 44 below if—

(a) his detention without charge is necessary to secure or preserve evidence relating to an offence for which he is under arrest or to obtain such evidence by questioning him;

(b) an offence for which he is under arrest is a serious arrestable offence; and

(c) the investigation is being conducted diligently and expeditiously.

(5) Subject to subsection (7) below, an application for a warrant of further detention may be made—

(a) at any time before the expiry of 36 hours after the relevant time; or

(b) in a case where—

(i) it is not practicable for the magistrates' court to which the application will be made to sit at the expiry of 36 hours after the relevant time; but

(ii) the court will sit during the 6 hours following the end of that period,

at any time before the expiry of the said 6 hours.

(6) In a case to which subsection (5)(b) above applies—

(a) the person to whom the application relates may be kept in police detention until the application is heard; and

(b) the custody officer shall make a note in that person's custody record—

(i) of the fact that he was kept in police detention for more than 36 hours after the relevant time; and

(ii) of the reason why he was so kept.

(7) If—

(a) an application for a warrant of further detention is made after the expiry of 36 hours after the relevant time; and

(b) it appears to the magistrates' court that it would have been reasonable for the police to make it before the expiry of that period,

the court shall dismiss the application.

(8) Where on an application such as is mentioned in subsection (1) above a magistrates' court is not satisfied that there are reasonable grounds for believing that the further detention of the person to whom the application relates is justified, it shall be its duty—

(a) to refuse the application; or

(b) to adjourn the hearing of it until a time not later than 36 hours after the relevant time.

(9) The person to whom the application relates may be kept in police detention during the adjournment.

(10) A warrant of further detention shall—

(a) state the time at which it is issued;

(b) authorise the keeping in police detention of the person to whom it relates for the period stated in it.

(11) Subject to subsection (12) below, the period stated in a warrant of further detention shall be such period as the magistrates' court thinks fit, having regard to the evidence before it.

(12) The period shall not be longer than 36 hours.

(13) If it is proposed to transfer a person in police detention to a police area other than that in which he is detained when the application for a warrant of further detention is made, the court hearing the application shall have regard to the distance and the time the journey would take.

(14) Any information submitted in support of an application under this section shall state—

(a) the nature of the offence for which the person to whom the application relates has been arrested;

(b) the general nature of the evidence on which that person was arrested;

(c) what inquiries relating to the offence have been made by the police and what further inquiries are proposed by them;

(d) the reasons for believing the continued detention of that person to be necessary for the purposes of such further inquiries.

(15) Where an application under this section is refused, the person to whom the application relates shall forthwith be charged or, subject to subsection (16) below, released, either on bail or without bail.

(16) A person need not be released under subsection (15) above—

(a) before the expiry of 24 hours after the relevant time; or

(b) before the expiry of any longer period for which his continued detention is or has been authorised under section 42 above.

(17) Where an application under this section is refused, no further application shall be made under this section in respect of the person to whom the refusal relates, unless supported by evidence which has come to light since the refusal.

(18) Where a warrant of further detention is issued, the person to whom it relates shall be released from police detention, either on bail or without bail, upon or before the expiry of the warrant unless he is charged.

(19) A person released under subsection (18) above shall not be re-arrested without a warrant for the offence for which he was previously arrested unless new evidence justifying a further arrest has come to light since his release; but this subsection does not prevent an arrest under section 46A below.

44 Extension of warrants of further detention

(1) On an application on oath made by a constable and supported by an information a magistrates' court may extend a warrant of further detention issued under section 43 above if it is satisfied that there are reasonable grounds for believing that the further detention of the person to whom the application relates is justified.

(2) Subject to subsection (3) below, the period for which a warrant of further detention may be extended shall be such period as the court thinks fit, having regard to the evidence before it.

(3) The period shall not—
  (a) be longer than 36 hours; or
  (b) end later than 96 hours after the relevant time.

(4) Where a warrant of further detention has been extended under subsection (1) above, or further extended under this subsection, for a period ending before 96 hours after the relevant time, on an application such as is mentioned in that subsection a magistrates' court may further extend the warrant if it is satisfied as there mentioned; and subsections (2) and (3) above apply to such further extensions as they apply to extensions under subsection (1) above.

(5) A warrant of further detention shall, if extended or further extended under this section, be endorsed with a note of the period of the extension.

(6) Subsections (2), (3) and (14) of section 43 above shall apply to an application made under this section as they apply to an application made under that section.

(7) Where an application under this section is refused, the person to whom the application relates shall forthwith be charged or, subject to subsection (8) below, released, either on bail or without bail.

(8) A person need not be released under subsection (7) above before the expiry of any period for which a warrant of further detention issued in relation to him has been extended or further extended on an earlier application made under this section.

45   Detention before charge—supplementary

(1) In sections 43 and 44 of this Act "magistrates' court" means a court consisting of two or more justices of the peace sitting otherwise than in open court.

(2) Any reference in this Part of this Act to a period of time or a time of day is to be treated as approximate only.

46   Detention after charge

(1) Where a person—
  (a) is charged with an offence; and
  (b) after being charged—
    (i) is kept in police detention; or
    (ii) is detained by a local authority in pursuance of arrangements made under section 38(6) above,
he shall be brought before a magistrates' court in accordance with the provisions of this section.

(2) If he is to be brought before a magistrates' court for the petty sessions area in which the police station at which he was charged is situated, he shall be brought before such a court as soon as is practicable and in any event not later than the first sitting after he is charged with the offence.

(3) If no magistrates' court for that area is due to sit either on the day on which he is charged or on the next day, the custody officer for the police station at which he was charged shall inform the clerk to the justices for the area that there is a person in the area to whom subsection (2) above applies.

(4) If the person charged is to be brought before a magistrates' court for a petty sessions area other than that in which the police station at which he was charged is situated, he shall be removed to that area as soon as is practicable and brought before such a court as soon as is practicable after his arrival in the area and in any event not later than the first sitting of a magistrates' court for that area after his arrival in the area.

(5) If no magistrates' court for that area is due to sit either on the day on which he arrives in the area or on the next day—

    (a) he shall be taken to a police station in the area; and

    (b) the custody officer at that station shall inform the clerk to the justices for the area that there is a person in the area to whom subsection (4) applies.

(6) Subject to subsection (8) below, where a clerk to the justices for a petty sessions area has been informed—

    (a) under subsection (3) above that there is a person in the area to whom subsection (2) above applies; or

    (b) under subsection (5) above that there is a person in the area to whom subsection (4) above applies,

the clerk shall arrange for a magistrates' court to sit not later than the day next following the relevant day.

(7) In this section "the relevant day"—

    (a) in relation to a person who is to be brought before a magistrates' court for the petty sessions area in which the police station at which he was charged is situated, means the day on which he was charged; and

    (b) in relation to a person who is to be brought before a magistrates' court for any other petty sessions area, means the day on which he arrives in the area.

(8) Where the day next following the relevant day is Christmas Day, Good Friday or a Sunday, the duty of the justices' chief executive under subsection (6) above is a duty to arrange for a magistrates' court to sit not later than the first day after the relevant day which is not one of those days.

(9) Nothing in this section requires a person who is in hospital to be brought before a court if he is not well enough.

46A   Power of arrest for failure to answer to police bail.

(1) A constable may arrest without a warrant any person who, having been released on bail under this Part of this Act subject to a duty to attend at a police station, fails to attend at that police station at the time appointed for him to do so.

(2) A person who is arrested under this section shall be taken to the police station appointed as the place at which he is to surrender to custody as soon as practicable after the arrest.

(3) For the purposes of—

    (a) section 30 above (subject to the obligation in subsection (2) above), and

    (b) section 31 above,

an arrest under this section shall be treated as an arrest for an offence.

CODES OF PRACTICE, CODE C

2   Custody records

2.1   A separate custody record must be opened as soon as practicable for each person who is brought to a police station under arrest or is arrested at the police station having attended there voluntarily. All information which has to be recorded under this code must be recorded as soon as practicable in the custody record unless otherwise specified. Any audio or video recording made in the custody area is not part of the custody record.

2.2   In the case of any action requiring the authority of an officer of a specified rank, his name and rank must be noted in the custody record. The recording of names does not apply to officers dealing with people detained under the Prevention of Terrorism (Temporary Provisions) Act 1989. Instead the record shall state the warrant or other identification number and duty station of such officers.

2.3   The custody officer is responsible for the accuracy and completeness of the custody record and for ensuring that the record or a copy of the record accompanies a detained person if he is transferred to another police station. The record shall show the time of and reason for transfer and the time a person is released from detention.

2.4   A solicitor or appropriate adult must be permitted to consult the custody record of a person detained as soon as practicable after their arrival at the police station. When a person leaves police detention or is taken before a court, he or his legal representative or his appropriate adult shall be supplied on request with a copy of the custody record as soon as practicable. This entitlement lasts for 12 months after his release.

2.5   The person who has been detained, the appropriate adult, or the legal representative shall be permitted to inspect the original custody record after the person has left police detention provided they give reasonable notice of their request. A note of any such inspection shall be made in the custody record.

2.6   All entries in custody records must be timed and signed by the maker. In the case of a record entered on a computer this shall be timed and contain the operator's identification. Warrant or other identification numbers shall be used rather than names in the case of detention under the Prevention of Terrorism (Temporary Provisions) Act 1989.

2.7   The fact and time of any refusal by a person to sign a custody record when asked to do so in accordance with the provisions of this code must itself be recorded.

Initial action
For paragraph 3, see page 34.

5   Right not to be held incommunicado

(a) Action

5.1   Any person arrested and held in custody at a police station or other premises may on request have one person known to him or who is likely to take an interest in his welfare informed at public expense of his whereabouts as soon as practicable. If the person cannot be contacted the person who has made the request may choose up to two alternatives. If they too cannot be contacted the person in charge of detention or of the investigation has discretion to allow further attempts until the information has been conveyed. [See *Notes 5C and 5D*]

5.2   The exercise of the above right in respect of each of the persons nominated may be delayed only in accordance with *Annex B* to this code.

5.3   The above right may be exercised on each occasion that a person is taken to another police station.

5.4   The person may receive visits at the custody officer's discretion. [See *Note 5B*]

5.5   Where an enquiry as to the whereabouts of the person is made by a friend, relative or person with an interest in his welfare, this information shall be given, if he agrees and if *Annex B* does not apply. [See *Note 5D*]

5.6   Subject to the following condition, the person shall be supplied with writing materials on request and allowed to speak on the telephone for a reasonable time to one person [See *Notes 5A and 5E*]. Where an officer of the rank of Inspector or above considers that the sending of a letter or the making of a telephone call may result in:

(a) any of the consequences set out in the first and second paragraphs of *Annex B* and the person is detained in connection with an arrestable or a serious arrestable offence, for which purpose, any reference to a serious arrestable offence in *Annex B* includes an arrestable offence; or

(b) either of the consequences set out in paragraph 8 of *Annex B* and the person is detained under the Prevention of Terrorism (Temporary Provisions) Act 1989;

that officer can deny or delay the exercise of either or both these privileges. However, nothing in this section permits the restriction or denial of the rights set out in paragraphs 5.1 and 6.1.

5.7   Before any letter or message is sent, or telephone call made, the person shall be informed that what he says in any letter, call or message (other than in the case of a communication to a solicitor) may be read or listened to as appropriate and may be given in evidence. A telephone call may be terminated if it is being abused. The costs can be at public expense at the discretion of the custody officer.

(b) Documentation

5.8   A record must be kept of:

(a)   any request made under this section and the action taken on it;

(b)   any letters, messages or telephone calls made or received or visits received; and

(c)   any refusal on the part of the person to have information about himself or his whereabouts given to an outside enquirer. The person must be asked to countersign the record accordingly and any refusal to sign shall be recorded.

Notes for guidance

5A   An interpreter may make a telephone call or write a letter on a person's behalf.

5B   In the exercise of his discretion the custody officer should allow visits where possible in the light of the availability of sufficient manpower to supervise a visit and any possible hindrance to the investigation.

5C   If the person does not know of anyone to contact for advice or support or cannot contact a friend or relative, the custody officer should bear in mind any local voluntary bodies or other organisations who might be able to offer help in such cases. But if it is specifically legal advice that is wanted, then paragraph 6.1 below will apply.

5D   In some circumstances it may not be appropriate to use the telephone to disclose information under paragraphs 5.1 and 5.5 above.

5E   The telephone call at paragraph 5.6 is in addition to any communication under paragraphs 5.1 and 6.1.

6   Right to legal advice

(a) Action

6.1   Subject to the provisos in *Annex B* all people in police detention must be informed that they may at any time consult and communicate privately, whether in person, in writing or by telephone with a solicitor, and that independent legal advice is available free of charge from the duty solicitor. [See paragraph 3.1 and *Note 6B and Note 6J*]

6.2   [Not Used]

6.3   A poster advertising the right to have legal advice must be prominently displayed in the charging area of every police station. [See *Note 6H*]

6.4   No police officer shall at any time do or say anything with the intention of dissuading a person in detention from obtaining legal advice.

6.5   The exercise of the right of access to legal advice may be delayed only in accordance with *Annex B* to this code. Whenever legal advice is requested (and unless *Annex B* applies) the custody officer must act without delay to secure the provision of such advice to the person concerned. If, on being informed or reminded of the right to legal advice, the person declines to speak to a solicitor in person, the officer shall point out that the right to legal advice includes the right to speak with a solicitor on the telephone and ask him if he wishes to do so. If the person continues to waive his right to legal advice the officer shall ask him the reasons for doing so, and any reasons shall be recorded on the custody record or the interview record as appropriate. Reminders of the right to legal advice must be given in accordance with paragraphs 3.5, 11.2, 15.3, 16.4 and 16.5 of this code and paragraphs 2.15(ii) and 5.2 of Code D. Once it is clear that a person neither wishes to speak to a solicitor in person nor by telephone he should cease to be asked his reasons. [See *Note 6K*]

6.6   A person who wants legal advice may not be interviewed or continue to be interviewed until he has received it unless:

(a)   *Annex B* applies; or

(b)   an officer of the rank of superintendent or above has reasonable grounds for believing that:

(i)   delay will involve an immediate risk of harm to persons or serious loss of, or damage to, property; or

> > (ii) where a solicitor, including a duty solicitor, has been contacted and has agreed to attend, awaiting his arrival would cause unreasonable delay to the process of investigation; or
> (c) the solicitor nominated by the person, or selected by him from a list:
> > (i) cannot be contacted; or
> > (ii) has previously indicated that he does not wish to be contacted; or
> > (iii) having been contacted, has declined to attend;

and the person has been advised of the Duty Solicitor Scheme but has declined to ask for the duty solicitor, or the duty solicitor is unavailable. (In these circumstances the interview may be started or continued without further delay provided that an officer of the rank of Inspector or above has given agreement for the interview to proceed in those circumstances – see *Note 6B*).

> (d) the person who wanted legal advice changes his mind.
> > In these circumstances the interview may be started or continued without further delay provided that the person has given his agreement in writing or on tape to being interviewed without receiving legal advice and that an officer of the rank of Inspector or above, having inquired into the person's reasons for his change of mind, has given authority for the interview to proceed. Confirmation of the person's agreement, his change of mind, his reasons where given and the name of the authorising officer shall be recorded in the taped or written interview record at the beginning or re-commencement of interview. [See *Note 6I*]

6.7   Where 6.6(b)(i) applies, once sufficient information to avert the risk has been obtained, questioning must cease until the person has received legal advice unless 6.6(a), (b)(ii), (c) or (d) apply.

6.8   Where a person has been permitted to consult a solicitor and the solicitor is available (i.e. present at the station or on his way to the station or easily contactable by telephone) at the time the interview begins or is in progress, the solicitor must be allowed to be present while he is interviewed.

6.9   The solicitor may only be required to leave the interview if his conduct is such that the investigating officer is unable properly to put questions to the suspect. [See *Notes 6D* and *6E*]

6.10   If the investigating officer considers that a solicitor is acting in such a way, he will stop the interview and consult an officer not below the rank of superintendent, if one is readily available, and otherwise an officer not below the rank of inspector who is not connected with the investigation. After speaking to the solicitor, the officer who has been consulted will decide whether or not the interview should continue in the presence of that solicitor. If he decides that it should not, the suspect will be given the opportunity to consult another solicitor before the interview continues and that solicitor will be given an opportunity to be present at the interview.

6.11   The removal of a solicitor from an interview is a serious step and, if it occurs, the officer of superintendent rank or above who took the decision will consider whether the incident should be reported to the Law Society. If the decision to remove the solicitor has been taken by an officer below the rank of superintendent, the facts must be reported to an officer of superintendent rank or above who will similarly consider whether a report to the Law Society would be appropriate. Where the solicitor concerned is a duty solicitor, the report should be both to the Law Society and to the Legal Aid Board.

6.12   In Codes of Practice issued under the Police and Criminal Evidence Act 1984, "solicitor" means a solicitor who holds a current practising certificate, a trainee solicitor, a duty solicitor representative or an accredited representative included on the register of representatives maintained by the Legal Aid Board. If a solicitor wishes to send a non-accredited or probationary representative to provide advice on his behalf, then that person shall be admitted to the police station for this purpose unless an officer of the rank of inspector or above considers that such a visit will hinder the investigation of crime and directs otherwise. (Hindering the investigation of a crime does not include giving proper legal advice to a detained person in accordance with *Note 6D*.) Once admitted to the police station, the provisions of paragraphs 6.6 to 6.10 apply.

6.13 In exercising his discretion under paragraph 6.12, the officer should take into account in particular whether the identity and status of the non-accredited or probationary representative have been satisfactory established; whether he is of suitable character to provide legal advice (a person with a criminal record is unlikely to be suitable unless the conviction was for a minor offence and is not of recent date); and any other matters in any written letter of authorisation provided by the solicitor on whose behalf the person is attending the police station. [See *Note 6F*]

6.14 If the inspector refuses access to a non-accredited or probationary representative or a decision is taken that such a person should not be permitted to remain at an interview, he must forthwith notify a solicitor on whose behalf the non-accredited or probationary representative was to have acted or was acting, and give him an opportunity to make alternative arrangements. The detained person must also be informed and the custody record noted.

6.15 If a solicitor arrives at the station to see a particular person, that person must (unless *Annex B* applies) be informed of the solicitor's arrival whether or not he is being interviewed and asked whether he would like to see him. This applies even if the person concerned has already declined legal advice or having requested it, subsequently agreed to be interviewed without having received advice. The solicitor's attendance and the detained person's decision must be noted in the custody record.

(b) Documentation

6.16 Any request for legal advice and the action taken on it shall be recorded.

6.17 If a person has asked for legal advice and an interview is begun in the absence of a solicitor or his representative (or the solicitor or his representative has been required to leave an interview), a record shall be made in the interview record.

Notes for guidance

6A In considering whether paragraph 6.6(b) applies, the officer should where practicable ask the solicitor for an estimate of the time that he is likely to take, in coming to the station, and relate this information to the time for which detention is permitted, the time of day (i.e. whether the period of rest required by paragraph 12.2 is imminent) and the requirements of other investigations in progress. If the solicitor says that he is on his way to the station or that he will set off immediately it will not normally be appropriate to begin an interview before he arrives. If it appears that it will be necessary to begin an interview before the solicitor's arrival he should be given an indication of how long the police would be able to wait before paragraph 6.6(b) applies so that he has an opportunity to make arrangements for legal advice to be provided by someone else.

6B A person who asks for legal advice should be given an opportunity to consult a specific solicitor or another solicitor from that solicitor's firm or the duty solicitor. If advice is not available by these means, or he does not wish to consult the duty solicitor, the person should be given an opportunity to choose a solicitor from a list of those willing to provide legal advice. If the solicitor is unavailable, he may choose up to two alternatives. If these attempts to secure legal advice are unsuccessful, the custody officer has discretion to allow further attempts until a solicitor has been contacted and agrees to provide legal advice. Apart from carrying out his duties under Note 6B, a police officer must not advise the suspect about any particular firm of solicitors.

6C [Not Used]

6D A detained person has a right to free legal advice and to be represented by a solicitor. The solicitor's only role in the police station is to protect and advance the legal rights of his client. On occasions this may require the solicitor to give advice which has the effect of his client avoiding giving evidence which strengthens a prosecution case. The solicitor may intervene in order to seek clarification or to challenge an improper question to his client or the manner in which it is put, or to advise his client not to reply to particular questions, or if he wishes to give his client further legal advice. Paragraph 6.9 will only apply if the solicitor's approach or conduct prevents or unreasonably obstructs proper questions being put to the suspect or his response being recorded. Examples of unacceptable conduct include answering questions on a suspect's behalf or providing written replies for him to quote.

6E   In a case where an officer takes the decision to exclude a solicitor, he must be in a position to satisfy the court that the decision was properly made. In order to do this he may need to witness what is happening himself.

6F   If an officer of at least the rank of inspector considers that a particular solicitor or firm of solicitors is persistently sending non-accredited or probationary representatives who are unsuited to provide legal advice, he should inform an officer of at least the rank of superintendent, who may wish to take the matter up with the Law Society.

6G   Subject to the constraints of Annex B, a solicitor may advise more than one client in an investigation if he wishes. Any question of a conflict of interest is for the solicitor under his professional code of conduct. If, however, waiting for a solicitor to give advice to one client may lead to unreasonable delay to the interview with another, the provisions of paragraph 6.6(b) may apply.

6H   In addition to a poster in English advertising the right to legal advice, a poster or posters containing translations into Welsh, the main ethnic minority languages and the principal European languages should be displayed wherever they are likely to be helpful and it is practicable to do so.

6I   Paragraph 6.6(d) requires the authorisation of an officer of the rank of inspector or above, to the continuation of an interview, where a person who wanted legal advice changes his mind. It is permissible for such authorisation to be given over the telephone, if the authorising officer is able to satisfy himself as to the reason for the person's change of mind and is satisfied that it is proper to continue the interview in those circumstances.

6J   Where a person chooses to speak to a solicitor on the telephone, he should be allowed to do so in private unless this is impractical because of the design and layout of the custody area or the location of telephones.

6K   A person is not obliged to give reasons for declining legal advice and should not be pressed if he does not wish to do so.

8   Conditions of detention

(a) Action

8.1   So far as is practicable, not more than one person shall be detained in each cell.

8.2   Cells in use must be adequately heated, cleaned and ventilated. They must be adequately lit, subject to such dimming as is compatible with safety and security to allow people detained overnight to sleep. No additional restraints shall be used within a locked cell unless absolutely necessary, and then only suitable handcuffs. In the case of a mentally handicapped or mentally disorded person, particular care must be taken when deciding whether to use handcuffs. [See Annex E paragraph 13]

8.3   Blankets, mattresses, pillows and other bedding supplied shall be of a reasonable standard and in a clean and sanitary condition. [See *Note 8B*]

8.4   Access to toilet and washing facilities must be provided.

8.5   If it is necessary to remove a person's clothes for the purposes of investigation, for hygiene or health reasons or for cleaning, replacement clothing of a reasonable standard of comfort and cleanliness shall be provided. A person may not be interviewed unless adequate clothing has been offered to him.

8.6   At least two light meals and one main meal shall be offered in any period of 24 hours. [See *Note 8C*] Drinks should be provided at meal times and upon reasonable request between meal times. Whenever necessary, advice shall be sought from the police surgeon on medical and dietary matters. As far as practicable, meals provided shall offer a varied diet and meet any special dietary needs or religious beliefs that the person may have; he may also have meals supplied by his family or friends at his or their own expense. [See *Note 8B*]

8.7   Brief outdoor exercise shall be offered daily if practicable.

8.8   A juvenile shall not be placed in a police cell unless no other secure accommodation is available and the custody officer considers that it is not practicable to supervise him if he is not placed in a cell or the custody officer considers that a cell provides more comfortable accommodation than other secure accommodation in the police station. He may not be placed in a cell with a detained adult.

8.9   Reasonable force may be used if necessary for the following purposes:
  (i)   to secure compliance with reasonable instructions, including instructions given in pursuance of the provisions of a code of practice; or
  (ii) to prevent escape, injury, damage to property or the destruction of evidence.

8.10   People detained shall be visited every hour, and those who are drunk, at least every half hour. A person who is drunk shall be roused and spoken to on each visit. [see *Note 8A*] Should the custody officer feel in any way concerned about the person's condition, for example because he fails to respond adequately when roused, then the officer shall arrange for medical treatment in accordance with paragraph 9.2 of this code.

(b) Documentation

8.11   A record must be kept of replacement clothing and meals offered.

8.12   If a juvenile is placed in a cell, the reason must be recorded.

Notes for guidance

8A   Whenever possible juveniles and other people at risk should be visited more frequently.

8B   The provisions in paragraphs 8.3 and 8.6 respectively regarding bedding and a varied diet are of particular importance in the case of a person detained under the Prevention of Terrorism (Temporary Provisions) Act 1989, immigration detainees and others who are likely to be detained for an extended period.

8C   Meals should so far as practicable be offered at recognised meal times.

ANNEX B   DELAY IN NOTIFYING ARREST OR ALLOWING ACCESS
TO LEGAL ADVICE

A   Persons detained under the Police and Criminal Evidence Act 1984

(a) Action

1   The rights set out in sections 5 or 6 of the code or both may be delayed if the person is in police detention in connection with a serious arrestable offence, has not yet been charged with an offence and an officer of the rank of superintendent or above has reasonable grounds for believing that the exercise of either right:
  (i)   will lead to interference with or harm to evidence connected with a serious arrestable offence or interference with or physical injury to other people; or
  (ii) will lead to the alerting of other people suspected of having committed such an offence but not yet arrested for it; or
  (iii) will hinder the recovery of property obtained as a result of such an offence.
[See *Note B3*]

2   These rights may also be delayed where the serious arrestable offence is either,
  (i)   a drug trafficking offence and the officer has reasonable grounds for believing that the detained person has benefited from drug trafficking, and that the recovery of the value of that person's proceeds of drug trafficking will be hindered by the exercise of either right.
  (ii) an offence to which Part VI of the Criminal Justice Act 1988 (covering confiscation orders) applies and the officer has reasonable grounds for believing that the detained person has benefited from the offence, and that the recovery of the value of the property obtained by that person from or in connection with the offence, or if the pecuniary advantage derived by him from or in connection with it, will be hindered by the exercise of either right.

3   Access to a solicitor may not be delayed on the grounds that he might advise the person not to answer any questions or that the solicitor was initially asked to attend the police station by someone else, provided that the person himself then wishes to see the solicitor. In the latter case the detained person must be told that the solicitor has come to the police station at another person's request, and must be asked to sign the custody record to signify whether or not he wishes to see the solicitor.

4   These rights may be delayed only for as long as is necessary and, subject to paragraph 9 below, in no case beyond 36 hours after the relevant time as defined in section 41 of the Police and Criminal Evidence Act 1984. If the above grounds cease to apply within this time, the person must as soon as practicable be asked if he wishes to exercise either right, the custody record must be noted accordingly, and action must be taken in accordance with the relevant section of the code.

5   A detained person must be permitted to consult a solicitor for a reasonable time before any court hearing.

(b) Documentation

6   The grounds for action under this Annex shall be recorded and the person informed of them as soon as practicable.

7   Any reply given by a person under paragraphs 4 or 9 must be recorded and the person asked to endorse the record in relation to whether he wishes to receive legal advice at this point.

B   Persons detained under the Prevention of Terrorism (Temporary Provisions) Act 1989

(a) Action

8   The rights set out in sections 5 or 6 of this code or both may be delayed if paragraph 1 above applies or if an officer of the rank of superintendent or above has reasonable grounds for believing that the exercise of either right;

(a) will lead to interference with the gathering of information about the commission, preparation or instigation of acts of terrorism; or

(b) by alerting any person, will make it more difficult to prevent an act of terrorism or to secure the apprehension, prosecution or conviction of any person in connection with the commission, preparation or instigation of an act of terrorism.

9   These rights may be delayed only for as long as is necessary and in no case beyond 48 hours from the time of arrest. If the above grounds cease to apply within this time, the person must as soon as practicable be asked if he wishes to exercise either right, the custody record must be noted accordingly, and action must be taken in accordance with the relevant section of this code.

10   Paragraphs 3 and 5 above apply.

(b) Documentation

11   Paragraphs 6 and 7 above apply.

Notes for guidance

B1   Even if Annex B *applies in the case of a juvenile or a person who is mentally disordered or mentally handicapped, action to inform the appropriate adult (and the person responsible for a juvenile's welfare, if that is a different person) must nevertheless be taken in accordance with paragraph 3.7 and 3.9 of this code.*

B2   In the case of Commonwealth citizens and foreign nationals see Note 7A.

B3   Police detention is defined in section 118(2) of the Police and Criminal Evidence Act 1984.

B4   The effect of paragraph 1 above is that the officer may authorise delaying access to a specific solicitor only if he has reasonable grounds to believe that specific solicitor will, inadvertently or otherwise, pass on a message from the detained person or act in some other way which will lead to any of the three results in paragraph 1 coming about. In these circumstances the officer should offer the detained person access to a solicitor (who is not the specific solicitor reffered to above) on the Duty Solicitor Scheme.

B5   The fact that the grounds for delaying notification of arrest under paragraph 1 above may be satisfied does not automatically mean that the grounds for delaying access to legal advice will also be satisfied.

Identification

CODES OF PRACTICE, CODE D

2   Identification by witnesses

2.0   A record shall be made of the description of the suspect as first given by a potential witness. This must be done before the witness takes part in the forms of identification listed in paragraph 2.1 or *Annex D* of this code. The record may be made or kept in any form provided that details of the description as first given by the witness can accurately be produced from it in a written form which can be provided to the suspect or his solicitor in accordance with this code. A copy shall be provided to the suspect or his solicitor before any procedures under paragraph 2.1 of this code are carried out. [See *Note 2D*]

(a) Cases where the suspect is known

2.1   In a case which involves disputed identification evidence, and where the identity of the suspect is known to the police and he is available (See *Note 2E*), the methods of identification by witnesses which may be used are:

    (i)   a parade;

    (ii) a group identification;

    (iii) a video film;

    (iv) a confrontation.

2.2   The arrangements for, and conduct of, these types of identification shall be the responsibility of an officer in uniform not below the rank of inspector who is not involved with the investigation ("the identification officer"). No officer involved with the investigation of the case against the suspect may take any part in these procedures.

Identification parade

2.3   Whenever a suspect disputes an identification, an identification parade shall be held if the suspect consents unless paragraphs 2.4 or 2.7 or 2.10 apply. A parade may also be held if the officer in charge of the investigation considers that it would be useful, and the suspect consents.

2.4   A parade need not be held if the identification officer considers that, whether by reason of the unusual appearance of the suspect or for some other reason, it would not be practicable to assemble sufficient people who resembled him to make a parade fair.

2.5   Any parade must be carried out in accordance with *Annex A*. A video recording or colour photograph shall be taken of the parade.

2.6   If a suspect refuses or, having agreed, fails to attend an identification parade or the holding of a parade is impracticable, arrangements must if practicable be made to allow the witnesses an opportunity of seeing him in a group identification, a video identification, or a confrontation (see below).

Group identification

2.7   A group identification takes place where the suspect is viewed by a witness amongst an informal group of people. The procedure may take place with the consent and co-operation of a suspect or covertly where a suspect has refused to co-operate with an identification parade or a group identification or has failed to attend. A group identification may also be arranged if the officer in charge of the investigation considers, whether because of fear on the part of the witness or for some other reason, that it is, in the circumstances, more satisfactory than a parade.

2.8   The suspect should be asked for his consent to a group identification and advised in accordance with paragraphs 2.15 and 2.16 of this code. However, where consent is refused the identification officer has the discretion to proceed with a group identification if it is practicable to do so.

2.9   A group identification shall be carried out in accordance with *Annex E*. A video recording or colour photograph shall be taken of the group identification in accordance with *Annex E*.

Video film identification

2.10   The identification officer may show a witness a video film of a suspect if the investigating officer considers, whether because of the refusal of the suspect to take part in an identification parade or group identification or other reasons, that this would in the circumstances be the most satisfactory course of action.

2.11   The suspect should be asked for his consent to a video identification and advised in accordance with paragraphs 2.15 and 2.16. However, where such consent is refused the identification officer has the discretion to proceed with a video identification if it is practicable to do so.

2.12   A video identification must be carried out in accordance with *Annex B*.

Confrontation

2.13   If neither a parade, a group identification nor a video identification procedure is arranged, the suspect may be confronted by the witness. Such a confrontation does not require the suspect's consent, but may not take place unless none of the other procedures are practicable.

2.14   A confrontation must be carried out in accordance with *Annex C*.

Notice to suspect

2.15   Before a parade takes place or a group identification or video identification is arranged, the identification officer shall explain to the suspect:

    (i)   the purposes of the parade or group identification or video identification;

    (ii)   that he is entitled to free legal advice (see paragraph 6.5 of Code C);

    (iii)   the procedures for holding it (including his right to have a solicitor or friend present);

    (iv)   where appropriate the special arrangements for juveniles;

    (v)   where appropriate the special arrangements for mentally disordered and mentally handicapped people;

    (vi)   that he does not have to take part in a parade, or co-operate in a group identification, or with the making of a video film and, if it is proposed to hold a group identification or video identification, his entitlement to a parade if this can practicably be arranged;

    (vii)   if he does not consent to take part in a parade or co-operate in a group identification or with the making of a video film, his refusal may be given in evidence in any subsequent trial and police may proceed covertly without his consent or make other arrangements to test whether a witness identifies him;

    (vii)a that if he should significantly alter his appearance between the taking of any photograph at the time of his arrest or after charge and any attempt to hold an identification procedure, this may be given in evidence if the case comes to trial; and the officer may then consider other forms of identification;

(vii)b   that a video or photograph may be taken of him when he attends for any identification procedure;

(viii)   whether the witness had been shown photographs, photofit, identikit or similar pictures by the police during the investigation before the identity of the suspect became known; [See *Note 2B*]

(ix)   that if he changes his appearance before a parade it may not be practicable to arrange one on the day in question or subsequently and, because of his change of appearance, the identification officer may then consider alternative methods of identification;

(x)   that he or his solicitor will be provided with details of the description of the suspect as first given by any witnesses who are to attend the parade, group identification, video identification or confrontation.

2.16   This information must also be contained in a written notice which must be handed to the suspect. The identification officer shall give the suspect a reasonable opportunity to read the notice, after which he shall be asked to sign a second copy of the notice to indicate whether or not he is willing to take part in the parade or group identification or co-operate with the making of a video film. The signed copy shall be retained by the identification officer.

(b) Cases where the identity of the suspect is not known

2.17   A police officer may take a witness to a particular neighbourhood or place to see whether he can identify the person whom he said he saw on the relevant occasion. Before doing so, where practicable a record shall be made of any description given by the witness of the suspect. Care should be taken not to direct the witness's attention to any individual.

2.18   A witness must not be shown photographs, photofit, identikit or similar pictures if the identity of the suspect is known to the police and he is available to stand on an identification parade. If the identity of the suspect is not known, the showing of such pictures to a witness must be done in accordance with *Annex D*. [See paragraph 2.15 (viii) and *Note 2E*]

(c) Documentation

2.19   The identification officer shall make a record of the parade, group identification or video identification on the forms provided.

2.20   If the identification officer considers that it is not practicable to hold a parade, he shall tell the suspect why and record the reason.

2.21   A record shall be made of a person's refusal to co-operate in a parade, group identification or video identification.

(d) Showing films and photographs of incidents

2.21A   Nothing in this code inhibits an investigating officer from showing a video film or photographs of an incident to the public at large through the national, or local media, or to police officers, for the purposes of recognition and tracing suspects. However when such material is shown to potential witnesses (including police officers [see *Note 2A*] for the purpose of obtaining identification evidence, it shall be shown on an individual basis so as to avoid any possibility of collusion, and the showing shall, as far as possible, follow the principles for Video Film Identification (see paragraph 2.10) or Identification by Photographs (see paragraph 2.18) as appropriate).

2.21B   Where such a broadcast or publication is made a copy of the material released by the police to the media for the purposes of recognising or tracing the suspect shall be kept and the suspect or his solicitor should be allowed to view such material before any procedures under paragraph 2.1 of this Code are carried out [see *Notes 2D* and *2E*] provided it is practicable to do so and would not unreasonably delay the investigation. Each witness who is involved in the procedure shall be asked by the investigating officer after they have taken part whether they have seen any broadcast or published films or photographs relating to the offence and their replies shall be recorded.

Notes for guidance

2A   Except for the provisions of Annex D paragraph 1, a police officer who is a witness for the purposes of this part of the code is subject to the same principles and procedures as a civilian witness.

2B   Where a witness attending an identification parade has previously been shown photographs or photofit, identikit or similar pictures, it is the responsibility of the officer in charge of the investigation to make the identification officer aware that this is the case.

2C   [Not Used]

2D   Where it is proposed to show photographs to a witness in accordance with Annex D, it is the responsibility of the officer in charge of the investigation to confirm to the officer responsible for supervising and directing the showing that the first description of the suspect given by that witness has been recorded. If this description has not been recorded, the procedure under Annex D must be postponed. (See Annex D paragraph 1A)

2E   References in this section to a suspect being "known" means there is sufficient information known to the police to justify the arrest of a particular person for suspected involvement in the offence. A suspect being "available" means that he is immediately available to take part in the procedure or he will become available within a reasonably short time.

3   Identification by fingerprints

(a) Action

3.1   A person's fingerprints may be taken only with his consent or if paragraph 3.2 applies. If he is at a police station consent must be in writing. In either case the person must be informed of the reason before they are taken and that they will be destroyed as soon as practicable if paragraph 3.4 applies. He must be told that he may witness their destruction if he asks to do so within five days of being cleared or informed that he will not be prosecuted.

3.2   Powers to take fingerprints without consent from any person over the age of ten years are provided by sections 27 and 61 of the Police and Criminal Evidence Act 1984. These provide that fingerprints may be taken without consent:

  (a) from a person detained at a police station if an officer of at least the rank of superintendent has reasonable grounds for suspecting that the fingerprints will tend to confirm or disprove his involvement in a criminal offence and the officer authorises the fingerprints to be taken;

  (b) from a person detained at a police station who has been charged with a recordable offence or informed that he will be reported for such an offence and he has not previously had his fingerprints taken in relation to that offence;

  (c) from a person convicted of a recordable offence. Section 27 of the Police and Criminal Evidence Act 1984 provides power to require such a person to attend a police station for the purposes of having his fingerprints taken if he has not been in police detention for the offence nor had his fingerprints taken in the course of the investigation of the offence or since conviction.

Reasonable force may be used if necessary to take a person's fingerprints without his consent.

3.2A   A person whose fingerprints are to be taken with or without consent shall be informed beforehand that his prints may be subject of a speculative search against other fingerprints. [See *Note 3B*]

3.3   [Not Used]

3.4   The fingerprints of a person and all copies of them taken in that case must be destroyed as soon as practicable if:

  (a) he is prosecuted for the offence concerned and cleared; or

  (b) he is not prosecuted (unless he admits the offence and is cautioned for it).

An opportunity of witnessing the destruction must be given to him if he wishes and if, in accordance with paragraph 3.1, he applies within five days of being cleared or informed that he will not be prosecuted.

3.5   When fingerprints are destroyed, access to relevant computer data shall be made impossible as soon as it is practicable to do so.

3.6   References to fingerprints include palm prints.

(b) Documentation

3.7   A record must be made as soon as possible of the reason for taking a person's fingerprints without consent and of their destruction. If force is used a record shall be made of the circumstances and those present.

3.8   A record shall be made when a person has been informed under the terms of paragraph 3.2A that his fingerprints may be subject of a speculative search.

Notes for guidance

3A   References to recordable offences in this code relate to those offences for which convictions may be recorded in national police records. (See section 27(4) of the Police and Criminal Evidence Act 1984.) The recordable offences to which this code applies at the time when the code was prepared, are any offences which carry a sentence of imprisonment on conviction (irrespective of the period, or the age of the offender or actual sentence passed) and non-imprisonable offences under section 1 of the Street Offences Act 1959 (loitering or soliciting for purposes of prostitution), section 43 of the Telecommunications Act 1984 (improper use of public telecommunications system), section 25 of the Road Traffic Act 1988 (tampering with motor vehicles), section 1 of the Malicious Communications Act 1988 (sending letters etc with intent to cause distress or anxiety) and section 139(1) of the Criminal Justice Act 1988 (having article with a blade or point in a public place).

3B   A speculative search means that a check may be made against other fingerprints contained in records held by or on behalf of the police or held in connection with or as a result of an investigation of an offence.

4   Photographs

(a) Action

4.1   The photograph of a person who has been arrested may be taken at a police station only with his written consent or if paragraph 4.2 applies. In either case he must be informed of the reason for taking it and that the photograph will be destroyed if paragraph 4.4 applies. He must be told that if he should significantly alter his appearance between the taking of the photograph and any attempt to hold an identification procedure this may be given in evidence if the case comes to trial. He must be told that he may witness the destruction of the photograph or be provided with a certificate confirming its destruction if he applies within five days of being cleared or informed that he will not be prosecuted.

4.2   The photograph of a person who has been arrested may be taken without consent if:

    (i)   he is arrested at the same time as other people, or at a time when it is likely that other people will be arrested, and a photograph is necessary to establish who was arrested, at what time and at what place; or

    (ii) he has been charged with, or reported for a recordable offence and has not yet been released or brought before a court [see *Note 3A*]; or

    (iii) he is convicted of such an offence and his photograph is not already on record as a result of (i) or (ii). There is no power of arrest to take a photograph in pursuance of this provision which applies only where the person is in custody as a result of the exercise of another power (e.g. arrest for fingerprinting under section 27 of the Police and Criminal Evidence Act 1984); or

    (iv) an officer of at least the rank of superintendent authorises it, having reasonable grounds for suspecting the involvement of the person in a criminal offence and where there is identification evidence in relation to that offence.

4.3   Force may not be used to take a photograph.

4.4   Where a person's photograph has been taken in accordance with this section, the photograph, negatives and all copies taken in that particular case must be destroyed if:

(a) he is prosecuted for the offence and cleared unless he has a previous conviction for a recordable offence; or

(b) he has been charged but not prosecuted (unless he admits the offence and is cautioned for it or he has a previous conviction for a recordable offence).

An opportunity of witnessing the destruction or a certificate confirming the destruction must be given to him if he so requests, provided that, in accordance with paragraph 4.1, he applies within five days of being cleared or informed that he will not be prosecuted. [See *Note 4B*]

(b) Documentation

4.5   A record must be made as soon as possible of the reason for taking a person's photograph under this section without consent and of the destruction of any photographs.

Notes for guidance

4A   The admissibility and value of identification evidence may be compromised if a potential witness in an identification procedure views any photographs of the suspect otherwise than in accordance with the provisions of this code.

4B   This paragraph is not intended to require the destruction of copies of a police gazette in cases where, for example, a remand prisoner has escaped from custody, or a person in custody is suspected of having committed offences in other force areas, and a photograph of the person concerned is circulated in a police gazette for information.

5   Identification by body samples and impressions

(a) Action

Intimate samples

5.1   Intimate samples may be taken from a person in police detention only:

(i) if an officer of the rank of superintendent or above has reasonable grounds to believe that such an impression or sample will tend to confirm or disprove the suspect's involvement in a recordable offence and gives authorisation for a sample to be taken; and

(ii) with the suspect's written consent.

5.1A   Where two or more non-intimate samples have been taken from a person in the course of an investigation of an offence and the samples have proved unsuitable or insufficient for a particular form of analysis and that person is not in police detention, an intimate sample may be taken from him if a police officer of at least the rank of superintendent authorises it to be taken, and the person concerned gives his written consent. [See *Note 5B and Note 5E*]

5.2   Before a person is asked to provide an intimate sample he must be warned that if he refuses without good cause, his refusal may harm his case if it comes to trial. [See *Note 5A*] If he is in police detention and not legally represented, he must also be reminded of his entitlement to have free legal advice (see paragraph 6.5 of Code C) and the reminder must be noted in the custody record. If paragraph 5.1A above applies and the person is attending a police station voluntarily, the officer shall explain the entitlement to free legal advice as provided for in accordance with paragraph 3.15 of Code C.

5.3   Except for samples of urine, intimate samples or dental impressions may be taken only by a registered medical or dental practitioner as appropriate.

Non-intimate samples

5.4   A non-intimate sample may be taken from a detained person only with his written consent or if paragraph 5.5 applies.

5.5   A non-intimate sample may be taken from a person without consent in accordance with the provisions of section 63 of the Police and Criminal Evidence Act 1984, as amended by section 55 of the Criminal Justice and Public Order Act 1994. The principal circumstances provided for are as follows:

(i)   if an officer of the rank of superintendent or above has reasonable grounds to believe that the sample will tend to confirm or disprove the person's involvement in a recordable offence and gives authorisation for a sample to be taken; or

(ii) where the person has been charged with a recordable offence or informed that he will be reported for such an offence; and he has not had a non-intimate sample taken from him in the course of the investigation or if he has had a sample taken from him, it has proved unsuitable or insufficient for the same form of analysis [See *Note 5B*]; or

(iii) if the person has been convicted of a recordable offence after the date on which this code comes into effect. Section 63A of the Police and Criminal Evidence Act 1984, as amended by section 56 of the Criminal Justice and Public Order Act 1994, describes the circumstances in which a constable may require a person convicted of a recordable offence to attend a police station in order that a non-intimate sample may be taken.

5.6   Where paragraph 5.5 applies, reasonable force may be used if necessary to take non-intimate samples.

(b) Destruction

5.7   [Not Used]

5.8   Except in accordance with paragraph 5.8A below, where a sample or impression has been taken in accordance with this section it must be destroyed as soon as practicable if:

(a)   the suspect is prosecuted for the offence concerned and cleared; or

(b)   he is not prosecuted (unless he admits the offence and is cautioned for it).

5.8A   In accordance with section 64 of the Police and Criminal Evidence Act 1984 as amended by section 57 of the Criminal Justice and Public Order Act 1994 samples need not be destroyed if they were taken for the purpose of an investigation of an offence for which someone has been convicted, and from whom a sample was also taken.[See *Note 5F*]

(c) Documentation

5.9   A record must be made as soon as practicable of the reasons for taking a sample or impression and of its destruction. If force is used a record shall be made of the circumstances and those present. If written consent is given to the taking of a sample or impression, the fact must be recorded in writing.

5.10   A record must be made of the giving of a warning required by paragraph 5.2 above. A record shall be made of the fact that a person has been informed under the terms of paragraph 5.11A below that samples may be subject of a speculative search.

(d) General

5.11   The terms intimate and non-intimate samples are defined in section 65 of the Police and Criminal Evidence Act 1984, as amended by section 58 of the Criminal Justice and Public Order Act 1994, as follows:

(a)   "intimate sample" means a dental impression or a sample of blood, semen or any other tissue fluid, urine, or pubic hair, or a swab taken from a person's body orifice other than the mouth;

(b)   "non-intimate sample" means:

(i)   a sample of hair (other than pubic hair) which includes hair plucked with the root [See *Note 5C*];

(ii) a sample taken from a nail or from under a nail;

(iii) a swab taken from any part of a person's body including the mouth but not any other body orifice;

(iv) saliva;

(v) a footprint or similar impression of any part of a person's body other than a part of his hand.

5.11A   A person from whom an intimate or non-intimate sample is to be taken shall be informed beforehand that any sample taken may be the subject of a speculative search. [See *Note 5D*]

5.11B   The suspect must be informed, before an intimate or non-intimate sample is taken, of the grounds on which the relevant authority has been given, including where appropriate the nature of the suspected offence.

5.12   Where clothing needs to be removed in circumstances likely to cause embarrassment to the person, no person of the opposite sex who is not a medical practitioner or nurse shall be present, (unless in the case of a juvenile or a mentally disordered or mentally handicapped person, that person specifically requests the presence of an appropriate adult of the opposite sex who is readily available) nor shall anyone whose presence is unnecessary. However, in the case of a juvenile this is subject to the overriding proviso that such a removal of clothing may take place in the absence of the appropriate adult only if the person signifies in the presence of the appropriate adult that he prefers his absence and the appropriate adult agrees.

Notes for guidance

5A   In warning a person who is asked to provide an intimate sample in accordance with paragraph 5.2, the following form of words may be used:

"You do not have to [provide this sample] [allow this swab or impression to be taken], but I must warn you that if you refuse without good cause, your refusal may harm your case if it comes to trial."

5B   An insufficient sample is one which is not sufficient either in quantity or quality for the purpose of enabling information to be provided for the purpose of a particular form of analysis such as DNA analysis. An unsuitable sample is one which, by its nature, is not suitable for a particular form of analysis.

5C   Where hair samples are taken for the purpose of DNA analysis (rather than for other purposes such as making a visual match) the suspect should be permitted a reasonable choice as to what part of the body he wishes the hairs to be taken from. When hairs are plucked they should be plucked individually unless the suspect prefers otherwise and no more should be plucked than the person taking them reasonably considers necessary for a sufficient sample.

5D   A speculative search means that a check may be made against other samples and information derived from other samples contained in records or held by or on behalf of the police or held in connection with or as a result of an investigation of an offence.

5E   Nothing in paragraph 5.1A prevents intimate samples being taken for elimination purposes with the consent of the person concerned but the provisions of paragraph 1.11, relating to the role of the appropriate adult, should be applied.

5F   The provisions for the retention of samples in 5.8A allow for all samples in a case to be available for any subsequent miscarriage of justice investigation. But such samples – and the information derived from them – may not be used in the investigation of any offence or in evidence against the person who would otherwise be entitled to their destruction.

ANNEX A   IDENTIFICATION PARADES

(a) General

1   A suspect must be given a reasonable opportunity to have a solicitor or friend present, and the identification officer shall ask him to indicate on a second copy of the notice whether or not he so wishes.

2   A parade may take place either in a normal room or in one equipped with a screen permitting witnesses to see members of the parade without being seen. The procedures for the composition and conduct of the parade are the same in both cases, subject to paragraph 7 below (except that a parade involving a screen may take place only when the suspect's solicitor, friend or appropriate adult is present or the parade is recorded on video).

2A   Before the parade takes place the suspect or his solicitor shall be provided with details of the first description of the suspect by any witnesses who are to attend the parade. The suspect or his solicitor should also be allowed to view any material released to the media by the police for the purpose of recognising or tracing the suspect, provided it is practicable to do so and would not unreasonably delay the investigation.

(b) Parades involving prison inmates

3   If an inmate is required for identification, and there are no security problems about his leaving the establishment, he may be asked to participate in a parade or video identification.

4   A parade may be held in a Prison Department establishment, but shall be conducted as far as practicable under normal parade rules. Members of the public shall make up the parade unless there are serious security or control objections to their admission to the establishment. In such cases, or if a group or video identification is arranged within the establishment, other inmates may participate. If an inmate is the suspect, he shall not be required to wear prison uniform for the parade unless the other people taking part are other inmates in uniform or are members of the public who are prepared to wear prison uniform for the occasion.

(c) Conduct of the parade

5   Immediately before the parade, the identification officer must remind the suspect of the procedures governing its conduct and caution him in the terms of paragraph 10.4 of Code C.

6   All unauthorised people must be excluded from the place where the parade is held.

7   Once the parade has been formed, everything afterwards in respect of it shall take place in the presence and hearing of the suspect and of any interpreter, solicitor, friend or appropriate adult who is present (unless the parade involves a screen, in which case everything said to or by any witness at the place where the parade is held must be said in the hearing and presence of the suspect's solicitor, friend or appropriate adult or be recorded on video).

8   The parade shall consist of at least eight people (in addition to the suspect) who so far as possible resemble the suspect in age, height, general appearance and position in life. One suspect only shall be included in a parade unless there are two suspects of roughly similar appearance in which case they may be paraded together with at least twelve other people. In no circumstances shall more than two suspects be included in one parade and where there are separate parades they shall be made up of different people.

9   Where all members of a similar group are possible suspects, separate parades shall be held for each member of the group unless there are two suspects of similar appearance when they may appear on the same parade with at least twelve other members of the group who are not suspects. Where police officers in uniform form an identification parade, any numerals or other identifying badges shall be concealed.

10   When the suspect is brought to the place where the parade is to be held, he shall be asked by the identification officer whether he has any objection to the arrangements for the parade or to any of the other participants in it. The suspect may obtain advice from his solicitor or friend, if present, before the parade proceeds. Where practicable, steps shall be taken to remove the grounds for objection. Where it is not practicable to do so, the officer shall explain to the suspect why his objections cannot be met.

11   The suspect may select his own position in the line. Where there is more than one witness, the identification officer must tell the suspect, after each witness has left the room, that he can if he wishes change position in the line. Each position in the line must be clearly numbered, whether by means of a numeral laid on the floor in front of each parade member or by other means.

12   The identification officer is responsible for ensuring that, before they attend the parade, witnesses are not able to:
  (i) communicate with each other about the case or overhear a witness who has already seen the parade;
  (ii) see any member of the parade;
  (iii) on that occasion see or be reminded of any photograph or description of the suspect or be given any other indication of his identity; or
  (iv) on that occasion, see the suspect either before or after the parade.

13   The officer conducting a witness to a parade must not discuss with him the composition of the parade, and in particular he must not disclose whether a previous witness has made any identification.

14   Witnesses shall be brought in one at a time. Immediately before the witness inspects the parade, the identification officer shall tell him that the person he saw may or may not be on the parade and if he cannot make a positive identification he should say so but that he should not make a decision before looking at each member of the parade at least twice. The officer shall then ask him to look at each member of the parade at least twice, taking as much care and time as he wishes. When the officer is satisfied that the witness has properly looked at each member of the parade, he shall ask him whether the person he himself saw on an earlier relevant occasion is on the parade.

15   The witness should make an identification by indicating the number of the person concerned.

16   If the witness makes an identification after the parade has ended the suspect and, if present, his solicitor, interpreter or friend shall be informed. Where this occurs, consideration should be given to allowing the witness a second opportunity to identify the suspect.

17   If a witness wishes to hear any parade member speak, adopt any specified posture or see him move, the identification officer shall first ask whether he can identify any persons on the parade on the basis of appearance only. When the request is to hear members of the parade speak, the witness shall be reminded that the participants in the parade have been chosen on the basis of physical appearance only. Members of the parade may then be asked to comply with the witness's request to hear them speak, to see them move or to adopt any specified posture.

17A   Where video films or photographs have been released to the media by the police for the purpose of recognising or tracing the suspect, the investigating officer shall ask each witness after the parade whether he has seen any broadcast or published films or photographs relating to the offence and shall record his reply.

18   When the last witness has left, the identification officer shall ask the suspect whether he wishes to make any comments on the conduct of the parade.

(d) Documentation

19   A colour photograph or a video film of the parade shall be taken. A copy of the photograph or video film shall be supplied on request to the suspect or his solicitor within a reasonable time.

20   The photograph or video film taken in accordance with paragraph 19 and held by the police shall be destroyed or wiped clean at the conclusion of the proceedings unless the person concerned is convicted or admits the offence and is cautioned for it.

21   If the identification officer asks any person to leave a parade because he is interfering with its conduct the circumstances shall be recorded.

22   A record must be made of all those present at a parade whose names are known to the police.

23   If prison inmates make up a parade the circumstances must be recorded.

24   A record of the conduct of any parade must be made on the forms provided.

ANNEX B   VIDEO IDENTIFICATION

(a) General

1   Where a video parade is to be arranged the following procedures must be followed.

2   Arranging, supervising and directing the making and showing of a video film to be used in a video identification must be the responsibility of an identification officer or identification officers who have no direct involvement with the relevant case.

3   The film must include the suspect and at least eight other people who so far as possible resemble the suspect in age, height, general appearance and position in life. Only one suspect shall appear on any film unless there are two suspects of roughly similar appearance in which case they may be shown together with at least twelve other people.

4   The suspect and other people shall as far as possible be filmed in the same positions or carrying out the same activity and under identical conditions.

5   Provisions must be made for each person filmed to be identified by number.

6   If police officers are filmed, any numerals or other identifying badges must be concealed. If a prison inmate is filmed either as a suspect or not, then either all or none of the people filmed should be in prison uniform.

7   The suspect and his solicitor, friend, or appropriate adult must be given a reasonable opportunity to see the complete film before it is shown to witnesses. If he has a reasonable objection to the video film or any of its participants, steps shall, if practicable be taken to remove the grounds for objection. If this is not practicable the identification officer shall explain to the suspect and/or his representative why his objections cannot be met and record both the objection and the reason on the forms provided.

8   The suspect's solicitor, or where one is not instructed the suspect himself, where practicable shall be given reasonable notification of the time and place that it is intended to conduct the video identification in order that a representative may attend on behalf of the suspect. The suspect himself may not be present when the film is shown to the witness(es). In the absence of a person representing the suspect the viewing itself shall be recorded on video. No unauthorised people may be present.

8A   Before the video identification takes place the suspect or his solicitor shall be provided with details of the first description of the suspect by any witnesses who are to attend the parade. The suspect or his solicitor should also be allowed to view any material released to the media by the police for the purpose of recognising or tracing the suspect, provided it is practicable to do so and would not unreasonably delay the investigation.

(b) Conducting the video identification

9   The identification officer is responsible for ensuring that, before they see the film, witnesses are not able to communicate with each other about the case or overhear a witness who has seen the film. He must not discuss with the witness the composition of the film and must not disclose whether a previous witness has made any identification.

10   Only one witness may see the film at a time. Immediately before the video identification takes place the identification officer shall tell the witness that the person he saw may or may not be on the video film. The witness shall be advised that at any point he may ask to see a particular part of the tape again or to have a particular picture frozen for him to study. Furthermore, it should be pointed out that there is no limit on how many times he can view the whole tape or any part of it. However, he should be asked to refrain from making a positive identification or saying that he cannot make a positive identification until he has seen the entire film at least twice.

11   Once the witness has seen the whole film at least twice and has indicated that he does not want to view it or any part of it again, the identification officer shall ask the witness to say whether the individual he saw in person on an earlier occasion has been shown on the film and, if so, to identify him by number. The identification officer will then show the film of the person identified again to confirm the identification with the witness.

12   The identification officer must take care not to direct the witness's attention to any one individual on the video film, or give any other indication of the suspect's identity. Where a witness has previously made an identification by photographs, or a photofit, identikit or similar picture has been made, the witness must not be reminded of such a photograph or picture once a suspect is available for identification by other means in accordance with this code. Neither must he be reminded of any description of the suspect.

12A   Where video films or photographs have been released to the media by the police for the purpose of recognising or tracing the suspect, the investigating officer shall ask each witness after the parade whether he has seen any broadcast or published films or photographs relating to the offence and shall record his reply.

(c) Tape security and destruction

13   It shall be the responsibility of the identification officer to ensure that all relevant tapes are kept securely and their movements accounted for. In particular, no officer involved in the investigation against the suspect shall be permitted to view the video film prior to it being shown to any witness.

14   Where a video film has been made in accordance with this section all copies of it held by the police must be destroyed if the suspect:

(a) is prosecuted for the offence and cleared; or

(b) is not prosecuted (unless he admits the offence and is cautioned for it).

An opportunity of witnessing the destruction must be given to him if he so requests within five days of being cleared or informed that he will not be prosecuted.

(d) Documentation

15   A record must be made of all those participating in or seeing the video whose names are known to the police.

16   A record of the conduct of the video identification must be made on the forms provided.

ANNEX C   CONFRONTATION BY A WITNESS

1   The identification officer is responsible for the conduct of any confrontation of a suspect by a witness.

2   Before the confrontation takes place, the identification officer must tell the witness that the person he saw may or may not be the person he is to confront and that if he cannot make a positive identification he should say so.

2A   Before the confrontation takes place, the suspect or his solicitor shall be provided with details of the first description of the suspect given by any witness who is to attend the confrontation. The suspect or his solicitor should also be allowed to view any material released by the police to the media for the purposes of recognising or tracing the suspect provided that it is practicable to do so and would not unreasonably delay the investigation.

3   The suspect shall be confronted independently by each witness, who shall be asked "Is this the person?" Confrontation must take place in the presence of the suspect's solicitor, interpreter or friend, unless this would cause unreasonable delay.

4   The confrontation should normally take place in the police station, either in a normal room or in one equipped with a screen permitting a witness to see the suspect without being seen. In both cases the procedures are the same except that a room equipped with a screen may be used only when the suspect's solicitor, friend or appropriate adult is present or the confrontation is recorded on video.

5   Where video films or photographs have been released to the media by the police for the purposes of recognising or tracing the suspect, the investigating officer shall ask

each witness after the procedure whether he has seen any broadcast or published films or photographs relating to the offence and shall record his reply.

ANNEX D   SHOWING OF PHOTOGRAPHS

(a) Action

1   An officer of the rank of sergeant or above shall be responsible for supervising and directing the showing of photographs. The actual showing may be done by a constable or a civilian police employee.

1A   The officer must confirm that the first description of the suspect given by the witness has been recorded before the witness is shown the photographs. If he is unable to confirm that the description has been recorded, he shall postpone the showing.

2   Only one witness shall be shown photographs at any one time. He shall be given as much privacy as practicable and shall not be allowed to communicate with any other witness in the case.

3   The witness shall be shown not less than twelve photographs at a time, which shall, as far as possible, all be of a similar type.

4   When the witness is shown the photographs, he shall be told that the photograph of the person he saw may or may not be amongst them. He shall not be prompted or guided in any way but shall be left to make any selection without help.

5   If a witness makes a positive identification from photographs, then, unless the person identified is otherwise eliminated from enquiries, other witnesses shall not be shown photographs. But both they and the witness who has made the identification shall be asked to attend an identification parade or group or video identification if practicable unless there is no dispute about the identification of the suspect.

6   Where the use of a photofit, identikit or similar picture has led to there being a suspect available who can be asked to appear on a parade, or participate in a group or video identification, the picture shall not be shown to other potential witnesses.

7   Where a witness attending an identification parade has previously been shown photographs or photofit, identikit or similar pictures (and it is the responsibility of the officer in charge of the investigation to make the identification officer aware that this is the case) then the suspect and his solicitor must be informed of this fact before the identity parade takes place.

8   None of the photographs used shall be destroyed, whether or not an identification is made, since they may be required for production in court. The photographs shall be numbered and a separate photograph taken of the frame or part of the album from which the witness made an identification as an aid to reconstituting it.

(b) Documentation

9   Whether or not an identification is made, a record shall be kept of the showing of photographs and of any comment made by the witness.

ANNEX E   GROUP IDENTIFICATION

(a) General

1   The purpose of the provisions of this Annex is to ensure that as far as possible, group identifications follow the principles and procedures for identification parades so that the conditions are fair to the suspect in the way they test the witness's ability to make an identification.

2   Group identifications may take place either with the suspect's consent and cooperation or covertly without his consent.

3   The location of the group identification is a matter for the identification officer, although he may take into account any representations made by the suspect, appropriate

adult, his solicitor or friend. The place where the group identification is held should be one where other people are either passing by, or waiting around informally, in groups such that the suspect is able to join them and be capable of being seen by the witness at the same time as others in the group. Examples include people leaving an escalator, pedestrians walking through a shopping centre, passengers on railway and bus stations waiting in queues or groups or where people are standing or sitting in groups in other public places.

4   If the group identification is to be held covertly, the choice of locations will be limited by the places where the suspect can be found and the number of other people present at that time. In these cases, suitable locations might be along regular routes travelled by the suspect, including buses or trains, or public places he frequents.

5   Although the number, age, sex, race and general description and style of clothing of other people present at the location cannot be controlled by the identification officer, in selecting the location he must consider the general appearance and numbers of people likely to be present. In particular, he must reasonably expect that over the period the witness observes the group, he will be able to see, from time to time, a number of others (in addition to the suspect) whose appearance is broadly similar to that of the suspect.

6   A group identification need not be held if the identification officer believes that because of the unusual appearance of the suspect, none of the locations which it would be practicable to use satisfy the requirements of paragraph 5 necessary to make the identification fair.

7   Immediately after a group identification procedure has taken place (with or without the suspect's consent), a colour photograph or a video should be taken of the general scene, where this is practicable, so as to give a general impression of the scene and the number of people present. Alternatively, if it is practicable, the group identification may be video recorded.

8   If it is not practicable to take the photograph or video film in accordance with paragraph 7, a photograph or film of the scene should be taken later at a time determined by the identification officer, if he considers that it is practicable to do so.

9   An identification carried out in accordance with this code remains a group identification notwithstanding that at the time of being seen by the witness the suspect was on his own rather than in a group.

10   The identification officer need not be in uniform when conducting a group identification.

11   Before the group identification takes place the suspect or his solicitor should be provided with details of the first description of the suspect by any witnesses who are to attend the identification. The suspect or his solicitor should also be allowed to view any material released by the police to the media for the purposes of recognising or tracing the suspect provided that it is practicable to do so and would not unreasonably delay the investigation.

12   Where video films or photographs have been released to the media by the police for the purposes of recognising or tracing the suspect, the investigating officer shall ask each witness after the procedure whether he has seen any broadcast or published films or photographs relating to the offence and shall record his reply.

(b) Identification with the consent of the suspect

13   A suspect must be given a reasonable opportunity to have a solicitor or friend present. The identification officer shall ask him to indicate on a second copy of the notice whether or not he so wishes.

14   The witness, identification officer and suspect's solicitor, appropriate adult, friend or any interpreter for the witness, if present may be concealed from the sight of the persons in the group which they are observing if the identification officer considers that this facilitates the conduct of the identification.

15   The officer conducting a witness to a group identification must not discuss with the witness the forthcoming group identification and in particular he must not disclose whether a previous witness has made any identification.

16   Anything said to or by the witness during the procedure regarding the identification should be said in the presence and hearing of the identification officer and, if present, the suspect's solicitor, appropriate adult, friend or any interpreter for the witness.

17   The identification officer is responsible for ensuring that before they attend the group identification witnesses are not able to:

    (i)   communicate with each other about the case or overhear a witness who has already been given an opportunity to see the suspect in the group;

    (ii)   on that occasion see the suspect; or

    (iii)   on that occasion see or be reminded of any photographs or description of the suspect or be given any other indication of his identity.

18   Witnesses shall be brought to the place where they are to observe the group one at a time. Immediately before the witness is asked to look at the group, the identification officer shall tell him that the person he saw may or may not be in the group and if he cannot make a positive identification he should say so. The witness shall then be asked to observe the group in which the suspect is to appear. The way in which the witness should do this will depend on whether the group is moving or stationary.

Moving group

19   When the group in which the suspect is to appear is moving, for example, leaving an escalator, the provisions of paragraphs 20 to 23 below should be followed.

20   If two or more suspects consent to a group identification, each should be the subject of separate identification procedures. These may however be conducted consecutively on the same occasion.

21   The identification officer shall tell the witness to observe the group and ask him to point out any person he thinks he saw on the earlier relevant occasion. When the witness makes such an indication the officer shall, if it is practicable, arrange for the witness to take a closer look at the person he has indicated and ask him whether he can make a positive identification. If this is not practicable, the officer shall ask the witness how sure he is that the person he has indicated is the relevant person.

22   The witness should continue to observe the group for the period which the identification officer reasonably believes is necessary in the circumstances for the witness to be able to make comparisons between the suspect and other persons of broadly similar appearance to the suspect in accordance with paragraph 5.

23   Once the identification officer has informed the witness in accordance with paragraph 21, the suspect should be allowed to take any position in the group he wishes.

Stationary groups

24   When the group in which the suspect is to appear is stationary, for example, people waiting in a queue, the provisions of paragraphs 25 to 28 below should be followed.

25   If two or more suspects consent to a group identification, each should be the subject of separate identification procedures unless they are of broadly similar appearance when they may appear in the same group. Where separate group identifications are held, the groups must be made up of different persons.

26   The suspect may take any position in the group he wishes. Where there is more than one witness, the identification officer must tell the suspect, out of the sight and hearing of any witness, that he can if he wishes change his position in the group.

27   The identification officer shall ask the witness to pass along or amongst the group and to look at each person in the group at least twice, taking as much care and time as is

possible according to the circumstances, before making an identification. When he has done this, the officer shall ask him whether the person he saw on an earlier relevant occasion is in the group and to indicate any such person by whatever means the identification officer considers appropriate in the circumstances. If this is not practicable, the officer shall ask the witness to point out any person he thinks he saw on the earlier relevant occasion.

28   When the witness makes an indication in accordance with paragraph 27, the officer shall, if it is practicable, arrange for the witness to take a closer look at the person he has indicated and ask him whether he can make a positive identification. If this is not practicable, the officer shall ask the witness how sure he is that the person he has indicated is the relevant person.

All Cases

29   If the suspect unreasonably delays joining the group, or having joined the group, deliberately conceals himself from the sight of the witness, the identification officer may treat this as a refusal to co-operate in a group identification.

30   If the witness identifies a person other than the suspect, an officer should inform that person what has happened and ask if they are prepared to give their name and address. There is no obligation upon any member of the public to give these details. There shall be no duty to record any details of any other member of the public present in the group or at the place where the procedure is conducted.

31   When the group identification has been completed, the identification officer shall ask the suspect whether he wishes to make any comments on the conduct of the procedure.

32   If he has not been previously informed the identification officer shall tell the suspect of any identifications made by the witnesses.

(c) Identification without suspect's consent

33   Group identifications held covertly without the suspect's consent should so far as is practicable follow the rules for conduct of group identification by consent.

34   A suspect has no right to have a solicitor, appropriate adult or friend present as the identification will, of necessity, take place without the knowledge of the suspect.

35   Any number of suspects may be identified at the same time.

(d) Identifications in police stations

36   Group identifications should only take place in police stations for reasons of safety, security, or because it is impracticable to hold them elsewhere.

37   The group identification may take place either in a room equipped with a screen permitting witnesses to see members of the group without being seen, or anywhere else in the police station that the identification officer considers appropriate.

38   Any of the additional safeguards applicable to identification parades should be followed if the identification officer considers it is practicable to do so in the circumstances.

(e) Identifications involving prison inmates

39   A group identification involving a prison inmate may only be arranged in the prison or at a police station.

40   Where a group identification takes place involving a prison inmate, whether in a prison or in a police station, the arrangements should follow those in paragraphs 36 to 38 of this Annex. If a group identification takes place within a prison other inmates may participate. If an inmate is the suspect he should not be required to wear prison uniform for the group identification unless the other persons taking part are wearing the same uniform.

(f) Documentation

41   Where a photograph or video film is taken in accordance with paragraph 7 or 8, a copy of the photograph or video film shall be supplied on request to the suspect or his solicitor within a reasonable time.

42   If the photograph or film includes the suspect, it and all copies held by the police shall be destroyed or wiped clean at the conclusion of the proceedings unless the person is convicted or admits the offence and is cautioned for it.

43   A record of the conduct of any group identification must be made on the forms provided. This shall include anything said by the witness or the suspect about any identifications or the conduct of the procedure and any reasons why it was not practicable to comply with any of the provisions of this code governing the conduct of group identifications.

Questioning

Police and Criminal Evidence Act 1984

58   Access to legal advice
(1) A person arrested and held in custody in a police station or other premises shall be entitled, if he so requests, to consult a solicitor privately at any time.

(2) Subject to subsection (3) below, a request under subsection (1) above and the time at which it was made shall be recorded in the custody record.

(3) Such a request need not be recorded in the custody record of a person who makes it at a time while he is at a court after being charged with an offence.

(4) If a person makes such a request, he must be permitted to consult a solicitor as soon as is practicable except to the extent that delay is permitted by this section.

(5) In any case he must be permitted to consult a solicitor within 36 hours from the relevant time, as defined in section 41(2) above.

(6) Delay in compliance with a request is only permitted—
  (a) in the case of a person who is in police detention for a serious arrestable offence; and
  (b) if an officer of at least the rank of superintendent authorises it.

(7) An officer may give an authorisation under subsection (6) above orally or in writing but, if he gives it orally, he shall confirm it in writing as soon as is practicable.

(8) Subject to subsection (8A) below, an officer may only authorise delay where he has reasonable grounds for believing that the exercise of the right conferred by subsection (1) above at the time when the person detained desires to exercise it—
  (a) will lead to interference with or harm to evidence connected with a serious arrestable offence or interference with or physical injury to other persons; or
  (b) will lead to the alerting of other persons suspected of having committed such an offence but not yet arrested for it; or
  (c) will hinder the recovery of any property obtained as a result of such an offence.

(8A) An officer may also authorise delay where the serious arrestable offence is a drug trafficking offence or an offence to which Part VI of the Criminal Justice Act 1988 applies and the officer has reasonable grounds for believing—
  (a) where the offence is a drug trafficking offence, that the detained person has benefited from drug trafficking and that the recovery of the value of that person's proceeds of drug trafficking will be hindered by the exercise of the right conferred by subsection (1) above; and
  (b) where the offence is one to which Part VI of the Criminal Justice Act 1988 applies, that the detained person has benefited from the offence and that the recovery of the value of the property obtained by that person from or in connection with the offence or of the pecuniary advantage derived by him from or in connection with it will be hindered by the exercise of the right conferred by subsection (1) above.

(9) If delay is authorised—

    (a) the detained person shall be told the reason for it; and

    (b) the reason shall be noted on his custody record.

(10) The duties imposed by subsection (9) above shall be performed as soon as is practicable.

(11) There may be no further delay in permitting the exercise of the right conferred by subsection (1) above once the reason for authorising delay ceases to subsist.

(12) Nothing in this section applies to a person arrested or detained under the terrorism provisions.

Right to legal advice

See page 47 for Codes of Practice, Code C para 6.

CODES OF PRACTICE, CODE C

10 Cautions

(a) When a caution must be given

10.1   A person whom there are grounds to suspect of an offence must be cautioned before any questions about it (or further questions if it is his answers to previous questions which provide the grounds for suspicion) are put to him regarding his involvement or suspected involvement in that offence if his answers or his silence (i.e. failure or refusal to answer a question or to answer satisfactorily) may be given in evidence to a court in a prosecution. He therefore need not be cautioned if questions are put for other purposes, for example, solely to establish his identity or his ownership of any vehicle or to obtain information in accordance with any relevant statutory requirement (see paragraph 10.5C) or in furtherance of the proper and effective conduct of a search, (for example to determine the need to search in the exercise of powers of stop and search or to seek cooperation while carrying out a search) or to seek verification of a written record in accordance with paragraph 11.13.

10.2   Whenever a person who is not under arrest is initially cautioned or is reminded that he is under caution (see paragraph 10.5) he must at the same time be told that he is not under arrest and is not obliged to remain with the officer (see paragraph 3.15).

10.3   A person must be cautioned upon arrest for an offence unless:

    (a) it is impracticable to do so by reason of his condition or behaviour at the time; or

    (b) he has already been cautioned immediately prior to arrest in accordance with paragraph 10.1 above.

(b) Action: general

10.4   The caution shall be in the following terms:

"You do not have to say anything. But it may harm your defence if you do not mention when questioned something which you later rely on in court. Anything you do say may be given in evidence."

Minor deviations do not constitute a breach of this requirement provided that the sense of the caution is preserved. [See *Note 10C*]

10.5   When there is a break in questioning under caution the interviewing officer must ensure that the person being questioned is aware that he remains under caution. If there is any doubt the caution shall be given again in full when the interview resumes. [See *Note 10A*]

Special warnings under sections 36 and 37 of the Criminal Justice and Public Order Act 1994

10.5A   When a suspect who is interviewed after arrest fails or refuses to answer certain questions, or to answer them satisfactorily, after due warning, a court or jury may draw such inferences as appear proper under sections 36 and 37 of the Criminal Justice and Public Order Act 1994. This applies when:

 (a) a suspect is arrested by a constable and there is found on his person, or in or on his clothing or footwear, or otherwise in his possession, or in the place where he was arrested, any objects, marks or substances, or marks on such objects, and the person fails or refuses to account for the objects, marks or substances found; or

 (b) an arrested person was found by a constable at a place at or about the time the offence for which he was arrested, is alleged to have been committed, and the person fails or refuses to account for his presence at that place.

 10.5B For an inference to be drawn from a suspect's failure or refusal to answer a question about one of these matters or to answer it satisfactorily, the interviewing officer must first tell him in ordinary language:

 (a) what offence he is investigating;

 (b) what fact he is asking the suspect to account for;

 (c) that he believes this fact may be due to the suspect's taking part in the commission of the offence in question;

 (d) that a court may draw a proper inference if he fails or refuses to account for the fact about which he is being questioned;

 (e) that a record is being made of the interview and that it may be given in evidence if he is brought to trial.

 10.5C Where, despite the fact that a person has been cautioned, failure to cooperate may have an effect on his immediate treatment, he should be informed of any relevant consequence and that they are not affected by the caution. Examples are when his refusal to provide his name and address when charged may render him liable to detention, or when his refusal to provide particulars and information in accordance with a statutory requirement, for example, under the Road Traffic Act 1988, may amount to an offence or may make him liable to arrest.

(c) Juveniles, the mentally disordered and the mentally handicapped

 10.6 If a juvenile or a person who is mentally disordered or mentally handicapped is cautioned in the absence of the appropriate adult, the caution must be repeated in the adult's presence.

(d) Documentation

 10.7 A record shall be made when a caution is given under this section, either in the officer's pocket book or in the interview record as appropriate.

Notes for guidance

 10A In considering whether or not to caution again after a break, the officer should bear in mind that he may have to satisfy a court that the person understood that he was still under caution when the interview resumed.

 10B [Not Used]

 10C If it appears that a person does not understand what the caution means, the officer who has given it should go on to explain it in his own words.

 10D [Not Used]

11 Interviews: general

(a) Action

 11.1A An interview is the questioning of a person regarding his involvement or suspected involvement in a criminal offence or offences which, by virtue of paragraph 10.1 of Code C, is required to be carried out under caution. Procedures undertaken under section 7 of the Road Traffic Act 1988 do not constitute interviewing for the purpose of this code.

11.1   Following a decision to arrest a suspect he must not be interviewed about the relevant offence except at a police station or other authorised place of detention unless the consequent delay would be likely:

(a) to lead to interference with or harm to evidence connected with an offence or interference with or physical harm to other people; or

(b) to lead to the alerting of other people suspected of having committed an offence but not yet arrested for it; or

(c) to hinder the recovery of property obtained in consequence of the commission of an offence.

Interviewing in any of these circumstances shall cease once the relevant risk has been averted or the necessary questions have been put in order to attempt to avert that risk.

11.2   Immediately prior to the commencement or re-commencement of any interview at a police station or other authorised place of detention, the interviewing officer shall remind the suspect of his entitlement to free legal advice and that the interview can be delayed for him to obtain legal advice (unless the exceptions in paragraph 6.6 or *Annex C* apply). It is the responsibility of the interviewing officer to ensure that all such reminders are noted in the record of interview.

11.2A   At the beginning of an interview carried out in a police station, the interviewing officer, after cautioning the suspect, shall put to him any significant statement or silence which occurred before his arrival at the police station, and shall ask him whether he confirms or denies that earlier statement or silence and whether he wishes to add anything. A "significant" statement or silence is one which appears capable of being used in evidence against the suspect, in particular a direct admission of guilt, or failure or refusal to answer a question or to answer it satisfactorily, which might give rise to an inference under Part III of the Criminal Justice and Public Order Act 1994.

11.3   No police officer may try to obtain answers to questions or to elicit a statement by the use of oppression. Except as provided for in paragraph 10.5C, no police officer shall indicate, except in answer to a direct question, what action will be taken on the part of the police if the person being interviewed answers questions, makes a statement or refuses to do either. If the person asks the officer directly what action will be taken in the event of his answering questions, making a statement or refusing to do either, then the officer may inform the person what action the police propose to take in that event provided that action is itself proper and warranted.

11.4   As soon as a police officer who is making enquiries of any person about an offence believes that a prosecution should be brought against him and that there is sufficient evidence for it to succeed, he shall ask the person if he has anything further to say. If the person indicates that he has nothing more to say the officer shall without delay cease to question him about that offence. This should not, however, be taken to prevent officers in revenue cases or acting under the confiscation provisions of the Criminal Justice Act 1988 or the Drug Trafficking Offences Act 1986 from inviting suspects to complete a formal question and answer record after the interview is concluded.

(b) Interview records

11.5 (a) An accurate record must be made of each interview with a person suspected of an offence, whether or not the interview takes place at a police station.

(b) The record must state the place of the interview, the time it begins and ends, the time the record is made (if different), any breaks in the interview and the names of all those present; and must be made on the forms provided for this purpose or in the officer's pocket book or in accordance with the code of practice for the tape-recording of police interviews with suspects (Code E).

(c) The record must be made during the course of the interview, unless in the investigating officer's view this would not be practicable or would interfere with conduct of the interview, and must constitute either a verbatim record of what has been said or, failing this, an account of the interview which adequately and accurately summarises it.

11.6   The requirement to record the names of all those present at any interview does not apply to police officers interviewing people detained under the Prevention of Terrorism (Temporary Provisions) Act 1989. Instead the record shall state the warrant or other identification number and duty station of such officers.

11.7   If an interview record is not made during the course of the interview it must be made as soon as practicable after its completion.

11.8   Written interview records must be timed and signed by the maker.

11.9   If an interview record is not completed in the course of the interview the reason must be recorded in the officer's pocket book.

11.10   Unless it is impracticable the person interviewed shall be given the opportunity to read the interview record and to sign it as correct or to indicate the respects in which he considers it inaccurate. If the interview is tape-recorded the arrangements set out in Code E apply. If the person concerned cannot read or refuses to read the record or to sign it, the senior police officer present shall read it to him and ask him whether he would like to sign it as correct (or make his mark) or to indicate the respects in which he considers it inaccurate. The police officer shall then certify on the interview record itself what has occurred. [*See Note 11D*]

11.11   If the appropriate adult or the person's solicitor is present during the interview, he shall also be given an opportunity to read and sign the interview record (or any written statement taken down by a police officer).

11.12   Any refusal by a person to sign an interview record when asked to do so in accordance with the provisions of the code must itself be recorded.

11.13   A written record shall also be made of any comments made by a suspected person, including unsolicited comments, which are outside the context of an interview but which might be relevant to the offence. Any such record must be timed and signed by the maker. Where practicable the person shall be given the opportunity to read that record and to sign it as correct or to indicate the respects in which he considers it inaccurate. Any refusal to sign shall be recorded. [*See Note 11D*]

(c) Juveniles, mentally disordered people and mentally handicapped people

11.14   A juvenile or a person who is mentally disordered or mentally handicapped, whether suspected or not, must not be interviewed or asked to provide or sign a written statement in the absence of the appropriate adult unless paragraph 11.1 or *Annex C* applies.

11.15   Juveniles may only be interviewed at their places of education in exceptional circumstances and then only where the principal or his nominee agrees. Every effort should be made to notify both the parent(s) or other person responsible for the juvenile's welfare and the appropriate adult (if this is a different person) that the police want to interview the juvenile and reasonable time should be allowed to enable the appropriate adult to be present at the interview. Where awaiting the appropriate adult would cause unreasonable delay and unless the interviewee is suspected of an offence against the educational establishment, the principal or his nominee can act as the appropriate adult for the purposes of the interview.

11.16   Where the appropriate adult is present at an interview, he shall be informed that he is not expected to act simply as an observer; and also that the purposes of his presence are, first, to advise the person being questioned and to observe whether or not the interview is being conducted properly and fairly, and secondly, to facilitate communication with the person being interviewed.

Notes for guidance

11A   [Not Used]

11B   It is important to bear in mind that, although juveniles or people who are mentally disordered or mentally handicapped are often capable of providing reliable evidence, they may, without knowing or wishing to do so, be particularly prone in certain circumstances to provide information which is unreliable, misleading or self-incriminating. Special care should therefore always be exercised in questioning such a person, and the appropriate adult should be involved, if there is any doubt about a person's age, mental state or capacity. Because of the risk of unreliable evidence it is also important to obtain corroboration of any facts admitted whenever possible.

11C   It is preferable that a juvenile is not arrested at his place of education unless this is unavoidable. Where a juvenile is arrested at his place of education, the principal or his nominee must be informed.

11D   When a suspect agrees to read records of interviews and of other comments and to sign them as correct, he should be asked to endorse the record with words such as "I agree that this is a correct record of what was said" and add his signature. Where the suspect does not agree with the record, the officer should record the details of any disagreement and then ask the suspect to read these details and then sign them to the effect that they accurately reflect his disagreement. Any refusal to sign when asked to do so shall be recorded.

12   Interviews in police stations

(a) Action

12.1   If a police officer wishes to interview, or conduct enquiries which require the presence of a detained person, the custody officer is responsible for deciding whether to deliver him into his custody.

12.2   In any period of 24 hours a detained person must be allowed a continuous period of at least 8 hours for rest, free from questioning, travel or any interruption by police officers in connection with the investigation concerned. This period should normally be at night. The period of rest may not be interrupted or delayed, except at the request of the person, his appropriate adult or his legal representative, unless there are reasonable grounds for believing that it would:

   (i)   involve a risk of harm to people or serious loss of, or damage to, property; or
   (ii)   delay unnecessarily the person's release from custody; or
   (iii) otherwise prejudice the outcome of the investigation.

If a person is arrested at a police station after going there voluntarily, the period of 24 hours runs from the time of his arrest and not the time of arrival at the police station. Any action which is required to be taken in accordance with section 8 of this code, or in accordance with medical advice or at the request of the detained person, his appropriate adult or his legal representative, does not constitute an interruption to the rest period such that a fresh period must be allowed.

12.3   A detained person may not be supplied with intoxicating liquor except on medical directions. No person, who is unfit through drink or drugs to the extent that he is unable to appreciate the significance of questions put to him and his answers, may be questioned about an alleged offence in that condition except in accordance with *Annex C*. [See *Note 12B*]

12.4   As far as practicable interviews shall take place in interview rooms which must be adequately heated, lit and ventilated.

12.5   People being questioned or making statements shall not be required to stand.

12.6   Before the commencement of an interview each interviewing officer shall identify himself and any other officers present by name and rank to the person being interviewed, except in the case of people detained under the Prevention of Terrorism (Temporary Provisions) Act 1989 when each officer shall identify himself by his warrant or other identification number and rank rather than his name.

12.7   Breaks from interviewing shall be made at recognised meal times. Short breaks for refreshment shall also be provided at intervals of approximately two hours, subject to the interviewing officer's discretion to delay a break if there are reasonable grounds for believing that it would:

(i)   involve a risk of harm to people or serious loss of, or damage to property;

(ii) delay unnecessarily the person's release from custody; or

(iii) otherwise prejudice the outcome of the investigation.

[See *Note 12C*]

12.8   If in the course of the interview a complaint is made by the person being questioned or on his behalf concerning the provisions of this code then the interviewing officer shall:

(i)   record it in the interview record; and

(ii) inform the custody officer, who is then responsible for dealing with it in accordance with section 9 of this code.

(b) Documentation

12.9   A record must be made of the time at which a detained person is not in the custody of the custody officer, and why; and of the reason for any refusal to deliver him out of that custody.

12.10   A record must be made of any intoxicating liquor supplied to a detained person, in accordance with paragraph 12.3 above.

12.11   Any decision to delay a break in an interview must be recorded, with grounds, in the interview record.

12.12   All written statements made at police stations under caution shall be written on the forms provided for the purpose.

12.13   All written statements made under caution shall be taken in accordance with *Annex D* to this code.

Notes for guidance

12A   If the interview has been contemporaneously recorded and the record signed by the person interviewed in accordance with paragraph 11.10 above, or has been tape recorded, it is normally unnecessary to ask for a written statement. Statements under caution should normally be taken in these circumstances only at the person's express wish. An officer may, however, ask him whether or not he wants to make such a statement.

12B   The police surgeon can give advice about whether or not a person is fit to be interviewed in accordance with paragraph 12.3 above.

12C   Meal breaks should normally last at least 45 minutes and shorter breaks after two hours should last at least 15 minutes. If the interviewing officer delays a break in accordance with paragraph 12.7 of this code and prolongs the interview, a longer break should then be provided. If there is a short interview, and a subsequent short interview is contemplated, the length of the break may be reduced if there are reasonable grounds to believe that this is necessary to avoid any of the consequences in paragraph 12.7 (i) to (iii).

CODES OF PRACTICE, CODE E

3   Interviews to be tape recorded

3.1   Subject to paragraph 3.2 below, tape recording shall be used at police stations for any interview:

(a)   with a person who has been cautioned in accordance with section 10 of Code C in respect of an indictable offence (including an offence triable either way) [see *Notes 3A and 3B*];

(b)   which takes place as a result of a police officer exceptionally putting further questions to a suspect about an offence described in sub-paragraph (a) above after he has been charged with, or informed he may be prosecuted for, that offence [see *Note 3C*]; or

(c)   in which a police officer wishes to bring to the notice of a person, after he has been charged with, or informed he may be prosecuted for an offence described in sub-paragraph (a) above, any written statement made by another person, or the content of an interview with another person [see *Note 3D*].

3.2   Tape recording is not required in respect of the following:

(a) an interview with a person arrested under section 14(1)(a) or Schedule 5 paragraph 6 of the Prevention of Terrorism (Temporary Provisions) Act 1989 or an interview with a person being questioned in respect of an offence where there are reasonable grounds for suspecting that it is connected to terrorism or was committed in furtherance of the objectives of an organisation engaged in terrorism. This sub-paragraph applies only where the terrorism is connected with the affairs of Northern Ireland or is terrorism of any other description except terrorism connected solely with the affairs of the United Kingdom or any part of the United Kingdom other than Northern Ireland. "Terrorism" has the meaning given by section 20(1) of the Prevention of Terrorism (Temporary Provisions) Act 1989 [see *Notes 3E, 3F, 3G and 3H*];

(b) an interview with a person suspected on reasonable grounds of an offence under section 1 of the Official Secrets Act 1911 [see *Note 3H*].

3.3   The custody officer may authorise the interviewing officer not to tape record the interview:

(a) where it is not reasonably practicable to do so because of failure of the equipment or the non-availability of a suitable interview room or recorder and the authorising officer considers on reasonable grounds that the interview should not be delayed until the failure has been rectified or a suitable room or recorder becomes available [see *Note 3J*]; or

(b) where it is clear from the outset that no prosecution will ensue.

In such cases the interview shall be recorded in writing and in accordance with section 11 of Code C. In all cases the custody officer shall make a note in specific terms of the reasons for not tape recording. [see *Note 3K*].

3.4   Where an interview takes place with a person voluntarily attending the police station and the police officer has grounds to believe that person has become a suspect (i.e. the point at which he should be cautioned in accordance with paragraph 10.1 of Code C) the continuation of the interview shall be tape recorded, unless the custody officer gives authority in accordance with the provisions of paragraph 3.3 above for the continuation of the interview not to be recorded.

3.5   The whole of each interview shall be tape recorded, including the taking and reading back of any statement.

3J   Where practicable, priority should be given to tape recording interviews with people who are suspected of more serious offences.

3K   A decision not to tape record an interview for any reason may be the subject of comment in court. The authorising officer should therefore be prepared to justify his decision in each case.

4   The interview

(a)   Commencement of interviews

4.1   When the suspect is brought into the interview room the police officer shall without delay, but in the sight of the suspect, load the tape recorder with clean tapes and set it to record. The tapes must be unwrapped or otherwise opened in the presence of the suspect. [See *Note 4A*].

4.2   The police officer shall then tell the suspect formally about the tape recording. He shall say:

(a) that the interview is being tape recorded;

(b) his name and rank and the name and rank of any other police officer present except in the case of enquiries linked to the investigation of terrorism where warrant or other identification numbers shall be stated rather than names;

(c) the name of the suspect and any other party present (e.g. a solicitor);

(d) the date, time of commencement and place of the interview; and

(e) that the suspect will be given a notice about what will happen to the tapes.

[See *Note 4B*].

4.3   The police officer shall then caution the suspect in the following terms:

"You do not have to say anything. But it may harm your defence if you do not mention when questioned something which you later rely on in court. Anything you do say may be given in evidence.'

Minor deviations do not constitute a breach of this requirement provided that the sense of the caution is preserved. [See *Note 4C*].

4.3A   The police officer shall remind the suspect of his right to free and independent legal advice and that he can speak to a solicitor on the telephone in accordance with paragraph 6.5 of Code C.

4.3B   The police officer shall then put to the suspect any significant statement or silence (i.e. failure or refusal to answer a question or to answer it satisfactorily) which occurred before the start of the tape-recorded interview, and shall ask him whether he confirms or denies that earlier statement or silence or whether he wishes to add anything. A 'significant' statement or silence means one which appears capable of being used in evidence against the suspect, in particular a direct admission of guilt, or failure or refusal to answer a question or to answer it satisfactorily, which might give rise to an inference under Part III of the Criminal Justice and Public Order Act 1994.

Special warnings under Sections 36 and 37 of the Criminal Justice and Public Order Act 1994

4.3C   When a suspect who is interviewed after arrest fails or refuses to answer certain questions, or to answer them satisfactorily, after due warning, a court or jury may draw a proper inference from this silence under sections 36 and 37 of the Criminal Justice and Public Order Act 1994. This applies when:

(a) a suspect is arrested by a constable and there is found on his person, or in or on his clothing or footwear, or otherwise in his possession, or in the place where he was arrested, any objects, marks or substances, or marks on such objects, and the person fails or refuses to account for the objects, marks or substances found; or

(b) an arrested person was found by a constable at a place at or about the time the offence for which he was arrested, is alleged to have been committed, and the person fails or refuses to account for his presence at that place.

4.3D   For an inference to be drawn from a suspect's failure or refusal to answer a question about one of these matters or to answer it satisfactorily, the interviewing officer must first tell him in ordinary language:

(a) what offence he is investigating;

(b) what fact he is asking the suspect to account for;

(c) that he believes this fact may be due to the suspect's taking part in the commission of the offence in question;

(d) that a court may draw a proper inference from his silence if he fails or refuses to account for the fact about which he is being questioned;

(e) that a record is being made of the interview and may be given in evidence if he is brought to trial.

4.3E   Where, despite the fact that a person has been cautioned, failure to co-operate may have an effect on his immediate treatment, he should be informed of any relevant consequences and that they are not affected by the caution. Examples are when his refusal to provide his name and address when charged may render him liable to detention, or when his refusal to provide particulars and information in accordance with a statutory requirement, for example, under the Road Traffic Act 1988, may amount to an offence or may make him liable to arrest.

(b) Interviews with the deaf

4.4   If the suspect is deaf or there is doubt about his hearing ability, the police officer shall take a contemporaneous note of the interview in accordance with the requirements of Code C, as well as tape record it in accordance with the provisions of this code. [See *Notes 4E and 4F*].

(c) Objections and complaints by the suspect

4.5   If the suspect raises objections to the interview being tape recorded either at the outset or during the interview or during a break in the interview, the police officer shall explain the fact that the interview is being tape recorded and that the provisions of this code require that the suspect's objections shall be recorded on tape. When any objections have been recorded on tape or the suspect has refused to have his objections recorded, the police officer may turn off the recorder. In this eventuality he shall say that he is turning off the recorder and give his reasons for doing so and then turn it off. The police officer shall then make a written record of the interview in accordance with section 11 of Code C. If, however, the police officer reasonably considers that he may proceed to put questions to the suspect with the tape recorder still on, he may do so. [See *Note 4G*].

4.6   If in the course of an interview a complaint is made by the person being questioned, or on his behalf, concerning the provisions of this code or of Code C, then the officer shall act in accordance with paragraph 12.8 of Code C. [See *Notes 4H and 4J*].

4.7   If the suspect indicates that he wishes to tell the police officer about matters not directly connected with the offence of which he is suspected and that he is unwilling for these matters to be recorded on tape, he shall be given the opportunity to tell the police officer about these matters after the conclusion of the formal interview.

(d) Changing tapes

4.8   When the recorder indicates that the tapes have only a short time left to run, the police officer shall tell the suspect that the tapes are coming to an end and round off that part of the interview. If the police officer wishes to continue the interview but does not already have a second set of tapes, he shall obtain a set. The suspect shall not be left unattended in the interview room. The police officer will remove the tapes from the tape recorder and insert the new tapes which shall be unwrapped or otherwise opened in the suspect's presence. The tape recorder shall then be set to record on the new tapes. Care must be taken, particularly when a number of sets of tapes have been used, to ensure that there is no confusion between the tapes. This may be done by marking the tapes with an identification number immediately they are removed from the tape recorder.

(e) Taking a break during interview

4.9   When a break is to be taken during the course of an interview and the interview room is to be vacated by the suspect, the fact that a break is to be taken, the reason for it and the time shall be recorded on tape. The tapes shall then be removed from the tape recorder and the procedures for the conclusion of an interview set out in paragraph 4.14 below followed.

4.10   When a break is to be a short one and both the suspect and a police officer are to remain in the interview room the fact that a break is to be taken, the reasons for it and the time shall be recorded on tape. The tape recorder may be turned off; there is, however, no need to remove the tapes and when the interview is recommenced the tape recording shall be continued on the same tapes. The time at which the interview recommences shall be recorded on tape.

4.11   When there is a break in questioning under caution the interviewing officer must ensure that the person being questioned is aware that he remains under caution and of his right to legal advice. If there is any doubt the caution must be given again in full when the interview resumes. [See *Notes 4K and 4L*].

(f) Failure of recording equipment

4.12   If there is a failure of equipment which can be rectified quickly, for example by inserting new tapes, the appropriate procedures set out in paragraph 4.8 shall be followed, and when the recording is resumed the officer shall explain what has happened and record the time the interview recommences. If, however, it will not be possible to continue recording on that particular tape recorder and no replacement recorder or recorder in another interview room is readily available, the interview may continue without being tape recorded. In such circumstances the procedures in paragraphs 3.3 above for seeking the authority of the custody officer will be followed. [See *Note 4M*].

(g) Removing tapes from the recorder

4.13   Where tapes are removed from the recorder in the course of an interview, they shall be retained and the procedures set out in paragraph 4.15 below followed.

(h) Conclusion of interview

4.14   At the conclusion of the interview, the suspect shall be offered the opportunity to clarify anything he has said and to add anything he may wish.

4.15   At the conclusion of the interview, including the taking and reading back of any written statement, the time shall be recorded and the tape recorder switched off. The master tape shall be sealed with a master tape label and treated as an exhibit in accordance with the force standing orders. The police officer shall sign the label and ask the suspect and any third party present to sign it also. If the suspect or third party refuses to sign the label, an officer of at least the rank of inspector, or if one is not available the custody officer, shall be called into the interview room and asked to sign it. In the case of enquiries linked to the investigation of terrorism, an officer who signs the label shall use his warrant or other identification number.

4.16   The suspect shall be handed a notice which explains the use which will be made of the tape recording and the arrangements for access to it and that a copy of the tape shall be supplied as soon as practicable if the person is charged or informed that he will be prosecuted.

Control of abuse of police powers

Police Act 1996

67   Preliminary

(1) Where a complaint is submitted to the chief officer of police for a police area, he shall taken any steps that appear to him to be desirable for the purpose of obtaining or preserving evidence relating to the conduct complained of.

(2) After complying with subsection (1), the chief officer shall determine whether he is the appropriate authority in relation to the member of a police force whose conduct is the subject of the complaint.

(3) If the chief officer determines that he is not the appropriate authority, he shall—

(a) send the complaint or, if it was submitted orally, particulars of it, to the appropriate authority, and

(b) give notice that he has done so to the person by whom or on whose behalf the complaint was submitted.

(4) Nothing in this Chapter shall have effect in relation to a complaint in so far as it relates to the direction or control of a police force by the chief officer of police or the person performing the functions of the chief officer of police.

(5) If any conduct to which a complaint wholly or partly relates is or has been the subject

of criminal or disciplinary proceedings, none of the provisions of this Chapter which relate to the recording and investigation of complaints shall have effect in relation to the complaint in so far as it relates to that conduct.

68   Investigation of complaints senior officers

(1) Where a complaint about the conduct of a senior officer—

   (a) is submitted to the appropriate authority, or

   (b) is sent to the appropriate authority under section 67(3), the appropriate authority shall record and, subject to subsection (2), investigate it.

(2) If satisfied that the conduct complained of, even if proved, would not justify criminal or disciplinary proceedings, the appropriate authority may deal with the complaint according to the appropriate authority's discretion.

(2A) In any other case, subsection (2B) or (3) shall apply.

(2B) If the complaint is about the conduct of the Commissioner of Police of the Metropolis or the Deputy Commissioner of Police of the Metropolis—

   (a) the appropriate authority shall notify the Secretary of State; and

   (b) the Secretary of State shall appoint a person to investigate the complaint.

(3) In any other case, the appropriate authority shall appoint a member of the appropriate authority's force or of some other force to investigate the complaint.

(4) If

   (a) in a case where subsection (2B) applies, the Secretary of State, or

   (b) in a case where subsection (3) applies, the appropriate authority, requests the chief officer of police of a police force to provide a member of his force for appointment under subsection[(2B) or] (3), the chief officer shall comply with the request.

(5) No member of a police force of a rank lower than that of the member whose conduct is the subject of the complaint may be appointed under subsection (3).

(6) Unless an investigation under this section is supervised by the Authority under section 72, the investigating officer shall submit his report on it to the appropriate authority.

69   Investigation of complaints: standard procedure

(1) If a chief officer of police determines that he is the appropriate authority in relation to a member of a police force—

   (a) whose conduct is the subject of a complaint, and

   (b) who is not a senior officer,

he shall record the complaint.

(2) After recording a complaint under subsection (1), the chief officer of police shall consider whether the complaint is suitable for informal resolution and may appoint a member of his force to assist him.

(3) A complaint is not suitable for informal resolution unless—

   (a) the member of the public concerned gives his consent, and

   (b) the chief officer of police is satisfied that the conduct complained of, even if proved, would not justify criminal or disciplinary proceedings.

(4) If it appears to the chief officer of police that the complaint is suitable for informal resolution, he shall seek to resolve it informally and may appoint a member of his force to do so on his behalf.

(5) If it appears to the chief officer of police that the complaint is not suitable for informal resolution, he shall appoint a member of his own or some other force to investigate it formally.

(6) If, after attempts have been made to resolve a complaint informally, it appears to the chief officer of police—

   (a) that informal resolution of the complaint is impossible, or

(b) that the complaint is for any other reason not suitable for informal resolution, he shall appoint a member of his own or some other force to investigate it formally.

(7) A member of a police force may not be appointed to investigate a complaint formally if he has previously been appointed to act in relation to it under subsection (4).

(8) If a chief officer of police requests the chief officer of police of some other force to provide a member of that other force for appointment under subsection (5) or (6), that chief officer shall comply with the request.

(9) Unless the investigation is supervised by the Authority under section 72, the investigating officer shall submit his report on it to the chief officer of police who appointed him.

70   References of complaints to Authority

(1) The appropriate authority—
  (a) shall refer to the Authority—
    (i) any complaint alleging that the conduct complained of resulted in the death of, or serious injury to, some other person, and
    (ii) any complaint of a description specific for the purposes of this section in regulations made by the Secretary of State, and
  (b) may refer to the Authority any complaint which is not required to be referred to them.

(2) The Authority may require the submission to them for consideration of any complaint not referred to them by the appropriate authority; and the appropriate authority shall comply with any such requirement not later than the end of the period specified for the purposes of this subsection in regulations made by the Secretary of State.

(3) Where a complaint falls to be referred to the Authority under subsection (1)(a), the appropriate authority shall refer it to them not later than the end of the period specified for the purposes of sub-paragraph (i) or, as the case may be, (ii) of that subsection in regulations made by the Secretary of State.

71   References of other matters to Authority

(1) The appropriate authority may refer to the Authority any matter to which this section applies, if it appears to the appropriate authority that the matter ought to be referred by reason—
  (a) of its gravity, or
  (b) of exceptional circumstances.

(2) This section applies to any matter which—
  (a) appears to the appropriate authority to indicate that a member of a police force may have committed a criminal offence or behaved in a manner which would justify disciplinary proceedings, and
  (b) is not the subject of a complaint.

72   Supervision of investigations by Authority

(1) The Authority shall supervise the investigation of—
  (a) any complaint alleging that the conduct of a member of a police force resulted in the death of, or serious injury to, some other person,
  (b) any other description of complaint specified for the purposes of this section in regulations made by the Secretary of State, and
  (c) any complaint which is not within paragraph (a) or (b), and any matter referred to the Authority under section 71, if the Authority determine that it is desirable in the public interest that they should do so.

(2) Where the Authority have made a determination under subsection (1)(c), they shall notify it to the appropriate authority.

(3) Where an investigation is to be supervised by the Authority, they may require—
  (a) that no appointment is made under section 68(2B) or (3) or 69(5) unless they have

given notice to the appropriate authority that they approve the person whom that authority propose to appoint, or

(b) if such an appointment has already been made and the Authority are not satisfied with the person appointed, that—

(i) the appropriate authority, as soon as is reasonably practicable, select another member of a police force and notify the Authority that it proposes to appoint him, and

(ii) the appointment is not made unless the Authority give notice to the appropriate authority that they approve that person.

(3A) In the application of subsection (3) in relation to appointment under section 68(2B)—

(a) any reference to the appropriate authority shall be taken as a reference to the Secretary of State; and

(b) the reference in paragraph (b)(i) to another member of a police force shall be taken as a reference to another person.

(4) The Secretary of State shall by regulations authorise the Authority, subject to any restrictions or conditions specified in the regulations, to impose requirements as to a particular investigation additional to any requirements imposed by virtue of subsection (3).

(5) A member of a police force shall comply with any requirement imposed on him by virtue of regulations under subsection (4).

73   Reports on investigations etc.

(1) At the end of an investigation which the Authority have supervised, the investigating officer shall—

(a) submit a report on the investigation to the Authority, and

(b) send a copy of the report to the appropriate authority.

(2) After considering a report submitted to them under subsection (1), the Authority shall submit an appropriate statement to the appropriate authority.

(3) If it is practicable to do so, the Authority, when submitting the appropriate statement under subsection (2), shall send a copy of it to the member of a police force whose conduct has been investigated.

(4) If—

(a) the investigation related to a complaint, and

(b) it is practicable to do so,

the Authority shall also send a copy of the appropriate statement to the person by or on behalf of whom the complaint was submitted.

(5) The power to issue an appropriate statement includes power to issue separate statements in respect of the disciplinary and criminal aspects of an investigation.

(6) No disciplinary proceedings shall be brought before the appropriate statement is submitted to the appropriate authority.

(7) Subject to subsection (8) neither the appropriate authority nor the Director of Public Prosecutions shall bring criminal proceedings before the appropriate statement is submitted to the appropriate authority.

(8) The restriction imposed by subsection (7) does not apply if it appears to the Director that there are exceptional circumstances which make it undesirable to wait for the submission of the appropriate statement.

(9) In this section "appropriate statement" means a statement—

(a) as to whether the investigation was or was not conducted to the Authority's satisfaction,

(b) specifying any respect in which it was not so conducted, and

(c) dealing with any such other matters as the Secretary of State may by regulations provide.

74   Steps to be taken after investigation: senior officers
On receiving—
>   (a) a report concerning the conduct of a senior officer which is submitted to it under section 68(6), or
>   (b) a copy of a report concerning the conduct of a senior officer which is sent to it under section 73(1),

the appropriate authority shall send a copy of the report to the Director of Public Prosecutions unless the report satisfies the appropriate authority that no criminal offence has been committed.

75   Steps to be taken after investigation: standard procedure
>   (1) Nothing in this section or section 76 has effect in relation to senior officers.
>   (2) On receiving—
>   (a) a report concerning the conduct of a member of a police force who is not a senior officer which is submitted to him under section 69(9), or
>   (b) a copy of a report concerning the conduct of such a member which is sent to him under section 73(1).

a chief officer of police shall determine whether the report indicates that a criminal offence may have been committed by a member of the police force for his area.

>   (3) If the chief officer determines that the report indicates that a criminal offence may have been committed by a member of the police force for his area, he shall send a copy of the report to the Director of Public Prosecutions.
>   (4) After the Director has dealt with the question of criminal proceedings, the chief officer shall, in such cases as may be prescribed by regulations made by the Secretary of State, send the Authority a memorandum which—
>   (a) is signed by the chief officer,
>   (b) states whether he has brought (or proposes to bring) disciplinary proceedings in respect of the conduct which was the subject of the investigation, and
>   (c) if he has not brought (or does not propose to bring) such proceedings, gives his reasons.
>   (5) If the chief officer considers that the report does not indicate that a criminal offence may have been committed by a member of the police force for his area, he shall, in such cases as may be prescribed by regulations made by the Secretary of State, send the Authority a memorandum to that effect which—
>   (a) is signed by the chief officer,
>   (b) states whether he has brought (or proposes to bring) disciplinary proceedings in respect of the conduct which was the subject of the investigation, and
>   (c) if he has not brought (or does not propose to bring) such proceedings, gives his reasons.
>   (6) Where the investigation—
>   (a) related to conduct which was the subject of a complaint, and
>   (b) was not supervised by the Authority, the chief officer shall, if he is required by virtue of regulations under subsection (4) or (5) to send the Authority a memorandum, at the same time send them a copy of the complaint, or of the record of the complaint, and a copy of the report of the investigation.
>   (7) Where a chief officer has sent the Authority a memorandum under subsection (4) or (5), he shall—
>   (a) if the memorandum states that he proposes to bring disciplinary proceedings, bring and proceed with them, and
>   (b) if the memorandum states that he has brought such proceedings, proceed with them.

76   Powers of Authority as to disciplinary proceedings

(1) Where a memorandum under section 75 states that a chief officer of police has not brought disciplinary proceedings or does not propose to bring such proceedings, the Authority may recommend him to bring such proceedings.

(2) Where a chief officer has brought disciplinary proceedings in accordance with a recommendation under subsection (1), he shall proceed with them.

(3) If after the Authority have made a recommendation under this section and consulted the chief officer he is still unwilling to bring disciplinary proceedings, they may direct him to do so.

(4) Where the Authority give a chief officer a direction under this section, they shall supply him with a written statement of their reasons for doing so.

(5) Subject to subsection (6), it shall be the duty of a chief officer to comply with such a direction.

(6) The Authority may withdraw a direction given under this section.

(7) A chief officer shall—

  (a) advise the Authority of what action he has taken in response to a recommendation or direction under this section, and

  (b) supply the Authority with such other information as they may reasonably require for the purposes of discharging their functions under this section.

77   Information as to the manner of dealing with complaints etc.

Every police authority in carrying out its duty with respect to the maintenance of an efficient and effective police force, and inspectors of constabulary in carrying out their duties with respect to the efficiency and effectiveness of any police force, shall keep themselves informed as to the working of sections 67 to 76 in relation to the force.

78   Constabularies maintained by authorities other than police authorities

(1) An agreement for the establishment in relation to any body of constables maintained by an authority, other than a police authority, of procedures corresponding or similar to any of those established by or by virtue of this Chapter may, with the approval of the Secretary of State, be made between the Authority and the authority maintaining the body of constables.

(2) Where no such procedures are in force in relation to a body of constables, the Secretary of State may by order establish such procedures.

(3) An agreement under this section may at any time be varied or terminated with the approval of the Secretary of State.

(4) Before making an order under this section the Secretary of State shall consult—

  (a) the Authority, and

  (b) the authority maintaining the body of constables to whom the order would relate.

(5) A statutory instrument containing an order under this section shall be subject to annulment in pursuance of a resolution of either House of Parliament.

(6) Nothing in any other enactment passed or made before 31st October 1984 shall prevent an authority who maintain a body of constables from carrying into effect procedures established by virtue of this section.

(7) No such procedures shall have effect in relation to anything done by a constable outside England and Wales.

79   Reports

(1) The Authority shall, at the request of the Secretary of State, report to him on such matters relating generally to their functions as the Secretary of State may specify, and the Authority may for that purpose carry out research into any such matters.

(2) The Authority may make a report to the Secretary of State on any matters coming to their notice under this Chapter to which they consider that his attention should be drawn by reason of their gravity or of other exceptional circumstances.

(3) The Authority shall send a copy of any report under subsection (2)—

    (a) to the police authority and the chief officer of police of any police force which appears to the Authority to be concerned, or

    (b) if the report concerns a body of constables such as is mentioned in section 78, to the authority maintaining it and the officer having the direction and the control of it.

(4) As soon as practicable after the end of each calendar year the Authority shall make to the Secretary of State a report on the discharge of their functions during that year.

(5) The Secretary of State shall lay before Parliament a copy of every report received by him under this section and shall cause every such report to be published.

(6) The Authority shall send to each police authority—

    (a) a copy of every report made under subsection (4), and

    (b) any statistical or other general information—

        (i) which relates to the year dealt with by the report and to the area of that police authority, and

        (ii) which the Authority consider should be brought to the police authority's attention in connection with its functions under section 77.

80 Restriction on disclosure of information

(1) No information received by the Authority in connection with any of their functions under sections 67 to 79 or regulations made by virtue of section 81 shall be disclosed by any person who is or has been a member, officer or servant of the Authority except—

    (a) to the Secretary of State or to a member, officer or servant of the Authority or, so far as may be necessary for the proper discharge of the functions of the Authority, to other persons.

    (b) for the purposes of any criminal, civil or disciplinary proceedings, or

    (c) in the form of a summary or other general statement made by the Authority which does not identify the person from whom the information was received or any person to whom it relates.

(2) Any person who discloses information in contravention of this section shall be guilty of an offence and liable on summary conviction to a fine of an amount not exceeding level 5 on the standard scale.

81 Regulations

(1) The Secretary of State may make regulations as to the procedure to be followed under this Chapter.

(2) The Secretary of State shall by regulations provide—

    (a) that, subject to such exceptions, and in accordance with such procedures, as may be specified in the regulations, the chief officer of police of a police force shall supply a copy of, or of the record of, any complaint concerning the conduct of a member of his force—

        (i) to that member, and

        (ii) to the person by or on behalf of whom the complaint was submitted;

    (b) procedures for the informal resolution of complaints of such descriptions as may be specified in the regulations, and for giving the person by or on behalf of whom the complaint was submitted a record of the outcome of any such procedure if he applies for one within such period as the regulations may provide;

    (c) procedures for giving a member of a police force, whose conduct is the subject of a complaint which falls to be resolved informally, an opportunity to comment orally or in writing on the complaint;

    (d) for cases in which any provision of this Chapter is not to apply where—

        (i)   a complaint, other than a complaint which fails to be resolved informally, is withdrawn, or

        (ii) the complainant indicates that he does not wish any further steps to be taken;

  (e) for enabling the Authority to dispense with any requirement of this Chapter;

  (f) for enabling the Authority to relinquish the supervision of the investigation of any complaint or other matter;

  (g) procedures for the reference or submission of complaints or other matters to the Authority;

  (h) for the time within which the Authority are to give a notification under section 72(2);

  (i) that the Authority shall be supplied with such information or documents of such description as may be specified in the regulations at such time or in such circumstances as may be so specified;

  (j) that any action or decision of the Authority which they take in consequence of their receipt of a memorandum under section 75 shall, if it is an action or decision of a description specified in the regulations, be notified to the person concerned and that, in connection with such a notification, the Authority shall have power to supply that person with any relevant information;

  (k) that chief officers of police shall have power to delegate any functions conferred on them by or by virtue of this Chapter.

(3) In this section "document" means anything in which information of any description is recorded.

82   Regulations—supplementary

(1) Regulations under this Chapter may make different provision for different circumstances and may authorise the Secretary of State to make provision for any purposes specified in the regulations.

(2) Subject to subsection (3), a statutory instrument containing regulations under this Chapter shall be subject to annulment in pursuance of a resolution of either House of Parliament.

(3) Regulations to which this subsection applies shall not be made unless a draft of them has been laid before and approved by resolution of each House of Parliament.

(4) Subsection (3) applies to regulations made by virtue of section 70(1)(a)(ii), 72(1)(b) or (4), 75(4) or (5) or 81(2)(b), (e) or (f).

83   Guidance concerning complaints etc

(1) The Secretary of State may issue guidance to police authorities, chief officers of police and other members of police forces concerning the discharge of their functions under this Chapter and they shall have regard to any such guidance in the discharge of their functions.

(2) Guidance may not be issued under subsection (1) in relation to the handling of a particular case.

(3) A failure on the part of a person to whom guidance is issued under subsection (1) to have regard to such guidance shall be admissible in evidence on any appeal from a decision taken in proceedings under regulations made in accordance with section 50(3).

(4) In discharging their functions under section 76 the Authority shall have regard to any guidance given to them by the Secretary of State with respect to such matters as are for the time being the subject of guidance under subsection (1), and they shall have regard in particular, but without prejudice to the generality of this subsection, to any such guidance as to the principles to be applied in cases that involve any question of criminal proceedings.

(5) The report of the Authority under section 79(4) shall contain a statement of any guidance given to the Authority under subsection (4) above during the year to which the report relates.

Prosecutorial review

Prosecution of Offences Act 1985

1   The Crown Prosecution Service

(1) There shall be a prosecuting service for England and Wales (to be known as the "Crown Prosecution Service") consisting of—

(a)   the Director of Public Prosecutions, who shall be head of the Service;

(b)   the Chief Crown Prosecutors, designated under subsection (4) below, each of whom shall be the member of the Service responsible to the Director for supervising the operation of the Service in his area; and

(c)   the other staff appointed by the Director under this section.

(2) The Director shall appoint such staff for the Service as, with the approval of the Treasury as to numbers, remuneration and other terms and conditions of service, he considers necessary for the discharge of his functions.

(3) The Director may designate any member of the Service who has a general qualification within the meaning of section 71 of the Courts and Legal Services Act 1990 for the purposes of this subsection, and any person so designated shall be known as a Crown Prosecutor.

(4) The Director shall divide England and Wales into areas and, for each of those areas, designate a Crown Prosecutor for the purposes of this subsection and any person so designated shall be known as a Chief Crown Prosecutor.

(5) The Director may, from time to time, vary the division of England and Wales made for the purposes of subsection (4) above.

(6) Without prejudice to any functions which may have been assigned to him in his capacity as a member of the Service, every Crown Prosecutor shall have all the powers of the Director as to the institution and conduct of proceedings but shall exercise those powers under the direction of the Director.

(7) Where any enactment (whenever passed)—

(a)   prevents any step from being taken without the consent of the Director or without his consent or the consent of another; or

(b)   requires any step to be taken by or in relation to the Director;

any consent given by or, as the case may be, step taken by or in relation to, a Crown Prosecutor shall be treated, for the purposes of that enactment, as given by or, as the case may be, taken by or in relation to the Director.

2   The Director of Public Prosecutions

(1) The Director of Public Prosecutions shall be appointed by the Attorney General.

(2) The Director must be a person who has a 10 year general qualification within the meaning of section 71 of the Courts and Legal Services Act 1990.

(3) There shall be paid to the Director such remuneration as the Attorney General may, with the approval of the Treasury, determine.

3   Functions of the director

(1) The Director shall discharge his functions under this or any other enactment under the superintendence of the Attorney General.

(2) It shall be the duty of the Director, subject to any provisions contained in the Criminal Justice Act 1987—

(a)   to take over the conduct of all criminal proceedings, other than specified proceedings, instituted on behalf of a police force (whether by a member of that force or by any other person);

    (b) to institute and have the conduct of criminal proceedings in any case where it appears to him that—
        (i) the importance or difficulty of the case makes it appropriate that proceedings should be instituted by him; or
        (ii) it is otherwise appropriate for proceedings to be instituted by him;
    (c) to take over the conduct of all binding over proceedings instituted on behalf of a police force (whether by a member of that force or by any other person);
    (d) to take over the conduct of all proceedings begun by summons issued under section 3 of the Obscene Publications Act 1959 (forfeiture of obscene articles);
    (e) to give, to such extent as he considers appropriate, advice to police forces on all matters relating to criminal offences;
    (f) to appear for the prosecution, when directed by the court to do so, on any appeal under—
        (i) section 1 of the Administration of Justice Act 1960 (appeal from the High Court in criminal cases):
        (ii) Part I or Part II of the Criminal Appeal Act 1968 (appeals from the Crown Court to the criminal division of the Court of Appeal and thence to the House of Lords); or
        (iii) section 108 of the Magistrates' Courts Act 1980 (right of appeal to Crown Court) as it applies, by virtue of subsection (5) of section 12 of the Contempt of Court Act 1981, to orders made under section 12 (contempt of magistrates' courts); and
    (g) to discharge such other functions as may from time to time be assigned to him by the Attorney General in pursuance of this paragraph.
    (3) In this section—
"the court" means—
    (a) in the case of an appeal to or from the criminal division of the Court of Appeal, that division;
    (b) in the case of an appeal from a Divisional Court of the Queen's Bench Division, the Divisional Court; and
    (c) in the case of an appeal against an order of a magistrates' court, the Crown Court;

"police force" means any police force maintained by a police authority under the Police Act 1996, the National Crime Squad and any other body of constables for the time being specified by order made by the Secretary of State for the purposes of this section; and

"specified proceedings" means proceedings which fall within any category for the time being specified by order made by the Attorney General for the purposes of this section.

    (4) The power to make orders under subsection (3) above shall be exercisable by statutory instrument subject to annulment in pursuance of a resolution of either House of Parliament.

10 Guidelines for Crown Prosecutors

    (1) The Director shall issue a Code for Crown Prosecutors giving guidance on general principles to be applied by them—
    (a) in determining, in any case—
        (i) whether proceedings for an offence should be instituted or, where proceedings have been instituted, whether they should be discontinued; or
        (ii) what charges should be preferred; and
    (b) in considering, in any case, representations to be made by them to any magistrates' court about the mode of trial suitable for that case.
    (2) The Director may from time to time make alterations in the Code.
    (3) The provisions of the Code shall be set out in the Director's report under section 9 of this Act for the year in which the Code is issued; and any alteration in the Code shall be set out in his report under that section for the year in which the alteration is made.

Bail

Bail Act 1976

Incidents of bail in criminal proceedings

3   General provisions

(1) A person granted bail in criminal proceedings shall be under a duty to surrender to custody, and that duty is enforceable in accordance with section 6 of this Act.

(2) No recognizance for his surrender to custody shall be taken from him.

(3) Except as provided by this section—

(a) no security for his surrender to custody shall be taken from him.

(b) he shall not be required to provide a surety or sureties for his surrender to custody, and

(c) no other requirement shall be imposed on him as a condition of bail.

(4) He may be required, before release on bail, to provide a surety or sureties to secure his surrender to custody.

(5) He may be required, before release on bail, to give security for his surrender to custody.

The security may be given by him or on his behalf.

(6) He may be required to comply, before release on bail or later, with such requirements as appear to the court to be necessary to secure that—

(a) he surrenders to custody.

(b) he does not commit an offence while on bail,

(c) he does not interfere with witnesses or otherwise obstruct the course of justice whether in relation to himself or any other person,

(d) he makes himself available for the purpose of enabling inquiries or a report to be made to assist the court in dealing with him for the offence.

(e) before the time appointed for him to surrender to custody, he attends an interview with an authorised advocate or authorised litigator, as defined by section 119(1) of the Courts and Legal Services Act 1990;

and, in any Act, "the normal powers to impose conditions of bail" means the powers to impose conditions under paragraph (a), (b) or (c) above.

(6ZAA) Subject to section 3AA below, if he is a child or young person he may be required to comply with requirements imposed for the purpose of securing the electronic monitoring of his compliance with any other requirement imposed on him as a condition of bail.

(6ZA) Where he is required under subsection (6) above to reside in a bail hostel or probation hostel, he may also be required to comply with the rules of the hostel.

(6A) In the case of a person accused of murder the court granting bail shall, unless it considers that satisfactory reports on his mental condition have already been obtained, impose as conditions of bail—

(a) a requirement that the accused shall undergo examination by two medical practitioners, for the purpose of enabling such reports to be prepared; and

(b) a requirement that he shall for that purpose attend such an institution or place as the court directs and comply with any other directions which may be given to him for that purpose by either of those practitioners.

(6B) Of the medical practitioners referred to in subsection (6A) above at least one shall be practitioner approved for the purposes of section 12 of the Mental Health Act 1983.

(7) If a parent or guardian of a child or young person consents to be surety for the child or

young person for the purposes of this subsection, the parent or guardian may be required to secure that the child or young person complies with any requirement imposed on him by virtue of subsection (6), (6ZAA) or (6A) above, but—

(a) no requirement shall be imposed on the parent or the guardian of a young person by virtue of this subsection where it appears that the young person will attain the age of seventeen before the time to be appointed for him to surrender to custody; and

(b) the parent or guardian shall not be required to secure compliance with any requirement to which his consent does not extend and shall not, in respect of those requirements to which his consent does extend, be bound in a sum greater than £50.

(8) Where a court has granted bail in criminal proceedings it may on application—

(a) by or on behalf of the person to whom it was granted, or

(b) by the prosecutor or a constable,

vary the conditions of bail or impose conditions in respect of bail which it has granted unconditionally.

(8A) Where a notice of transfer is given under a relevant transfer provision, subsection (8) above shall have effect in relation to a person in relation to whose case the notice is given as if he has been committed on bail on the Crown Court for trial.

(8B) Subsection (8) above applies where a court has sent a person on bail to the Crown Court for trial under section 51 of the Crime and Disorder Act 1998 as it applies where a court has committed a person on bail to the Crown Court for trial.

(9) This section is subject to subsection (3) of section 11 of the Powers of Criminal Courts (Sentencing) Act 2000 (conditions of bail on remand for medical examination).

(10) This section is subject, in its application to bail granted by a constable, to section 3A of this Act.

(10) In subsection (8A) above "relevant transfer provision" means—

(a) section 4 of the Criminal Justice Act 1987, or

(b) section 53 of the Criminal Justice Act 1991.

3A   Conditions of bail in case of police bail

(1) Section 3 of this Act applies, in relation to bail granted by a custody officer under Part IV of the Police and Criminal Evidence Act 1984 in cases where the normal powers to impose conditions of bail are available to him, subject to the following modifications.

(2) Subsection (6) does not authorise the imposition of a requirement to reside in a bail hostel or any requirement under paragraph (d) or (e).

(3) Subsections (6ZAA), (6ZA), (6A) and (6B) shall be omitted.

(4) For subsection (8), substitute the following—

"(8) Where a custody officer has granted bail in criminal proceedings he or another custody officer serving at the same police station may, at the request of the person to whom it was granted, vary the conditions of bail; and in doing so he may impose conditions or more onerous conditions.".

(5) Where a constable grants bail to a person no conditions shall be imposed under subsections (4), (5), (6) or (7) of section 3 of this Act unless it appears to the constable that it is necessary to do so for the purpose of preventing that person from—

(a) failing to surrender to custody, or

(b) committing an offence while on bail, or

(c) interfering with witnesses or otherwise obstructing the course of justice, whether in relation to himself or any other person.

(6) Subsection (5) above also applies on any request to a custody officer under subsection (8) of section 3 of this Act to vary the conditions of bail.

3AA Electronic monitoring of compliance with bail conditions

(1) A court shall not impose on a child or young person a requirement under section 3(6ZAA) above (an "electronic monitoring requirement") unless each of the following conditions is satisfied.

(2) The first condition is that the child or young person has attained the age of twelve years.

(3) The second condition is that—

    (a) the child or young person is charged with or has been convicted of a violent or sexual offence, or an offence punishable in the case of an adult with imprisonment for a term of fourteen years or more; or

    (b) he is charged with or has been convicted of one or more imprisonable offences which, together with any other imprisonable offences of which he has been convicted in any proceedings—

        (i) amount, or

        (ii) would, if he were convicted of the offences with which he is charged, amount, to a recent history of repeatedly committing imprisonable offences while remanded on bail or to local authority accommodation.

(4) The third condition is that the court—

    (a) has been notified by the Secretary of State that electronic monitoring arrangements are available in each petty sessions area which is a relevant area; and

    (b) is satisfied that the necessary provision can be made under those arrangements.

(5) The fourth condition is that a youth offending team has informed the court that in its opinion the imposition of such a requirement will be suitable in the case of the child or young person.

(6) Where a court imposes an electronic monitoring requirement, the requirement shall include provision for making a person responsible for the monitoring; and a person who is made so responsible shall be of a description specified in an order made by the Secretary of State.

(7) The Secretary of State may make rules for regulating—

    (a) the electronic monitoring of compliance with requirements imposed on a child or young person as a condition of bail; and

    (b) without prejudice to the generality of paragraph (a) above, the functions of persons made responsible for securing the electronic monitoring of compliance with such requirements.

(8) Rules under this section may make different provision for different cases.

(9) Any power of the Secretary of State to make an order or rules under this section shall be exercisable by statutory instrument.

(10) A statutory instrument containing rules made under this section shall be subject to annulment in pursuance of a resolution of either House of Parliament.

(11) In this section "local authority accommodation" has the same meaning as in the Children and Young Persons Act 1969 (c. 54).

(12) For the purposes of this section a petty sessions area is a relevant area in relation to a proposed electronic monitoring requirement if the court considers that it will not be practicable to secure the electronic monitoring in question unless electronic monitoring arrangements are available in that area.

Bail for accused persons and others

4 General right to bail of accused persons and others

(1) A person to whom this section applies shall be granted bail except as provided in Schedule 1 to this Act.

(2) This section applies to a person who is accused of an offence when—

(a) he appears or is brought before a magistrates' court or the Crown Court in the course of or in connection with proceedings for the offence, or

(b) he applies to a court for bail in connection with the proceedings.

This subsection does not apply as respects proceedings on or against a person's conviction of the offence or proceedings against a fugitive offender for the offence.

(3) This section also applies to a person who, having been convicted of an offence, appears or is brought before a magistrates' court to be dealt with under Part II of Schedule 3 to the Powers of Criminal Courts (Sentencing) Act 2000 (breach of certain community orders).

(4) This section also applies to a person who has been convicted of an offence of enabling inquiries or a report to be made for the purpose of enabling inquiries or a report to be made to assist the court in dealing with him for the offence.

(5) Schedule 1 to this Act also has effect as respects conditions of bail for a person to whom this section applies.

(6) In Schedule 1 to this Act "the defendant" means a person to whom this section applies and any reference to a defendant whose case is adjourned for inquiries or a report is a reference to a person to whom this section applies by virtue of subsection (4) above.

(7) This section is subject to section 41 of the Magistrates' Courts Act 1980 (restriction of bail by magistrates' court in cases of treason).

(8) This section is subject to section 25 of the Criminal Justice and Public Order Act 1994 (exclusion of bail in cases of homicide and rape).

(9) In taking any decisions required by Part I or II of Schedule 1 to this Act, the considerations to which the court is to have regard include, so far as relevant, any misuse of controlled drugs by the defendant ("controlled drugs" and "misuse" having the same meanings as in the Misuse of Drugs Act 1971).

5   Supplementary provisions about decisions on bail

(1) Subject to subsection (2) below, where—

(a) a court or constable grants bail in criminal proceedings, or

(b) a court withholds bail in criminal proceedings from a person to whom section 4 of this Act applies, or

(c) a court, officer of a court or constable appoints a time or place or a court or officer of a court appoints a different time or place for a person granted bail in criminal proceedings to surrender to custody, or

(d) a court or constable varies any conditions of bail or imposes conditions in respect of bail in criminal proceedings,

that court, officer or constable shall make a record of the decision in the prescribed manner and containing the prescribed particulars and, if requested to do so by the person in relation to whom the decision was taken, shall cause him to be given a copy of the record of the decision as soon as practicable after the record is made.

(2) Where bail in criminal proceedings is granted by endorsing a warrant of arrest for bail the constable who releases on bail the person arrested shall make the record required by subsection (1) above instead of the judge or justice who issued the warrant.

(2A) Where a magistrates' court or the Crown Court grants bail in criminal proceedings to a person to whom section 4 of this Act applies after hearing representations from the prosecutor in favour of withholding bail, then the court shall give reasons for granting bail.

(2B) A court which is by virtue of subsection (2A) above required to give reasons for its decision shall include a note of those reasons in the record of its decision and, if requested to do so by the prosecutor, shall cause the prosecutor to be given a copy of the record of the decision as soon as practicable after the record is made.

(3) Where a magistrates' court or the Crown Court—

(a) withholds bail in criminal proceedings, or

(b) imposes conditions in granting bail in criminal proceedings, or

(c) varies any conditions of bail or imposes conditions in respect of bail in criminal proceedings,

and does so in relation to a person to whom section 4 of this Act applies, then the court shall, with a view to enabling him to consider making an application in the matter to another court, give reasons for withholding bail or for imposing or varying the conditions.

(4) A court which is by virtue of subsection (3) above required to give reasons for its decision shall include a note of those reasons in the record of its decision and shall (except in a case where, by virtue of subsection (5) below, this need not be done) give a copy of that note to the person in relation to whom the decision was taken.

(5) The Crown Court need not give a copy of the note of the reasons for its decision to the person in relation to whom the decision was taken where that person is represented by counsel or a solicitor unless his counsel or solicitor requests the court to do so.

(6) Where a magistrates' court withholds bail in criminal proceedings from a person who is not represented by counsel or a solicitor, the court shall—

(a) if it is committing him for trial to the Crown Court, inform him that he may apply to the High Court or to the Crown Court to be granted bail;

(b) in any other case, inform him that he may apply to the High Court for that purpose.

(6A) Where in criminal proceedings—

(a) a magistrates' court remands a person in custody under section 11 of the Powers of Criminal Courts (Sentencing) Act 2000 (remand for medical examination) or any of the following provisions of the Magistrates' Courts Act 1980—

(i) section 5 (adjournment of inquiry into offence);

(ii) section 10 (adjournment of trial); or

(iii) section 18 (initial procedure on information against adult for offence triable either way),

after hearing full argument on an application for bail from him; and

(b) either—

(i) it has not previously heard such argument on an application for bail from him in those proceedings; or

(ii) it has previously heard full argument from him on such an application but it is satisfied that there has been a change in his circumstances or that new considerations have been placed before it,

it shall be the duty of the court to issue a certificate in the prescribed form that they heard full argument on his application for bail before they refused the application.

(6B) Where the court issues a certificate under subsection (6A) above in a case to which paragraph (b)(ii) of that subsection applies, it shall state in the certificate the nature of the change of circumstances or the new considerations which caused it to hear a further fully argued bail application.

(6C) Where a court issues a certificate under subsection (6A) above it shall cause the person to whom it refuses bail to be given a copy of the certificate.

(7) Where a person has given security in pursuance of section 3(5) above and a court is satisfied that he failed to surrender to custody then, unless it appears that he had reasonable cause for his failure, the court may order the forfeiture of the security.

(8) If a court orders the forfeiture of a security under subsection (7) above, the court may declare that the forfeiture extends to such amount less than the full value of the security as it thinks fit to order.

(8A) An order under subsection (7) above shall, unless previously revoked, have effect at the end of twenty-one days beginning with the day on which it is made.

(8B) A court which has ordered the forfeiture of a security under subsection (7) above may, if satisfied on an application made by or on behalf of the person who gave it that he did after all have reasonable cause for his failure to surrender to custody, by order remit the forfeiture or declare that it extends to such amount less than the full value of the security as it thinks fit to order.

(8C) An application under subsection (8B) above may be made before or after the order for forfeiture has taken effect, but shall not be entertained unless the court is satisfied that the prosecution was given reasonable notice of the applicant's intention to make it.

(9) A security which has been ordered to be forfeited by a court under subsection (7) above shall, to the extent of the forfeiture—

> (a) if it consists of money, be accounted for and paid in the same manner as a fine imposed by that court would be;
> (b) if it does not consist of money, be enforced by such magistrates' court as may be specified in the order.

(9A) Where an order is made under subsection (8B) above after the order for forfeiture of the security in question has taken effect, any money which would have fallen to be repaid or paid over to the person who gave the security if the order under subsection (8B) had been made before the order for forfeiture took effect shall be repaid or paid over to him.

(10) In this section "prescribed" means, in relation to the decision of a court or an officer of a court, prescribed by Supreme Court rules. Courts-Martial Appeal rules, Crown Court rules or magistrates' courts rules, as the case requires or, in relation to a decision of a constable, prescribed by direction of the Secretary of State.

(11) This section is subject, in its application to bail granted by a constable, to section 5A of this Act.

5A Supplementary provisions in cases of police bail

(1) Section 5 of this Act applies, in relation to bail granted by a custody officer under Part IV of the Police and Criminal Evidence Act 1984 in cases where the normal powers to impose conditions of bail are available to him, subject to the following modifications.

(1A) Subsections (2A) and (2B) shall be omitted.

(2) For subsection (3) substitute the following—

"(3) Where a custody officer, in relation to any person,—

> (a) imposes conditions in granting bail in criminal proceedings, or
> (b) varies any conditions of bail or imposes conditions in respect of bail in criminal proceedings, the custody officer shall, with a view to enabling that person to consider requesting him or another custody officer, or making an application to a magistrates' court, to vary the conditions, give reasons for imposing or varying the conditions."

(3) For subsection (4) substitute the following—

"(4) A custody officer who is by virtue of subsection (3) above required to give reasons for his decision shall include a note of those reasons in the custody record and shall give a copy of that note to the person in relation to whom the decision was taken."

(4) Subsections (5) and (6) shall be omitted.

5B Reconsideration of decisions granting bail

(1) Where a magistrates' court has granted bail in criminal proceedings in connection with an offence, or proceedings for an offence, to which this section applies or a constable has granted bail in criminal proceedings in connection with proceedings for such an offence, that court or the appropriate court in relation to the constable may, on application by the prosecutor for the decision to be reconsidered,—

> (a) vary the conditions of bail,

(b) impose conditions in respect of bail which has been granted unconditionally, or

(c) withhold bail.

(2) The offences to which this section applies are offences triable on indictment and offences triable either way.

(3) No application for the reconsideration of a decision under this section shall be made unless it is based on information which was not available to the court or constable when the decision was taken.

(4) Whether or not the person to whom the application relates appears before it, the magistrates' court shall take the decision in accordance with section 4(1) (and Schedule 1) of this Act.

(5) Where the decision of the court on a reconsideration under this section is to withhold bail from the person to whom it was originally granted the court shall—

(a) if that person is before the court, remand him in custody, and

(b) if that person is not before the court, order him to surrender himself forthwith into the custody of the court.

(6) Where a person surrenders himself into the custody of the court in compliance with an order under subsection (5) above, the court shall remand him in custody.

(7) A person who has been ordered to surrender to custody under subsection (5) above may be arrested without warrant by a constable if he fails without reasonable cause to surrender to custody in accordance with the order.

(8) A person arrested in pursuance of subsection (7) above shall be brought as soon as practicable, and in any event within 24 hours after his arrest, before a justice of the peace for the petty sessions area in which he was arrested and the justice shall remand him in custody.

In reckoning for the purposes of this subsection any period of 24 hours, no account shall be taken of Christmas Day, Good Friday or any Sunday.

(8A) Where the court, on a reconsideration under this section, refuses to withhold bail from a relevant person after hearing representations from the prosecutor in favour of withholding bail, then the court shall give reasons for refusing to withhold bail.

(8B) In subsection (8A) above, "relevant person" means a person to whom section 4(1) (and Schedule 1) of this Act is applicable in accordance with subsection (4) above.

(8C) A court which is by virtue of subsection (8A) above required to give reasons for its decision shall include a note of those reasons in any record of its decision and, if requested to do so by the prosecutor, shall cause the prosecutor to be given a copy of any such record as soon as practicable after the record is made.

(9) Magistrates' court rules shall include provision—

(a) requiring notice of an application under this section and of the grounds for it to be given to the person affected, including notice of the powers available to the court under it;

(b) for securing that any representations made by the person affected (whether in writing or orally) are considered by the court before making its decision; and

(c) designating the court which is the appropriate court in relation to the decision of any constable to grant bail.

6 Offence of absconding by person released on bail

(1) If a person who has been released on bail in criminal proceedings fails without reasonable cause to surrender to custody he shall be guilty of an offence.

(2) If a person who—

(a) has been released on bail in criminal proceedings, and

(b) having reasonable cause therefor, has failed to surrender to custody,

fails to surrender to custody at the appointed place as soon after the appointed time as is reasonably practicable he shall be guilty of an offence.

(3) It shall be for the accused to prove that he had reasonable cause for his failure to surrender to custody.

(4) A failure to give to a person granted bail in criminal proceedings a copy of the record of the decision shall not constitute a reasonable cause for that person's failure to surrender to custody.

(5) An offence under subsection (1) or (2) above shall be punishable either on summary conviction or as if it were a criminal contempt of court.

(6) Where a magistrates' court convicts a person of an offence under subsection (1) or (2) above the court may, if it thinks—

> (a) that the circumstances of the offence are such that greater punishment should be inflicted for that offence than the court has power to inflict, or
>
> (b) in a case where it commits that person for trial to the Crown Court for another offence, that it would be appropriate for him to be dealt with for the offence under subsection (1) or (2) above by the court before which he is tried for the other offence,

commit him in custody or on bail to the Crown Court for sentence.

(7) A person who is convicted summarily of an offence under subsection (1) or (2) above and is committed to the Crown Court for sentence shall be liable to imprisonment for a term not exceeding 3 months or to a fine not exceeding level 5 on the standard scale or to both and a person who is so committed for sentence or is dealt with as for such a contempt shall be liable to imprisonment for a term not exceeding 12 months or to a fine or to both.

(8) In any proceedings for an offence under subsection (1) or (2) above a document purporting to be a copy of the part of the prescribed record which relates to the time and place appointed for the person specified in the record to surrender to custody and to be duly certified to be a true copy of that part of the record shall be evidence of the time and place appointed for that person to surrender to custody.

(9) For the purposes of subsection (8) above—

> (a) "the prescribed record" means the record of the decision of the court, officer or constable made in pursuance of section 5(1) of this Act:
>
> (b) the copy of the prescribed record is duly certified if it is certified by the appropriate officer of the court or, as the case may be, by the constable who took the decision or a constable designated for the purpose by the officer in charge of the police station from which the person to whom the record relates was released;
>
> (c) "the appropriate officer" of the court is—
>
> > (i) in the case of a magistrates' court, the justices' chief executive or such other officer as may be authorised by him to act for the purpose;
> >
> > (ii) in the case of the Crown Court, such officer as may be designated for the purpose in accordance with arrangements made by the Lord Chancellor;
> >
> > (iii) in the case of the High Court, such officer as may be designated for the purpose in accordance with arrangements made by the Lord Chancellor;
> >
> > (iv) in the case of the Court of Appeal, the registrar of criminal appeals or such other officer as may be authorised by him to act for the purpose;
> >
> > (v) in the case of the Courts-Martial Appeal Court, the registrar or such other officer as may be authorised by him to act for the purpose.

7   Liability to arrest for absconding or breaking conditions of bail

(1) If a person who has been released on bail in criminal proceedings and is under a duty to surrender into the custody of a court fails to surrender to custody at the time appointed for him to do so the court may issue a warrant for his arrest.

(2) If a person who has been released on bail in criminal proceedings absents himself from the court at any time after he has surrendered into the custody of the court and before

the court is ready to begin or to resume the hearing of the proceedings, the court may issue a warrant for his arrest; but no warrant shall be issued under this subsection where that person is absent in accordance with leave given to him by or on behalf of the court.

(3) A person who has been released on bail in criminal proceedings and is under a duty to surrender into the custody of a court may be arrested without warrant by a constable—

    (a) if the constable has reasonable grounds for believing that that person is not likely to surrender to custody;

    (b) if the constable has reasonable grounds for believing that that person is likely to break any of the conditions of his bail or has reasonable grounds for suspecting that that person has broken any of those conditions; or

    (c) in a case where that person was released on bail with one or more surety or sureties, if a surety notifies a constable in writing that that person is unlikely to surrender to custody and that for that reason the surety wishes to be relieved of his obligations as a surety.

(4) A person arrested in pursuance of subsection (3) above—

    (a) shall, except where he was arrested within 24 hours of the time appointed for him to surrender to custody, be brought as soon as practicable and in any event within 24 hours after his arrest before a justice of the peace for the petty sessions area in which he was arrested; and

    (b) in the said excepted case shall be brought before the court at which he was to have surrendered to custody. In reckoning for the purposes of this subsection any period of 24 hours, no account shall be taken of Christmas Day, Good Friday or any Sunday.

(5) A justice of the peace before whom a person is brought under subsection (4) above may, subject to subsection (6) below, if of the opinion that that person—

    (a) is not likely to surrender to custody, or

    (b) has broken or is likely to break any condition of his bail,

remand him in custody or commit him to custody, as the case may require, or alternatively, grant him bail subject to the same or to different conditions, but if not of that opinion shall grant him bail subject to the same conditions (if any) as were originally imposed.

(6) Where the person so brought before the justice is a child or young person and the justice does not grant him bail, subsection (5) above shall have effect subject to the provisions of section 23 of the Children and Young Persons Act 1969 (remands to the care of local authorities).

SCHEDULE 1

PERSONS ENTITLED TO BAIL: SUPPLEMENTARY PROVISIONS

PART I   DEFENDANTS ACCUSED OR CONVICTED OF IMPRISONABLE OFFENCES

Exceptions to right to bail

2 The defendant need not be granted bail if the court is satisfied that there are substantial grounds for believing that the defendant, if released on bail (whether subject to conditions or not) would—

    (a) fail to surrender to custody, or

    (b) commit an offence while on bail, or

    (c) interfere with witnesses or otherwise obstruct the course of justice, whether in relation to himself or any other person.

2A The defendant need not be granted bail if—

    (a) the offence is an indictable offence or an offence triable either way; and

    (b) it appears to the court that he was on bail in criminal proceedings on the date of the offence.

3   The defendant need not be granted bail if the court is satisfied that the defendant should be kept in custody for his own protection or, if he is a child or young person, for his own welfare.

4   The defendant need not be granted bail if he is in custody in pursuance of the sentence of a court or of any authority acting under any of the Services Acts.

5   The defendant need not be granted bail where the court is satisfied that it has not been practicable to obtain sufficient information for the purpose of taking the decisions required by this Part of this Schedule for want of time since the institution of the proceedings against him.

6   The defendant need not be granted bail if, having been released on bail in or in connection with the proceedings for the offence, he has been arrested in pursuance of section 7 of this Act.

7   Omitted

Restrictions of conditions of bail

8   (1) Subject to sub-paragraph (3) below, where the defendant is granted bail, no conditions shall be imposed under subsections (4) to (7) (except subsection (6)(d) or (e)) of section 3 of this Act unless it appears to the court that it is necessary to do so for the purpose of preventing the occurrence of any of the events mentioned in paragraph 2 of this Part of this Schedule.

(1A) No condition shall be imposed under section 3(6)(d) of this Act unless it appears to be necessary to do so for the purpose of enabling inquiries or a report to be made.

(2) Sub-paragraphs (1) and (1A) above also apply on any application to the court to vary the conditions of bail or to impose conditions in respect of bail which has been granted unconditionally.

(3) The restriction imposed by sub-paragraph (1A) above shall not apply to the conditions required to be imposed under section 3(6A) of this Act or operate to override the direction in section 11(3) of the Powers of Criminal Courts (Sentencing) Act 2000 to a magistrates' court to impose conditions of bail under section 3(6)(d) of this Act of the description specified in [the said section 11(3) in the circumstances so specified].

9   In taking the decisions required by paragraph 2 or 2A of this Part of this Schedule, the court shall have regard to such of the following considerations as appear to it to be relevant, that is to say—

   (a) the nature and seriousness of the offence or default (and the probable method of dealing with the defendant for it),
   (b) the character, antecedents, associations and community ties of the defendant,
   (c) the defendant's record as respects the fulfilment of his obligations under previous grants of bail in criminal proceedings,
   (d) except in the case of a defendant whose case is adjourned for inquiries or a report, the strength of the evidence of his having committed the offence or having defaulted,

as well as to any others which appear to be relevant.

Criminal Justice and Public Order Act 1994

25   No bail for defendants charged with or convicted of homicide or rape after previous conviction of such offences

(1) A person who in any proceedings has been charged with or convicted of an offence to which this section applies in circumstances to which it applies shall be granted bail in those proceedings only if the court or, as the case may be, the constable considering the grant of bail is satisfied that there are exceptional circumstances which justify it.

(2) This section applies, subject to subsection (3) below, to the following offences, that is to say—

    (a) murder;

    (b) attempted murder;

    (c) manslaughter;

    (d) rape; or

    (e) attempted rape.

(3) This section applies to a person charged with or convicted of any such offence only if he has been previously convicted by or before a court in any part of the United Kingdom of any such offence or of culpable homicide and, in the case of a previous conviction of manslaughter or of culpable homicide, if he was then sentenced to imprisonment or, if he was then a child or young person, to long-term detention under any of the relevant enactments.

(4) This section applies whether or not an appeal is pending against conviction or sentence.

(5) In this section—

"conviction" includes—

    (a) a finding that a person is not guilty by reason of insanity;

    (b) a finding under section 4A(3) of the Criminal Procedure (Insanity) Act 1964 (cases of unfitness to plead) that a person did the act or made the omission charged against him; and

    (c) a conviction of an offence for which an order is made placing the offender on probation or discharging him absolutely or conditionally;

  and "convicted" shall be construed accordingly; and

"the relevant enactments" means—

    (a) as respects England and Wales, section 91 of the Powers of Criminal Courts (Sentencing) Act 2000;

    (b) as respects Scotland, sections 205(1) to (3) and 208 of the Criminal Procedure (Scotland) Act 1995;

    (c) as respects Northern Ireland, section 73(2) of the Children and Young Persons Act (Northern Ireland) 1968.

(6) This section does not apply in relation to proceedings instituted before its commencement.

Police and Criminal Evidence Act 1984

46A   Power of arrest for failure to answer to police bail

(1) A constable may arrest without a warrant any person who, having been released on bail under this Part of this Act subject to a duty to attend at a police station, fails to attend at that police station at the time appointed for him to do so.

(2) A person who is arrested under this section shall be taken to the police station appointed as the place at which he is to surrender to custody as soon as practicable after the arrest.

(3) For the purposes of—

    (a) section 30 above (subject to the obligation in subsection (2) above), and

    (b) section 31 above,

an arrest under this section shall be treated as an arrest for an offence.

47   Bail after arrest

(1) Subject to subsection (2) below, a release on bail of a person under this Part of this Act

shall be a release on bail granted in accordance with sections 3, 3A, 5 and 5A of the Bail Act 1976 as they apply to bail granted by a constable.

(1A) The normal powers to impose conditions of bail shall be available to him where a custody officer releases a person on bail under section 38(1) above (including that subsection as applied by section 40(10) above) but not in any other cases.

In this subsection, "the normal powers to impose conditions of bail" has the meaning given in section 3(6) of the Bail Act 1976.

(2) Nothing in the Bail Act 1976 shall prevent the re-arrest without warrant of a person released on bail subject to a duty to attend at a police station if new evidence justifying a further arrest has come to light since his release.

(3) Subject to subsections (3A) and (4) below, in this Part of this Act references to "bail" are references to bail subject to a duty—

    (a) to appear before a magistrates' court at such time and such place; or

    (b) to attend at such police station at such time, as the custody officer may appoint.

(3A) Where a custody officer grants bail to a person subject to a duty to appear before a magistrates' court, he shall appoint for the appearance—

    (a) a date which is not later than the first sitting of the court after the person is charged with the offence; or

    (b) where he is informed by the justices' chief executive for the relevant petty sessions area that the appearance cannot be accommodated until a later date, that later date.

(4) Where a custody officer has granted bail to a person subject to a duty to appear at a police station, the custody officer may give notice in writing to that person that his attendance at the police station is not required.

(6) Where a person who has been granted bail and either has attended at the police station in accordance with the grant of bail or has been arrested under section 46A above is detained at a police station, any time during which he was in police detention prior to being granted bail shall be included as part of any period which falls to be calculated under this Part of this Act.

(7) Where a person who was released on bail subject to a duty to attend at a police station is re-arrested, the provisions of this Part of this Act shall apply to him as they apply to a person arrested for the first time; but this subsection does not apply to a person who is arrested under section 46A above or has attended a police station in accordance with the grant of bail (and who accordingly is deemed by section 34(7) above to have been arrested for an offence).

47A Early administrative hearings conducted by justices' clerks

Where a person has been charged with an offence at a police station, any requirement imposed under this Part for the person to appear or be brought before a magistrates' court shall be taken to be satisfied if the person appears or is brought before the clerk to the justices for a petty sessions area in order for the clerk to conduct a hearing under section 50 of the Crime and Disorder Act 1998 (early administrative hearings).

Bail (Amendment) Act 1993

1 Prosecution right of appeal

(1) Where a magistrates' court grants bail to a person who is charged with or convicted of—

    (a) an offence punishable by a term of imprisonment of 5 years or more, or

    (b) an offence under section 12 (taking a conveyance without authority) or 12A (aggravated vehicle taking) of the Theft Act 1968,

the prosecution may appeal to a judge of the Crown Court against the granting of bail.

(2) Subsection (1) above applies only where the prosecution is conducted—

    (a) by or on behalf of the Director of Public Prosecutions; or

    (b) by a person who falls within such class or description of person as may be prescribed for the purposes of this section by order made by the Secretary of State.

(3) Such an appeal may be made only if—

    (a) the prosecution made representations that bail should not be granted; and

    (b) the representations were made before it was granted.

(4) In the event of the prosecution wishing to exercise the right of appeal set out in subsection (1) above, oral notice of appeal shall be given to the magistrates' court at the conclusion of the proceedings in which such bail has been granted and before the release from custody of the person concerned.

(5) Written notice of appeal shall thereafter be served on the magistrates' court and the person concerned within two hours of the conclusion of such proceedings.

(6) Upon receipt from the prosecution of oral notice of appeal from its decision to grant bail the magistrates' court shall remand in custody the person concerned, until the appeal is determined or otherwise disposed of.

(7) Where the prosecution fails, within the period of two hours mentioned in subsection (5) above, to serve one or both of the notices required by that subsection, the appeal shall be deemed to have been disposed of.

(8) The hearing of an appeal under subsection (1) above against a decision of the magistrates' court to grant bail shall be commenced within forty-eight hours, excluding weekends and any public holiday (that is to say, Christmas Day, Good Friday or a bank holiday), from the date on which oral notice of appeal is given.

(9) At the hearing of any appeal by the prosecution under this section, such appeal shall be by way of re-hearing, and the judge hearing any such appeal may remand the person concerned in custody or may grant bail subject to such conditions (if any) as he thinks fit.

(10) In relation to a child or young person (within the meaning of the Children and Young Persons Act 1969)—

    (a) the reference in subsection (1) above to an offence punishable by a term of imprisonment is to be read as a reference to an offence which would be so punishable in the case of an adult; and

    (b) the reference in subsection (6) above to remand in custody is to be read subject to the provisions of section 23 of the Act of 1969 (remands to local authority accommodation).

(11) The power to make an order under subsection (2) above shall be exercisable by statutory instrument and any instrument shall be subject to annulment in pursuance of a resolution of either House of Parliament.

2 Citation, commencement and extent

(1) This Act may be cited as the Bail (Amendment) Act 1993.

(2) This Act (except this section) shall come into force on such day as the Secretary of State may by order made by statutory instrument appoint.

(3) This Act extends to England and Wales only.

The Children and Young Persons Act 1969 (as amended)

23 Remands and committals to local authority accommodation

(1) Where—

    (a) a court remands a child or young person charged with or convicted of one or more offences or commits him for trial or sentence; and

    (b) he is not released on bail,

the remand or committal shall be to local authority accommodation; and in the following provisions of this section, any reference (however expressed) to a remand shall be construed as including a reference to a committal.

(2) A court remanding a person to local authority accommodation shall designate the local authority who are to receive him; and that authority shall be—

(a) in the case of a person who is being looked after by a local authority, that authority; and

(b) in any other case, the local authority in whose area it appears to the court that he resides or the offence or one of the offences was committed.

(3) Where a person is remanded to local authority accommodation, it shall be lawful for any person acting on behalf of the designated authority to detain him.

(4) Subject to subsections (5) and (5A) below, a court remanding a person to local authority accommodation may, after consultation with the designated authority, require that authority to comply with a security requirement, that is to say, a requirement that the person in question be placed and kept in secure accommodation.

(5) A court shall not impose a security requirement except in respect of a child who has attained the age of twelve, or a young person, who (in either case) is of a prescribed description, and then only if—

(a) he is charged with or has been convicted of a violent or sexual offence, or an offence punishable in the case of an adult with imprisonment for a term of fourteen years or more; or

(b) he has a recent history of absconding while remanded to local authority accommodation, and is charged with or has been convicted of an imprisonable offence alleged or found to have been committed while he was so remanded,

and (in either case) the court is of opinion that only such a requirement would be adequate to protect the public from serious harm from him.

(5A) A court shall not impose a security requirement in respect of a child or young person who is not legally represented in the court unless—

(a) he was granted a right to representation funded by the Legal Services Commission as part of the Criminal Defence Service but the right was withdrawn because of his conduct; or

(b) having been informed of his right to apply for such representation and had the opportunity to do so, he refused or failed to apply.

(6) Where a court imposes a security requirement in respect of a person, it shall be its duty—

(a) to state in open court that it is of such opinion as is mentioned in subsection (5) above; and

(b) to explain to him in open court and in ordinary language why it is of that opinion; and a magistrates' court shall cause a reason stated by it under paragraph (b) above to be specified in the warrant of commitment and to be entered in the register.

(7) Subject to section 23AA below, a court remanding a person to local authority accommodation without imposing a security requirement may, after consultation with the designated authority, require that person to comply with—

(a) any such conditions as could be imposed under section 3(6) of the Bail Act 1976 (c. 63) if he were then being granted bail; and

(b) any conditions imposed for the purpose of securing the electronic monitoring of his compliance with any other condition imposed under this subsection.

(7A) Where a person is remanded to local authority accommodation and a security requirement is imposed in respect of him—

(a) the designated local authority may, with the consent of the Secretary of State, arrange for the person to be detained, for the whole or any part of the period of the remand or committal, in a secure training centre; and

(b) his detention there pursuant to the arrangements shall be lawful.

(7B) Arrangements under subsection (7A) above may include provision for payments to be made by the authority to the Secretary of State.

(8) Where a court imposes on a person any such conditions as are mentioned in subsection (7) above, it shall be its duty to explain to him in open court and in ordinary language why it is imposing those conditions; and a magistrates' court shall cause a reason stated by it under this subsection to be specified in the warrant of commitment and to be entered in the register.

(9) A court remanding a person to local authority accommodation without imposing a security requirement may, after consultation with the designated authority, impose on that authority requirements—

(a) for securing compliance with any conditions imposed on that person under subsection (7) above; or

(b) stipulating that he shall not be placed with a named person.

(10) Where a person is remanded to local authority accommodation, a relevant court—

(a) may, on the application of the designated authority, impose on that person any such conditions as could be imposed under subsection (7) above if the court were then remanding him to such accommodation; and

(b) where it does so, may impose on that authority any requirements for securing compliance with the conditions so imposed.

(11) Where a person is remanded to local authority accommodation, a relevant court may, on the application of the designated authority or that person, vary or revoke any conditions or requirements imposed under subsection (7), (9) or (10) above.

(12) In this section—

"court" and "magistrates' court" include a justice;

"imprisonable offence" means an offence punishable in the case of an adult with imprisonment;

"prescribed description" means a description prescribed by reference to age or sex or both by an order of the Secretary of State;

"relevant court", in relation to a person remanded to local authority accommodation, means the court by which he was so remanded, or any magistrates' court having jurisdiction in the place where he is for the time being;

"secure accommodation" means accommodation which is provided in a community home for the purpose of restricting liberty, and is approved for that purpose by the Secretary of State;

"sexual offence' and "violent offence' have the same meanings as in the Powers of Criminal Courts (Sentencing) Act 2000;

"young person" means a person who has attained the age of fourteen years and is under the age of seventeen years.

(13) In this section—

(a) any reference to a person who is being looked after by a local authority shall be construed in accordance with section 22 of the Children Act 1989;

(b) any reference to consultation shall be construed as a reference to such consultation (if any) as is reasonably practicable in all the circumstances of the case; and

(c) any reference, in relation to a person charged with or convicted of a violent or sexual offence, to protecting the public from serious harm from him shall be construed as a reference to protecting members of the public from death or serious personal injury, whether physical or psychological, occasioned by further such offences committed by him.

(14) This section has effect subject to—

(b) section 128(7) of that Act (remands to the custody of a constable for periods of not more than three days), but section 128(7) shall have effect in relation to a child or young person as if for the reference to three clear days there were substituted a reference to twenty-four hours.

Mode of trial

European Convention on Human Rights

Article 6   Right to a fair trail

1. In the determination of his civil rights and obligations or of any criminal charge against him, everyone is entitled to a fair and public hearing within a reasonable time by an independent and impartial tribunal established by law. Judgment shall be pronounced publicly but the press and public may be excluded from all or part of the trial in the interests of morals, public order or national security in a democratic society, where the interests of juveniles or the protection of the private life of the parties so require, or to the extent strictly necessary in the opinion of the court in special circumstances where publicity would prejudice the interests of justice.

2. Everyone charged with a criminal offence shall be presumed innocent until proved guilty according to law.

3. Everyone charged with a criminal offence has the following minimum rights:

(a) to be informed promptly, in a language which he understands and in detail, of the nature and cause of the accusation against him;

(b) to have adequate time and facilities for the preparation of his defence;

(c) to defend himself in person or through legal assistance of his own choosing or, if he has not sufficient means to pay for legal assistance, to be given it free when the interests of justice so require;

(d) to examine or have examined witnesses against him and to obtain the attendance and examination of witnesses on his behalf under the same conditions as witnesses against him;

(e) to have the free assistance of an interpreter if he cannot understand or speak the language used in court.

Criminal Law Act 1977

PART III

CRIMINAL PROCEDURE, PENALTIES, ETC.

15   Allocation of offences to classes as regards mode of trial: offences which are to become triable only summarily

(1) The following offences shall be triable only summarily (instead of either way), namely—

(a) the offences mentioned (and broadly described) in column 1 of Schedule 1 to this Act; and

(4) The following offences under the Night Poaching Act 1828 shall be triable only summarily (instead of only on indictment), namely—

(a) offences under section 2 of that Act (assaults by persons committing offences under the Act);

(b) offences under section 9 of that Act (entering land, with others, armed and for the purpose of taking or destroying game or rabbits).

(5) Subsections (1) and (4) above are without prejudice to any other enactment by virtue of which any offence is triable only summarily.

Magistrates' Courts Act 1980 (as amended)

17   Certain offences triable either way

(1) The offences listed in Schedule 1 to this Act shall be triable either way.

(2) Subsection (1) above is without prejudice to any other enactment by virtue of which any offence is triable either way.

17A   Initial procedure: accused to indicate intention as to plea

(1) This section shall have effect where a person who has attained the age of 18 years appears or is brought before a magistrates' court on an information charging him with an offence triable either way.

(2) Everything that the court is required to do under the following provisions of this section must be done with the accused present in court.

(3) The court shall cause the charge to be written down, if this has not already been done, and to be read to the accused.

(4) The court shall then explain to the accused in ordinary language that he may indicate whether (if the offence were to proceed to trial) he would plead guilty or not guilty, and that if he indicates that he would plead guilty—

(a) the court must proceed as mentioned in subsection (6) below; and

(b) he may be committed for sentence to the Crown Court under [section 3 of the Powers of Criminal Courts (Sentencing) Act 2000] below if the court is of such opinion as is mentioned in subsection (2) of that section.

(5) The court shall then ask the accused whether (if the offence were to proceed to trial) he would plead guilty or not guilty.

(6) If the accused indicates that he would plead guilty the court shall proceed as if—

(a) the proceedings constituted from the beginning the summary trial of the information; and

(b) section 9(1) above was complied with and he pleaded guilty under it.

(7) If the accused indicates that he would plead not guilty section 18(1) below shall apply.

(8) If the accused in fact fails to indicate how he would plead, for the purposes of this section and section 18(1) below he shall be taken to indicate that he would plead not guilty.

(9) Subject to subsection (6) above, the following shall not for any purpose be taken to constitute the taking of a plea—

(a) asking the accused under this section whether (if the offence were to proceed to trial) he would plead guilty or not guilty;

(b) an indication by the accused under this section of how he would plead.

17B   Intention as to plea: absence of accused

(1) This section shall have effect where—

(a) a person who has attained the age of 18 years appears or is brought before a magistrates' court on an information charging him with an offence triable either way.

(b) the accused is represented by a legal representative,

(c) the court considers that by reason of the accused's disorderly conduct before the court it is not practicable for proceedings under section 17A above to be conducted in his presence, and

(d) the court considers that it should proceed in the absence of the accused.

(2) In such a case—

(a) the court shall cause the charge to be written down, if this has not already been done, and to be read to the representative;

(b) the court shall ask the representative whether (if the offence were to proceed to trial) the accused would plead guilty or not guilty;

(c) if the representative indicates that the accused would plead guilty the court shall proceed as if the proceedings constituted from the beginning the summary trial of the information, and as if section 9(1) above was complied with and the accused pleaded guilty under it;

(d) if the representative indicates that the accused would plead not guilty section 18(1) below shall apply.

(3) If the representative in fact fails to indicate how the accused would plead, for the purposes of this section and section 18(1) below he shall be taken to indicate that the accused would plead not guilty.

(4) Subject to subsection (2)(c) above, the following shall not for any purpose be taken to constitute the taking of a plea—

(a) asking the representative under this section whether (if the offence were to proceed to trial) the accused would plead guilty or not guilty;

(b) an indication by the representative under this section of how the accused would plead.

17C   Intention as to plea adjournment

A magistrates' court proceeding under section 17A or 17B above may adjourn the proceedings at any time, and on doing so on any occasion when the accused is present may remand the accused, and shall remand him if—

(a) on the occasion on which he first appeared, or was brought, before the court to answer to the information he was in custody or, having been released on bail, surrendered to the custody of the court; or

(b) he has been remanded at any time in the course of proceedings on the information;

and where the court remands the accused, the time fixed for the resumption of proceedings shall be that at which he is required to appear or be brought before the court in pursuance of the remand or would be required to be brought before the court but for section 128(3A) below.

18   Initial procedure on information against adult for offence triable either way

(1) Sections 19 to 23 below shall have effect where a person who has attained the age of 18 years appears or is brought before a magistrates' court on an information charging him with an offence triable either way and—

(a) he indicates under section 17A above that (if the offence were to proceed to trial) he would plead not guilty, or

(b) his representative indicates under section 17B above that (if the offence were to proceed to trial) he would plead not guilty.

(2) Without prejudice to section 11(1) above, everything that the court is required to do under sections 19 to 22 below must be done before any evidence is called and, subject to subsection (3) below and section 23 below, with the accused present in court.

(3) The court may proceed in the absence of the accused in accordance with such of the provisions of sections 19 to 22 below as are applicable in the circumstances if the court considers that by reason of his disorderly conduct before the court it is not practicable for the proceedings to be conducted in his presence; and subsections (3) to (5) of section 23 below, so far as applicable, shall have effect in relation to proceedings conducted in the absence of the accused by virtue of this subsection (references in those subsections to the person representing the accused being for this purpose read as references to the person, if any, representing him).

(4) A magistrates' court proceeding under sections 19 to 23 below may adjourn the proceedings at any time, and on doing so on any occasion when the accused is present may remand the accused, and shall remand him if—

(a) on the occasion on which he first appeared, or was brought, before the court to answer to the information he was in custody or, having been released on bail, surrendered to the custody of the court; or

(b) he has been remanded at any time in the course of proceedings on the information; and where the court remands the accused, the time fixed for the resumption of the proceedings shall be that at which he is required to appear or be brought before the court in pursuance of the remand or would be required to be brought before the court but for section 128(3A) below.

(5) The functions of a magistrates' court under sections 19 to 23 below may be discharged by a single justice, but the foregoing provision shall not be taken to authorise the summary trial of an information by a magistrates' court composed of less than two justices.

19 Court to begin by considering which mode of trial appears more suitable

(1) The court shall consider whether, having regard to the matters mentioned in subsection (3) below and any representations made by the prosecutor or the accused, the offence appears to the court more suitable for summary trial or for trial on indictment.

(2) Before so considering, the court—

[ ]

(b) shall afford first the prosecutor and then the accused an opportunity to make representations as to which mode of trial would be more suitable.

(3) The matters to which the court is to have regard under subsection (1) above are the nature of the case; whether the circumstances make the offence one of serious character; whether the punishment which a magistrates' court would have power to inflict for it would be adequate; and any other circumstances which appear to the court to make it more suitable for the offence to be tried in one way rather than the other.

(4) If the prosecution is being carried on by the Attorney General, the Solicitor General or the Director of Public Prosecutions and he applies for the offence to be tried on indictment, the preceding provisions of this section and sections 20 and 21 below shall not apply, and the court shall proceed to inquire into the information as examining justices.

(5) The power of the Director of Public Prosecutions under subsection (4) above to apply for an offence to be tried on indictment shall not be exercised except with the consent of the Attorney General.

20 Procedure where summary trial appears more suitable

(1) If, where the court has considered as required by section 19(1) above, it appears to the court that the offence is more suitable for summary trial, the following provisions of this section shall apply (unless excluded by section 23 below).

(2) The court shall explain to the accused in ordinary language—

    (a) that it appears to the court more suitable for him to be tried summarily for the offence, and that he can either consent to be so tried or, if he wishes, be tried by a jury; and

    (b) that if he is tried summarily and is convicted by the court, he may be committed for sentence to the Crown Court under [section 3 of the Powers of Criminal Courts (Sentencing) Act 2000] if the convicting court, is of such opinion as is mentioned in subsection (2) of that section.

(3) After explaining to the accused as provided by subsection (2) above the court shall ask him whether he consents to be tried summarily or wishes to be tried by a jury, and—

    (a) if he consents to be tried summarily, shall proceed to the summary trial of the information;

    (b) if he does not so consent, shall proceed to inquire into the information as examining justices.

21   Procedure where trial on indictment appears more suitable

If, where the court has considered as required by section 19(1) above, it appears to the court that the offence is more suitable for trial on indictment, the court shall tell the accused that the court has decided that it is more suitable for him to be tried for the offence by a jury, and shall proceed to inquire into the information as examining justices.

22   Certain offences triable either way to be tried summarily if value involved is small

(1) If the offence charged by the information is one of those mentioned in the first column of Schedule 2 to this Act (in this section referred to as "scheduled offences") then, the court shall, before proceeding in accordance with section 19 above, consider whether, having regard to any representations made by the prosecutor or the accused, the value involved (as defined in subsection (10) below) appears to the court to exceed the relevant sum.

For the purposes of this section the relevant sum is £5,000.

(2) If, where subsection (1) above applies, it appears to the court clear that, for the offence charged, the value involved does not exceed the relevant sum, the court shall proceed as if the offence were triable only summarily, and sections 19 to 21 above shall not apply.

(3) If, where subsection (1) above applies, it appears to the court clear that, for the offence charged, the value involved exceeds the relevant sum, the court shall thereupon proceed in accordance with section 19 above in the ordinary way without further regard to the provisions of this section.

(4) If, where subsection (1) above applies, it appears to the court for any reason not clear whether, for the offence charged, the value involved does or does not exceed the relevant sum, the provisions of subsections (5) and (6) below shall apply.

(5) The court shall cause the charge to be written down, if this has not already been done, and read to the accused, and shall explain to him in ordinary language—

    (a) that he can, if he wishes, consent to be tried summarily for the offence and that if he consents to be so tried, he will definitely be tried in that way; and

    (b) that if he is tried summarily and is convicted by the court, his liability to imprisonment or a fine will be limited as provided in section 33 below.

(6) After explaining to the accused as provided by subsection (5) above the court shall ask him whether he consents to be tried summarily and—

    (a) if he so consents, shall proceed in accordance with subsection (2) above as if that subsection applied;

    (b) if he does not so consent, shall proceed in accordance with subsection (3) above as if that subsection applied.

(8) Where a person is convicted by a magistrates' court of a scheduled offence, it shall not be open to him to appeal to the Crown Court against the conviction on the ground that the convicting court's decision as to the value involved was mistaken.

(9) If, where subsection (1) above applies, the offence charged is one with which the accused is charged jointly with a person who has not attained the age of 18 years, the reference in that subsection to any representations made by the accused shall be read as including any representations made by the person under 18.

(10) In this section "the value involved", in relation to any scheduled offence, means the value indicated in the second column of Schedule 2 to this Act, measured as indicated in the third column of that Schedule; and in that Schedule "the material time" means the time of the alleged offence.

(11) Where—
  (a) the accused is charged on the same occasion with two or more scheduled offences and it appears to the court that they constitute or form part of a series of two or more offences of the same or a similar character; or
  (b) the offence charged consists in incitement to commit two or more scheduled offences,
this section shall have effect as if any reference in it to the value involved were a reference to the aggregate of the values involved.

(12) Subsection (8) of section 12A of the Theft Act 1968 (which determines when a vehicle is recovered) shall apply for the purposes of paragraph 3 of Schedule 2 to this Act as it applies for the purposes of that section.

23 Power of court, with consent of legally represented accused, to proceed in his absence

(1) Where—
  (a) the accused is represented by a legal representative who in his absence signifies to the court the accused's consent to the proceedings for determining how he is to be tried for the offence being conducted in his absence; and
  (b) the court is satisfied that there is good reason for proceeding in the absence of the accused,
the following provisions of this section shall apply.

(2) Subject to the following provisions of this section, the court may proceed in the absence of the accused in accordance with such of the provisions of sections 19 to 22 above as are applicable in the circumstances.

(3) If, in a case where subsection (1) of section 22 above applies, it appears to the court as mentioned in subsection (4) of that section, subsections (5) and (6) of that section shall not apply and the court—
  (a) if the accused's consent to be tried summarily has been or is signified by the person representing him, shall proceed in accordance with subsection (2) of that section as if that subsection applied; or
  (b) if that consent has not been and is not so signified, shall proceed in accordance with subsection (3) of that section as if that subsection applied.

(4) If, where the court has considered as required by section 19(1) above, it appears to the court that the offence is more suitable for summary trial then—
  (a) if the accused's consent to be tried summarily has been or is signified by the person representing him, section 20 above shall not apply, and the court shall proceed to the summary trial of the information; or
  (b) if that consent has not been and is not so signified, section 20 above shall not apply and the court shall proceed to inquire into the information as examining justices and may adjourn the hearing without remanding the accused.

(5) If, where the court has considered as required by section 19(1) above, it appears to the court that the offence is more suitable for trial on indictment, section 21 above shall not apply, and the court shall proceed to inquire into the information as examining justices and may adjourn the hearing without remanding the accused.

25 Power to change from summary trial to committal proceedings, and vice versa

(1) Subsections (2) to (4) below shall have effect where a person who has attained the age of 18 years appears or is brought before a magistrates' court on an information charging him with an offence triable either way.

(2) Where the court has (otherwise than in pursuance of section 22(2) above) begun to try the information summarily, the court may, at any time before the conclusion of the evidence for the prosecution, discontinue the summary trial and proceed to inquire into the information as examining justices and, on doing so, shall adjourn the hearing.

(3) Where the court has begun to inquire into the information as examining justices, then, if at any time during the inquiry it appears to the court, having regard to any representations made in the presence of the accused by the prosecutor, or made by the accused, and to the nature of the case, that the offence is after all more suitable for summary trial, the court may, after doing as provided in subsection (4) below, ask the accused whether he consents to be tried summarily and, if he so consents, may subject to subsection (3A) below proceed to try the information summarily;

(3A) Where the prosecution is being carried on by the Attorney General or the Solicitor General, the court shall not exercise the power conferred by subsection (3) above without his consent and, where the prosecution is being carried on by the Director of Public Prosecutions, shall not exercise that power if the Attorney General directs that it should not be exercised.

(4) Before asking the accused under subsection (3) above whether he consents to be tried summarily, the court shall in ordinary language—

(a) explain to him that it appears to the court more suitable for him to be tried summarily for the offence, but that this can only be done if he consents to be so tried; and

(b) unless it has already done so, explain to him, as provided in section 20(2)(b) above, about the court's power to commit to the Crown Court for sentence.

(5) Where a person under the age of 18 years appears or is brought before a magistrates' court on an information charging him with an indictable offence other than homicide, and the court—

(a) has begun to try the information summarily on the footing that the case does not fall within paragraph (a) or (b) of section 24(1) above and must therefore be tried summarily, as required by the said section 24(1); or

(b) has begun to inquire into the case as examining justices on the footing that the case does so fall, subsection (6) or (7) below, as the case may be, shall have effect.

(6) If, in a case falling within subsection (5)(a) above, it appears to the court at any time before the conclusion of the evidence for the prosecution that the case is after all one which under the said section 24(1) ought not to be tried summarily, the court may discontinue the summary trial and proceed to inquire into the information as examining justices and, on doing so, shall adjourn the hearing.

(7) If, in a case falling within subsection (5)(b) above, it appears to the court at any time during the inquiry that the case is after all one which under the said section 24(1) ought to be tried summarily, the court may proceed to try the information summarily.

(8) If the court adjourns the hearing under subsection (2) or (6) above it may (if it thinks fit) do so without remanding the accused.

26   Power to issue summons to accused in certain circumstances

(1) Where—

  (a) in the circumstances mentioned in section 23(1)(a) above the court is not satisfied that there is good reason for proceeding in the absence of the accused; or

  (b) subsection (4)(b) or (5) of section 23 or subsection (2) or (6) of section 25 above applies, and the court adjourns the hearing in pursuance of that subsection without remanding the accused, the justice or any of the justices of which the court is composed may issue a summons directed to the accused requiring his presence before the court.

(2) If the accused is not present at the time and place appointed—

  (a) in a case within subsection (1)(a) above, for the proceedings under section 19(1) or 22(1) above, as the case may be; or

  (b) in a case within subsection (1)(b) above, for the resumption of the hearing, the court may issue a warrant for his arrest.

SCHEDULE 1

(5) Offences under the following provisions of the Offences against the Person Act 1861—

  (a) section 16 (threats to kill);

  (b) section 20 (inflicting bodily injury, with or without a weapon);

  (c) section 26 (not providing apprentices or servants with food etc.);

  (d) section 27 (abandoning or exposing child);

  (e) section 34 (doing or omitting to do anything so as to endanger railway passengers);

  (f) section 36 (assaulting a clergyman at a place of worship etc);

  (g) section 38 (assault with intent to resist apprehension);

  (h) section 47 (assault occasioning bodily harm [. . .]);

  (i) section 57 (bigamy);

  (j) section 60 (concealing the birth of a child).

(6) Offences under section 20 of the Telegraph Act 1868 (disclosing or intercepting messages).

(19) Offences under section 36 of the Criminal Justice Act 1925 (forgery of passports etc.).

(23) Offences under the following provisions of the Sexual Offences Act 1956—

  (a) section 6 (unlawful sexual intercourse with a girl under 16);

  (b) section 13 (indecency between men);

  (c) section 26 (permitting a girl under 16 to use premises for sexual intercourse).

(26) The following offences under the Criminal Law Act 1967—

  (a) offences under section 4(1) (assisting offenders); and

  (b) offences under section 5(1) (concealing arrestable offences and giving false information),

where the offence to which they relate is triable either way.

(27) Offences under section 4(1) of the Sexual Offences Act 1967 (procuring others to commit homosexual acts).

(28) All indictable offences under the Theft Act 1968 except:—

  (a) robbery, aggravated burglary, blackmail and assault with intent to rob;

  (b) burglary comprising the commission of, or an intention to commit, an offence which is triable only on indictment;

  (c) burglary in a dwelling if any person in the dwelling was subjected to violence or the threat of violence.

(29) Offences under the following provisions of the Criminal Damage Act 1971—

  (a) section 1(1) (destroying or damaging property);

(b) section 1(1) and (3) (arson);

(c) section 2 (threats to destroy or damage property);

(d) section 3 (possessing anything with intent to destroy or damage property).

(32) Committing an indecent assault upon a person whether male or female

(33) Aiding, abetting, counselling or procuring the commission of any offence listed in the preceding paragraphs of this Schedule except paragraph 26.

(35) Any offence consisting in the incitement to commit an offence triable either way except an offence mentioned in paragraph 33 above.

Trial by jury

Juries Act 1974

1   Qualification for jury service

Subject to the provisions of this Act, every person shall be qualified to serve as a juror in the Crown Court, the High Court and county courts and be liable accordingly to attend for jury service when summoned under this Act, if—

(a) he is for the time being registered as a parliamentary or local government elector and is not less than eighteen nor more than seventy years of age; and

(b) he has been ordinarily resident in the United Kingdom, the Channel Islands or the Isle of Man for any period of at least five years since attaining the age of thirteen,

but not if he is for the time being ineligible or disqualified for jury service; and the persons who are ineligible, and those who are disqualified, are those respectively listed in Parts I and II of Schedule 1 to this Act.

3   Electoral register as basis of jury selection

(1) Every electoral registration officer under the Representation of the People Act 1983 shall as soon as practicable after the publication of any register of electors for his area deliver to such officer as the Lord Chancellor may designate such number of copies of the register as the designated officer may require for the purpose of summoning jurors, and on each copy there shall be indicated those persons on the register whom the registration officer has ascertained to be, or to have been on a date also indicated on the copy, less than eighteen or more than seventy years of age.

(2) The reference in subsection (1) above to a register of electors does not include a ward list within the meaning of section 4(1) of the City of London (Various Powers) Act 1957.

8   Excusal for previous jury service

(1) If a person summoned under this Act shows to the satisfaction of the appropriate officer, or of the court (or any of the courts) to which he is summoned—

(a) that he has served on a jury, or duly attended to serve on a jury, in the prescribed period ending with the service of the summons on him, or

(b) that the Crown Court or any other court has excused him from jury service for a period which has not terminated,

the officer or court shall excuse him from attending, or further attending, in pursuance of the summons.

(2) In subsection (1) above "the prescribed period" means two years or such longer period as the Lord Chancellor may prescribe by order made by statutory instrument subject to

annulment in pursuance of a resolution of either House of Parliament, and any such order may be varied or revoked by a subsequent order under this subsection.

(3) Records of persons summoned under this Act, and of persons included in panels, shall be kept in such manner as the Lord Chancellor may direct, and the Lord Chancellor may, if he thinks fit, make arrangements for allowing inspection of the records so kept by members of the public in such circumstances and subject to such conditions as he may prescribe.

(4) A person duly attending in compliance with a summons under this Act shall be entitled on application to the appropriate officer to a certificate recording that he has so attended.

(5) In subsection (1) above the words "served on a jury" refer to service on a jury in any court, including any court of assize or other court abolished by the Courts Act 1971, but excluding service on a jury in a coroner's court.

9 Excusal for certain persons and discretionary excusal

(1) A person summoned under this Act shall be entitled, if he so wishes, to be excused from jury service if he is among the persons listed in Part III of Schedule 1 to this Act but, except as provided by that Part of that Schedule in the case of members of the forces, a person shall not by this section be exempt from his obligation to attend if summoned unless he is excused from attending under subsection (2) below.

(2) If any person summoned under this Act shows to the satisfaction of the appropriate officer that there is good reason why he should be excused from attending in pursuance of the summons, the appropriate officer may excuse him from so attending and shall do so if the reason shown is that the person is entitled under subsection (1) above to excusal.

(3) Crown Court rules shall provide a right of appeal to the court (or one of the courts) before which the person is summoned to attend against any refusal of the appropriate officer to excuse him under subsection (2) above.

(4) Without prejudice to the preceding provisions of this section, the court (or any of the courts) before which a person is summoned to attend under this Act may excuse that person from so attending.

17 Majority verdicts

(1) Subject to subsections (3) and (4) below, the verdict of a jury in proceedings in the Crown Court or the High Court need not be unanimous if—

(a) in a case where there are not less than eleven jurors, ten of them agree on the verdict; and

(b) in a case where there are ten jurors, nine of them agree on the verdict.

(2) Subject to subsection (4) below, the verdict of a jury (that is to say a complete jury of eight) in proceedings in a county court need not be unanimous if seven of them agree on the verdict.

(3) The Crown Court shall not accept a verdict of guilty by virtue of subsection (1) above unless the foreman of the jury has stated in open court the number of jurors who respectively agreed to and dissented from the verdict.

(4) No court shall accept a verdict by virtue of subsection (1) or (2) above unless it appears to the court that the jury have had such period of time for deliberation as the court thinks reasonable having regard to the nature and complexity of the case; and the Crown Court shall in any event not accept such a verdict unless it appears to the court that the jury have had at least two hours for deliberation.

(5) This section is without prejudice to any practice in civil proceedings by which a court may accept a majority verdict with the consent of the parties, or by which the parties may agree to proceed in any case with an incomplete jury.

SCHEDULE 1, PART I   PERSONS INELIGIBLE

A   THE JUDICIARY

1.

Holders of high judicial office within the meaning of the Appellate Jurisdiction Act 1876.

Circuit judges and Recorders.

Masters of the Supreme Court.

Registrars and assistant registrars of any court.

[District Judges (Magistrates' Courts)].

Justices of the peace.

The Chairman or President, the Vice-Chairman or Vice-President, and the registrar and assistant registrar of any Tribunal.

A person who has at any time been a person falling within any description specified above in this Group.

B   OTHERS CONCERNED WITH ADMINISTRATION OF JUSTICE

1.

Barristers and solicitors, whether or not in actual practice as such.

Any person who is not a barrister or solicitor but who is an authorised advocate or authorised litigator (as defined by section 119(1) of the Courts and Legal Services Act 1990) and—

      (a) any legal executive or person corresponding to a legal executive; or

      (b) any person corresponding to a barristers' clerk or assistant clerk,

who is employed by such an authorised advocate or authorised litigator.

Solicitors' articled clerks.

Barristers' clerks and their assistants.

Legal executives in the employment of solicitors.

Public notaries

The Director of Public Prosecutions and members of his staff.

Officers employed under the Lord Chancellor and concerned wholly or mainly with the day-to-day administration of the legal system or any part of it.

Officers and staff of any court, if their work is wholly or mainly concerned with the day-to-day administration of the court.

Coroners, deputy coroners and assistant coroners.

Justices' chief executives, justices' clerks and justices' clerks' assistants.

Active Elder Brethren of the Corporation of Trinity House of Deptford Strond.

A shorthandwriter in any court.

A court security officer within the meaning of Part IV of the Criminal Justice Act 1991.

Governors, chaplains, medical officers and other officers of penal establishments; members of boards of visitors for penal establishments.

("Penal establishment" for this purpose means any establishment regulated by the Prison Act 1952.

Prisoner custody officers within the meaning of Part IV of the Criminal Justice Act 1991.

Custody officers within the meaning of Part I of the Criminal Justice and Public Order Act 1994.

The warden or a member of the staff of a, probation hostel or bail hostel [. . .].

The warden or a member of the staff of approved premises (within the meaning of Part I of the Criminal Justice and Court Services Act 2000).

Probation officers and persons appointed to assist them.

Members of the Parole Board; members of local review committees established under the Criminal Justice Act 1967.

The chief officer and members of the staff of a local probation board established under section 4 of the Criminal Justice and Court Services Act 2000.

Any person who performs the functions of a chief officer of a local probation board in accordance with a management order made under section 10 of the Criminal Justice and Court Services Act 2000.

Any person who performs the functions of an officer of a local probation board under section 5(2) of the Criminal Justice and Court Services Act 2000.

Members and employees of the Criminal Cases Review Commission.

A member of any police force(including a person on relevant service within paragraph (b), (c) or (d) of section 97(1) of the Police Act 1996); special constables; a member of any constabulary maintained under statute; a person employed in any capacity by virtue of which he has the powers and privileges of a constable.

A member of a police authority within the meaning of the Police Act 1996; a member of any body (corporate or other) with responsibility for appointing members of a constabulary maintained under statute.

Inspectors of Constabulary appointed by Her Majesty: assistant inspectors of constabulary appointed by the Secretary of State.

Civilians employed for police purposes under section 15 of the Police Act 1996 members of the metropolitan civil staffs within the meaning of section 15 of the Superannuation (Miscellaneous Provisions) Act 1967 (persons employed under the Commissioner of Police of the Metropolis, Inner London justices' clerks, etc.).

A member of the National Criminal Intelligence Service or the National Crime Squad.

A member of the Service Authority for the National Criminal Intelligence Service; a member of the Service Authority for the National Crime Squad; a person employed by the Service Authority for the National Criminal Intelligence Service under section 13 of the Police Act 1997 or by the Service Authority for the National Crime Squad under section 58 of that Act.

A person in charge of, or employed in, any forensic science laboratory.

A person who at any time within the last ten years has been a person falling within any description specified above in this Group.

C   THE CLERGY, ETC

1.

A man in holy orders.

A regular minister of any religious denomination.

A vowed member of any religious order living in a monastery, convent or other religious community.

D   MENTALLY DISORDERED PERSONS

1.

A person who suffers or has suffered from mental illness, psychopathic disorder, mental handicap or severe mental handicap and on account of that condition either—

     (a) is resident in a hospital or other similar institution; or

     (b) regularly attends for treatment by a medical practitioner.

A person for the time being in guardianship under [section 7 of the Mental Health Act 1983].

A person who, under [Part VII of that Act], has been determined by a judge to be incapable, by reason of mental disorder, of managing and administering his property and affairs.

(In this Group—

     (a) "mental handicap" means a state of arrested or incomplete development of mind (not amounting to severe mental handicap) which includes significant impairment of intelligence and social functioning;

(b) "severe mental handicap" means a state of arrested or incomplete development of mind which includes severe impairment of intelligence and social functioning;

(c) other expressions are to be construed in accordance with [the said Act of 1983])

PART II   PERSONS DISQUALIFIED

1.

A person who has at any time been sentenced in the United Kingdom, the Channel Islands or the Isle of Man—

(a) to imprisonment for life , custody for life or to a term of imprisonment or youth custody of five years or more: or

(b) to be detained during Her Majesty's pleasure, during the pleasure of the Secretary of State or during the pleasure of the Governor of Northern Ireland.

A person who at any time in the last ten years has, in the United Kingdom or the Channel Islands or the Isle of Man—

(a) served any part of a sentence of imprisonment, youth custody or detention, or

(b) been detained in a Borstal institution; or

(c) had passed on him or (as the case may be) made in respect of him a suspended sentence of imprisonment or order for detention; or

(d) had made in respect of him a community service order.

A person who at any time in the last five years has, in the United Kingdom or the Channel Islands or the Isle of Man, [had made in respect of him a probation order].

PART III   PERSONS EXCUSABLE AS OF RIGHT
GENERAL

1.

Persons more than sixty-five years of age.

PARLIAMENT

1.

Peers and peeresses entitled to receive writs of summons to attend the House of Lords.
Members of the House of Commons.
Officers of the House of Lords.
Officers of the House of Commons.

SCOTTISH PARLIAMENT AND SCOTTISH EXECUTIVE

1.

Members of the Scottish Parliament.
Members of the Scottish Executive.
Junior Scottish Ministers.

EUROPEAN ASSEMBLY

1.

Representatives to the [European Parliament].

NATIONAL ASSEMBLY FOR WALES

1.

Members of the National Assembly for Wales.
The Auditor General for Wales.
Public Officials The Auditor General for Scotland.

THE FORCES

1.

Full-time serving members of—
any of Her Majesty's naval, military or air forces,
[. . .]
(A person excusable under this head shall be under no obligation to attend in pursuance
of a summons for jury service if his commanding officer certifies to the officer issuing the
summons that it would be prejudicial to the efficiency of the service if the person were
required to be absent from duty.)

MEDICAL AND OTHER SIMILAR PROFESSIONS

1.

The following, if actually practising their profession and registered (including provisionally
or temporarily registered), enrolled or certified under the enactments relating to that
profession—
    medical practitioners,
    dentists,
    nurses,
    midwives,
    veterinary surgeons and veterinary practitioners,
    pharmaceutical chemists.

EXCUSAL ON RELIGIOUS GROUNDS

1.

A practising member of a religious society or order the tenets or beliefs of which are
incompatible with jury service.

Contempt of Court Act 1981

8 Confidentiality of jury's deliberations

(1) Subject to subsection (2) below, it is a contempt of court to obtain, disclose or solicit
any particulars of statements made, opinions expressed, arguments advanced or votes cast by
members of a jury in the course of their deliberations in any legal proceedings.

(2) This section does not apply to any disclosure of any particulars—

(a) in the proceedings in question for the purpose of enabling the jury to arrive at
their verdict, or in connection with the delivery of that verdict, or

(b) in evidence in any subsequent proceedings for an offence alleged to have been
committed in relation to the jury in the first mentioned proceedings,

or to the publication of any particulars so disclosed.

(3) Proceedings for a contempt of court under this section (other than Scottish proceedings) shall not be instituted except by or with the consent of the Attorney General or on the motion of a court having jurisdiction to deal with it.

(c) ISSUES DURING TRIAL, EVIDENCE AND PROCEDURE

Disclosure

Criminal Procedure and Investigations Act 1996

1 Application of this Part

(1) This Part applies where—

> (a) a person is charged with a summary offence in respect of which a court proceeds to summary trial and in respect of which he pleads not guilty,
>
> (b) a person who has attained the age of 18 is charged with an offence which is triable either way, in respect of which a court proceeds to summary trial and in respect of which he pleads not guilty, or
>
> (c) a person under the age of 18 is charged with an indictable offence in respect of which a court proceeds to summary trial and in respect of which he pleads not guilty.

(2) This Part also applies where—

> (a) a person is charged with an indictable offence and he is committed for trial for the offence concerned,
>
> (b) a person is charged with an indictable offence and proceedings for the trial of the person on the charge concerned are transferred to the Crown Court by virtue of a notice of transfer given under section 4 of the Criminal Justice Act 1987 (serious or complex fraud),
>
> (c) a person is charged with an indictable offence and proceedings for the trial of the person on the charge concerned are transferred to the Crown Court by virtue of a notice of transfer served on a magistrates' court under section 53 of the Criminal Justice Act 1991 (certain cases involving children),
>
> (cc) a person is charged with an offence for which he is sent for trial under section 51 (no committal proceedings for indictable-only offences) of the Crime and Disorder Act 1998,
> or
>
> (d) a count charging a person with a summary offence is included in an indictment under the authority of section 40 of the Criminal Justice Act 1988 (common assault etc.), or
>
> (e) a bill of indictment charging a person with an indictable offence is preferred under the authority of section 2(2)(b) of the Administration of Justice (Miscellaneous Provisions) Act 1933 (bill preferred by direction of Court of Appeal, or by direction or with consent of a judge), or
>
> (f) a bill of indictment charging a person with an indictable offence is preferred under section 22B(3)(a) of the Prosecution of Offences Act 1985.

(3) This Part applies in relation to alleged offences into which no criminal investigation has begun before the appointed day.

(4) For the purposes of this section a criminal investigation is an investigation which police officers or other persons have a duty to conduct with a view to it being ascertained—

    (a) whether a person should be charged with an offence, or

    (b) whether a person charged with an offence is guilty of it.

(5) The reference in subsection (3) to the appointed day is to such day as is appointed for the purposes of this Part by the Secretary of State by order.

3 Primary disclosure by prosecutor

(1) The prosecutor must—

    (a) disclose to the accused any prosecution material which has not previously been disclosed to the accused and which in the prosecutor's opinion might undermine the case for the prosecution against the accused, or

    (b) give to the accused a written statement that there is no material of a description mentioned in paragraph (a).

(2) For the purposes of this section prosecution material is material—

    (a) which is in the prosecutor's possession, and came into his possession in connection with the case for the prosecution against the accused, or

    (b) which, in pursuance of a code operative under Part II, he has inspected in connection with the case for the prosecution against the accused.

(3) Where material consists of information which has been recorded in any form the prosecutor discloses it for the purposes of this section—

    (a) by securing that a copy is made of it and that the copy is given to the accused, or

    (b) if in the prosecutor's opinion that is not practicable or not desirable, by allowing the accused to inspect it at a reasonable time and a reasonable place or by taking steps to secure that he is allowed to do so;

and a copy may be in such form as the prosecutor thinks fit and need not be in the same form as that in which the information has already been recorded.

(4) Where material consists of information which has not been recorded the prosecutor discloses it for the purposes of this section by securing that it is recorded in such form as he thinks fit and—

    (a) by securing that a copy is made of it and that the copy is given to the accused, or

    (b) if in the prosecutor's opinion that is not practicable or not desirable, by allowing the accused to inspect it at a reasonable time and a reasonable place or by taking steps to secure that he is allowed to do so.

(5) Where material does not consist of information the prosecutor discloses it for the purposes of this section by allowing the accused to inspect it at a reasonable time and a reasonable place or by taking steps to secure that he is allowed to do so.

(6) Material must not be disclosed under this section to the extent that the court, on an application by the prosecutor, concludes it is not in the public interest to disclose it and orders accordingly.

(7) Material must not be disclosed under this section to the extent that it is material the disclosure of which is prohibited by section 17 of the Regulation of Investigatory Powers Act 2000.

(8) The prosecutor must act under this section during the period which, by virtue of section 12, is the relevant period for this section.

4 Primary disclosure: further provisions

(1) This section applies where—

    (a) the prosecutor acts under section 3, and

    (b) before so doing he was given a document in pursuance of provision included, by virtue of section 24(3), in a code operative under Part II.

(2) In such a case the prosecutor must give the document to the accused at the same time as the prosecutor acts under section 3.

5 Compulsory disclosure by accused

(1) Subject to subsections (2) to (4), this section applies where—
  (a) this Part applies by virtue of section 1(2), and
  (b) the prosecutor complies with section 3 or purports to comply with it.

(2) Where this Part applies by virtue of section 1(2)(b), this section does not apply unless—
  (a) a copy of the notice of transfer, and
  (b) copies of the documents containing the evidence,
have been given to the accused under regulations made under section 5(9) of the Criminal Justice Act 1987.

(3) Where this Part applies by virtue of section 1(2)(c), this section does not apply unless—
  (a) a copy of the notice of transfer, and
  (b) copies of the documents containing the evidence,
have been given to the accused under regulations made under paragraph 4 of Schedule 6 to the Criminal Justice Act 1991.

(3A) Where this Part applies by virtue of section 1(2)(cc), this section does not apply unless—
  (a) copies of the documents containing the evidence have been served on the accused under regulations made under paragraph 1 of Schedule 3 to the Crime and Disorder Act 1998; and
  (b) a copy of the notice under subsection (7) of section 51 of that Act has been served on him under that subsection.

(4) Where this Part applies by virtue of section 1(2)(e), this section does not apply unless the prosecutor has served on the accused a copy of the indictment and a copy of the set of documents containing the evidence which is the basis of the charge.

(5) Where this section applies, the accused must give a defence statement to the court and the prosecutor.

(6) For the purposes of this section a defence statement is a written statement—
  (a) setting out in general terms the nature of the accused's defence,
  (b) indicating the matters on which he takes issue with the prosecution, and
  (c) setting out, in the case of each such matter, the reason why he takes issue with the prosecution.

(7) If the defence statement discloses an alibi the accused must give particulars of the alibi in the statement, including—
  (a) the name and address of any witness the accused believes is able to give evidence in support of the alibi, if the name and address are known to the accused when the statement is given;
  (b) any information in the accused's possession which might be of material assistance in finding any such witness, if his name or address is not known to the accused when the statement is given.

(8) For the purposes of this section evidence in support of an alibi is evidence tending to show that by reason of the presence of the accused at a particular place or in a particular area at a particular time he was not, or was unlikely to have been, at the place where the offence is alleged to have been committed at the time of its alleged commission.

(9) The accused must give a defence statement under this section during the period which, by virtue of section 12, is the relevant period for this section.

6 Voluntary disclosure by accused

(1) This section applies where—

   (a) this Part applies by virtue of section 1(1), and

   (b) the prosecutor complies with section 3 or purports to comply with it.

  (2) The accused—

   (a) may give a defence statement to the prosecutor, and

   (b) if he does so, must also give such a statement to the court.

  (3) Subsections (6) to (8) of section 5 apply for the purposes of this section as they apply for the purposes of that.

  (4) If the accused gives a defence statement under this section he must give it during the period which, by virtue of section 12, is the relevant period for this section.

7 Secondary disclosure by prosecutor

  (1) This section applies where the accused gives a defence statement under section 5 or 6.

  (2) The prosecutor must—

   (a) disclose to the accused any prosecution material which has not previously been disclosed to the accused and which might be reasonably expected to assist the accused's defence as disclosed by the defence statement given under section 5 or 6, or

   (b) give to the accused a written statement that there is no material of a description mentioned in paragraph (a).

  (3) For the purposes of this section prosecution material is material—

   (a) which is in the prosecutor's possession and came into his possession in connection with the case for the prosecution against the accused, or

   (b) which, in pursuance of a code operative under Part II, he has inspected in connection with the case for the prosecution against the accused.

  (4) Subsections (3) to (5) of section 3 (method by which prosecutor discloses) apply for the purposes of this section as they apply for the purposes of that.

  (5) Material must not be disclosed under this section to the extent that the court, on an application by the prosecutor, concludes it is not in the public interest to disclose it and orders accordingly.

  (6) Material must not be disclosed under this section to the extent that it is material the disclosure of which is prohibited by section 17 of the Regulation of Investigatory Powers Act 2000.

  (7) The prosecutor must act under this section during the period which, by virtue of section 12, is the relevant period for this section.

8 Application by accused for disclosure

  (1) This section applies where the accused gives a defence statement under section 5 or 6 and the prosecutor complies with section 7 or purports to comply with it or fails to comply with it.

  (2) If the accused has at any time reasonable cause to believe that—

   (a) there is prosecution material which might be reasonably expected to assist the accused's defence as disclosed by the defence statement given under section 5 or 6, and

   (b) the material has not been disclosed to the accused,

the accused may apply to the court for an order requiring the prosecutor to disclose such material to the accused.

  (3) For the purposes of this section prosecution material is material—

   (a) which is in the prosecutor's possession and came into his possession in connection with the case for the prosecution against the accused,

   (b) which, in pursuance of a code operative under Part II, he has inspected in connection with the case for the prosecution against the accused, or

   (c) which falls within subsection (4).

  (4) Material falls within this subsection if in pursuance of a code operative under Part II

the prosecutor must, if he asks for the material, be given a copy of it or be allowed to inspect it in connection with the case for the prosecution against the accused.

(5) Material must not be disclosed under this section to the extent that the court, on an application by the prosecutor, concludes it is not in the public interest to disclose it and orders accordingly.

(6) Material must not be disclosed under this section to the extent that it is material the disclosure of which is prohibited by section 17 of the Regulation of Investigatory Powers Act 2000.

9   Continuing duty of prosecutor to disclose

(1) Subsection (2) applies at all times—
   (a) after the prosecutor complies with section 3 or purports to comply with it, and
   (b) before the accused is acquitted or convicted or the prosecutor decides not to proceed with the case concerned.

(2) The prosecutor must keep under review the question whether at any given time there is prosecution material which—
   (a) in his opinion might undermine the case for the prosecution against the accused, and
   (b) has not been disclosed to the accused;
and if there is such material at any time the prosecutor must disclose it to the accused as soon as is reasonably practicable.

(3) In applying subsection (2) by reference to any given time the state of affairs at that time (including the case for the prosecution as it stands at that time) must be taken into account.

(4) Subsection (5) applies at all times—
   (a) after the prosecutor complies with section 7 or purports to comply with it, and
   (b) before the accused is acquitted or convicted or the prosecutor decides not to proceed with the case concerned.

(5) The prosecutor must keep under review the question whether at any given time there is prosecution material which—
   (a) might be reasonably expected to assist the accused's defence as disclosed by the defence statement given under section 5 or 6, and
   (b) has not been disclosed to the accused;
and if there is such material at any time the prosecutor must disclose it to the accused as soon as is reasonably practicable.

(6) For the purposes of this section prosecution material is material—
   (a) which is in the prosecutor's possession and came into his possession in connection with the case for the prosecution against the accused, or
   (b) which, in pursuance of a code operative under Part II, he has inspected in connection with the case for the prosecution against the accused.

(7) Subsections (3) to (5) of section 3 (method by which prosecutor discloses) apply for the purposes of this section as they apply for the purposes of that.

(8) Material must not be disclosed under this section to the extent that the court, on an application by the prosecutor, concludes it is not in the public interest to disclose it and orders accordingly.

(9) Material must not be disclosed under this section to the extent that it is material the disclosure of which is prohibited by section 17 of the Regulation of Investigatory Powers Act 2000.

10   Prosecutor's failure to observe time limits

(1) This section applies if the prosecutor—
   (a) purports to act under section 3 after the end of the period which, by virtue of section 12, is the relevant period for section 3, or

(b) purports to act under section 7 after the end of the period which, by virtue of section 12, is the relevant period for section 7.

(2) Subject to subsection (3), the failure to act during the period concerned does not on its own constitute grounds for staying the proceedings for abuse of process.

(3) Subsection (2) does not prevent the failure constituting such grounds if it involves such delay by the prosecutor that the accused is denied a fair trial.

11 Faults in disclosure by accused

(1) This section applies where section 5 applies and the accused—

(a) fails to give a defence statement under that section,

(b) gives a defence statement under that section but does so after the end of the period which, by virtue of section 12, is the relevant period for section 5,

(c) sets out inconsistent defences in a defence statement given under section 5,

(d) at his trial puts forward a defence which is different from any defence set out in a defence statement given under section 5,

(e) at his trial adduces evidence in support of an alibi without having given particulars of the alibi in a defence statement given under section 5, or

(f) at his trial calls a witness to give evidence in support of an alibi without having complied with subsection (7)(a) or (b) of section 5 as regards the witness in giving a defence statement under that section.

(2) This section also applies where section 6 applies, the accused gives a defence statement under that section, and the accused—

(a) gives the statement after the end of the period which, by virtue of section 12, is the relevant period for section 6,

(b) sets out inconsistent defences in the statement,

(c) at his trial puts forward a defence which is different from any defence set out in the statement,

(d) at his trial adduces evidence in support of an alibi without having given particulars of the alibi in the statement, or

(e) at his trial calls a witness to give evidence in support of an alibi without having complied with subsection (7)(a) or (b) of section 5 (as applied by section 6) as regards the witness in giving the statement.

(3) Where this section applies—

(a) the court or, with the leave of the court, any other party may make such comment as appears appropriate;

(b) the court or jury may draw such inferences as appear proper in deciding whether the accused is guilty of the offence concerned.

(4) Where the accused puts forward a defence which is different from any defence set out in a defence statement given under section 5 or 6, in doing anything under subsection (3) or in deciding whether to do anything under it the court shall have regard—

(a) to the extent of the difference in the defences, and

(b) to whether there is any justification for it.

(5) A person shall not be convicted of an offence solely on an inference drawn under subsection (3).

(6) Any reference in this section to evidence in support of an alibi shall be construed in accordance with section 5.

12 Time limits

(1) This section has effect for the purpose of determining the relevant period for sections 3, 5, 6 and 7.

(2) Subject to subsection (3), the relevant period is a period beginning and ending with such days as the Secretary of State prescribes by regulations for the purposes of the section concerned.

(3) The regulations may do one or more of the following—

    (a) provide that the relevant period for any section shall if the court so orders be extended (or further extended) by so many days as the court specifies;

    (b) provide that the court may only make such an order if an application is made by a prescribed person and if any other prescribed conditions are fulfilled;

    (c) provide that an application may only be made if prescribed conditions are fulfilled;

    (d) provide that the number of days by which a period may be extended shall be entirely at the court's discretion;

    (e) provide that the number of days by which a period may be extended shall not exceed a prescribed number;

    (f) provide that there shall be no limit on the number of applications that may be made to extend a period;

    (g) provide that no more than a prescribed number of applications may be made to extend a period;

and references to the relevant period for a section shall be construed accordingly.

(4) Conditions mentioned in subsection (3) may be framed by reference to such factors as the Secretary of State thinks fit.

(5) Without prejudice to the generality of subsection (4), so far as the relevant period for section 3 or 7 is concerned—

    (a) conditions may be framed by reference to the nature or volume of the material concerned;

    (b) the nature of material may be defined by reference to the prosecutor's belief that the question of non-disclosure on grounds of public interest may arise.

(6) In subsection (3) "prescribed" means prescribed by regulations under this section.

13   Time limits: transitional

(1) As regards a case in relation to which no regulations under section 12 have come into force for the purposes of section 3, section 3(8) shall have effect as if it read—

"(8) The prosecutor must act under this section as soon as is reasonably practicable after—

    (a) the accused pleads not guilty (where this Part applies by virtue of section 1(1)),

    (b) the accused is committed for trial (where this Part applies by virtue of section 1(2)(a)),

    (c) the proceedings are transferred (where this Part applies by virtue of section 1(2)(b) or (c)),

    (ca) copies of the documents containing the evidence on which the charge or charges are based are served on the accused (where this Part applies by virtue of section 1(2)(cc)).

    (d) the count is included in the indictment (where this Part applies by virtue of section 1(2)(d)), or

    (e) the bill of indictment is preferred (where this Part applies by virtue of section 1(2)(e))."

(2) As regards a case in relation to which no regulations under section 12 have come into force for the purposes of section 7, section 7(7) shall have effect as if it read—

"(7) The prosecutor must act under this section as soon as is reasonably practicable after the accused gives a defence statement under section 5 or 6."

14   Public interest: review for summary trials

(1) This section applies where this Part applies by virtue of section 1(1).

(2) At any time—

    (a) after a court makes an order under section 3(6), 7(5), 8(5) or 9(8), and

    (b) before the accused is acquitted or convicted or the prosecutor decides not to proceed with the case concerned, the accused may apply to the court for a review of the question whether it is still not in the public interest to disclose material affected by its order.

(3) In such a case the court must review that question, and if it concludes that it is in the public interest to disclose material to any extent—

(a) it shall so order, and

(b) it shall take such steps as are reasonable to inform the prosecutor of its order.

(4) Where the prosecutor is informed of an order made under subsection (3) he must act accordingly having regard to the provisions of this Part (unless he decides not to proceed with the case concerned).

15 Public interest: review in other cases

(1) This section applies where this Part applies by virtue of section 1(2).

(2) This section applies at all times—

(a) after a court makes an order under section 3(6), 7(5), 8(5) or 9(8), and

(b) before the accused is acquitted or convicted or the prosecutor decides not to proceed with the case concerned.

(3) The court must keep under review the question whether at any given time it is still not in the public interest to disclose material affected by its order.

(4) The court must keep the question mentioned in subsection (3) under review without the need for an application; but the accused may apply to the court for a review of that question.

(5) If the court at any time concludes that it is in the public interest to disclose material to any extent—

(a) it shall so order, and

(b) it shall take such steps as are reasonable to inform the prosecutor of its order.

(6) Where the prosecutor is informed of an order made under subsection (5) he must act accordingly having regard to the provisions of this Part (unless he decides not to proceed with the case concerned).

16 Applications: opportunity to be heard

Where—

(a) an application is made under section 3(6), 7(5), 8(5), 9(8), 14(2) or 15(4),

(b) a person claiming to have an interest in the material applies to be heard by the court, and

(c) he shows that he was involved (whether alone or with others and whether directly or indirectly) in the prosecutor's attention being brought to the material,

the court must not make an order under section 3(6), 7(5), 8(5), 9(8), 14(3) or 15(5) (as the case may be) unless the person applying under paragraph (b) has been given an opportunity to be heard.

17 Confidentiality of disclosed information

(1) If the accused is given or allowed to inspect a document or other object under—

(a) section 3, 4, 7, 9, 14 or 15, or

(b) an order under section 8,

then, subject to subsections (2) to (4), he must not use or disclose it or any information recorded in it.

(2) The accused may use or disclose the object or information—

(a) in connection with the proceedings for whose purposes he was given the object or allowed to inspect it,

(b) with a view to the taking of further criminal proceedings (for instance, by way of appeal) with regard to the matter giving rise to the proceedings mentioned in paragraph (a), or

(c) in connection with the proceedings first mentioned in paragraph (b).

(3) The accused may use or disclose—

(a) the object to the extent that it has been displayed to the public in open court, or

(b) the information to the extent that it has been communicated to the public in open court;

but the preceding provisions of this subsection do not apply if the object is displayed or the information is communicated in proceedings to deal with a contempt of court under section 18.

(4) If—

(a) the accused applies to the court for an order granting permission to use or disclose the object or information, and

(b) the court makes such an order,

the accused may use or disclose the object or information for the purpose and to the extent specified by the court.

(5) An application under subsection (4) may be made and dealt with at any time, and in particular after the accused has been acquitted or convicted or the prosecutor has decided not to proceed with the case concerned; but this is subject to rules made by virtue of section 19(2).

(6) Where—

(a) an application is made under subsection (4), and

(b) the prosecutor or a person claiming to have an interest in the object or information applies to be heard by the court,

the court must not make an order granting permission unless the person applying under paragraph (b) has been given an opportunity to be heard.

(7) References in this section to the court are to—

(a) a magistrates' court, where this Part applies by virtue of section 1(1);

(b) the Crown Court, where this Part applies by virtue of section 1(2).

(8) Nothing in this section affects any other restriction or prohibition on the use or disclosure of an object or information, whether the restriction or prohibition arises under an enactment (whenever passed) or otherwise.

18 Confidentiality: contravention

(1) It is a contempt of court for a person knowingly to use or disclose an object or information recorded in it if the use or disclosure is in contravention of section 17.

(2) The following courts have jurisdiction to deal with a person who is guilty of a contempt under this section—

(a) a magistrates' court, where this Part applies by virtue of section 1(1);

(b) the Crown Court, where this Part applies by virtue of section 1(2).

(3) A person who is guilty of a contempt under this section may be dealt with as follows—

(a) a magistrates' court may commit him to custody for a specified period not exceeding six months or impose on him a fine not exceeding £5,000 or both;

(b) the Crown Court may commit him to custody for a specified period not exceeding two years or impose a fine on him or both.

(4) If—

(a) a person is guilty of a contempt under this section, and

(b) the object concerned is in his possession,

the court finding him guilty may order that the object shall be forfeited and dealt with in such manner as the court may order.

(5) The power of the court under subsection (4) includes power to order the object to be destroyed or to be given to the prosecutor or to be placed in his custody for such period as the court may specify.

(6) If—

(a) the court proposes to make an order under subsection (4), and

(b) the person found guilty, or any other person claiming to have an interest in the object, applies to be heard by the court,

the court must not make the order unless the applicant has been given an opportunity to be heard.

(7) If—

(a) a person is guilty of a contempt under this section, and

(b) a copy of the object concerned is in his possession,

the court finding him guilty may order that the copy shall be forfeited and dealt with in such manner as the court may order.

(8) Subsections (5) and (6) apply for the purposes of subsection (7) as they apply for the purposes of subsection (4), but as if references to the object were references to the copy.

(9) An object or information shall be inadmissible as evidence in civil proceedings if to adduce it would in the opinion of the court be likely to constitute a contempt under this section; and "the court" here means the court before which the civil proceedings are being taken.

(10) The powers of a magistrates' court under this section may be exercised either of the court's own motion or by order on complaint.

Vulnerable witnesses

Criminal Justice Act 1988

32 Evidence through television links

(1) A person other than the accused may give evidence through a live television link in proceedings to which subsection (1A) below applies if–

(a) the witness is outside the United Kingdom; or

(b) the witness is a child, or is to be cross-examined following the admission under section 32A below of a video recording of testimony from him, and the offence is one to which subsection (2) below applies,

but evidence may not be so given without the leave of the court.

"(1A) This subsection applies—

(a) to trials on indictment, appeals to the criminal division of the Court of Appeal and hearings of references under section 17 of the Criminal Appeal Act 1995; and

(b) to proceedings in youth courts and appeals to the Crown Court arising out of such proceedings, and hearings of references under section 11 of the Criminal Appeal Act 1995 so arising.

(2) This subsection applies—

(a) to an offence which involves an assault on, or injury or a threat of injury to, a person;

(b) to an offence under section 1 of the Children and Young Persons Act 1933 (cruelty to persons under 16);

(c) to an offence under the Sexual Offences Act 1956, the Indecency with Children Act 1960, the Sexual Offences Act 1967, section 54 of the Criminal Law Act 1977 or the Protection of Children Act 1978; and

(d) to an offence which consists of attempting or conspiring to commit, or of aiding, abetting, counselling, procuring or inciting the commission of, an offence falling within paragraph (a), (b) or (c) above.

(3) A statement made on oath by a witness outside the United Kingdom and given in evidence through a link by virtue of this section shall be treated for the purposes of section 1 of the Perjury Act 1911 as having been made in the proceedings in which it is given in evidence.

(3A) Where, in the case of any proceedings before a youth court—

  (a) leave is given by virtue of subsection (1)(b) above for evidence to be given through a television link; and

  (b) suitable facilities for receiving such evidence are not available at any petty-sessional court-house in which the court can (apart from this subsection) lawfully sit,

the court may sit for the purposes of the whole or any part of those proceedings at any place at which such facilities are available and which has been appointed for the purposes of this subsection by the justices acting for the petty sessions area for which the court acts.

(3B) A place appointed under subsection (3) above may be outside the petty sessions area for which it is appointed; but it shall be deemed to be in that area for the purpose of the jurisdiction of the justices acting for that area.

(3C) Where—

  (a) the court gives leave for a person to give evidence through a live television link, and

  (b) the leave is given by virtue of subsection (1)(b) above,

then, subject to subsection (3D) below, the person concerned may not give evidence otherwise than through a live television link.

(3D) In a case falling within subsection (3C) above the court may give permission for the person to give evidence otherwise than through a live television link if it appears to the court to be in the interests of justice to give such permission.

(3E) Permission may be given under subsection (3D) above—

  (a) on an application by a party to the case, or

  (b) of the court's own motion;

but no application may be made under paragraph (a) above unless there has been a material change of circumstances since the leave was given by virtue of subsection (1)(b) above.

(4) Without prejudice to the generality of any enactment conferring power to make rules to which this subsection applies, such rules may make such provision as appears to the authority making them to be necessary or expedient for the purposes of this section.

(5) The rules to which subsection (4) above applies are Magistrates' Courts Rules, Crown Court Rules and Criminal Appeal Rules.

(6) Subsection (7) of section 32A below shall apply for the purposes of this section as it applies for the purposes of that section, but with the omission of the references to a person being, in the cases there mentioned, under the age of fifteen years or under the age of eighteen years.

32A Video recordings of testimony from child witnesses

(1) This section applies in relation to the following proceedings, namely—

  (a) trials on indictment for any offence to which section 32(2) above applies;

  (b) appeals to the criminal division of the Court of Appeal and hearings of references under section 9 of the Criminal Appeal Act 1995 in respect of any such offence; and

  (c) proceedings in youth courts for any such offence appeals to the Crown Court arising out of such proceedings, and hearings of references under section 11 of the Criminal Appeal Act 1995 so arising.

(2) In any such proceedings a video recording of an interview which—

  (a) is conducted between an adult and a child who is not the accused or one of the accused ('the child witness'); and

  (b) relates to any matter in issue in the proceedings,

may, with the leave of the court, be given in evidence in so far as it is not excluded by the court under subsection (3) below.

(3) Where a video recording is tendered in evidence under this section, the court shall (subject to the exercise of any power of the court to exclude evidence which is otherwise admissible) give leave under subsection (2) above unless—

(a) it appears that the child witness will not be available for cross-examination;

(b) any rules of court requiring disclosure of the circumstances in which the recording was made have not been complied with to the satisfaction of the court; or

(c) the court is of the opinion, having regard to all the circumstances of the case, that in the interests of justice the recording ought not to be admitted;

and where the court gives such leave it may, if it is of the opinion that in the interests of justice any part of the recording ought not to be admitted, direct that that part shall be excluded.

(4) In considering whether any part of a recording ought to be excluded under subsection (3) above, the court shall consider whether any prejudice to the accused, or one of the accused, which might result from the admission of that part is outweighed by the desirability of showing the whole, or substantially the whole, of the recorded interview.

(5) Where a video recording is admitted under this section—

(a) the child witness shall be called by the party who tendered it in evidence;

(b) that witness shall not be examined in chief on any matter which, in the opinion of the court, has been dealt with adequately in his recorded testimony.

(6) Where a video recording is given in evidence under this section, any statement made by the child witness which is disclosed by the recording shall be treated as if given by that witness in direct oral testimony; and accordingly—

(a) any such statement shall be admissible evidence of any fact of which such testimony from him would be admissible;

(b) no such statement shall be capable of corroborating any other evidence given by him;

and in estimating the weight, if any, to be attached to such a statement, regard shall be had to all the circumstances from which any inference can reasonably be drawn (as to its accuracy or otherwise).

(6A) Where the court gives leave under subsection (2) above the child witness shall not give relevant evidence (within the meaning given by subsection (6D) below) otherwise than by means of the video recording; but this is subject to subsection (6B) below.

(6B) In a case falling within subsection (6A) above the court may give permission for the child witness to give relevant evidence (within the meaning given by subsection (6D) below) otherwise than by means of the video recording if it appears to the court to be in the interests of justice to give such permission.

(6C) Permission may be given under subsection (6B) above—

(a) on an application by a party to the case, or

(b) of the court's own motion;

but no application may be made under paragraph (a) above unless there has been a material change of circumstances since the leave was given under subsection (2) above.

(6D) For the purposes of subsections (6A) and (6B) above evidence is relevant evidence if—

(a) it is evidence in chief on behalf of the party who tendered the video recording, and

(b) it relates to matter which, in the opinion of the court, is dealt with in the recording and which the court has not directed to be excluded under subsection (3) above.

(7) In this section "child" means a person who—

(a) in the case of an offence falling within section 32(2)(a) or (b) above, is under fourteen years of age or, if he was under that age when the video recording was made, is under fifteen years of age; or

(b) in the case of an offence falling within section 32(2)(c) above, is under seventeen years of age or, if he was under that age when the video recording was made, is under eighteen years of age.

(8) Any reference in subsection (7) above to an offence falling within paragraph (a), (b) or (c) of section 32(2) above includes a reference to an offence which consists of attempting or conspiring to commit, or of aiding, abetting, counselling, procuring or inciting the commission of, an offence falling within that paragraph.

(9) In this section—

'statement' includes any representation of fact, whether made in words or otherwise;

'video recording' means any recording, on any medium, from which a moving image may by any means be produced and includes the accompanying sound-track.

(10) A magistrates' court inquiring into an offence as examining justices under section 6 of the Magistrates' Courts Act 1980 may consider any video recording as respects which leave under subsection (2) above is to be sought at the trial.

(11) Without prejudice to the generality of any enactment conferring power to make rules of court, such rules may make such provision as appears to the authority making them to be necessary or expedient for the purposes of this section.

(12) Nothing in this section shall prejudice the admissibility of any video recording which would be admissible apart from this section.

33 Omitted

33A Evidence given by children

(1) A child's evidence in criminal proceedings shall be given unsworn.

(2) A deposition of a child's unsworn evidence may be taken for the purposes of criminal proceedings as if that evidence had been given on oath.

(2A) A child's evidence shall be received unless it appears to the court that the child is incapable of giving intelligible testimony.

(3) In this section 'child' means a person under fourteen years of age.

34 Abolition of requirement of corroboration for unsworn evidence of children

(2) Any requirement whereby at a trial on indictment it is obligatory for the court to give the jury a warning about convicting the accused on the uncorroborated evidence of a child is abrogated.

(3) Unsworn evidence admitted by virtue of [section 56 of the Youth Justice and Criminal Evidence Act 1999] may corroborate evidence (sworn or unsworn) given by any other person.

Youth Justice and Criminal Evidence Act 1999

PART II

SPECIAL MEASURES DIRECTIONS IN CASE OF VULNERABLE AND INTIMIDATED WITNESSES

16 Witnesses eligible for assistance on grounds of age or incapacity

(1) For the purposes of this Chapter a witness in criminal proceedings (other than the accused) is eligible for assistance by virtue of this section—

(a) if under the age of 17 at the time of the hearing; or

(b) if the court considers that the quality of evidence given by the witness is likely to be diminished by reason of any circumstances falling within subsection (2).

(2) The circumstances falling within this subsection are—

(a) that the witness—

(i)   suffers from mental disorder within the meaning of the Mental Health Act 1983, or

(ii) otherwise has a significant impairment of intelligence and social functioning;

(b) that the witness has a physical disability or is suffering from a physical disorder.

(3) In subsection (1)(a) "the time of the hearing", in relation to a witness, means the time when it falls to the court to make a determination for the purposes of section 19(2) in relation to the witness.

(4) In determining whether a witness falls within subsection (1)(b) the court must consider any views expressed by the witness.

(5) In this Chapter references to the quality of a witness's evidence are to its quality in terms of completeness, coherence and accuracy; and for this purpose "coherence" refers to a witness's ability in giving evidence to give answers which address the questions put to the witness and can be understood both individually and collectively.

17   Witnesses eligible for assistance on grounds of fear or distress about testifying

(1) For the purposes of this Chapter a witness in criminal proceedings (other than the accused) is eligible for assistance by virtue of this subsection if the court is satisfied that the quality of evidence given by the witness is likely to be diminished by reason of fear or distress on the part of the witness in connection with testifying in the proceedings.

(2) In determining whether a witness falls within subsection (1) the court must take into account, in particular—

(a) the nature and alleged circumstances of the offence to which the proceedings relate;

(b) the age of the witness;

(c) such of the following matters as appear to the court to be relevant, namely—

(i)   the social and cultural background and ethnic origins of the witness,

(ii) the domestic and employment circumstances of the witness, and

(iii) any religious beliefs or political opinions of the witness;

(d) any behaviour towards the witness on the part of—

(i)   the accused,

(ii) members of the family or associates of the accused, or

(iii) any other person who is likely to be an accused or a witness in the proceedings.

(3) In determining that question the court must in addition consider any views expressed by the witness.

(4) Where the complainant in respect of a sexual offence is a witness in proceedings relating to that offence (or to that offence and any other offences), the witness is eligible for assistance in relation to those proceedings by virtue of this subsection unless the witness has informed the court of the witness' wish not to be so eligible by virtue of this subsection.

18   Special measures available to eligible witnesses

(1) For the purposes of this Chapter—

(a) the provision which may be made by a special measures direction by virtue of each of sections 23 to 30 is a special measure available in relation to a witness eligible for assistance by virtue of section 16; and

(b) the provision which may be made by such a direction by virtue of each of sections 23 to 28 is a special measure available in relation to a witness eligible for assistance by virtue of section 17;

but this subsection has effect subject to subsection (2).

(2) Where (apart from this subsection) a special measure would, in accordance with subsection (1)(a) or (b), be available in relation to a witness in any proceedings, it shall not be taken by a court to be available in relation to the witness unless—

(a) the court has been notified by the Secretary of State that relevant arrangements may be made available in the area in which it appears to the court that the proceedings will take place, and

(b) the notice has not been withdrawn.

(3) In subsection (2) "relevant arrangements" means arrangements for implementing the measure in question which cover the witness and the proceedings in question.

(4) The withdrawal of a notice under that subsection relating to a special measure shall not affect the availability of that measure in relation to a witness if a special measures direction providing for that measure to apply to the witness's evidence has been made by the court before the notice is withdrawn.

(5) The Secretary of State may by order make such amendments of this Chapter as he considers appropriate for altering the special measures which, in accordance with subsection (1)(a) or (b), are available in relation to a witness eligible for assistance by virtue of section 16 or (as the case may be) section 17, whether—

(a) by modifying the provisions relating to any measure for the time being available in relation to such a witness,

(b) by the addition—

(i) (with or without modifications) of any measure which is for the time being available in relation to a witness eligible for assistance by virtue of the other of those sections, or

(ii) of any new measure, or

(c) by the removal of any measure.

19   Special measures direction relating to eligible witness

(1) This section applies where in any criminal proceedings—

(a) a party to the proceedings makes an application for the court to give a direction under this section in relation to a witness in the proceedings other than the accused, or

(b) the court of its own motion raises the issue whether such a direction should be given.

(2) Where the court determines that the witness is eligible for assistance by virtue of section 16 or 17, the court must then—

(a) determine whether any of the special measures available in relation to the witness (or any combination of them) would, in its opinion, be likely to improve the quality of evidence given by the witness; and

(b) if so—

(i) determine which of those measures (or combination of them) would, in its opinion, be likely to maximise so far as practicable the quality of such evidence; and

(ii) give a direction under this section providing for the measure or measures so determined to apply to evidence given by the witness.

(3) In determining for the purposes of this Chapter whether any special measure or measures would or would not be likely to improve, or to maximise so far as practicable, the quality of evidence given by the witness, the court must consider all the circumstances of the case, including in particular—

(a) any views expressed by the witness; and

(b) whether the measure or measures might tend to inhibit such evidence being effectively tested by a party to the proceedings.

(4) A special measures direction must specify particulars of the provision made by the direction in respect of each special measure which is to apply to the witness's evidence.

(5) In this Chapter "special measures direction" means a direction under this section.

(6) Nothing in this Chapter is to be regarded as affecting any power of a court to make an

order or give leave of any description (in the exercise of its inherent jurisdiction or otherwise)—

(a) in relation to a witness who is not an eligible witness, or

(b) in relation to an eligible witness where (as, for example, in a case where a foreign language interpreter is to be provided) the order is made or the leave is given otherwise than by reason of the fact that the witness is an eligible witness.

20 Further provisions about directions: general

(1) Subject to subsection (2) and section 21(8), a special measures direction has binding effect from the time it is made until the proceedings for the purposes of which it is made are either—

(a) determined (by acquittal, conviction or otherwise), or

(b) abandoned,

in relation to the accused or (if there is more than one) in relation to each of the accused.

(2) The court may discharge or vary (or further vary) a special measures direction if it appears to the court to be in the interests of justice to do so, and may do so either—

(a) on an application made by a party to the proceedings, if there has been a material change of circumstances since the relevant time, or

(b) of its own motion.

(3) In subsection (2) "the relevant time" means—

(a) the time when the direction was given, or

(b) if a previous application has been made under that subsection, the time when the application (or last application) was made.

(4) Nothing in section 24(2) and (3), 27(4) to (7) or 28(4) to (6) is to be regarded as affecting the power of the court to vary or discharge a special measures direction under subsection (2).

(5) The court must state in open court its reasons for—

(a) giving or varying,

(b) refusing an application for, or for the variation or discharge of, or

(c) discharging,

a special measures direction and, if it is a magistrates' court, must cause them to be entered in the register of its proceedings.

(6) Rules of court may make provision—

(a) for uncontested applications to be determined by the court without a hearing;

(b) for preventing the renewal of an unsuccessful application for a special measures direction except where there has been a material change of circumstances;

(c) for expert evidence to be given in connection with an application for, or for varying or discharging, such a direction;

(d) for the manner in which confidential or sensitive information is to be treated in connection with such an application and in particular as to its being disclosed to, or withheld from, a party to the proceedings.

21 Special provisions relating to child witnesses

(1) For the purposes of this section—

(a) a witness in criminal proceedings is a "child witness" if he is an eligible witness by reason of section 16(1)(a) (whether or not he is an eligible witness by reason of any other provision of section 16 or 17);

(b) a child witness is "in need of special protection" if the offence (or any of the offences) to which the proceedings relate is—

(i) an offence falling within section 35(3)(a) (sexual offences etc.), or

(ii) an offence falling within section 35(3)(b), (c) or (d) (kidnapping, assaults etc.); and

(c) a "relevant recording", in relation to a child witness, is a video recording of an interview of the witness made with a view to its admission as evidence in chief of the witness.

(2) Where the court, in making a determination for the purposes of section 19(2), determines that a witness in criminal proceedings is a child witness, the court must—

(a) first have regard to subsections (3) to (7) below; and

(b) then have regard to section 19(2);

and for the purposes of section 19(2), as it then applies to the witness, any special measures required to be applied in relation to him by virtue of this section shall be treated as if they were measures determined by the court, pursuant to section 19(2)(a) and (b)(i), to be ones that (whether on their own or with any other special measures) would be likely to maximise, so far as practicable, the quality of his evidence.

(3) The primary rule in the case of a child witness is that the court must give a special measures direction in relation to the witness which complies with the following requirements—

(a) it must provide for any relevant recording to be admitted under section 27 (video recorded evidence in chief); and

(b) it must provide for any evidence given by the witness in the proceedings which is not given by means of a video recording (whether in chief or otherwise) to be given by means of a live link in accordance with section 24.

(4) The primary rule is subject to the following limitations—

(a) the requirement contained in subsection (3)(a) or (b) has effect subject to the availability (within the meaning of section 18(2)) of the special measure in question in relation to the witness;

(b) the requirement contained in subsection (3)(a) also has effect subject to section 27(2); and

(c) the rule does not apply to the extent that the court is satisfied that compliance with it would not be likely to maximise the quality of the witness's evidence so far as practicable (whether because the application to that evidence of one or more other special measures available in relation to the witness would have that result or for any other reason).

(5) However, subsection (4)(c) does not apply in relation to a child witness in need of special protection.

(6) Where a child witness is in need of special protection by virtue of subsection (1)(b)(i), any special measures direction given by the court which complies with the requirement contained in subsection (3)(a) must in addition provide for the special measure available under section 28 (video recorded cross-examination or re-examination) to apply in relation to—

(a) any cross-examination of the witness otherwise than by the accused in person, and

(b) any subsequent re-examination.

(7) The requirement contained in subsection (6) has effect subject to the following limitations—

(a) it has effect subject to the availability (within the meaning of section 18(2)) of that special measure in relation to the witness; and

(b) it does not apply if the witness has informed the court that he does not want that special measure to apply in relation to him.

(8) Where a special measures direction is given in relation to a child witness who is an eligible witness by reason only of section 16(1)(a), then—

(a) subject to subsection (9) below, and

(b) except where the witness has already begun to give evidence in the proceedings,

the direction shall cease to have effect at the time when the witness attains the age of 17.

(9) Where a special measures direction is given in relation to a child witness who is an eligible witness by reason only of section 16(1)(a) and—

    (a) the direction provides—

        (i) for any relevant recording to be admitted under section 27 as evidence in chief of the witness, or

        (ii) for the special measure available under section 28 to apply in relation to the witness, and

    (b) if it provides for that special measure to so apply, the witness is still under the age of 17 when the video recording is made for the purposes of section 28,

then, so far as it provides as mentioned in paragraph (a)(i) or (ii) above, the direction shall continue to have effect in accordance with section 20(1) even though the witness subsequently attains that age.

22 Extension of provisions of section 21 to certain witnesses over 17

(1) For the purposes of this section—

    (a) a witness in criminal proceedings (other than the accused) is a "qualifying witness" if he—

        (i) is not an eligible witness at the time of the hearing (as defined by section 16(3)), but

        (ii) was under the age of 17 when a relevant recording was made;

    (b) a qualifying witness is "in need of special protection" if the offence (or any of the offences) to which the proceedings relate is—

        (i) an offence falling within section 35(3)(a) (sexual offences etc.), or

        (ii) an offence falling within section 35(3)(b), (c) or (d) (kidnapping, assaults etc.); and

    (c) a "relevant recording", in relation to a witness, is a video recording of an interview of the witness made with a view to its admission as evidence in chief of the witness.

(2) Subsections (2) to (7) of section 21 shall apply as follows in relation to a qualifying witness—

    (a) subsections (2) to (4), so far as relating to the giving of a direction complying with the requirement contained in subsection (3)(a), shall apply to a qualifying witness in respect of the relevant recording as they apply to a child witness (within the meaning of that section);

    (b) subsection (5), so far as relating to the giving of such a direction, shall apply to a qualifying witness in need of special protection as it applies to a child witness in need of special protection (within the meaning of that section); and

    (c) subsections (6) and (7) shall apply to a qualifying witness in need of special protection by virtue of subsection (1)(b)(i) above as they apply to such a child witness as is mentioned in subsection (6).

23 Screening witness from accused

(1) A special measures direction may provide for the witness, while giving testimony or being sworn in court, to be prevented by means of a screen or other arrangement from seeing the accused.

(2) But the screen or other arrangement must not prevent the witness from being able to see, and to be seen by—

    (a) the judge or justices (or both) and the jury (if there is one);

    (b) legal representatives acting in the proceedings; and

    (c) any interpreter or other person appointed (in pursuance of the direction or otherwise) to assist the witness.

(3) Where two or more legal representatives are acting for a party to the proceedings,

subsection (2)(b) is to be regarded as satisfied in relation to those representatives if the witness is able at all material times to see and be seen by at least one of them.

24   Evidence by live link

(1) A special measures direction may provide for the witness to give evidence by means of a live link.

(2) Where a direction provides for the witness to give evidence by means of a live link, the witness may not give evidence in any other way without the permission of the court.

(3) The court may give permission for the purposes of subsection (2) if it appears to the court to be in the interests of justice to do so, and may do so either—

    (a) on an application by a party to the proceedings, if there has been a material change of circumstances since the relevant time, or

    (b) of its own motion.

(4) In subsection (3) "the relevant time" means—

    (a) the time when the direction was given, or

    (b) if a previous application has been made under that subsection, the time when the application (or last application) was made.

(5) Where in proceedings before a magistrates' court—

    (a) evidence is to be given by means of a live link in accordance with a special measures direction, but

    (b) suitable facilities for receiving such evidence are not available at any petty-sessional court-house in which that court can (apart from this subsection) lawfully sit,

the court may sit for the purposes of the whole or any part of those proceedings at a place where such facilities are available and which has been appointed for the purposes of this subsection by the justices acting for the petty sessions area for which the court acts.

(6) A place appointed under subsection (5) may be outside the petty sessions area for which it is appointed; but (if so) it is to be regarded as being in that area for the purpose of the jurisdiction of the justices acting for that area.

(7) In this section "petty-sessional court-house" has the same meaning as in the Magistrates' Courts Act 1980 and "petty sessions area" has the same meaning as in the Justices of the Peace Act 1997.

(8) In this Chapter "live link" means a live television link or other arrangement whereby a witness, while absent from the courtroom or other place where the proceedings are being held, is able to see and hear a person there and to be seen and heard by the persons specified in section 23(2)(a) to (c).

25   Evidence given in private

(1) A special measures direction may provide for the exclusion from the court, during the giving of the witness's evidence, of persons of any description specified in the direction.

(2) The persons who may be so excluded do not include—

    (a) the accused,

    (b) legal representatives acting in the proceedings, or

    (c) any interpreter or other person appointed (in pursuance of the direction or otherwise) to assist the witness.

(3) A special measures direction providing for representatives of news gathering or reporting organisations to be so excluded shall be expressed not to apply to one named person who—

    (a) is a representative of such an organisation, and

    (b) has been nominated for the purpose by one or more such organisations,

unless it appears to the court that no such nomination has been made.

(4) A special measures direction may only provide for the exclusion of persons under this section where—

(a) the proceedings relate to a sexual offence; or

(b) it appears to the court that there are reasonable grounds for believing that any person other than the accused has sought, or will seek, to intimidate the witness in connection with testifying in the proceedings.

(5) Any proceedings from which persons are excluded under this section (whether or not those persons include representatives of news gathering or reporting organisations) shall nevertheless be taken to be held in public for the purposes of any privilege or exemption from liability available in respect of fair, accurate and contemporaneous reports of legal proceedings held in public.

26   Removal of wigs and gowns

A special measures direction may provide for the wearing of wigs or gowns to be dispensed with during the giving of the witness's evidence.

27   Video recorded evidence in chief

(1) A special measures direction may provide for a video recording of an interview of the witness to be admitted as evidence in chief of the witness.

(2) A special measures direction may, however, not provide for a video recording, or a part of such a recording, to be admitted under this section if the court is of the opinion, having regard to all the circumstances of the case, that in the interests of justice the recording, or that part of it, should not be so admitted.

(3) In considering for the purposes of subsection (2) whether any part of a recording should not be admitted under this section, the court must consider whether any prejudice to the accused which might result from that part being so admitted is outweighed by the desirability of showing the whole, or substantially the whole, of the recorded interview.

(4) Where a special measures direction provides for a recording to be admitted under this section, the court may nevertheless subsequently direct that it is not to be so admitted if—

(a) it appears to the court that—

(i)   the witness will not be available for cross-examination (whether conducted in the ordinary way or in accordance with any such direction), and

(ii) the parties to the proceedings have not agreed that there is no need for the witness to be so available; or

(b) any rules of court requiring disclosure of the circumstances in which the recording was made have not been complied with to the satisfaction of the court.

(5) Where a recording is admitted under this section—

(a) the witness must be called by the party tendering it in evidence, unless—

(i)   a special measures direction provides for the witness's evidence on cross-examination to be given otherwise than by testimony in court, or

(ii) the parties to the proceedings have agreed as mentioned in subsection (4)(a)(ii); and

(b) the witness may not give evidence in chief otherwise than by means of the recording—

(i)   as to any matter which, in the opinion of the court, has been dealt with adequately in the witness's recorded testimony, or

(ii) without the permission of the court, as to any other matter which, in the opinion of the court, is dealt with in that testimony.

(6) Where in accordance with subsection (2) a special measures direction provides for part only of a recording to be admitted under this section, references in subsections (4) and (5) to the recording or to the witness's recorded testimony are references to the part of the recording or testimony which is to be so admitted.

(7) The court may give permission for the purposes of subsection (5)(b)(ii) if it appears to the court to be in the interests of justice to do so, and may do so either—

    (a) on an application by a party to the proceedings, if there has been a material change of circumstances since the relevant time, or

    (b) of its own motion.

(8) In subsection (7) "the relevant time" means—

    (a) the time when the direction was given, or

    (b) if a previous application has been made under that subsection, the time when the application (or last application) was made.

(9) The court may, in giving permission for the purposes of subsection (5)(b)(ii), direct that the evidence in question is to be given by the witness by means of a live link; and, if the court so directs, subsections (5) to (7) of section 24 shall apply in relation to that evidence as they apply in relation to evidence which is to be given in accordance with a special measures direction.

(10) A magistrates' court inquiring into an offence as examining justices under section 6 of the Magistrates' Courts Act 1980 may consider any video recording in relation to which it is proposed to apply for a special measures direction providing for it to be admitted at the trial in accordance with this section.

(11) Nothing in this section affects the admissibility of any video recording which would be admissible apart from this section.

28   Video recorded cross-examination or re-examination

(1) Where a special measures direction provides for a video recording to be admitted under section 27 as evidence in chief of the witness, the direction may also provide—

    (a) for any cross-examination of the witness, and any re-examination, to be recorded by means of a video recording; and

    (b) for such a recording to be admitted, so far as it relates to any such cross-examination or re-examination, as evidence of the witness under cross-examination or on re-examination, as the case may be.

(2) Such a recording must be made in the presence of such persons as rules of court or the direction may provide and in the absence of the accused, but in circumstances in which—

    (a) the judge or justices (or both) and legal representatives acting in the proceedings are able to see and hear the examination of the witness and to communicate with the persons in whose presence the recording is being made, and

    (b) the accused is able to see and hear any such examination and to communicate with any legal representative acting for him.

(3) Where two or more legal representatives are acting for a party to the proceedings, subsection (2)(a) and (b) are to be regarded as satisfied in relation to those representatives if at all material times they are satisfied in relation to at least one of them.

(4) Where a special measures direction provides for a recording to be admitted under this section, the court may nevertheless subsequently direct that it is not to be so admitted if any requirement of subsection (2) or rules of court or the direction has not been complied with to the satisfaction of the court.

(5) Where in pursuance of subsection (1) a recording has been made of any examination of the witness, the witness may not be subsequently cross-examined or re-examined in respect of any evidence given by the witness in the proceedings (whether in any recording admissible under section 27 or this section or otherwise than in such a recording) unless the court gives a further special measures direction making such provision as is mentioned in subsection (1)(a) and (b) in relation to any subsequent cross-examination, and re-examination, of the witness.

(6) The court may only give such a further direction if it appears to the court—

(a) that the proposed cross-examination is sought by a party to the proceedings as a result of that party having become aware, since the time when the original recording was made in pursuance of subsection (1), of a matter which that party could not with reasonable diligence have ascertained by then, or

(b) that for any other reason it is in the interests of justice to give the further direction.

(7) Nothing in this section shall be read as applying in relation to any cross-examination of the witness by the accused in person (in a case where the accused is to be able to conduct any such cross-examination).

29   Examination of witness through intermediary

(1) A special measures direction may provide for any examination of the witness (however and wherever conducted) to be conducted through an interpreter or other person approved by the court for the purposes of this section ("an intermediary").

(2) The function of an intermediary is to communicate—

(a) to the witness, questions put to the witness, and

(b) to any person asking such questions, the answers given by the witness in reply to them.

and to explain such question or answers so far as necessary to enable them to be understood by the witness or person in question.

(3) Any examination of the witness in pursuance of subsection (1) must take place in the presence of such persons as rules of court or the direction may provide, but in circumstances in which—

(a) the judge or justices (or both) and legal representatives acting in the proceedings are able to see and hear the examination of the witness and to communicate with the intermediary, and

(b) (except in the case of a video recorded examination) the jury (if there is one) are able to see and hear the examination of the witness.

(4) Where two or more legal representatives are acting for a party to the proceedings, subsection (3)(a) is to be regarded as satisfied in relation to those representatives if at all material times it is satisfied in relation to at least one of them.

(5) A person may not act as an intermediary in a particular case except after making a declaration, in such form as may be prescribed by rules of court, that he will faithfully perform his function as intermediary.

(6) Subsection (1) does not apply to an interview of the witness which is recorded by means of a video recording with a view to its admission as evidence in chief of the witness; but a special measures direction may provide for such a recording to be admitted under section 27 if the interview was conducted through an intermediary and—

(a) that person complied with subsection (5) before the interview began, and

(b) the court's approval for the purposes of this section is given before the direction is given.

(7) Section 1 of the Perjury Act 1911 (perjury) shall apply in relation to a person acting as an intermediary as it applies in relation to a person lawfully sworn as an interpreter in a judicial proceeding; and for this purpose, where a person acts as an intermediary in any proceeding which is not a judicial proceeding for the purposes of that section, that proceeding shall be taken to be part of the judicial proceeding in which the witness's evidence is given.

30

A special measures direction may provide for the witness, while giving evidence (whether by testimony in court or otherwise), to be provided with such device as the court considers appropriate with a view to enabling questions or answers to be communicated to or by the witness despite any disability or disorder or other impairment which the witness has or suffers from.

CHAPTER II

PROTECTION OF WITNESSES FROM CROSS-EXAMINATION BY ACCUSED IN PERSON

34   Complainants in proceedings for sexual offences

No person charged with a sexual offence may in any criminal proceedings cross-examine in person a witness who is the complainant, either—

  (a) in connection with that offence, or

  (b) in connection with any other offence (of whatever nature) with which that person is charged in the proceedings.

35   Child complainants and other child witnesses

  (1) No person charged with an offence to which this section applies may in any criminal proceedings cross-examine in person a protected witness, either—

  (a) in connection with that offence, or

  (b) in connection with any other offence (of whatever nature) with which that person is charged in the proceedings.

  (2) For the purposes of subsection (1) a "protected witness" is a witness who—

  (a) either is the complainant or is alleged to have been a witness to the commission of the offence to which this section applies, and

  (b) either is a child or falls to be cross-examined after giving evidence in chief (whether wholly or in part)—

  (i) by means of a video recording made (for the purposes of section 27) at a time when the witness was a child, or

  (ii) in any other way at any such time.

  (3) The offences to which this section applies are—

  (a) any offence under—

  (i)   the Sexual Offences Act 1956,

  (ii) the Indecency with Children Act 1960,

  (iii) the Sexual Offences Act 1967,

  (iv) section 54 of the Criminal Law Act 1977, or

  (v)   the Protection of Children Act 1978;

  (b) kidnapping, false imprisonment or an offence under section 1 or 2 of the Child Abduction Act 1984;

  (c) any offence under section 1 of the Children and Young Persons Act 1933;

  (d) any offence (not within any of the preceding paragraphs) which involves an assault on, or injury or a threat of injury to, any person.

  (4) In this section "child" means—

  (a) where the offence falls within subsection (3)(a), a person under the age of 17; or

  (b) where the offence falls within subsection (3)(b), (c) or (d), a person under the age of 14.

  (5) For the purposes of this section "witness" includes a witness who is charged with an offence in the proceedings.

36   Direction prohibiting accused from cross-examining particular witness

  (1) This section applies where, in a case where neither of sections 34 and 35 operates to prevent an accused in any criminal proceedings from cross-examining a witness in person—

  (a) the prosecutor makes an application for the court to give a direction under this section in relation to the witness, or

  (b) the court of its own motion raises the issue whether such a direction should be given.

(2) If it appears to the court—
    (a) that the quality of evidence given by the witness on cross-examination—
        (i) is likely to be diminished if the cross-examination (or further cross-examination) is conducted by the accused in person, and
        (ii) would be likely to be improved if a direction were given under this section, and
    (b) that it would not be contrary to the interests of justice to give such a direction,
the court may give a direction prohibiting the accused from cross-examining (or further cross-examining) the witness in person.

(3) In determining whether subsection (2)(a) applies in the case of a witness the court must have regard, in particular, to—
    (a) any views expressed by the witness as to whether or not the witness is content to be cross-examined by the accused in person;
    (b) the nature of the questions likely to be asked, having regard to the issues in the proceedings and the defence case advanced so far (if any);
    (c) any behaviour on the part of the accused at any stage of the proceedings, both generally and in relation to the witness;
    (d) any relationship (of whatever nature) between the witness and the accused;
    (e) whether any person (other than the accused) is or has at any time been charged in the proceedings with a sexual offence or an offence to which section 35 applies, and (if so) whether section 34 or 35 operates or would have operated to prevent that person from cross-examining the witness in person;
    (f) any direction under section 19 which the court has given, or proposes to give, in relation to the witness.

(4) For the purposes of this section—
    (a) "witness", in relation to an accused, does not include any other person who is charged with an offence in the proceedings; and
    (b) any reference to the quality of a witness's evidence shall be construed in accordance with section 16(5).

37 Further provisions about directions under section 36

(1) Subject to subsection (2), a direction has binding effect from the time it is made until the witness to whom it applies is discharged.
In this section "direction" means a direction under section 36.

(2) The court may discharge a direction if it appears to the court to be in the interests of justice to do so, and may do so either—
    (a) on an application made by a party to the proceedings, if there has been a material change of circumstances since the relevant time, or
    (b) of its own motion.

(3) In subsection (2) "the relevant time" means—
    (a) the time when the direction was given, or
    (b) if a previous application has been made under that subsection, the time when the application (or last application) was made.

(4) The court must state in open court its reasons for—
    (a) giving, or
    (b) refusing an application for, or for the discharge of, or
    (c) discharging,
a direction and, if it is a magistrates' court, must cause them to be entered in the register of its proceedings.

(5) Rules of court may make provision—
    (a) for uncontested applications to be determined by the court without a hearing;
    (b) for preventing the renewal of an unsuccessful application for a direction except where there has been a material change of circumstances;

(c) for expert evidence to be given in connection with an application for, or for discharging, a direction;

(d) for the manner in which confidential or sensitive information is to be treated in connection with such an application and in particular as to its being disclosed to, or withheld from, a party to the proceedings.

38   Defence representation for purposes of cross-examination

(1) This section applies where an accused is prevented from cross-examining a witness in person by virtue of section 34, 35 or 36.

(2) Where it appears to the court that this section applies, it must—

(a) invite the accused to arrange for a legal representative to act for him for the purpose of cross-examining the witness; and

(b) require the accused to notify the court; by the end of such period as it may specify, whether a legal representative is to act for him for that purpose.

(3) If by the end of the period mentioned in subsection (2)(b) either—

(a) the accused has notified the court that no legal representative is to act for him for the purpose of cross-examining the witness, or

(b) no notification has been received by the court and it appears to the court that no legal representative is to so act,

the court must consider whether it is necessary in the interests of justice for the witness to be cross-examined by a legal representative appointed to represent the interests of the accused.

(4) If the court decides that it is necessary in the interests of justice for the witness to be so cross-examined, the court must appoint a qualified legal representative (chosen by the court) to cross-examine the witness in the interests of the accused.

(5) A person so appointed shall not be responsible to the accused.

(6) Rules of court may make provision—

(a) as to the time when, and the manner in which, subsection (2) is to be complied with;

(b) in connection with the appointment of a legal representative under subsection (4), and in particular for securing that a person so appointed is provided with evidence or other material relating to the proceedings.

(7) Rules of court made in pursuance of subsection (6)(b) may make provision for the application, with such modifications as are specified in the rules, of any of the provisions of—

(a) Part I of the Criminal Procedure and Investigations Act 1996 (disclosure of material in connection with criminal proceedings), or

(b) the Sexual Offences (Protected Material) Act 1997.

(8) For the purposes of this section—

(a) any reference to cross-examination includes (in a case where a direction is given under section 36 after the accused has begun cross-examining the witness) a reference to further cross-examination; and

(b) "qualified legal representative" means a legal representative who has a right of audience (within the meaning of the Courts and Legal Services Act 1990) in relation to the proceedings before the court.

39   Warning to jury

(1) Where on a trial on indictment an accused is prevented from cross-examining a witness in person by virtue of section 34, 35 or 36, the judge must give the jury such warning (if any) as the judge considers necessary to ensure that the accused is not prejudiced—

(a) by any inferences that might be drawn from the fact that the accused has been prevented from cross-examining the witness in person;

(b) where the witness has been cross-examined by a legal representative appointed under section 38(4), by the fact that the cross-examination was carried out by such a legal representative and not by a person acting as the accused's own legal representative.

(2) Subsection (8)(a) of section 38 applies for the purposes of this section as it applies for the purposes of section 38.

40   Funding of defence representation

(1) In section 19(3) of the Prosecution of Offences Act 1985 (regulations authorising payments out of central funds), after paragraph (d) there shall be inserted—

"(e) to cover the proper fee or costs of a legal representative appointed under section 38(4) of the Youth Justice and Criminal Evidence Act 1999 (defence representation for purposes of cross-examination) and any expenses properly incurred in providing such a person with evidence or other material in connection with his appointment."

CHAPTER III

PROTECTION OF COMPLAINANTS IN PROCEEDINGS FOR SEXUAL OFFENCES

41   Restriction on evidence or questions about complainant's sexual history

(1) If at a trial a person is charged with a sexual offence, then, except with the leave of the court—

(a) no evidence may be adduced, and

(b) no question may be asked in cross-examination,

by or on behalf of any accused at the trial, about any sexual behaviour of the complainant.

(2) The court may give leave in relation to any evidence or question only on an application made by or on behalf of an accused, and may not give such leave unless it is satisfied—

(a) that subsection (3) or (5) applies, and

(b) that a refusal of leave might have the result of rendering unsafe a conclusion of the jury or (as the case may be) the court on any relevant issue in the case.

(3) This subsection applies if the evidence or question relates to a relevant issue in the case and either—

(a) that issue is not an issue of consent; or

(b) it is an issue of consent and the sexual behaviour of the complainant to which the evidence or question relates is alleged to have taken place at or about the same time as the event which is the subject matter of the charge against the accused; or

(c) it is an issue of consent and the sexual behaviour of the complainant to which the evidence or question relates is alleged to have been, in any respect, so similar—

(i) to any sexual behaviour of the complainant which (according to evidence adduced or to be adduced by or on behalf of the accused) took place as part of the event which is the subject matter of the charge against the accused, or

(ii) to any other sexual behaviour of the complainant which (according to such evidence) took place at or about the same time as that event,

that the similarity cannot reasonably be explained as a coincidence.

(4) For the purposes of subsection (3) no evidence or question shall be regarded as relating to a relevant issue in the case if it appears to the court to be reasonable to assume that the purpose (or main purpose) for which it would be adduced or asked is to establish or elicit material for impugning the credibility of the complainant as a witness.

(5) This subsection applies if the evidence or question—

(a) relates to any evidence adduced by the prosecution about any sexual behaviour of the complainant; and

(b) in the opinion of the court, would go no further than is necessary to enable the evidence adduced by the prosecution to be rebutted or explained by or on behalf of the accused.

(6) For the purposes of subsections (3) and (5) the evidence or question must relate to a specific instance (or specific instances) of alleged sexual behaviour on the part of the complainant (and accordingly nothing in those subsections is capable of applying in relation to the evidence or question to the extent that it does not so relate).

(7) Where this section applies in relation to a trial by virtue of the fact that one or more of a number of persons charged in the proceedings is or are charged with a sexual offence—

(a) it shall cease to apply in relation to the trial if the prosecutor decides not to proceed with the case against that person or those persons in respect of that charge; but

(b) it shall not cease to do so in the event of that person or those persons pleading guilty to, or being convicted of, that charge.

(8) Nothing in this section authorises any evidence to be adduced or any question to be asked which cannot be adduced or asked apart from this section.

42   Interpretation and application of section 41

(1) In section 41—

(a) "relevant issue in the case" means any issue falling to be proved by the prosecution or defence in the trial of the accused;

(b) "issue of consent" means any issue whether the complainant in fact consented to the conduct constituting the offence with which the accused is charged (and accordingly does not include any issue as to the belief of the accused that the complainant so consented);

(c) "sexual behaviour" means any sexual behaviour or other sexual experience, whether or not involving any accused or other person, but excluding (except in section 41(3)(c)(i) and (5)(a)) anything alleged to have taken place as part of the event which is the subject matter of the charge against the accused; and

(d) subject to any order made under subsection (2), "sexual offence" shall be construed in accordance with section 62.

(2) The Secretary of State may by order make such provision as he considers appropriate for adding or removing, for the purposes of section 41, any offence to or from the offences which are sexual offences for the purposes of this Act by virtue of section 62.

(3) Section 41 applies in relation to the following proceedings as it applies to a trial, namely—

(a) proceedings before a magistrates' court inquiring into an offence as examining justices,

(b) the hearing of an application under paragraph 5(1) of Schedule 6 to the Criminal Justice Act 1991 (application to dismiss charge following notice of transfer of case to Crown Court),

(c) the hearing of an application under paragraph 2(1) of Schedule 3 to the Crime and Disorder Act 1998 (application to dismiss charge by person sent for trial under section 51 of that Act),

(d) any hearing held, between conviction and sentencing, for the purpose of determining matters relevant to the court's decision as to how the accused is to be dealt with, and

(e) the hearing of an appeal,

and references (in section 41 or this section) to a person charged with an offence accordingly include a person convicted of an offence.

43 Procedure on applications under section 41

(1) An application for leave shall be heard in private and in the absence of the complainant.

In this section "leave" means leave under section 41.

(2) Where such an application has been determined, the court must state in open court (but in the absence of the jury, if there is one)—

(a) its reasons for giving, or refusing, leave, and

(b) if it gives leave, the extent to which evidence may be adduced or questions asked in pursuance of the leave,

and, if it is a magistrates' court, must cause those matters to be entered in the register of its proceedings.

(3) Rules of court may make provision—

(a) requiring applications for leave to specify, in relation to each item of evidence or question to which they relate, particulars of the grounds on which it is asserted that leave should be given by virtue of subsection (3) or (5) of section 41;

(b) enabling the court to request a party to the proceedings to provide the court with information which it considers would assist it in determining an application for leave;

(c) for the manner in which confidential or sensitive information is to be treated in connection with such an application, and in particular as to its being disclosed to, or withheld from, parties to the proceedings.

Right to silence/drawing inferences

Criminal Justice and Public Order Act 1994

Inferences from accused's silence

34 Effect of accused's failure to mention facts when questioned or charged

(1) Where, in any proceedings against a person for an offence, evidence is given that the accused—

(a) at any time before he was charged with the offence, on being questioned under caution by a constable trying to discover whether or by whom the offence had been committed, failed to mention any fact relied on in his defence in those proceedings; or

(b) on being charged with the offence or officially informed that he might be prosecuted for it, failed to mention any such fact,

being a fact which in the circumstances existing at the time the accused could reasonably have been expected to mention when so questioned, charged or informed, as the case may be, subsection (2) below applies.

(2) Where this subsection applies—

(a) a magistrates' court, in deciding whether to grant an application for dismissal made by the accused under section 6 of the Magistrates' Courts Act 1980 (application for dismissal of charge in course of proceedings with a view to transfer for trial);

(b) a judge, in deciding whether to grant an application made by the accused under—

(i) section 6 of the Criminal Justice Act 1987 (application for dismissal of charge of serious fraud in respect of which notice of transfer has been given under section 4 of that Act); or

(ii) paragraph 5 of Schedule 6 of the Criminal Justice Act 1991 (application for dismissal of charge of violent or sexual offence involving child in respect of which notice of transfer has been given under section 53 of that Act);

(c) the court, in determining whether there is a case to answer; and

(d) the court or jury, in determining whether the accused is guilty of the offence charged,

may draw such inferences from the failure as appear proper.

(2A) Where the accused was at an authorised place of detention at the time of the failure, subsections (1) and (2) above do not apply if he had not been allowed an opportunity to consult a solicitor prior to being questioned, charged or informed as mentioned in subsection (1) above.

(3) Subject to any directions by the court, evidence tending to establish the failure may be given before or after evidence tending to establish the fact which the accused is alleged to have failed to mention.

(4) This section applies in relation to questioning by persons (other than constables) charged with the duty of investigating offences or charging offenders as it applies in relation to questioning by constables; and in subsection (1) above "officially informed" means informed by a constable or any such person.

(5) This section does not—

(a) prejudice the admissibility in evidence of the silence or other reaction of the accused in the face of anything said in his presence relating to the conduct in respect of which he is charged, in so far as evidence thereof would be admissible apart from this section; or

(b) preclude the drawing of any inference from any such silence or other reaction of the accused which could properly be drawn apart from this section.

(6) This section does not apply in relation to a failure to mention a fact if the failure occurred before the coming into force of the 1997 Order.

35 Effect of accused's silence at trial

(1) At the trial of any person for an offence, subsections (2) and (3) below apply unless—

(a) the accused's guilt is not in issue; or

(b) it appears to the court that the physical or mental condition of the accused makes it undesirable for him to give evidence;

but subsection (2) below does not apply if, at the conclusion of the evidence for the prosecution, his legal representative informs the court that the accused will give evidence or, where he is unrepresented, the court ascertains from him that he will give evidence.

(2) Where this subsection applies, the court shall, at the conclusion of the evidence for the prosecution, satisfy itself (in the case of proceedings on indictment, in the presence of the jury) that the accused is aware that the stage has been reached at which evidence can be given for the defence and that he can, if he wishes, give evidence and that, if he chooses not to give evidence, or having been sworn, without good cause refuses to answer any question, it will be permissible for the court or jury to draw such inferences as appear proper from his failure to give evidence or his refusal, without good cause, to answer any question.

(3) Where this subsection applies, the court or jury, in determining whether the accused is guilty of the offence charged, may draw such inferences as appear proper from the failure of the accused to give evidence or his refusal, without good cause, to answer any question.

(4) This section does not render the accused compellable to give evidence on his own behalf, and he shall accordingly not be guilty of contempt of court by reason of a failure to do so.

(5) For the purposes of this section a person who, having been sworn, refuses to answer any question shall be taken to do so without good cause unless—

(a) he is entitled to refuse to answer the question by virtue of any enactment, when-ever passed or made, or on the ground of privilege; or

(b) the court in the exercise of its general discretion excuses him from answering it.

(7) This section applies—

(a) in relation to proceedings on indictment for an offence, only if the person charged with the offence is arraigned on or after the commencement of this section;

(b) in relation to proceedings in a magistrates' court, only if the time when the court begins to receive evidence in the proceedings falls after the commencement of this section.

36 Effect of accused's failure or refusal to account for objects, substances or marks

(1) Where—

(a) a person is arrested by a constable, and there is—

(i) on his person; or

(ii) in or on his clothing or footwear; or

(iii) otherwise in his possession; or

(iv) in any place in which he is at the time of his arrest,

any object, substance or mark, or there is any mark on any such object; and

(b) that or another constable investigating the case reasonably believes that the presence of the object, substance or mark may be attributable to the participation of the person arrested in the commission of an offence specified by the constable; and

(c) the constable informs the person arrested that he so believes, and requests him to account for the presence of the object, substance or mark; and

(d) the person fails or refuses to do so,

then if, in any proceedings against the person for the offence so specified, evidence of those matters is given, subsection (2) below applies.

(2) Where this subsection applies—

(a) a magistrates' court, inquiring into the offence as examining justices;

(b) a judge, in deciding whether to grant an application made by the accused under—

(i) section 6 of the Criminal Justice Act 1987 (application for dismissal of charge of serious fraud in respect of which notice of transfer has been given under section 4 of that Act); or

(ii) paragraph 5 of Schedule 6 to the Criminal Justice Act 1991 (application for dismissal of charge of violent or sexual offence involving child in respect of which notice of transfer has been given under section 53 of that Act);

(c) the court, in determining whether there is a case to answer; and

(d) the court or jury, in determining whether the accused is guilty of the offence charged,

may draw such inferences from the failure or refusal as appear proper.

(3) Subsections (1) and (2) above apply to the condition of clothing or footwear as they apply to a substance or mark thereon.

(4) Subsections (1) and (2) above do not apply unless the accused was told in ordinary language by the constable when making the request mentioned in subsection (1)(c) above what the effect of this section would be if he failed or refused to comply with the request.

(4A) Where the accused was at an authorised place of detention at the time of the failure or refusal, subsections (1) and (2) above do not apply if he had not been allowed an opportunity to consult a solicitor prior to the request being made.

(5) This section applies in relation to officers of customs and excise as it applies in relation to constables.

(6) This section does not preclude the drawing of any inference from a failure or refusal of the accused to account for the presence of an object, substance or mark or from the condition of clothing or footwear which could properly be drawn apart from this section.

(7) This section does not apply in relation to a failure or refusal which occurred before the commencement of this section.

37 Effect of accused's failure or refusal to account for presence at a particular place

(1) Where—

    (a) a person arrested by a constable was found by him at a place at or about the time the offence for which he was arrested is alleged to have been committed; and

    (b) that or another constable investigating the offence reasonably believes that the presence of the person at that place and at that time may be attributable to his participation in the commission of the offence; and

    (c) the constable informs the person that he so believes, and requests him to account for that presence; and

    (d) the person fails or refuses to do so,

then if, in any proceedings against the person for the offence, evidence of those matters is given, subsection (2) below applies.

(2) Where this subsection applies—

    (a) a magistrates' court, inquiring into the offence as examining justices;

    (b) a judge, in deciding whether to grant an application made by the accused under—

        (i) section 6 of the Criminal Justice Act 1987 (application for dismissal of charge of serious fraud in respect of which notice of transfer has been given under section 4 of that Act); or

        (ii) paragraph 5 of Schedule 6 to the Criminal Justice Act 1991 (application for dismissal of charge of violent or sexual offence involving child in respect of which notice of transfer has been given under section 53 of that Act);

    (c) the court, in determining whether there is a case to answer; and

    (d) the court or jury, in determining whether the accused is guilty of the offence charged,

may draw such inferences from the failure or refusal as appear proper.

(3) Subsections (1) and (2) do not apply unless the accused was told in ordinary language by the constable when making the request mentioned in subsection (1)(c) above what the effect of this section would be if he failed or refused to comply with the request.

(3A) Where the accused was at an authorised place of detention at the time of the failure or refusal, subsections (1) and (2) do not apply if he had not been allowed an opportunity to consult a solicitor prior to the request being made.

(4) This section applies in relation to officers of customs and excise as it applies in relation to constables.

(5) This section does not preclude the drawing of any inference from a failure or refusal of the accused to account for his presence at a place which could properly be drawn apart from this section.

(6) This section does not apply in relation to a failure or refusal which occurred before the commencement of this section.

Youth Justice and Criminal Evidence Act 1999

59   Restriction on use of answers etc. obtained under compulsion
Schedule 3, which amends enactments providing for the use of answers and statements given under compulsion so as to restrict in criminal proceedings their use in evidence against the persons giving them, shall have effect.

Confessions

Police and Criminal Evidence Act 1984

76   Confessions
(1) In any proceedings a confession made by an accused person may be given in evidence against him in so far as it is relevant to any matter in issue in the proceedings and is not excluded by the court in pursuance of this section.

(2) If, in any proceedings where the prosecution proposes to give in evidence a confession made by an accused person, it is represented to the court that the confession was or may have been obtained—

(a) by oppression of the person who made it; or

(b) in consequence of anything said or done which was likely, in the circumstances existing at the time, to render unreliable any confession which might be made by him in consequence thereof,

the court shall not allow the confession to be given in evidence against him except in so far as the prosecution proves to the court beyond reasonable doubt that the confession (notwithstanding that it may be true) was not obtained as aforesaid.

(3) In any proceedings where the prosecution proposes to give in evidence a confession made by an accused person, the court may of its own motion require the prosecution, as a condition of allowing it to do so, to prove that the confession was not obtained as mentioned in subsection (2) above.

(4) The fact that a confession is wholly or partly excluded in pursuance of this section shall not affect the admissibility in evidence—

(a) of any facts discovered as a result of the confession; or

(b) where the confession is relevant as showing that the accused speaks, writes or expresses himself in a particular way, of so much of the confession as is necessary to show that he does so.

(5) Evidence that a fact to which this subsection applies was discovered as a result of a statement made by an accused person shall not be admissible unless evidence of how it was discovered is given by him or on his behalf.

(6) Subsection (5) above applies—

(a) to any fact discovered as a result of a confession which is wholly excluded in pursuance of this section; and

(b) to any fact discovered as a result of a confession which is partly so excluded, if the fact is discovered as a result of the excluded part of the confession.

(7) Nothing in Part VII of this Act shall prejudice the admissibility of a confession made by an accused person.

(8) In this section "oppression" includes torture, inhuman or degrading treatment, and the use or threat of violence (whether or not amounting to torture).

(9) Where the proceedings mentioned in subsection (1) above are proceedings before a magistrates' court inquiring into an offence as examining justices this section shall have effect with the omission of—

(a) in subsection (1) the words "and is not excluded by the court in pursuance of this section", and

(b) subsections (2) to (6) and (8).

77 Confessions by mentally handicapped persons

(1) Without prejudice to the general duty of the court at a trial on indictment to direct the jury on any matter on which it appears to the court appropriate to do so, where at such a trial—

(a) the case against the accused depends wholly or substantially on a confession by him; and

(b) the court is satisfied—

(i) that he is mentally handicapped; and

(ii) that the confession was not made in the presence of an independent person,

the court shall warn the jury that there is special need for caution before convicting the accused in reliance on the confession, and shall explain that the need arises because of the circumstances mentioned in paragraphs (a) and (b) above.

(2) In any case where at the summary trial of a person for an offence it appears to the court that a warning under subsection (1) above would be required if the trial were on indictment, the court shall treat the case as one in which there is a special need for caution before convicting the accused on his confession.

(3) In this section—

"independent person" does not include a police officer or a person employed for, or engaged on, police purposes;

"mentally handicapped", in relation to a person, means that he is in a state of arrested or incomplete development of mind which includes significant impairment of intelligence and social functioning; and

"police purposes" has the meaning assigned to it by section 101(2) of the Police Act 1996.

78 Exclusion of unfair evidence

(1) In any proceedings the court may refuse to allow evidence on which the prosecution proposes to rely to be given if it appears to the court that, having regard to all the circumstances, including the circumstances in which the evidence was obtained, the admission of the evidence would have such an adverse effect on the fairness of the proceedings that the court ought not to admit it.

(2) Nothing in this section shall prejudice any rule of law requiring a court to exclude evidence.

(3) This section shall not apply in the case of proceedings before a magistrates' court inquiring into an offences as examining justices.

PART VIII   SUPPLEMENTARY

82 Part VIII—interpretation

(1) In this Part of this Act—

"confession", includes any statement wholly or partly adverse to the person who made it, whether made to a person in authority or not and whether made in words or otherwise;. . . .

(3) Nothing in this Part of this Act shall prejudice any power of a court to exclude evidence (whether by preventing questions from being put or otherwise) at its discretion.

Jury's ignorance of the defendant's criminal record

Criminal Evidence Act 1898

1   Competency of witnesses in criminal cases

1   Every person charged with an offence, shall be a competent witness for the defence at every stage of the proceedings, whether the person so charged is charged solely or jointly with any other person. Provided as follows:—

(e) A person charged and being a witness in pursuance of this Act in criminal proceedings who is called as a witness in the proceedings may be asked any question in cross-examination notwithstanding that it would tend to criminate him as to any offence with which he is charged in proceedings.

(f) A person charged and called as a witness in pursuance of this Act in criminal proceedings who is called as a witness in the proceedings shall not be asked, and if asked shall not be required to answer, any question tending to show that he has committed or been convicted of or been charged with any offence other than that one with which he is then charged, or is of bad character, unless—

(i)   the proof that he has committed or been convicted of such other offence is admissible evidence to show that he is guilty of the offence with which he is then charged; or

(ii) he has personally or by his advocate asked questions of the witnesses for the prosecution with a view to establish his own good character, or has given evidence of his good character, or the nature or conduct of the defence is such as to involve imputations on the character of the prosecutor or the witnesses or the deceased victim of the alleged crime for the prosecution; or

(iii) he has given evidence against any other person charged in the same proceedings

Theft Act 1968

27   Evidence and procedure on charge of theft or handling stolen goods

(3) Where a person is being proceeded against for handling stolen goods (but not for any offence other than handling stolen goods), then at any stage of the proceedings, if evidence has been given of his having or arranging to have in his possession the goods the subject of the charge, or of his undertaking or assisting in, or arranging to undertake or assist in, their retention, removal, disposal or realisation, the following evidence shall be admissible for the purpose of proving that he knew or believed the goods to be stolen goods:—

(a) evidence that he has had in his possession, or has undertaken or assisted in the retention, removal, disposal or realisation of, stolen goods from any theft taking place not earlier than twelve months before the offence charged; and

(b) (provided that seven days' notice in writing has been given to him of the intention to prove the conviction) evidence that he has within the five years preceding the date of the offence charged been convicted of theft or of handling stolen goods.

Appeals and reviews

Magistrates' Courts Act 1980

108   Right of appeal to the Crown Court

(1) A person convicted by a magistrates' court may appeal to the Crown Court—

(a) if he pleaded guilty, against his sentence;

(b) if he did not, against the conviction or sentence.

(1A) Section 14 of the Powers of Criminal Courts (Sentencing) Act 2000] (under which a conviction of an offence for which an order for conditional or absolute discharge is made is deemed not to be a conviction except for certain purposes) shall not prevent an appeal under this Act, whether against conviction or otherwise.

(2) A person sentenced by a magistrates' court for an offence in respect of which a probation order or an order for conditional discharge has been previously made may appeal to the Crown Court against the sentence.

(3) In this section "sentence" includes any order made on conviction by a magistrates' court, not being—

(b) an order for the payment of costs;

(c) an order under section 2 of the Protection of Animals Act 1911 (which enables a court to order the destruction of an animal); or

(d) an order made in pursuance of any enactment under which the court has no discretion as to the making of the order or its terms, and also includes a declaration under the Football Spectators Act 1989.

111   Statement of case by magistrates' court

(1) Any person who was a party to any proceeding before a magistrates' court or is aggrieved by the conviction, order, determination or other proceeding of the court may question the proceeding on the ground that it is wrong in law or is in excess of jurisdiction by applying to the justices composing the court to state a case for the opinion of the High Court on the question of law or jurisdiction involved; but a person shall not make an application under this section in respect of a decision against which he has a right of appeal to the High Court or which by virtue of any enactment passed after 31st December 1879 is final.

(2) An application under subsection (1) above shall be made within 21 days after the day on which the decision of the magistrates' court was given.

(3) For the purpose of subsection (2) above, the day on which the decision of the magistrates' court is given shall, where the court has adjourned the trial of an information after conviction, be the day on which the court sentences or otherwise deals with the offender.

(4) On the making of an application under this section in respect of a decision any right of the applicant to appeal against the decision to the Crown Court shall cease.

(5) If the justices are of opinion that an application under this section is frivolous, they may refuse to state a case, and, if the applicant so requires, shall give him a certificate stating that the application has been refused; but the justices shall not refuse to state a case if the application is made by or under the direction of the Attorney General.

(6) Where justices refuse to state a case, the High Court may, on the application of the person who applied for the case to be stated, make an order of mandamus requiring the justices to state a case.

Supreme Court Act 1981

48 **Appeals to Crown Court**

(1) The Crown Court may, in the course of hearing any appeal, correct any error or mistake in the order or judgment incorporating the decision which is the subject of the appeal.

(2) On the termination of the hearing of an appeal the Crown Court—

(a) may confirm, reverse or vary the decision appealed against; or

(b) may remit the matter with its opinion thereon to the authority whose decision is appealed against; or

(c) may make such other order in the matter as the court thinks just, and by such order exercise any power which the said authority might have exercised.

(3) Subsection (2) has effect subject to any enactment relating to any such appeal which expressly limits or restricts the powers of the court on the appeal.

(4) Subject to section 11(6) of the Criminal Appeal Act 1995, if the appeal is against a conviction or a sentence, the preceding provisions of this section shall be construed as including power to award any punishment, whether more or less severe than that awarded by the magistrates' court whose decision is appealed against, if that is a punishment which that magistrates' court might have awarded.

(5) This section applies whether or not the appeal is against the whole of the decision.

(6) In this section "sentence" includes any order made by a court when dealing with an offender, including—

(a) a hospital order under Part V of the Mental Health 1959 c. 72. Act 1959, with or without an order restricting discharge; and

(b) a recommendation for deportation made when dealing with an offender.

(7) The fact that an appeal is pending against an interim hospital order under the said Act of 1983 shall not affect the power of the magistrates' court that made it to renew or terminate the order or to deal with the appellant on its termination; and where the Crown Court quashes such an order but does not pass any sentence or make any other order in its place the Court may direct the appellant to be kept in custody or released on bail pending his being dealt with by that magistrates' court.

(8) Where the Crown Court makes an interim hospital order by virtue of subsection (2)—

(a) the power of renewing or terminating the order and of dealing with the appellant on its termination shall be exercisable by the magistrates' court whose decision is appealed against and not by the Crown Court; and

(b) that magistrates' court shall be treated for the purposes of section 38(7) of the said Act of 1983 (absconding offenders) as the court that made the order.

Criminal Appeal Act 1968 (as amended)

2 **Grounds for allowing an appeal under s 1**

[(1) Subject to the provisions of this Act, the Court of Appeal—

(a) shall allow an appeal against conviction if they think that the conviction is unsafe; and

(b) shall dismiss such an appeal in any other case.]

(2) In the case of an appeal against conviction the Court shall, if they allow the appeal, quash the conviction.

(3) An order of the Court of Appeal quashing a conviction shall, except when under section 7 below the appellant is ordered to be retired, operate as a direction to the court of trial to enter, instead of the record of conviction, a judgment and verdict of acquittal.

7 Power to order retrial
(1) Where the Court of Appeal allow an appeal against conviction ... and it appears to the Court that the interests of justice so require, they may order the appellant to be retried.

23 Evidence
(1) For [the purposes of an appeal under] this Part of this Act the Court of Appeal may, if they think it necessary or expedient in the interests of justice—

    (a) order the production of any document, exhibit or other thing connected with the proceedings, the production of which appears to them necessary for the determination of the case;

    (b) order any witness who would have been a compellable witness in the proceedings from which the appeal lies to attend for examination and be examined before the Court, whether or not he was called in those proceedings; and

    [(c) receive any evidence which was not adduced in the proceedings from which the appeal lies.]

[(2) The Court of Appeal shall, in considering whether to receive any evidence, have regard in particular to—

    (a) whether the evidence appears to the Court to be capable of belief;

    (b) whether it appears to the Court that the evidence may afford any ground for allowing the appeal;

    (c) whether the evidence would have been admissible in the proceedings from which the appeal lies on an issue which is the subject of the appeal; and

    (d) whether there is a reasonable explanation for the failure to adduce the evidence in those proceedings.]

(3) Subsection (1)(c) above applies to any [evidence of a] witness (including the appellant) who is competent but not compellable . . .

(4) For [the purposes of an appeal under] this Part of this Act, the Court of Appeal may, if they think it necessary or expedient in the interests of justice, order the examination of any witness whose attendance might be required under subsection (1)(b) above to be conducted, in manner provided by rules of court, before any judge or officer of the Court or other person appointed by the Court for the purpose, and allow the admission of any depositions so taken as evidence before the Court.

[23A Power to order investigations
(1) On an appeal against conviction the Court of Appeal may direct the Criminal Cases Review Commission to investigate and report to the Court on any matter if it appears to the Court that—

    (a) the matter is relevant to the determination of the case and ought, if possible, to be resolved before the case is determined;

    (b) an investigation of the matter by the Commission is likely to result in the Court being able to resolve it; and

    (c) the matter cannot be resolved by the Court without an investigation by the Commission.

(2) A direction by the Court of Appeal under subsection (1) above shall be given in writing and shall specify the matter to be investigated.

(3) Copies of such a direction shall be made available to the appellant and the respondent.

(4) Where the Commission have reported to the Court of Appeal on any matter which they have been directed under subsection (1) above to investigate, the Court—

(a) shall notify the appellant and the respondent that the Commission have reported; and

(b) may make available to the appellant and the respondent the report of the Commission and any statements, opinions and reports which accompanied it.]

33   Right of appeal to House of Lords

(1) An appeal lies to the House of Lords, at the instance of the defendant or the prosecutor, from any decision of the Court of Appeal on an appeal to that court under Part I of this Act [or section 9 (preparatory hearings) of the Criminal Justice Act 1987] [or section 35 of the Criminal Procedure and Investigations Act 1996].

(2) The appeal lies only with the leave of the Court of Appeal or the House of Lords; and leave shall not be granted unless it is certified by the Court of Appeal that a point of law of general public importance is involved in the decision and it appears to the Court of Appeal or the House of Lords (as the case may be) that the point is one which ought to be considered by that House.

[(3) Except as provided by this Part of this Act and section 13 of the Administration of Justice Act 1960 (appeal in cases of contempt of court), no appeal shall lie from any decision of the criminal division of the Court of Appeal.]

Criminal Appeal Act 1995

8   The Commission

(1) There shall be a body corporate to be known as the Criminal Cases Commission.

(2) The Commission shall not be regarded as the servant or agent of the Crown or as enjoying any status, immunity or privilege of the Crown; and the Commission's property shall not be regarded as property of, or held on behalf of, the Crown.

(3) The Commission shall consist of not fewer than eleven members.

(4) The members of the Commission shall be appointed by Her Majesty on the recommendation of the Prime Minister.

(5) At least one third of the members of the Commission shall be persons who are legally qualified; and for this purpose a person is legally qualified if—

(a) he has a ten year general qualification, within the meaning of section 71 of the Courts and Legal Services Act 1990, or

(b) he is a member of the Bar of Northern Ireland, or solicitor of the Supreme Court of Northern Ireland, of at least ten years' standing.

(6) At least two thirds of the members of the Commission shall be persons who appear to the Prime Minister to have knowledge or experience of any aspect of the criminal justice system and of them at least one shall be a person who appears to him to have knowledge or experience of any aspect of the criminal justice system in Northern Ireland; and for the purposes of this subsection the criminal justice system includes, in particular, the investigation of offences and the treatment of offenders.

(7) Schedule 1 (further provisions with respect to the Commission) shall have effect.

13   Conditions for making of references

(1) A reference of a conviction, verdict, finding or sentence shall not be made under any of sections 9 to 12 unless—

(a) the Commission consider that there is a real possibility that the conviction, verdict, finding or sentence would not be upheld were the reference to be made,

   (b) the Commission so consider—

      (i) in the case of a conviction, verdict or finding, because of an argument, or evidence, not raised in the proceedings which led to it or on any appeal or application for leave to appeal against it, or

     (ii) in the case of a sentence, because of an argument on a point of law, or information, not so raised, and

   (b) an appeal against the conviction, verdict, finding or sentence has been determined or leave to appeal against it has been refused.

   (2) Nothing in subsection (1)(b)(i) or (c) shall prevent the making of a reference if it appears to the Commission that there are exceptional circumstances which justify making it.

PART II

Sentencing

(a) DEFERMENT AND POSTPONEMENT OF SENTENCING

Powers of Criminal Courts (Sentencing) Act 2000

DEFERMENT OF SENTENCE

1 Deferment of Sentence

(1) The Crown Court or a magistrates' court may defer passing sentence on an offender for the purpose of enabling the court, or any other court to which it falls to deal with him, to have regard in dealing with him to—

(a) his conduct after conviction (including, where appropriate, the making by him of reparation for his offence); or

(b) any change in his circumstances;

but this is subject to subsections (2) and (3) below.

(2) The power conferred by subsection (1) above shall be exercisable only if—

(a) the offender consents; and

(b) the court is satisfied, having regard to the nature of the offence and the character and circumstances of the offender, that it would be in the interests of justice to exercise the power.

(3) Any deferment under this section shall be until such date as may be specified by the court, not being more than six months after the date on which the deferment is announced by the court; and, subject to section 2(7) below, where the passing of sentence has been deferred under this section it shall not be further so deferred.

(4) Notwithstanding any enactment, a court which under this section defers passing sentence on an offender shall not on the same occasion remand him.

(5) Where the passing of sentence on an offender has been deferred by a court under this section, the court's power under this section to deal with the offender at the end of the period of deferment—

(a) is power to deal with him, in respect of the offence for which passing of sentence has been deferred, in any way in which it could have dealt with him if it had not deferred passing sentence; and

(b) without prejudice to the generality of paragraph (a) above, in the case of a magistrates' court includes the power conferred by section 3 below to commit him to the Crown Court for sentence.

(6) Nothing in this section or section 2 below shall affect—

(a) the power of the Crown Court to bind over an offender to come up for judgment when called upon; or

(b) the power of any court to defer passing sentence for any purpose for which it may lawfully do so apart from this section.

2 Further powers of court where sentence deferred

(1) A court which under section 1 above has deferred passing sentence on an offender may deal with him before the end of the period of deferment if during that period he is convicted in Great Britain of any offence.

(2) Subsection (3) below applies where a court has under section 1 above deferred passing sentence on an offender in respect of one or more offences and during the period of deferment the offender is convicted in England or Wales of any offence ("the later offence").

(3) Where this subsection applies, then (without prejudice to subsection (1) above and whether or not the offender is sentenced for the later offence during the period of deferment), the court which passes sentence on him for the later offence may also, if this has not already been done, deal with him for the offence or offences for which passing of sentence has been deferred, except that—

    (a) the power conferred by this subsection shall not be exercised by a magistrates' court if the court which deferred passing sentence was the Crown Court; and

    (b) the Crown Court, in exercising that power in a case in which the court which deferred passing sentence was a magistrates' court, shall not pass any sentence which could not have been passed by a magistrates' court in exercising that power.

(4) Where—

    (a) a court which under section 1 above has deferred passing sentence on an offender proposes to deal with him, whether on the date originally specified by the court or by virtue of subsection (1) above before that date, or

    (b) the offender does not appear on the date so specified,

the court may issue a summons requiring him to appear before the court, or may issue a warrant for his arrest.

(5) In deferring the passing of sentence under section 1 above a magistrates' court shall be regarded as exercising the power of adjourning the trial conferred by section 10(1) of the Magistrates' Courts Act 1980, and accordingly sections 11(1) and 13(1) to (3A) and (5) of that Act (non-appearance of the accused) apply (without prejudice to subsection (4) above) if the offender does not appear on the date specified under section 1(3) above.

(6) Any power of a court under this section to deal with an offender in a case where the passing of sentence has been deferred under section 1 above—

    (a) is power to deal with him, in respect of the offence for which passing of sentence has been deferred, in any way in which the court which deferred passing sentence could have dealt with him; and

    (b) without prejudice to the generality of paragraph (a) above, in the case of a magistrates' court includes the power conferred by section 3 below to commit him to the Crown Court for sentence.

(7) Where—

    (a) the passing of sentence on an offender in respect of one or more offences has been deferred under section 1 above, and

    (b) a magistrates' court deals with him in respect of the offence or any of the offences by committing him to the Crown Court under section 3 below,

the power of the Crown Court to deal with him includes the same power to defer passing sentence on him as if he had just been convicted of the offence or offences on indictment before the court.

COMMITTAL TO CROWN COURT FOR SENTENCE

3 Committal for sentence on summary trial of offence triable either way

(1) Subject to subsection (4) below, this section applies where on the summary trial of an offence triable either way a person aged 18 or over is convicted of the offence.

(2) If the court is of the opinion—

    (a) that the offence or the combination of the offence and one or more offences associated with it was so serious that greater punishment should be inflicted for the offence than the court has power to impose, or

    (b) in the case of a violent or sexual offence, that a custodial sentence for a term longer than the court has power to impose is necessary to protect the public from serious harm from him,

the court may commit the offender in custody or on bail to the Crown Court for sentence in accordance with section 5(1) below.

(3) Where the court commits a person under subsection (2) above, section 6 below (which enables a magistrates' court, where it commits a person under this section in respect of an offence, also to commit him to the Crown Court to be dealt with in respect of certain other offences) shall apply accordingly.

(4) This section does not apply in relation to an offence as regards which this section is excluded by section 33 of the Magistrates' Courts Act 1980 (certain offences where value involved is small).

(5) The preceding provisions of this section shall apply in relation to a corporation as if—

    (a) the corporation were an individual aged 18 or over; and

    (b) in subsection (2) above, paragraph (b) and the words "in custody or on bail" were omitted.

4 Committal for sentence on indication of guilty plea to offence triable either way

(1) This section applies where—

    (a) a person aged 18 or over appears or is brought before a magistrates' court ("the court") on an information charging him with an offence triable either way ("the offence");

    (b) he or his representative indicates that he would plead guilty if the offence were to proceed to trial; and

    (c) proceeding as if section 9(1) of the Magistrates' Courts Act 1980 were complied with and he pleaded guilty under it, the court convicts him of the offence.

(2) If the court has committed the offender to the Crown Court for trial for one or more related offences, that is to say, one or more offences which, in its opinion, are related to the offence, it may commit him in custody or on bail to the Crown Court to be dealt with in respect of the offence in accordance with section 5(1) below.

(3) If the power conferred by subsection (2) above is not exercisable but the court is still to inquire, as examining justices, into one or more related offences—

    (a) it shall adjourn the proceedings relating to the offence until after the conclusion of its inquiries; and

    (b) if it commits the offender to the Crown Court for trial for one or more related offences, it may then exercise that power.

(4) Where the court—

    (a) under subsection (2) above commits the offender to the Crown Court to be dealt with in respect of the offence, and

    (b) does not state that, in its opinion, it also has power so to commit him under section 3(2) above,

section 5(1) below shall not apply unless he is convicted before the Crown Court of one or more of the related offences.

(5) Where section 5(1) below does not apply, the Crown Court may deal with the offender in respect of the offence in any way in which the magistrates' court could deal with him if it had just convicted him of the offence.

(6) Where the court commits a person under subsection (2) above, section 6 below (which enables a magistrates' court, where it commits a person under this section in respect of an offence, also to commit him to the Crown Court to be dealt with in respect of certain other offences) shall apply accordingly.

(7) For the purposes of this section one offence is related to another if, were they both to be prosecuted on indictment, the charges for them could be joined in the same indictment.

5   Power of Crown Court on committal for sentence under sections 3 and 4

(1) Where an offender is committed by a magistrates' court for sentence under section 3 or 4 above, the Crown Court shall inquire into the circumstances of the case and may deal with the offender in any way in which it could deal with him if he had just been convicted of the offence on indictment before the court.

(2) In relation to committals under section 4 above, subsection (1) above has effect subject to section 4(4) and (5) above.

6   Committal for sentence in certain cases where offender committed in respect of another offence

(1) This section applies where a magistrates' court ("the committing court") commits a person in custody or on bail to the Crown Court under any enactment mentioned in subsection (4) below to be sentenced or otherwise dealt with in respect of an offence ("the relevant offence").

(2) Where this section applies and the relevant offence is an indictable offence, the committing court may also commit the offender, in custody or on bail as the case may require, to the Crown Court to be dealt with in respect of any other offence whatsoever in respect of which the committing court has power to deal with him (being an offence of which he has been convicted by that or any other court).

(3) Where this section applies and the relevant offence is a summary offence, the committing court may commit the offender, in custody or on bail as the case may require, to the Crown Court to be dealt with in respect of—

  (a) any other offence of which the committing court has convicted him, being either—
    (i) an offence punishable with imprisonment; or
    (ii) an offence in respect of which the committing court has a power or duty to order him to be disqualified under section 34, 35 or 36 of the Road Traffic Offenders Act 1988 (disqualification for certain motoring offences); or
  (b) any suspended sentence in respect of which the committing court has under section 120(1) below power to deal with him.

(4) The enactments referred to in subsection (1) above are—

  (a) the Vagrancy Act 1824 (incorrigible rogues);
  (b) sections 3 and 4 above (committal for sentence for offences triable either way);
  (c) section 13(5) below (conditionally discharged person convicted of further offence);
  (d) section 116(3)(b) below (offender convicted of offence committed during currency of original sentence); and
  (e) section 120(2) below (offender convicted during operational period of suspended sentence).

7   Power of Crown Court on committal for sentence under section 6

(1) Where under section 6 above a magistrates' court commits a person to be dealt with by the Crown Court in respect of an offence, the Crown Court may after inquiring into the circumstances of the case deal with him in any way in which the magistrates' court could deal with him if it had just convicted him of the offence.

(2) Subsection (1) above does not apply where under section 6 above a magistrates' court commits a person to be dealt with by the Crown Court in respect of a suspended sentence, but

in such a case the powers under section 119 below (power of court to deal with suspended sentence) shall be exercisable by the Crown Court.

(3) Without prejudice to subsections (1) and (2) above, where under section 6 above or any enactment mentioned in subsection (4) of that section a magistrates' court commits a person to be dealt with by the Crown Court, any duty or power which, apart from this subsection, would fall to be discharged or exercised by the magistrates' court shall not be discharged or exercised by that court but shall instead be discharged or may instead be exercised by the Crown Court.

(4) Where under section 6 above a magistrates' court commits a person to be dealt with by the Crown Court in respect of an offence triable only on indictment in the case of an adult (being an offence which was tried summarily because of the offender's being under 18 years of age), the Crown Court's powers under subsection (1) above in respect of the offender after he attains the age of 18 shall be powers to do either or both of the following—

    (a) to impose a fine not exceeding £5,000;

    (b) to deal with the offender in respect of the offence in any way in which the magistrates' court could deal with him if it had just convicted him of an offence punishable with imprisonment for a term not exceeding six months.

REMISSION FOR SENTENCE: YOUNG OFFENDERS ETC.

8 Power and duty to remit young offenders to youth courts for sentence

(1) Subsection (2) below applies where a child or young person (that is to say, any person aged under 18) is convicted by or before any court of an offence other than homicide.

(2) The court may and, if it is not a youth court, shall unless satisfied that it would be undesirable to do so, remit the case—

    (a) if the offender was committed for trial or sent to the Crown Court for trial under section 51 of the Crime and Disorder Act 1998, to a youth court acting for the place where he was committed for trial or sent to the Crown Court for trial;

    (b) in any other case, to a youth court acting either for the same place as the remitting court or for the place where the offender habitually resides;

but in relation to a magistrates' court other than a youth court this subsection has effect subject to subsection (6) below.

(3) Where a case is remitted under subsection (2) above, the offender shall be brought before a youth court accordingly, and that court may deal with him in any way in which it might have dealt with him if he had been tried and convicted by that court.

(4) A court by which an order remitting a case to a youth court is made under subsection (2) above—

    (a) may, subject to section 25 of the Criminal Justice and Public Order Act 1994 (restrictions on granting bail), give such directions as appear to be necessary with respect to the custody of the offender or for his release on bail until he can be brought before the youth court; and

    (b) shall cause to be transmitted to the justices' chief executive for the youth court a certificate setting out the nature of the offence and stating—

        (i) that the offender has been convicted of the offence; and

        (ii) that the case has been remitted for the purpose of being dealt with under the preceding provisions of this section.

(5) Where a case is remitted under subsection (2) above, the offender shall have no right of appeal against the order of remission, but shall have the same right of appeal against any order of the court to which the case is remitted as if he had been convicted by that court.

(6) Without prejudice to the power to remit any case to a youth court which is conferred on a magistrates' court other than a youth court by subsections (1) and (2) above, where such a magistrates' court convicts a child or young person of an offence it must exercise that power unless the case falls within subsection (7) or (8) below.

(7) The case falls within this subsection if the court would, were it not so to remit the case, be required by section 16(2) below to refer the offender to a youth offender panel (in which event the court may, but need not, so remit the case).

(8) The case falls within this subsection if it does not fall within subsection (7) above but the court is of the opinion that the case is one which can properly be dealt with by means of—

    (a) an order discharging the offender absolutely or conditionally, or

    (b) an order for the payment of a fine, or

    (c) an order (under section 150 below) requiring the offender's parent or guardian to enter into a recognizance to take proper care of him and exercise proper control over him,

with or without any other order that the court has power to make when absolutely or conditionally discharging an offender.

(9) In subsection (8) above "care" and "control" shall be construed in accordance with section 150(11) below.

(10) A document purporting to be a copy of an order made by a court under this section shall, if it purports to be certified as a true copy by the justices' chief executive for the court, be evidence of the order.

9 Power of youth court to remit offender who attains age of 18 to magistrates' court other than youth court for sentence

(1) Where a person who appears or is brought before a youth court charged with an offence subsequently attains the age of 18, the youth court may, at any time after conviction and before sentence, remit him for sentence to a magistrates' court (other than a youth court) acting for the same petty sessions area as the youth court.

(2) Where an offender is remitted under subsection (1) above, the youth court shall adjourn proceedings in relation to the offence, and—

    (a) section 128 of the Magistrates' Courts Act 1980 (remand in custody or on bail) and all other enactments, whenever passed, relating to remand or the granting of bail in criminal proceedings shall have effect, in relation to the youth court's power or duty to remand the offender on that adjournment, as if any reference to the court to or before which the person remanded is to be brought or appear after remand were a reference to the court to which he is being remitted; and

    (b) subject to subsection (3) below, the court to which the offender is remitted ("the other court") may deal with the case in any way in which it would have power to deal with it if all proceedings relating to the offence which took place before the youth court had taken place before the other court.

(3) Where an offender is remitted under subsection (1) above, section 8(6) above (duty of adult magistrates' court to remit young offenders to youth court for sentence) shall not apply to the court to which he is remitted.

(4) Where an offender is remitted under subsection (1) above he shall have no right of appeal against the order of remission (but without prejudice to any right of appeal against an order made in respect of the offence by the court to which he is remitted).

(5) In this section—

    (a) "enactment" includes an enactment contained in any order, regulation or other instrument having effect by virtue of an Act; and

    (b) "bail in criminal proceedings" has the same meaning as in the Bail Act 1976.

10   Power of magistrates' court to remit case to another magistrates' court for sentence

(1) Where a person aged 18 or over ("the offender") has been convicted by a magistrates' court ("the convicting court") of an offence to which this section applies ("the instant offence") and—

   (a) it appears to the convicting court that some other magistrates' court ("the other court") has convicted him of another such offence in respect of which the other court has neither passed sentence on him nor committed him to the Crown Court for sentence nor dealt with him in any other way, and

   (b) the other court consents to his being remitted under this section to the other court,

the convicting court may remit him to the other court to be dealt with in respect of the instant offence by the other court instead of by the convicting court.

(2) This section applies to—

   (a) any offence punishable with imprisonment; and

   (b) any offence in respect of which the convicting court has a power or duty to order the offender to be disqualified under section 34, 35 or 36 of the Road Traffic Offenders Act 1988 (disqualification for certain motoring offences).

(3) Where the convicting court remits the offender to the other court under this section, it shall adjourn the trial of the information charging him with the instant offence, and—

   (a) section 128 of the Magistrates' Courts Act 1980 (remand in custody or on bail) and all other enactments, whenever passed, relating to remand or the granting of bail in criminal proceedings shall have effect, in relation to the convicting court's power or duty to remand the offender on that adjournment, as if any reference to the court to or before which the person remanded is to be brought or appear after remand were a reference to the court to which he is being remitted; and

   (b) subject to subsection (7) below, the other court may deal with the case in any way in which it would have power to deal with it if all proceedings relating to the instant offence which took place before the convicting court had taken place before the other court.

(4) The power conferred on the other court by subsection (3)(b) above includes, where applicable, the power to remit the offender under this section to another magistrates' court in respect of the instant offence.

(5) Where the convicting court has remitted the offender under this section to the other court, the other court may remit him back to the convicting court; and the provisions of subsections (3) and (4) above (so far as applicable) shall apply with the necessary modifications in relation to any remission under this subsection.

(6) The offender, if remitted under this section, shall have no right of appeal against the order of remission (but without prejudice to any right of appeal against any other order made in respect of the instant offence by the court to which he is remitted).

(7) Nothing in this section shall preclude the convicting court from making any order which it has power to make under section 148 below (restitution orders) by virtue of the offender's conviction of the instant offence.

(8) In this section—

   (a) "conviction" includes a finding under section 11(1) below (remand for medical examination) that the person in question did the act or made the omission charged, and "convicted" shall be construed accordingly;

   (b) "enactment" includes an enactment contained in any order, regulation or other instrument having effect by virtue of an Act; and

   (c) "bail in criminal proceedings" has the same meaning as in the Bail Act 1976.

REMAND BY MAGISTRATES' COURT FOR MEDICAL EXAMINATION

11   Remand by magistrates' court for medical examination
(1) If, on the trial by a magistrates' court of an offence punishable on summary conviction with imprisonment, the court—

(a) is satisfied that the accused did the act or made the omission charged, but

(b) is of the opinion that an inquiry ought to be made into his physical or mental condition before the method of dealing with him is determined,

the court shall adjourn the case to enable a medical examination and report to be made, and shall remand him.

(2) An adjournment under subsection (1) above shall not be for more than three weeks at a time where the court remands the accused in custody, nor for more than four weeks at a time where it remands him on bail.

(3) Where on an adjournment under subsection (1) above the accused is remanded on bail, the court shall impose conditions under paragraph (d) of section 3(6) of the Bail Act 1976 and the requirements imposed as conditions under that paragraph shall be or shall include requirements that the accused—

(a) undergo medical examination by a registered medical practitioner or, where the inquiry is into his mental condition and the court so directs, two such practitioners; and

(b) for that purpose attend such an institution or place, or on such practitioner, as the court directs and, where the inquiry is into his mental condition, comply with any other directions which may be given to him for that purpose by any person specified by the court or by a person of any class so specified.

(b) CUSTODIAL SENTENCING

General provisions

Powers of Criminal Courts (Sentencing) Act 2000

76   Meaning of "custodial sentence"
(1) In this Act "custodial sentence" means—

(a) a sentence of imprisonment (as to which, see section 89(1)(a) below);

(b) a sentence of detention under section 90 or 91 below;

(c) a sentence of custody for life under section 93 or 94 below;

(d) a sentence of detention in a young offender institution (under section 96 below or otherwise); or

(e) a detention and training order (under section 100 below).

(2) In subsection (1) above "sentence of imprisonment" does not include a committal for contempt of court or any kindred offence.

77   Liability to imprisonment on conviction on indictment
Where a person is convicted on indictment of an offence against any enactment and is for that offence liable to be sentenced to imprisonment, but the sentence is not by any enactment

either limited to a specified term or expressed to extend to imprisonment for life, the person so convicted shall be liable to imprisonment for not more than two years.

78   General limit on magistrates' court's power to impose imprisonment or detention in a young offender institution

(1) A magistrates' court shall not have power to impose imprisonment, or detention in a young offender institution, for more than six months in respect of any one offence.

(2) Unless expressly excluded, subsection (1) above shall apply even if the offence in question is one for which a person would otherwise be liable on summary conviction to imprisonment or detention in a young offender institution for more than six months.

(3) Subsection (1) above is without prejudice to section 133 of the Magistrates' Courts Act 1980 (consecutive terms of imprisonment).

(4) Any power of a magistrates' court to impose a term of imprisonment for non-payment of a fine, or for want of sufficient distress to satisfy a fine, shall not be limited by virtue of subsection (1) above.

(5) In subsection (4) above "fine" includes a pecuniary penalty but does not include a pecuniary forfeiture or pecuniary compensation.

(6) In this section "impose imprisonment" means pass a sentence of imprisonment or fix a term of imprisonment for failure to pay any sum of money, or for want of sufficient distress to satisfy any sum of money, or for failure to do or abstain from doing anything required to be done or left undone.

79   General restrictions on discretionary custodial sentences

(1) This section applies where a person is convicted of an offence punishable with a custodial sentence other than one—

    (a) fixed by law; or

    (b) falling to be imposed under section 109(2), 110(2) or 111(2) below.

(2) Subject to subsection (3) below, the court shall not pass a custodial sentence on the offender unless it is of the opinion—

    (a) that the offence, or the combination of the offence and one or more offences associated with it, was so serious that only such a sentence can be justified for the offence; or

    (b) where the offence is a violent or sexual offence, that only such a sentence would be adequate to protect the public from serious harm from him.

(3) Nothing in subsection (2) above shall prevent the court from passing a custodial sentence on the offender if he fails to express his willingness to comply with—

    (a) a requirement which is proposed by the court to be included in a probation order or supervision order and which requires an expression of such willingness; or

    (b) a requirement which is proposed by the court to be included in a drug treatment and testing order or an order under section 52(4) above (order to provide samples).

(4) Where a court passes a custodial sentence, it shall—

    (a) in a case not falling within subsection (3) above, state in open court that it is of the opinion that either or both of paragraphs (a) and (b) of subsection (2) above apply and why it is of that opinion; and

    (b) in any case, explain to the offender in open court and in ordinary language why it is passing a custodial sentence on him.

(5) A magistrates' court shall cause a reason stated by it under subsection (4) above to be specified in the warrant of commitment and to be entered in the register.

80   Length of discretionary custodial sentences: general provision

(1) This section applies where a court passes a custodial sentence other than one fixed by law or falling to be imposed under section 109(2) below.

(2) Subject to sections 110(2) and 111(2) below, the custodial sentence shall be—

    (a) for such term (not exceeding the permitted maximum) as in the opinion of the court is commensurate with the seriousness of the offence, or the combination of the offence and one or more offences associated with it; or

    (b) where the offence is a violent or sexual offence, for such longer term (not exceeding that maximum) as in the opinion of the court is necessary to protect the public from serious harm from the offender.

(3) Where the court passes a custodial sentence for a term longer than is commensurate with the seriousness of the offence, or the combination of the offence and one or more offences associated with it, the court shall—

    (a) state in open court that it is of the opinion that subsection (2)(b) above applies and why it is of that opinion; and

    (b) explain to the offender in open court and in ordinary language why the sentence is for such a term.

(4) A custodial sentence for an indeterminate period shall be regarded for the purposes of subsections (2) and (3) above as a custodial sentence for a term longer than any actual term.

(5) Subsection (3) above shall not apply in any case where the court passes a custodial sentence falling to be imposed under subsection (2) of section 110 or 111 below which is for the minimum term specified in that subsection.

81   Pre-sentence reports and other requirements

(1) Subject to subsection (2) below, a court shall obtain and consider a pre-sentence report before forming any such opinion as is mentioned in subsection (2) of section 79 or 80 above.

(2) Subsection (1) above does not apply if, in the circumstances of the case, the court is of the opinion that it is unnecessary to obtain a pre-sentence report.

(3) In a case where the offender is aged under 18 and the offence is not triable only on indictment and there is no other offence associated with it that is triable only on indictment, the court shall not form such an opinion as is mentioned in subsection (2) above unless—

    (a) there exists a previous pre-sentence report obtained in respect of the offender; and

    (b) the court has had regard to the information contained in that report, or, if there is more than one such report, the most recent report.

(4) In forming any such opinion as is mentioned in subsection (2) of section 79 or 80 above, a court—

    (a) shall take into account all such information as is available to it about the circumstances of the offence or (as the case may be) of the offence and the offence or offences associated with it, including any aggravating or mitigating factors; and

    (b) in the case of any such opinion as is mentioned in paragraph (b) of that subsection, may take into account any information about the offender which is before it.

(5) No custodial sentence shall be invalidated by the failure of a court to obtain and consider a pre-sentence report before forming an opinion referred to in subsection (1) above, but any court on an appeal against such a sentence—

    (a) shall, subject to subsection (6) below, obtain a pre-sentence report if none was obtained by the court below; and

    (b) shall consider any such report obtained by it or by that court.

(6) Subsection (5)(a) above does not apply if the court is of the opinion—

    (a) that the court below was justified in forming an opinion that it was unnecessary to obtain a pre-sentence report; or

    (b) that, although the court below was not justified in forming that opinion, in the circumstances of the case at the time it is before the court, it is unnecessary to obtain a pre-sentence report.

(7) In a case where the offender is aged under 18 and the offence is not triable only on indictment and there is no other offence associated with it that is triable only on indictment, the court shall not form such an opinion as is mentioned in subsection (6) above unless—

(a) there exists a previous pre-sentence report obtained in respect of the offender; and

(b) the court has had regard to the information contained in that report, or, if there is more than one such report, the most recent report.

(8) Section 156 below (disclosure of pre-sentence report to offender etc.) applies to any pre-sentence report obtained in pursuance of this section.

82A   Life sentences

(1) This section applies if a court passes a life sentence in circumstances where—

(a) the sentence is not fixed by law; or

(b) the offender was aged under 18 when he committed the offence.

(2) The court shall, unless it makes an order under subsection (4) below, order that the provisions of section 28(5) to (8) of the Crime (Sentences) Act 1997 (referred to in this section as the "early release provisions") shall apply to the offender as soon as he has served the part of his sentence which is specified in the order.

(3) The part of his sentence shall be such as the court considers appropriate taking into account—

(a) the seriousness of the offence, or of the combination of the offence and one or more offences associated with it;

(b) the effect of any direction which it would have given under section 87 below (crediting periods of remand in custody) if it had sentenced him to a term of imprisonment; and

(c) the early release provisions as compared with sections 33(2) and 35(1) of the Criminal Justice Act 1991.

(4) If the court is of the opinion that, because of the seriousness of the offence or of the combination of the offence and one or more offences associated with it, no order should be made under subsection (2) above, the court shall order that, subject to subsection (5) below, the early release provisions shall not apply to the offender.

(5) If, in a case where an order under subsection (4) above is in force, the offender was aged under 18 when he committed the offence, the Secretary of State shall at the appropriate stage direct that the early release provisions shall apply to the offender as soon as he has served the part of his sentence which is specified in the direction.

(6) The appropriate stage, for the purposes of subsection (5) above, is when the Secretary of State has formed the opinion, having regard to any factors determined by him to be relevant for the purpose, that it is appropriate for him to give the direction.

(7) In this section—

"court" includes a court-martial;

"life sentence" has the same meaning as in Chapter II of Part II of the Crime (Sentences) Act 1997.

83   Restriction on imposing custodial sentences on persons not legally represented

(1) A magistrates' court on summary conviction, or the Crown Court on committal for sentence or on conviction on indictment, shall not pass a sentence of imprisonment on a person who—

(a) is not legally represented in that court, and

(b) has not been previously sentenced to that punishment by a court in any part of the United Kingdom,

unless he is a person to whom subsection (3) below applies.

(2) A magistrates' court on summary conviction, or the Crown Court on committal for sentence or on conviction on indictment, shall not—

    (a) pass a sentence of detention under section 90 or 91 below,

    (b) pass a sentence of custody for life under section 93 or 94 below,

    (c) pass a sentence of detention in a young offender institution, or

    (d) make a detention and training order,

on or in respect of a person who is not legally represented in that court unless he is a person to whom subsection (3) below applies.

(3) This subsection applies to a person if either—

    (a) he was granted a right to representation funded by the Legal Services Commission as part of the Criminal Defence Service but the right was withdrawn because of his conduct; or

    (b) having been informed of his right to apply for such representation and having had the opportunity to do so, he refused or failed to apply.

(4) For the purposes of this section a person is to be treated as legally represented in a court if, but only if, he has the assistance of counsel or a solicitor to represent him in the proceedings in that court at some time after he is found guilty and before he is sentenced.

(5) For the purposes of subsection (1)(b) above a previous sentence of imprisonment which has been suspended and which has not taken effect under section 119 below or under section 19 of the Treatment of Offenders Act (Northern Ireland) 1968 shall be disregarded.

(6) In this section "sentence of imprisonment" does not include a committal for contempt of court or any kindred offence.

84   Restriction on consecutive sentences for released prisoners

(1) A court sentencing a person to a term of imprisonment shall not order or direct that the term shall commence on the expiry of any other sentence of imprisonment from which he has been released under Part II of the Criminal Justice Act 1991 (early release of prisoners).

(2) Expressions used in this section shall be construed as if they were contained in that Part.

(3) Without prejudice to the generality of subsection (2) above, any reference in this section to imprisonment shall be construed in accordance with section 43 (young offenders) and section 45 (fine defaulters and contemnors) of that Act.

85   Sexual or violent offences: extension of certain custodial sentences for licence purposes

(1) This section applies where a court—

    (a) proposes to impose a custodial sentence for a sexual or violent offence committed on or after 30th September 1998; and

    (b) considers that the period (if any) for which the offender would, apart from this section, be subject to a licence would not be adequate for the purpose of preventing the commission by him of further offences and securing his rehabilitation.

(2) Subject to subsections (3) to (5) below, the court may pass on the offender an extended sentence, that is to say, a custodial sentence the term of which is equal to the aggregate of—

    (a) the term of the custodial sentence that the court would have imposed if it had passed a custodial sentence otherwise than under this section ("the custodial term"); and

    (b) a further period ("the extension period") for which the offender is to be subject to a licence and which is of such length as the court considers necessary for the purpose mentioned in subsection (1) above.

(3) Where the offence is a violent offence, the court shall not pass an extended sentence the custodial term of which is less than four years.

(4) The extension period shall not exceed—
   (a) ten years in the case of a sexual offence; and
   (b) five years in the case of a violent offence.

(5) The term of an extended sentence passed in respect of an offence shall not exceed the maximum term permitted for that offence.

(6) Subsection (2) of section 80 above (length of discretionary custodial sentences) shall apply as if the term of an extended sentence did not include the extension period.

(7) The Secretary of State may by order amend paragraph (b) of subsection (4) above by substituting a different period, not exceeding ten years, for the period for the time being specified in that paragraph.

(8) In this section "licence" means a licence under Part II of the Criminal Justice Act 1991 (early release of prisoners).

Criminal Justice Act 1967 (as amended)

67   Effect of time spent in custody on remand on length of sentence

(1) The length of any sentence of imprisonment imposed on an offender by a court shall be treated as reduced by any relevant period, but where he was previously subject to a probation order, a community service order, an order for conditional discharge or a suspended sentence in respect of that offence, any such period falling before the order was made or suspended sentence passed shall be disregarded for the purposes of this section.

(1A) In subsection (1) above 'relevant period' means—
   (a) any period during which the offender was in police detention in connection with the offence for which the sentence was passed; or
   (b) any period during which he was in custody—
      (i) by reason only of having been committed to custody by an order of a court made in connection with any proceedings relating to that sentence or the offence for which it was passed or any proceedings from which those proceedings arose; or
      (ii) by reason of his having been so committed and having been concurrently detained otherwise than by order of a court; or
   (c) any period during which, in connection with the offence for which the sentence was passed, he was remanded or committed to local authority accommodation by virtue of an order under section 23 of the Children and Young Persons Act 1969 or section 37 of the Magistrates' Courts Act 1980 and in accommodation provided for the purpose of restricting liberty.

(2) For the purposes of this section a suspended sentence shall be treated as a sentence of imprisonment when it takes effect under section 119 of the Powers of Criminal Courts (Sentencing) Act 2000 and as being imposed by the order under which it takes effect.

Editors' note: Sections 87 & 88 of the **Powers of Criminal Courts (Sentencing) Act 2000** reproduced here in italics, will, at some point, replace section 67 of the Criminal Justice Act 1967.

87   Crediting of periods of remand in custody

(1) This section applies where—
   (a) a court sentences an offender to imprisonment for a term in respect of an offence committed after the commencement of this section; and
   (b) the offender has been remanded in custody (within the meaning given by section 88 below) in connection with the offence or a related offence, that is to say, any other offence the charge for which was founded on the same facts or evidence.

(2) It is immaterial for that purpose whether the offender—
- *(a) has also been remanded in custody in connection with other offences; or*
- *(b) has also been detained in connection with other matters.*

(3) Subject to subsection (4) below, the court shall direct that the number of days for which the offender was remanded in custody in connection with the offence or a related offence shall count as time served by him as part of the sentence.

(4) Subsection (3) above shall not apply if and to the extent that—
- *(a) rules made by the Secretary of State so provide in the case of—*
  - *(i) a remand in custody which is wholly or partly concurrent with a sentence of imprisonment; or*
  - *(ii) sentences of imprisonment for consecutive terms or for terms which are wholly or partly concurrent; or*
- *(b) it is in the opinion of the court just in all the circumstances not to give a direction under that subsection.*

(5) Where the court gives a direction under subsection (3) above, it shall state in open court—
- *(a) the number of days for which the offender was remanded in custody; and*
- *(b) the number of days in relation to which the direction is given.*

(6) Where the court does not give a direction under subsection (3) above, or gives such a direction in relation to a number of days less than that for which the offender was remanded in custody, it shall state in open court—
- *(a) that its decision is in accordance with rules made under paragraph (a) of subsection (4) above; or*
- *(b) that it is of the opinion mentioned in paragraph (b) of that subsection and what the circumstances are.*

88   Meaning of "remand in custody"

(1) References in section 87 above to an offender's being remanded in custody are references to his being—
- *(a) held in police detention;*
- *(b) remanded in or committed to custody by an order of a court;*
- *(c) remanded or committed to local authority accommodation under section 23 of the Children and Young Persons Act 1969 and placed and kept in secure accommodation; or*
- *(d) remanded, admitted or removed to hospital under section 35, 36, 38 or 48 of the Mental Health Act 1983.*

(2) A person is in police detention for the purposes of subsection (1) above–
- *(a) at any time when he is in police detention for the purposes of the Police and Criminal Evidence Act 1984; and*
- *(b) at any time when he is detained under section 14 of the Prevention of Terrorism (Temporary Provisions) Act 1989.*

Powers of Criminal Courts (Sentencing) Act 2000

89   Restriction on imposing imprisonment on persons under 21

(1) Subject to subsection (2) below, no court shall—
- (a) pass a sentence of imprisonment on a person for an offence if he is aged under 21 when convicted of the offence; or
- (b) commit a person aged under 21 to prison for any reason.

(2) Nothing in subsection (1) above shall prevent the committal to prison of a person aged under 21 who is—
- (a) remanded in custody;

(b) committed in custody for trial or sentence; or

(c) sent in custody for trial under section 51 of the Crime and Disorder Act 1998.

90 Offenders who commit murder etc. when under 18: duty to detain at Her Majesty's pleasure

Where a person convicted of murder or any other offence the sentence for which is fixed by law as life imprisonment appears to the court to have been aged under 18 at the time the offence was committed, the court shall (notwithstanding anything in this or any other Act) sentence him to be detained during Her Majesty's pleasure.

91 Offenders under 18 convicted of certain serious offences: power to detain for specified period

(1) Subsection (3) below applies where a person aged under 18 is convicted on indictment of—

(a) an offence punishable in the case of a person aged 21 or over with imprisonment for 14 years or more, not being an offence the sentence for which is fixed by law; or

(b) an offence under section 14 of the Sexual Offences Act 1956 (indecent assault on a woman); or

(c) an offence under section 15 of that Act (indecent assault on a man) committed after 30th September 1997.

(2) Subsection (3) below also applies where a person aged at least 14 but under 18 is convicted of an offence under—

(a) section 1 of the Road Traffic Act 1988 (causing death by dangerous driving); or

(b) section 3A of that Act (causing death by careless driving while under influence of drink or drugs).

(3) If the court is of the opinion that none of the other methods in which the case may legally be dealt with is suitable, the court may sentence the offender to be detained for such period, not exceeding the maximum term of imprisonment with which the offence is punishable in the case of a person aged 21 or over, as may be specified in the sentence.

92 Detention under sections 90 and 91: place of detention etc

(1) A person sentenced to be detained under section 90 or 91 above shall be liable to be detained in such place and under such conditions—

(a) as the Secretary of State may direct; or

(b) as the Secretary of State may arrange with any person.

(2) A person detained pursuant to the directions or arrangements made by the Secretary of State under this section shall be deemed to be in legal custody.

93 Duty to impose custody for life in certain cases where offender under 21

Where a person aged under 21 is convicted of murder or any other offence the sentence for which is fixed by law as imprisonment for life, the court shall sentence him to custody for life unless he is liable to be detained under section 90 above.

94 Power to impose custody for life in certain other cases where offender at least 18 but under 21

(1) Where a person aged at least 18 but under 21 is convicted of an offence—

(a) for which the sentence is not fixed by law, but

(b) for which a person aged 21 or over would be liable to imprisonment for life,

the court shall, if it considers that a sentence for life would be appropriate, sentence him to custody for life.

95 Custody for life: place of detention

(1) Subject to section 22(2)(b) of the Prison Act 1952 (removal to hospital etc.), an offender sentenced to custody for life shall be detained in a young offender institution unless a direction under subsection (2) below is in force in relation to him.

(2) The Secretary of State may from time to time direct that an offender sentenced to custody for life shall be detained in a prison or remand centre instead of a young offender institution.

96 Detention in a young offender institution for other cases where offender at least 18 but under 21

Subject to sections 90, 93 and 94 above, where—

(a) a person aged at least 18 but under 21 is convicted of an offence which is punishable with imprisonment in the case of a person aged 21 or over, and

(b) the court is of the opinion that either or both of paragraphs (a) and (b) of section 79(2) above apply or the case falls within section 79(3),

the sentence that the court is to pass is a sentence of detention in a young offender institution.

97 Term of detention in a young offender institution, and consecutive sentences

(1) The maximum term of detention in a young offender institution that a court may impose for an offence is the same as the maximum term of imprisonment that it may impose for that offence.

(2) Subject to subsection (3) below, a court shall not pass a sentence for an offender's detention in a young offender institution for less than 21 days.

(3) A court may pass a sentence of detention in a young offender institution for less than 21 days for an offence under section 65(6) of the Criminal Justice Act 1991 (breach of requirement imposed on young offender on his release from detention).

(4) Where—

(a) an offender is convicted of more than one offence for which he is liable to a sentence of detention in a young offender institution, or

(b) an offender who is serving a sentence of detention in a young offender institution is convicted of one or more further offences for which he is liable to such a sentence,

the court shall have the same power to pass consecutive sentences of detention in a young offender institution as if they were sentences of imprisonment.

(5) Subject to section 84 above (restriction on consecutive sentences for released prisoners), where an offender who—

(a) is serving a sentence of detention in a young offender institution, and

(b) is aged 21 or over,

is convicted of one or more further offences for which he is liable to imprisonment, the court shall have the power to pass one or more sentences of imprisonment to run consecutively upon the sentence of detention in a young offender institution.

100 Offenders under 18: detention and training orders

(1) Subject to sections 90, 91 and 93 above and subsection (2) below, where—

(a) a child or young person (that is to say, any person aged under 18) is convicted of an offence which is punishable with imprisonment in the case of a person aged 21 or over, and

(b) the court is of the opinion that either or both of paragraphs (a) and (b) of section 79(2) above apply or the case falls within section 79(3),

the sentence that the court is to pass is a detention and training order.

(2) A court shall not make a detention and training order—

(a) in the case of an offender under the age of 15 at the time of the conviction, unless it is of the opinion that he is a persistent offender;

(b) in the case of an offender under the age of 12 at that time, unless—

(i) it is of the opinion that only a custodial sentence would be adequate to protect the public from further offending by him; and

(ii) the offence was committed on or after such date as the Secretary of State may be order appoint.

101   Term of order, consecutive terms and taking account of remands

(1) Subject to subsection (2) below, the term of a detention and training order made in respect of an offence (whether by a magistrates' court or otherwise) shall be 4, 6, 8, 10, 12, 18 or 24 months.

(2) The term of a detention and training order may not exceed the maximum term of imprisonment that the Crown Court could (in the case of an offender aged 21 or over) impose for the offence.

(3) Subject to subsections (4) and (6) below, a court making a detention and training order may order that its term shall commence on the expiry of the term of any other detention and training order made by that or any other court.

(4) A court shall not make in respect of an offender a detention and training order the effect of which would be that he would be subject to detention and training orders for a term which exceeds 24 months.

(5) Where the term of the detention and training orders to which an offender would otherwise be subject exceeds 24 months, the excess shall be treated as remitted.

(6) A court making a detention and training order shall not order that its term shall commence on the expiry of the term of a detention and training order under which the period of supervision has already begun (under section 103(1) below).

(7) Where a detention and training order ("the new order") is made in respect of an offender who is subject to a detention and training order under which the period of supervision has begun ("the old order"), the old order shall be disregarded in determining—

(a) for the purposes of subsection (4) above whether the effect of the new order would be that the offender would be subject to detention and training orders for a term which exceeds 24 months; and

(b) for the purposes of subsection (5) above whether the term of the detention and training orders to which the offender would (apart from that subsection) be subject exceeds 24 months.

(8) In determining the term of a detention and training order for an offence, the court shall take account of any period for which the offender has been remanded in custody in connection with the offence, or any other offence the charge for which was founded on the same facts or evidence.

(9) Where a court proposes to make detention and training orders in respect of an offender for two or more offences—

(a) subsection (8) above shall not apply; but

(b) in determining the total term of the detention and training orders it proposes to make in respect of the offender, the court shall take account of the total period (if any) for which he has been remanded in custody in connection with any of those offences, or any other offence the charge for which was founded on the same facts or evidence.

102   The period of detention and training

(1) An offender shall serve the period of detention and training under a detention and training order in such secure accommodation as may be determined by the Secretary of State or by such other person as may be authorised by him for that purpose.

(2) Subject to subsections (3) to (5) below, the period of detention and training under a detention and training order shall be one-half of the term of the order.

(3) The Secretary of State may at any time release the offender if he is satisfied that exceptional circumstances exist which justify the offender's release on compassionate grounds.

(4) The Secretary of State may release the offender—

(a) in the case of an order for a term of 8 months or more but less than 18 months, one month before the half-way point of the term of the order; and

(b) in the case of an order for a term of 18 months or more, one month or two months before that point.

(5) If a youth court so orders on an application made by the Secretary of State for the purpose, the Secretary of State shall release the offender—

    (a) in the case of an order for a term of 8 months or more but less than 18 months, one month after the half-way point of the term of the order; and

    (b) in the case of an order for a term of 18 months or more, one month or two months after that point.

103 The period of supervision

(1) The period of supervision of an offender who is subject to a detention and training order—

    (a) shall begin with the offender's release, whether at the half-way point of the term of the order or otherwise; and

    (b) subject to subsection (2) below, shall end when the term of the order ends.

(2) The Secretary of State may by order provide that the period of supervision shall end at such point during the term of a detention and training order as may be specified in the order under this subsection.

(3) During the period of supervision, the offender shall be under the supervision of—

    (a) a probation officer;

    (b) a social worker of a local authority social services department; or

    (c) a member of a youth offending team;

and the category of person to supervise the offender shall be determined from time to time by the Secretary of State.

104 Breach of supervision requirements

(1) Where a detention and training order is in force in respect of an offender and it appears on information to a justice of the peace acting for a relevant petty sessions area that the offender has failed to comply with requirements under section 103(6)(b) above, the justice—

    (a) may issue a summons requiring the offender to appear at the place and time specified in the summons before a youth court acting for the area; or

    (b) if the information is in writing and on oath, may issue a warrant for the offender's arrest requiring him to be brought before such a court.

(3) If it is proved to the satisfaction of the youth court before which an offender appears or is brought under this section that he has failed to comply with requirements under section 103(6)(b) above, that court may—

    (a) order the offender to be detained, in such secure accommodation as the Secretary of State may determine, for such period, not exceeding the shorter of three months or the remainder of the term of the detention and training order, as the court may specify; or

    (b) impose on the offender a fine not exceeding level 3 on the standard scale.

105 Offences during currency of order

(1) This section applies to a person subject to a detention and training order if—

    (a) after his release and before the date on which the term of the order ends, he commits an offence punishable with imprisonment in the case of a person aged 21 or over ("the new offence"); and

    (b) whether before or after that date, he is convicted of the new offence.

(2) Subject to section 8(6) above (duty of adult magistrates' court to remit young offenders to youth court for sentence), the court by or before which a person to whom this section applies is convicted of the new offence may, whether or not it passes any other

sentence on him, order him to be detained in such secure accommodation as the Secretary of State may determine for the whole or any part of the period which—

(a) begins with the date of the court's order; and

(b) is equal in length to the period between the date on which the new offence was committed and the date mentioned in subsection (1) above.

(3) The period for which a person to whom this section applies is ordered under subsection (2) above to be detained in secure accommodation—

(a) shall, as the court may direct, either be served before and be followed by, or be served concurrently with, any sentence imposed for the new offence; and

(b) in either case, shall be disregarded in determining the appropriate length of that sentence.

106   Interaction with sentences of detention in a young offender institution

(1) Where a court passes a sentence of detention in a young offender institution in the case of an offender who is subject to a detention and training order, the sentence shall take effect as follows—

(a) if the offender has been released by virtue of subsection (2), (3), (4) or (5) of section 102 above, at the beginning of the day on which it is passed;

(b) if not, either as mentioned in paragraph (a) above or, if the court so orders, at the time when the offender would otherwise be released by virtue of subsection (2), (3), (4) or (5) of section 102.

(2) Where a court makes a detention and training order in the case of an offender who is subject to a sentence of detention in a young offender institution, the order shall take effect as follows—

(a) if the offender has been released under Part II of the Criminal Justice Act 1991 (early release of prisoners), at the beginning of the day on which it is made;

(b) if not, either as mentioned in paragraph (a) above or, if the court so orders, at the time when the offender would otherwise be released under that Part.

107   Meaning of "secure accommodation" and references to terms

(1) In sections 102, 104 and 105 above "secure accommodation" means—

(a) a secure training centre;

(b) a young offender institution;

(c) accommodation provided by a local authority for the purpose of restricting the liberty of children and young persons;

(d) accommodation provided for that purpose under subsection (5) of section 82 of the Children Act 1989 (financial support by the Secretary of State); or

(e) such other accommodation provided for the purpose of restricting liberty as the Secretary of State may direct.

108   Detention of persons aged at least 18 but under 21 for default or contempt

(1) In any case where, but for section 89(1) above, a court would have power—

(a) to commit a person aged at least 18 but under 21 to prison for default in payment of a fine or any other sum of money, or

(b) to make an order fixing a term of imprisonment in the event of such a default by such a person, or

(c) to commit such a person to prison for contempt of court or any kindred offence,

the court shall have power, subject to subsection (3) below, to commit him to be detained under this section or, as the case may be, to make an order fixing a term of detention under this section in the event of default, for a term not exceeding the term of imprisonment.

(3) No court shall commit a person to be detained under this section unless it is of the opinion that no other method of dealing with him is appropriate; and in forming any such opinion, the court—

    (a) shall take into account all such information about the circumstances of the default or contempt (including any aggravating or mitigating factors) as is available to it; and

    (b) may take into account any information about that person which is before it.

(4) Where a magistrates' court commits a person to be detained under this section, it shall—

    (a) state in open court the reason for its opinion that no other method of dealing with him is appropriate; and

    (b) cause that reason to be specified in the warrant of commitment and to be entered in the register.

(5) Subject to section 22(2)(b) of the Prison Act 1952 (removal to hospital etc.), a person in respect of whom an order has been made under this section is to be detained—

    (a) in a remand centre,

    (b) in a young offender institution, or

    (c) in any place in which a person aged 21 or over could be imprisoned or detained for default in payment of a fine or any other sum of money,

as the Secretary of State may from time to time direct.

109 Life sentence for second serious offence

(1) This section applies where—

    (a) a person is convicted of a serious offence committed after 30th September 1997; and

    (b) at the time when that offence was committed, he was 18 or over and had been convicted in any part of the United Kingdom of another serious offence.

(2) The court shall impose a life sentence, that is to say—

    (a) where the offender is 21 or over when convicted of the offence mentioned in subsection (1)(a) above, a sentence of imprisonment for life,

    (b) where he is under 21 at that time, a sentence of custody for life under section 94 above,

unless the court is of the opinion that there are exceptional circumstances relating to either of the offences or to the offender which justify its not doing so.

(3) Where the court does not impose a life sentence, it shall state in open court that it is of that opinion and what the exceptional circumstances are.

(5) An offence committed in England and Wales is a serious offence for the purposes of this section if it is any of the following, namely—

    (a) an attempt to commit murder, a conspiracy to commit murder or an incitement to murder;

    (b) an offence under section 4 of the Offences Against the Person Act 1861 (soliciting murder);

    (c) manslaughter;

    (d) an offence under section 18 of the Offences Against the Person Act 1861 (wounding, or causing grievous bodily harm, with intent);

    (e) rape or an attempt to commit rape;

    (f) an offence under section 5 of the Sexual Offences Act 1956 (intercourse with a girl under 13);

    (g) an offence under section 16 (possession of a firearm with intent to injure), section 17 (use of a firearm to resist arrest) or section 18 (carrying a firearm with criminal intent) of the Firearms Act 1968; and

    (h) robbery where, at some time during the commission of the offence, the offender had in his possession a firearm or imitation firearm within the meaning of that Act.

110   Minimum of seven years for third class A drug trafficking offence

(1) This section applies where—

    (a) a person is convicted of a class A drug trafficking offence committed after 30th September 1997;

    (b) at the time when that offence was committed, he was 18 or over and had been convicted in any part of the United Kingdom of two other class A drug trafficking offences; and

    (c) one of those other offences was committed after he had been convicted of the other.

(2) The court shall impose an appropriate custodial sentence for a term of at least seven years except where the court is of the opinion that there are particular circumstances which—

    (a) relate to any of the offences or to the offender; and

    (b) would make it unjust to do so in all the circumstances.

(3) Where the court does not impose such a sentence, it shall state in open court that it is of that opinion and what the particular circumstances are.

(4) Where—

    (a) a person is charged with a class A drug trafficking offence (which, apart from this subsection, would be triable either way), and

    (b) the circumstances are such that, if he were convicted of the offence, he could be sentenced for it under subsection (2) above,

the offence shall be triable only on indictment.

(5) In this section "class A drug trafficking offence" means a drug trafficking offence committed in respect of a class A drug; and for this purpose–

"class A drug" has the same meaning as in the Misuse of Drugs Act 1971;

"drug trafficking offence" means a drug trafficking offence within the meaning of the Drug Trafficking Act 1994, the Proceeds of Crime (Scotland) Act 1995 or the Proceeds of Crime (Northern Ireland) Order 1996.

111   Minimum of three years for third domestic burglary

(1) This section applies where—

    (a) a person is convicted of a domestic burglary committed after 30th November 1999;

    (b) at the time when that burglary was committed, he was 18 or over and had been convicted in England and Wales of two other domestic burglaries; and

    (c) one of those other burglaries was committed after he had been convicted of the other, and both of them were committed after 30th November 1999.

(2) The court shall impose an appropriate custodial sentence for a term of at least three years except where the court is of the opinion that there are particular circumstances which—

    (a) relate to any of the offences or to the offender; and

    (b) would make it unjust to do so in all the circumstances.

(3) Where the court does not impose such a sentence, it shall state in open court that it is of that opinion and what the particular circumstances are.

(4) Where—

    (a) a person is charged with a domestic burglary which, apart from this subsection, would be triable either way, and

    (b) the circumstances are such that, if he were convicted of the burglary, he could be sentenced for it under subsection (2) above,

the burglary shall be triable only on indictment.

(6) In this section "an appropriate custodial sentence" means—

    (a) in relation to a person who is 21 or over when convicted of the offence mentioned in subsection (1)(a) above, a sentence of imprisonment;

    (b) in relation to a person who is under 21 at that time, a sentence of detention in a young offender institution.

116   Power to order return to prison etc where offence committed during original sentence
   (1) This section applies to a person if—
      (a) he has been serving a determinate sentence of imprisonment which he began serving on or after 1st October 1992;
      (b) he is released under Part II of the Criminal Justice Act 1991 (early release of prisoners);
      (c) before the date on which he would (but for his release) have served his sentence in full, he commits an offence punishable with imprisonment ("the new offence"); and
      (d) whether before or after that date, he is convicted of the new offence.
   (2) Subject to subsection (3) below, the court by or before which a person to whom this section applies is convicted of the new offence may, whether or not it passes any other sentence on him, order him to be returned to prison for the whole or any part of the period which—
      (a) begins with the date of the order; and
      (b) is equal in length to the period between the date on which the new offence was committed and the date mentioned in subsection (1)(c) above.
   (3) A magistrates' court—
      (a) shall not have power to order a person to whom this section applies to be returned to prison for a period of more than six months; but
      (b) subject to section 25 of the Criminal Justice and Public Order Act 1994 (restrictions on granting bail), may commit him in custody or on bail to the Crown Court to be dealt with under subsection (4) below.
   (4) Where a person is committed to the Crown Court under subsection (3) above, the Crown Court may order him to be returned to prison for the whole or any part of the period which—
      (a) begins with the date of the order; and
      (b) is equal in length to the period between the date on which the new offence was committed and the date mentioned in subsection (1)(c) above.
   (10) This section and section 117 below apply to persons serving—
      (a) determinate sentences of detention under section 91 above, or
      (b) sentences of detention in a young offender institution,
as they apply to persons serving equivalent sentences of imprisonment; and references in this section and section 117 to imprisonment or prison shall be construed accordingly.

117   Treatment for purposes of section 116(1) of person serving two or more sentences or extended sentence
   (1) For the purposes of any reference in section 116(1) above (however expressed) to the term of imprisonment to which a person has been sentenced, consecutive terms and terms which are wholly or partly concurrent shall be treated as a single term if—
      (a) the sentences were passed on the same occasion; or
      (b) where they were passed on different occasions, the person has not been released under Part II of the Criminal Justice Act 1991 at any time during the period beginning with the first and ending with the last of those occasions; but this is subject to subsection (4) below.
   (2) Where a suspended sentence of imprisonment is ordered to take effect, with or without any variation of the original term, the occasion on which that order is made shall be treated for the purposes of subsection (1) above as the occasion on which the sentence is passed.
   (3) Where a person has been sentenced to two or more terms of imprisonment which are wholly or partly concurrent and do not fall to be treated as a single term, the date mentioned

in section 116(1)(c) above shall be taken to be that on which he would (but for his release) have served each of the sentences in full.

(4) Subsections (1) to (3) above apply only where one or more of the sentences concerned were passed on or after 30th September 1998; but where, by virtue of section 51(2) of the Criminal Justice Act 1991 as enacted, the terms of two or more sentences passed before 30th September 1998 have been treated as a single term for the purposes of Part II of that Act, they shall be treated as a single term for the purposes of section 116(1) above.

161   Interpretation
(2) In this Act, "sexual offence" means any of the following—
- (a) an offence under the Sexual Offences Act 1956, other than an offence under section 30, 31 or 33 to 36 of that Act;
- (b) an offence under section 128 of the Mental Health Act 1959;
- (c) an offence under the Indecency with Children Act 1960;
- (d) an offence under section 9 of the Theft Act 1968 of burglary with intent to commit rape;
- (e) an offence under section 54 of the Criminal Law Act 1977;
- (f) an offence under the Protection of Children Act 1978;
- (g) an offence under section 1 of the Criminal Law Act 1977 of conspiracy to commit any of the offences in paragraphs (a) to (f) above;
- (h) an offence under section 1 of the Criminal Attempts Act 1981 of attempting to commit any of those offences;
- (i) an offence of inciting another to commit any of those offences.

(3) In this Act, "violent offence" means an offence which leads, or is intended or likely to lead, to a person's death or to physical injury to a person, and includes an offence which is required to be charged as arson (whether or not it would otherwise fall within this definition).

Magistrates' Courts Act 1980

31   General limit on power of magistrates' court to impose imprisonment
(1) Without prejudice to section 133 below, a magistrates' court shall not have power to impose imprisonment for more than 6 months in respect of any one offence.

(2) Unless expressly excluded, subsection (1) above shall apply even if the offence in question is one for which a person would otherwise be liable on summary conviction to imprisonment for more than 6 months.

(3) Any power of a magistrates' court to impose a term of imprisonment for non-payment of a fine, or for want of sufficient distress to satisfy a fine, shall not be limited by virtue of subsection (1) above.

(4) In subsection (3) above "fine" includes a pecuniary penalty but does not include a pecuniary forfeiture or pecuniary compensation.

32   Penalties on summary conviction for offences triable either way
(1) On summary conviction of any of the offences triable either way listed in Schedule 1 to this Act a person shall be liable to imprisonment for a term not exceeding 6 months or to a fine not exceeding the prescribed sum or both, except that—
- (a) a magistrates' court shall not have power to impose imprisonment for an offence so listed if the Crown Court would not have that power in the case of an adult convicted of it on indictment;
- (b) on summary conviction of an offence consisting in the incitement to commit an offence triable either way a person shall not be liable to on summary conviction of the last-mentioned offence; and

    (c) on summary conviction of attempting to commit an offence triable either way a person shall not be liable to any greater penalty than he would be liable to on summary conviction of the completed offence.

(2) For any offence triable either way which is not listed in Schedule 1 to this Act, being an offence under a relevant enactment, the maximum fine which may be imposed on summary conviction shall by virtue of this subsection be the prescribed sum unless the offence is one for which by virtue of an enactment other than this subsection a larger fine may be imposed on summary conviction.

(3) Where, by virtue of any relevant enactment, a person summarily convicted of an offence triable either way would, apart from this section, be liable to a maximum fine of one amount in the case of a first conviction and of a different amount in the case of a second or subsequent conviction, subsection (2) above shall apply irrespective of whether the conviction is a first, second or subsequent one.

(4) Subsection (2) above shall not affect so much of any enactment as (in whatever words) makes a person liable on summary conviction to a fine not exceeding a specified amount for each day on which a continuing offence is continued after conviction or the occurrence of any other specified event.

(5) Subsection (2) above shall not apply on summary conviction of any of the following offences:—

    (a) offences under section 5 (2) of the Misuse of Drugs Act 1971 (having possession of a controlled drug) where the controlled drug in relation to which the offence was committed was a Class B or Class C drug;

    (b) offences under the following provisions of that Act, where the controlled drug in relation to which the offence was committed was a Class C drug, namely—

        (i) section 4 (2) (production, or being concerned in the production, of a controlled drug);

        (ii) section 4 (3) (supplying or offering a controlled drug or being concerned in the doing of either activity by another);

        (iii) section 5 (3) (having possession of a controlled drug with intent to supply it to another);

        (iv) section 8 (being the occupier, or concerned in the management, of premises and permitting or suffering certain activities to take place there);

        (v) section 12 (6) (contravention of direction prohibiting practitioner etc. from possessing, supplying etc. controlled drugs); or

        (vi) section 13 (3) (contravention of direction prohibiting practitioner etc. from prescribing, supplying etc. controlled drugs).

(9) In this section—

"fine" includes a pecuniary penalty but does not include a pecuniary forfeiture or pecuniary compensation;

"the prescribed sum" means £1,000 or such sum as is for the time being substituted in this definition by an order in force under section 143 (1) below;

"relevant enactment" means an enactment contained in the Criminal Law Act 1977 or in any Act passed before, or in the same Session as, that Act.

Murder (Abolition of Death Penalty) Act 1965 (as amended)

1 Abolition of death penalty for murder
(1) No person shall suffer death for murder, and a person convicted of murder shall be sentenced to imprisonment for life.

(2) On sentencing any person convicted of murder to imprisonment for life the Court may at the same time declare the period which it recommends to the Secretary of State as the minimum period which in its view should elapse before the Secretary of State orders the release of that person on licence under section 27 of the Prison Act, 1952, or section 21 of the Prisons (Scotland) Act, 1952.

Crime (Sentences) Act 1997

29 Power to release other life prisoners

(1) If recommended to do so by the Parole Board, the Secretary of State may, after consultation with the Lord Chief Justice together with the trial judge if available, release on licence a life prisoner who is not one to whom section 28 above applies.

(2) The Parole Board shall not make a recommendation under subsection (1) above unless the Secretary of State has referred the particular case, or the class of case to which that case belongs, to the Board for its advice.

Suspended sentences of imprisonment

Powers of Criminal Courts (Sentencing) Act 2000

118 Suspended sentences of imprisonment

(1) A court which passes a sentence of imprisonment for a term of not more than two years for an offence may (subject to subsection (4) below) order that the sentence shall not take effect unless, during a period specified in the order, the offender commits in Great Britain another offence punishable with imprisonment and thereafter a court having power to do so orders under section 119 below that the original sentence shall take effect.

(2) The period specified in an order under subsection (1) above must be a period of not less than one year nor more than two years beginning with the date of the order.

(3) In this Act—

"suspended sentence" means a sentence to which an order under subsection (1) above relates; and

"operational period", in relation to such a sentence, means the period specified in the order under subsection (1).

(4) A court shall not deal with an offender by means of a suspended sentence unless it is of the opinion—

   (a) that the case is one in which a sentence of imprisonment would have been appropriate even without the power to suspend the sentence; and

   (b) that the exercise of that power can be justified by the exceptional circumstances of the case.

(5) A court which passes a suspended sentence on any person for an offence shall consider whether the circumstances of the case are such as to warrant in addition the imposition of a fine or the making of a compensation order.

(6) A court which passes a suspended sentence on any person for an offence shall not impose a community sentence in his case in respect of that offence or any other offence of which he is convicted by or before the court or for which he is dealt with by the court.

(7) On passing a suspended sentence the court shall explain to the offender in ordinary language his liability under section 119 below if during the operational period he commits an offence punishable with imprisonment.

119   Power of court on conviction of further offence to deal with suspended sentence

(1) Where an offender is convicted of an offence punishable with imprisonment committed during the operational period of a suspended sentence and either he is so convicted by or before a court having power under section 120 below to deal with him in respect of the suspended sentence or he subsequently appears or is brought before such a court, then, unless the sentence has already taken effect, that court shall consider his case and deal with him by one of the following methods—

 (a) the court may order that the suspended sentence shall take effect with the original term unaltered;

 (b) the court may order that the sentence shall take effect with the substitution of a lesser term for the original term;

 (c) the court may by order vary the original order under section 118(1) above by substituting for the period specified in that order a period ending not later than two years from the date of the variation; or

 (d) the court may make no order with respect to the suspended sentence.

(2) The court shall make an order under paragraph (a) of subsection (1) above unless it is of the opinion that it would be unjust to do so in view of all the circumstances, including the facts of the subsequent offence; and where it is of that opinion that court shall state its reasons.

(3) Where a court orders that a suspended sentence shall take effect, with or without any variation of the original term, the court may order that that sentence shall take effect immediately or that the term of that sentence shall commence on the expiry of another term of imprisonment passed on the offender by that or another court.

(4) The power to make an order under subsection (3) above has effect subject to section 84 above (restriction on consecutive sentences for released prisoners).

120   Court by which suspended sentence may be dealt with

(1) An offender may be dealt with in respect of a suspended sentence by the Crown Court or, where the sentence was passed by a magistrates' court, by any magistrates' court before which he appears or is brought.

(2) Where an offender is convicted by a magistrates' court of an offence punishable with imprisonment and the court is satisfied that the offence was committed during the operational period of a suspended sentence passed by the Crown Court—

 (a) the court may, if it thinks fit, commit him in custody or on bail to the Crown Court; and

 (b) if it does not, shall give written notice of the conviction to the appropriate officer of the Crown Court.

121   Procedure where court convicting of further offence does not deal with suspended sentence

(1) If it appears to the Crown Court, where that court has jurisdiction in accordance with subsection (2) below, or to a justice of the peace having jurisdiction in accordance with that subsection—

 (a) that an offender has been convicted in Great Britain of an offence punishable with imprisonment committed during the operational period of a suspended sentence, and

 (b) that he has not been dealt with in respect of the suspended sentence, that court or justice may, subject to the following provisions of this section, issue a summons requiring the offender to appear at the place and time specified in it, or a warrant for his arrest.

(2) Jurisdiction for the purposes of subsection (1) above may be exercised—

(a) if the suspended sentence was passed by the Crown Court, by that court;

(b) if it was passed by a magistrates' court, by a justice acting for the area for which that court acted.

Suspended sentence supervision orders

---

122 Suspended sentence supervision orders

(1) Where a court passes on an offender a suspended sentence for a term of more than six months for a single offence, the court may make a suspended sentence supervision order, that is to say, an order placing the offender under the supervision of a supervising officer for a period which is specified in the order and does not exceed the operational period of the suspended sentence.

(2) A suspended sentence supervision order shall specify the petty sessions area in which the offender resides or will reside; and the supervising officer shall be a probation officer appointed for or assigned to the area for the time being specified in the order (whether under this subsection or by virtue of section 124(3) below (power to amend order)).

(3) An offender in respect of whom a suspended sentence supervision order is in force shall keep in touch with the supervising officer in accordance with such instructions as he may from time to time be given by that officer and shall notify him of any change of address.

(4) On making a suspended sentence supervision order, the court shall explain its effect to the offender in ordinary language.

(7) The Secretary of State may by order—

(a) direct that subsection (1) above be amended by substituting, for the number of months specified in that subsection as originally enacted or as previously amended under this paragraph, such other number (not more than six) as the order may specify; or

(b) make in that subsection the repeals necessary to enable a court to make a suspended sentence supervision order in the case of any suspended sentence, whatever the length of the term.

(8) Where under section 119 above a court deals with an offender in respect of a suspended sentence by varying the operational period of the sentence or by making no order with respect to the sentence, the court may make a suspended sentence supervision order in respect of the offender—

(a) in place of any such order made when the suspended sentence was passed; or

(b) if the court which passed the sentence could have made such an order but did not do so; or

(c) if that court could not then have made such an order but would have had power to do so if subsection (1) above had then had effect as it has effect at the time when the offender is dealt with under section 119.

123 Breach of requirement of suspended sentence supervision order

(1) If, at any time while a suspended sentence supervision order is in force in respect of an offender, it appears on information to a justice of the peace acting for the petty sessions area for the time being specified in the order that the offender has failed to comply with any of the requirements of section 122(3) above, the justice may—

    (a) issue a summons requiring the offender to appear at the place and time specified in it; or

    (b) if the information is in writing and on oath, issue a warrant for his arrest.

(2) Any summons or warrant issued under this section shall direct the offender to appear or be brought before a magistrates' court acting for the petty sessions area for the time being specified in the suspended sentence supervision order.

(3) If it is proved to the satisfaction of the court before which an offender appears or is brought under this section that he has failed without reasonable cause to comply with any of the requirements of section 122(3) above, the court may, without prejudice to the continuance of the order, impose on him a fine not exceeding £1000.

(4) A fine imposed under subsection (3) above shall be deemed, for the purposes of any enactment, to be a sum adjudged to be paid by a conviction.

124 Suspended sentence supervision orders: revocation, amendment and cessation

(1) A suspended sentence supervision order may be revoked on the application of the supervising officer or the offender—

    (a) if it was made by the Crown Court and includes a direction reserving the power of revoking it to that court, by the Crown Court;

    (b) in any other case, by a magistrates' court acting for the petty sessions area for the time being specified in the order.

(2) Where a suspended sentence supervision order has been made on appeal, for the purposes of subsection (1) above it shall be deemed—

    (a) if it was made on an appeal brought from a magistrates' court, to have been made by that magistrates' court;

    (b) if it was made on an appeal brought from the Crown Court or from the criminal division of the Court of Appeal, to have been made by the Crown Court.

(3) If a magistrates' court acting for the petty sessions area for the time being specified in a suspended sentence supervision order is satisfied that the offender proposes to change, or has changed, his residence from that petty sessions area to another petty sessions area, the court may, and on the application of the supervising officer shall, amend the order by substituting the other petty sessions area for the area specified in the order.

(4) Where a suspended sentence supervision order is amended by a court under subsection (3) above, the court shall send to the justices' chief executive for the new area specified in the order a copy of the order, together with such documents and information relating to the case as it considers likely to be of assistance to a court acting for that area in the exercise of its functions in relation to the order.

(5) A suspended sentence supervision order shall cease to have effect if before the end of the period specified in it—

    (a) a court orders under section 119 above that a suspended sentence passed in the proceedings in which the order was made shall have effect; or

    (b) the order is revoked under subsection (1) above or replaced under section 122(8) above.

125 Suspended sentences: supplementary

(1) For the purposes of any reference in this Chapter, however expressed, to the term of imprisonment to which a person has been sentenced, consecutive terms and terms which are wholly or partly concurrent shall, unless the context otherwise requires, be treated as a single term.

(c) SEX OFFENDERS

Notification requirements for sex offenders

Sex Offenders Act 1997

1 Sex offenders subject to notification requirements

(1) A person becomes subject to the notification requirements of this Part if, after the commencement of this Part—

- (a) he is convicted of a sexual offence to which this Part applies;
- (b) he is found not guilty of such an offence by reason of insanity, or to be under a disability and to have done the act charged against him in respect of such an offence; or
- (c) in England and Wales or Northern Ireland, he is cautioned by a constable in respect of such an offence which, at the time when the caution is given, he has admitted.

(2) A person becomes subject to those requirements if, at that commencement—

- (a) he has been convicted of a sexual offence to which this Part applies but has not been dealt with in respect of the offence; or
- (b) he has been found not guilty of such an offence by reason of insanity, or to be under a disability and to have done the act charged against him in respect of such an offence, but has not been dealt with in respect of the finding.

(3) A person becomes subject to those requirements if, at that commencement—

- (a) he is serving a sentence of imprisonment or a term of service detention, or is subject to a community order, in respect of a sexual offence to which this Part applies;
- (b) he is subject to supervision, having been released from prison after serving the whole or part of a sentence of imprisonment in respect of such an offence;
- (c) he is detained in a hospital, or is subject to a guardianship order, having been convicted of such an offence; or
- (d) he is detained in a hospital, having been found not guilty of such an offence by reason of insanity, or to be under a disability and to have done the act charged against him in respect of such an offence;

and a person who would fall within paragraph (a), (c) or (d) above but for the fact that, at that commencement, he is unlawfully at large or absent without leave, on temporary release or leave of absence, or on bail pending an appeal, shall be treated as falling within that paragraph.

(4) A person falling within subsections (1) to (3) above shall continue to be subject to those requirements for the period set out opposite a person of his description in the second column of the following Table (see p. 186).

(7) Where a person found to be under a disability, and to have done the act charged against him in respect of a sexual offence to which this Part applies, is subsequently tried for the offence, the finding, and any order made in respect of the finding, shall be disregarded for the purposes of this section.

(8) In this Part "the relevant date" means—

- (a) in a case of a person falling within subsection (1)(a), (2)(a) or (3)(a) to (c) above, the date of the conviction;

Table

Description of person	Applicable period
A person who, in respect of the offence, is or has been sentenced to imprisonment for life or for a term of 30 months or more	An indefinite period
A person who, in respect of the offence or finding, is or has been admitted to a hospital subject to a restriction order	An indefinite period
A person who, in respect of the offence, is or has been sentenced to imprisonment for a term of more than 6 months but less than 30 months	A period of 10 years beginning with the relevant date
A person who, in respect of the offence, is or has been sentenced to imprisonment for a term of 6 months or less	A period of 7 years beginning with that date
A person who, in respect of the offence or finding, is or has been admitted to a hospital without being subject to a restriction order	A period of 7 years beginning with that date
A person of any other description	A period of 5 years beginning with that date

  (b) in a case of a person falling within subsection (1)(b), (2)(b) or (3)(d) above, the date of the finding;

  (c) in a case of a person falling within subsection (1)(c) above, the date of the caution.

2   Effect of notification requirements

(1) A person who is subject to the notification requirements of this Part shall, before the end of the period of 14 days beginning with the relevant date or, if later, the commencement of this Part, notify to the police the following information, namely—

  (a) his name and, where he also uses one or more other names, each of those names; and

  (b) his home address.

(2) A person who is subject to those requirements shall also, before the end of the period of 14 days beginning with—

  (a) his using a name which has not been notified to the police under this section;

  (b) any change of his home address; or

  (c) his having resided or stayed, for a qualifying period, at any premises in the United Kingdom the address of which has not been notified to the police under this section,

notify that name, the effect of that change or, as the case may be, the address of those premises to the police.

(3) A notification given to the police by any person shall not be regarded as complying with subsection (1) or (2) above unless it also states—

  (a) his date of birth;

  (b) his name on the relevant date and, where he used one or more other names on that date, each of those names; and

  (c) his home address on that date.

(4) For the purpose of determining any period for the purposes of subsection (1) or (2) above, there shall be disregarded any time when the person in question—

  (a) is remanded in or committed to custody by an order of a court;

  (b) is serving a sentence of imprisonment or a term of service detention;

  (c) is detained in a hospital; or

  (d) is outside the United Kingdom.

(5) A person may give a notification under this section—

    (a) by attending at any police station in his local police area and giving an oral notification to any police officer, or to any person authorised for the purpose by the officer in charge of the station; or

    (b) by sending a written notification to any such police station.

(7) In this section—

"home address", in relation to any person, means the address of his home, that is to say, his sole or main residence in the United Kingdom or, where he has no such residence, premises in the United Kingdom which he regularly visits;

"local police area", in relation to any person, means the police area in which his home is situated;

"qualifying period" means—

    (a) a period of 14 days; or

    (b) two or more periods, in any period of 12 months, which (taken together) amount to 14 days.

3   Offences

(1) If a person—

    (a) fails, without reasonable excuse, to comply with section 2(1) or (2) above; or

    (b) notifies to the police, in purported compliance with section 2(1) or (2) above, any information which he knows to be false,

he shall be liable on summary conviction to a fine not exceeding level 5 on the standard scale, or to imprisonment for a term not exceeding six months, or to both.

(2) A person commits an offence under subsection (1)(a) above on the day on which he first fails, without reasonable excuse, to comply with section 2(1) or (2) above and continues to commit it throughout any period during which the failure continues; but a person shall not be prosecuted under that provision more than once in respect of the same failure.

4   Young sex offenders

(1) Subject to the provisions of this section, this Part applies to—

    (a) a period of detention which a person is liable to serve under a secure training order;

    (b) a period for which a person is ordered to be detained in residential accommodation under section 44(1) of the Criminal Procedure (Scotland) Act 1995;

    (c) a period of training in a training school, or of custody in a remand centre, which a person is liable to undergo or serve by virtue of an order under section 74(1)(a) or (e) of the Children and Young Persons Act (Northern Ireland) 1968;

    (d) a sentence of detention in a young offender institution, a young offenders institution or a young offenders centre;

    (e) a sentence under a custodial order within the meaning of section 71AA of the Army Act 1955 or the Air Force Act 1955 or section 43AA of the Naval Discipline Act 1957;

    (f) a sentence of detention under section 53 of the Children and Young Persons Act 1933, section 208 of the Criminal Procedure (Scotland) Act 1995 or section 73 of the Children and Young Persons Act (Northern Ireland) 1968;

    (g) a sentence of custody for life under section 8 of the Criminal Justice Act 1982; and

    (h) a sentence of detention, or custody for life, under section 71A of the Army Act 1955 or the Air Force Act 1955 or section 43A of the Naval Discipline Act 1957,

as it applies to an equivalent sentence of imprisonment; and references in this Part to prison or imprisonment shall be construed accordingly.

(2) In the case of a person who is under 18 on the relevant date, section 1(4) above shall have effect as if for any reference to a period of 10 years, 7 years or 5 years there were substituted a reference to one-half of that period.

(3) In the case of a person falling within section 1(1)(a) or (b) above who is under the relevant age on the relevant date, the court may direct that, until he attains that age, sections 2 and 3 above shall have effect as if an individual having parental responsibility or, in Scotland, parental responsibilities for him—

    (a) were authorised to comply on his behalf with the provisions of section 2 above; and

    (b) were liable in his stead for any failure to comply with those provisions;

and in this subsection "the relevant age" means 18 in England and Wales and Northern Ireland and 16 in Scotland.

5 Certificates for purposes of Part I

(2) If the court by or before which the person is so convicted or so found—

    (a) states in open court—

        (i) that on that date he has been convicted, found not guilty by reason of insanity or found to be under a disability and to have done the act charged against him; and

        (ii) that the offence in question is a sexual offence to which this Part applies; and

    (b) certifies those facts (whether at the time or subsequently),

the certificate shall, for the purposes of this Part, be evidence or, in Scotland, sufficient evidence of those facts.

(d) COMMUNITY SENTENCES

Powers of Criminal Courts (Sentencing) Act 2000 (as amended)

GENERAL PROVISIONS

33 Meaning of "community order" and "community sentence"

(1) In this Act, "community order" means any of the following orders—

    (a) a curfew order;

    (b) a community rehabilitation order;

    (c) a community punishment order;

    (d) a community punishment and rehabilitation order;

    (e) a drug treatment and testing order;

    (f) an attendance centre order;

    (g) a supervision order;

    (h) an action plan order.

(2) In this Act, "community sentence" means a sentence which consists of or includes one or more community orders.

34 Community orders not available where sentence fixed by law etc

None of the powers to make community orders which are conferred by this Part is exercisable in respect of an offence for which the sentence—

    (a) is fixed by law; or

    (b) falls to be imposed under section 109(2), 110(2) or 111(2) below (requirement to impose custodial sentences for certain repeated offences committed by offenders aged 18 or over).

35 Restrictions on imposing community sentences

(1) A court shall not pass a community sentence on an offender unless it is of the opinion

that the offence, or the combination of the offence and one or more offences associated with it, was serious enough to warrant such a sentence.

(2) In consequence of the provision made by section 51 below with respect to community punishment and rehabilitation orders, a community sentence shall not consist of or include both a community rehabilitation order and a community punishment order.

(3) Subject to subsection (2) above and to section 69(5) below (which limits the community orders that may be combined with an action plan order), where a court passes a community sentence—

   (a) the particular order or orders comprising or forming part of the sentence shall be such as in the opinion of the court is, or taken together are, the most suitable for the offender; and
   (b) the restrictions on liberty imposed by the order or orders shall be such as in the opinion of the court are commensurate with the seriousness of the offence, or the combination of the offence and one or more offences associated with it.

(4) Subsections (1) and (3)(b) above have effect subject to section 59 below (curfew orders and community punishment orders for persistent petty offenders).

36   Procedural requirements for community sentences: pre-sentence reports etc

(1) In forming any such opinion as is mentioned in subsection (1) or (3)(b) of section 35 above, a court shall take into account all such information as is available to it about the circumstances of the offence or (as the case may be) of the offence and the offence or offences associated with it, including any aggravating or mitigating factors.

(2) In forming any such opinion as is mentioned in subsection (3)(a) of that section, a court may take into account any information about the offender which is before it.

(3) The following provisions of this section apply in relation to—

   (a) a community rehabilitation order which includes additional requirements authorised by Schedule 2 to this Act;
   (b) a community punishment order;
   (c) a community punishment and rehabilitation order;
   (d) a drug treatment and testing order;
   (e) a supervision order which includes requirements authorised by Schedule 6 to this Act.

(4) Subject to subsection (5) below, a court shall obtain and consider a pre-sentence report before forming an opinion as to the suitability for the offender of one or more of the orders mentioned in subsection (3) above.

(5) Subsection (4) above does not apply if, in the circumstances of the case, the court is of the opinion that it is unnecessary to obtain a pre-sentence report.

(6) In a case where the offender is aged under 18 and the offence is not triable only on indictment and there is no other offence associated with it that is triable only on indictment, the court shall not form such an opinion as is mentioned in subsection (5) above unless—

   (a) there exists a previous pre-sentence report obtained in respect of the offender; and
   (b) the court has had regard to the information contained in that report, or, if there is more than one such report, the most recent report.

36A   Pre-sentence drug testing

(1) Where a person aged 18 or over is convicted of an offence and the court is considering passing a community sentence, it may make an order under subsection (2) below for the purpose of ascertaining whether the offender has any specified Class A drug in his body.

(2) The order shall require the offender to provide, in accordance with the order, samples of any description specified in the order.

(3) If it is proved to the satisfaction of the court that the offender has, without reasonable excuse, failed to comply with the order it may impose on him a fine of an amount not exceeding level 4.

In this subsection, "level 4" means the amount which, in relation to a fine for a summary offence, is level 4 on the standard scale.

(4) The court shall not make an order under subsection (2) above unless it has been notified by the Secretary of State that the power to make such orders is exercisable by the court and the notice has not been withdrawn.

36B   Electronic monitoring of requirements in community orders

(1) Subject to subsections (2) to (4) below, a community order may include requirements for securing the electronic monitoring of the offender's compliance with any other requirements imposed by the order.

(2) A court shall not include in a community order a requirement under subsection (1) above unless the court—

  (a) has been notified by the Secretary of State that electronic monitoring arrangements are available in the relevant areas specified in subsections (7) to (10) below; and

  (b) is satisfied that the necessary provision can be made under those arrangements.

(3) Where—

  (a) it is proposed to include in an exclusion order a requirement for securing electronic monitoring in accordance with this section; but

  (b) there is a person (other than the offender) without whose co-operation it will not be practicable to secure the monitoring,

the requirement shall not be included in the order without that person's consent.

(4) Where—

  (a) it is proposed to include in a community rehabilitation order or a community punishment and rehabilitation order a requirement for securing the electronic monitoring of the offender's compliance with a requirement such as is mentioned in paragraph 8(1) of Schedule 2 to this Act; but

  (b) there is a person (other than the offender) without whose co-operation it will not be practicable to secure the monitoring,

the requirement shall not be included in the order without that person's consent.

(5) An order which includes requirements under subsection (1) above shall include provision for making a person responsible for the monitoring; and a person who is made so responsible shall be of a description specified in an order made by the Secretary of State.

(6) The Secretary of State may make rules for regulating—

  (a) the electronic monitoring of compliance with requirements included in a community order; and

  (b) without prejudice to the generality of paragraph (a) above, the functions of persons made responsible for securing the electronic monitoring of compliance with requirements included in the order.

(7) In the case of a curfew order or an exclusion order, the relevant area is the area in which the place proposed to be specified in the order is situated.

In this subsection, "place", in relation to an exclusion order, has the same meaning as in section 40A below.

(8) In the case of a community rehabilitation order or a community punishment and rehabilitation order, the relevant areas are each of the following—

  (a) where it is proposed to include in the order a requirement for securing compliance with a requirement such as is mentioned in sub-paragraph (1) of paragraph 7 of Schedule 2 to this Act, the area mentioned in sub-paragraph (5) of that paragraph;

  (b) where it is proposed to include in the order a requirement for securing compliance with a requirement such as is mentioned in sub-paragraph (1) of paragraph 8 of that Schedule, the area mentioned in sub-paragraph (5) of that paragraph;

   (c) where it is proposed to include in the order a requirement for securing compliance with any other requirement, the area proposed to be specified under section 41(3) below.

(9) In the case of a community punishment order, a drug treatment and testing order, a drug abstinence order, a supervision order or an action plan order, the relevant area is the petty sessions area proposed to be specified in the order.

(10) In the case of an attendance centre order, the relevant area is the petty sessions area in which the attendance centre proposed to be specified in the order is situated.

CURFEW ORDERS

37 Curfew orders

(1) Where a person is convicted of an offence, the court by or before which he is convicted may (subject to sections 34 to 36 above) make an order requiring him to remain, for periods specified in the order, at a place so specified.

(3) A curfew order may specify different places or different periods for different days, but shall not specify—

   (a) periods which fall outside the period of six months beginning with the day on which it is made; or

   (b) periods which amount to less than two hours or more than twelve hours in any one day.

(4) In relation to an offender aged under 16 on conviction, subsection (3)(a) above shall have effect as if the reference to six months were a reference to three months.

(5) The requirements in a curfew order shall, as far as practicable, be such as to avoid—

   (a) any conflict with the offender's religious beliefs or with the requirements of any other community order to which he may be subject; and

   (b) any interference with the times, if any, at which he normally works or attends school or any other educational establishment.

(6) A curfew order shall include provision for making a person responsible for monitoring the offender's whereabouts during the curfew periods specified in the order; and a person who is made so responsible shall be of a description specified in an order made by the Secretary of State.

(7) A court shall not make a curfew order unless the court has been notified by the Secretary of State that arrangements for monitoring the offender's whereabouts are available in the area in which the place proposed to be specified in the order is situated and the notice has not been withdrawn.

(8) Before making a curfew order, the court shall obtain and consider information about the place proposed to be specified in the order (including information as to the attitude of persons likely to be affected by the enforced presence there of the offender).

(9) Before making a curfew order in respect of an offender who on conviction is under 16, the court shall obtain and consider information about his family circumstances and the likely effect of such an order on those circumstances.

(10) Before making a curfew order, the court shall explain to the offender in ordinary language—

   (a) the effect of the order (including any additional requirements proposed to be included in the order in accordance with section 38 below (electronic monitoring));

   (b) the consequences which may follow (under Part II of Schedule 3 to this Act) if he fails to comply with any of the requirements of the order; and

   (c) that the court has power (under Parts III and IV of that Schedule) to review the order on the application either of the offender or of the responsible officer.

38   Electronic monitoring of curfew orders

(1) Subject to subsection (2) below, a curfew order may in addition include requirements for securing the electronic monitoring of the offender's whereabouts during the curfew periods specified in the order.

(2) A court shall not make a curfew order which includes such requirements unless the court—

(a) has been notified by the Secretary of State that electronic monitoring arrangements are available in the area in which the place proposed to be specified in the order is situated; and

(b) is satisfied that the necessary provision can be made under those arrangements.

(3) Electronic monitoring arrangements made by the Secretary of State under this section may include entering into contracts with other persons for the electronic monitoring by them of offenders' whereabouts.

39   Breach, revocation and amendment of curfew orders

Schedule 3 to this Act (which makes provision for dealing with failures to comply with the requirements of certain community orders, for revoking such orders with or without the substitution of other sentences and for amending such orders) shall have effect so far as relating to curfew orders.

40   Curfew orders: supplementary

(1) The Secretary of State may make rules for regulating—

(a) the monitoring of the whereabouts of persons who are subject to curfew orders (including electronic monitoring in cases where arrangements for such monitoring are available); and

(b) without prejudice to the generality of paragraph (a) above, the functions of the responsible officers of persons who are subject to curfew orders.

(2) The Secretary of State may by order direct—

(a) that subsection (3) of section 37 above shall have effect with the substitution, for any period there specified, of such period as may be specified in the order; or

(b) that subsection (5) of that section shall have effect with such additional restrictions as may be so specified.

Criminal Justice and Court Services Act 2000

RENAMING CERTAIN COMMUNITY ORDERS

43   Probation orders renamed community rehabilitation orders

(1) An order under subsection (1) of section 41 of the Powers of Criminal Courts (Sentencing) Act 2000 (probation orders), whenever made, is to be referred to as a community rehabilitation order.

44   Community service orders renamed community punishment orders

(1) An order under subsection (1) of section 46 of the Powers of Criminal Courts (Sentencing) Act 2000 (community service orders), whenever made, is to be referred to as a community punishment order.

**45   Combination orders renamed community punishment and
rehabilitation orders.**

(1) An order under subsection (1) of section 51 of the Powers of Criminal Courts (Sentencing) Act 2000 (combination orders), whenever made, is to be referred to as a community punishment and rehabilitation order.

Powers of Criminal Courts (Sentencing) Act 2000

COMMUNITY REHABILITATION ORDERS

41 Community rehabilitation orders

(1) Where a person aged 16 or over is convicted of an offence and the court by or before which he is convicted is of the opinion that his supervision is desirable in the interests of—

    (a) securing his rehabilitation, or

    (b) protecting the public from harm from him or preventing the commission by him of further offences,

the court may (subject to sections 34 to 36 above) make an order requiring him to be under supervision for a period specified in the order of not less than six months nor more than three years.

(3) A community rehabilitation order shall specify the petty sessions area in which the offender resides or will reside.

(4) If the offender is aged 18 or over at the time when the community rehabilitation order is made, he shall, subject to paragraph 18 of Schedule 3 to this Act (offender's change of area), be required to be under the supervision of a probation officer appointed for or assigned to the petty sessions area specified in the order.

(5) If the offender is aged under 18 at that time, he shall, subject to paragraph 18 of Schedule 3, be required to be under the supervision of—

    (a) a probation officer appointed for or assigned to the petty sessions area specified in the order; or

    (b) a member of a youth offending team established by a local authority specified in the order;

and if an order specifies a local authority for the purposes of paragraph (b) above, the authority specified must be the local authority within whose area it appears to the court that the offender resides or will reside.

(6) In this Act, "responsible officer", in relation to an offender who is subject to a community rehabilitation order, means the probation officer or member of a youth offending team responsible for his supervision.

(7) Before making a community rehabilitation order, the court shall explain to the offender in ordinary language—

    (a) the effect of the order (including any additional requirements proposed to be included in the order in accordance with section 42 below);

    (b) the consequences which may follow (under Part II of Schedule 3 to this Act) if he fails to comply with any of the requirements of the order; and

    (c) that the court has power (under Parts III and IV of that Schedule) to review the order on the application either of the offender or of the responsible officer.

(8) On making a community rehabilitation order, the court may, if it thinks it expedient for the purpose of the offender's reformation, allow any person who consents to do so to give security for the good behaviour of the offender.

42 Additional requirements which may be included in community rehabilitation orders

(1) Subject to subsection (3) below, a community rehabilitation order may in addition require the offender to comply during the whole or any part of the community rehabilitation period with such requirements as the court, having regard to the circumstances of the case, considers desirable in the interests of—

    (a) securing the rehabilitation of the offender; or

    (b) protecting the public from harm from him or preventing the commission by him of further offences.

(2) Without prejudice to the generality of subsection (1) above,

    (a) the additional requirements which may be included in a community rehabilitation order shall include the requirements which are authorised by Schedule 2 to this Act.

    (b) subject to subsections (2D) and (2F) below, the order shall, if the first set of conditions is satisfied, include a drug abstinence requirement and may include such a requirement if the second set of conditions is satisfied.

(2A) For the purposes of this Part of this Act, a drug abstinence requirement is a requirement for the offender—

    (a) to abstain from misusing specified Class A drugs; and

    (b) to provide, when instructed to do so by the responsible officer, any sample mentioned in the instruction for the purpose of ascertaining whether he has any specified Class A drug in his body.

(2B) The first set of conditions is—

    (a) that the offender was aged 18 or over on the date of his conviction for the offence;

    (b) that, in the opinion of the court, the offender is dependent on or has a propensity to misuse specified Class A drugs; and

    (c) that the offence is a trigger offence.

(2C) The second set of conditions is—

    (a) that the offender was aged 18 or over on the date of his conviction for the offence; and

    (b) that, in the opinion of the court—

        (i) the offender is dependent on or has a propensity to misuse specified Class A drugs; and

        (ii) the misuse by the offender of any specified Class A drug caused or contributed to the offence.

(2D) The order may not include a drug abstinence requirement if—

    (a) the community rehabilitation order includes any requirement in respect of drugs under paragraph 6 of Schedule 2 to this Act; or

    (b) the community sentence includes a drug treatment and testing order or a drug abstinence order.

(2E) The function of giving instructions for the purposes of subsection (2A)(b) above shall be exercised in accordance with guidance given from time to time by the Secretary of State; and the Secretary of State may make rules for regulating the provision of samples in pursuance of such instructions.

(2F) The court shall not include a drug abstinence requirement in the order unless the court has been notified by the Secretary of State that arrangements for implementing such requirements are available in the area proposed to be specified under section 41(3) above and the notice has not been withdrawn.

(3) Without prejudice to the power of the court under section 130 below to make a compensation order, the payment of sums by way of damages for injury or compensation for loss shall not be included among the additional requirements of a community rehabilitation order.

SCHEDULE 2

ADDITIONAL REQUIREMENTS WHICH MAY BE INCLUDED IN COMMUNITY REHABILITATION ORDERS

1. *Requirements as to residence*

    (1) Subject to sub-paragraphs (2) and (3) below, a community rehabilitation order may include requirements as to the residence of the offender.

(2) Before making a community rehabilitation order containing any such requirement, the court shall consider the home surroundings of the offender.

(3) Where a community rehabilitation order requires the offender to reside in an approved hostel or any other institution, the period for which he is required to reside there shall be specified in the order.

2. *Requirements as to activities etc.*

(1) Subject to the provisions of this paragraph, a community rehabilitation order may require the offender—

    (a) to present himself to a person or persons specified in the order at a place or places so specified;

    (b) to participate or refrain from participating in activities specified in the order—

        (i) on a day or days so specified; or

        (ii) during the community rehabilitation period or such portion of it as may be so specified.

(2) A court shall not include in a community rehabilitation order a requirement such as is mentioned in sub-paragraph (1) above unless—

    (a) it has consulted—

        (i) in the case of an offender aged 18 or over, a probation officer; or

        (ii) in the case of an offender aged under 18, either a probation officer or a member of a youth offending team; and

    (b) it is satisfied that it is feasible to secure compliance with the requirement.

(3) A court shall not include a requirement such as is mentioned in sub-paragraph (1)(a) above or a requirement to participate in activities if it would involve the co-operation of a person other than the offender and the offender's responsible officer, unless that other person consents to its inclusion.

(4) A requirement such as is mentioned in sub-paragraph (1)(a) above shall operate to require the offender—

    (a) in accordance with instructions given by his responsible officer, to present himself at a place or places for not more than 60 days in the aggregate; and

    (b) while at any place, to comply with instructions given by, or under the authority of, the person in charge of that place.

(5) A place specified in an order shall have been approved by the probation committee for the area in which the premises are situated as providing facilities suitable for persons subject to community rehabilitation orders.

(6) A requirement to participate in activities shall operate to require the offender—

    (a) in accordance with instructions given by his responsible officer, to participate in activities for not more than 60 days in the aggregate; and

    (b) while participating, to comply with instructions given by, or under the authority of, the person in charge of the activities.

(7) Instructions given by the offender's responsible officer under sub-paragraph (4) or (6) above shall, as far as practicable, be such as to avoid—

    (a) any conflict with the offender's religious beliefs or with the requirements of any other community order to which he may be subject; and

    (b) any interference with the times, if any, at which he normally works or attends school or any other educational establishment.

3. *Requirements as to attendance at probation centre*

(1) Subject to the provisions of this paragraph, a community rehabilitation order may require the offender during the community rehabilitation period to attend at a probation centre specified in the order.

(2) A court shall not include in a community rehabilitation order such a requirement as is mentioned in sub-paragraph (1) above unless it has consulted—

(a) in the case of an offender aged 18 or over, a probation officer; or

(b) in the case of an offender aged under 18, either a probation officer or a member of a youth offending team.

(3) A court shall not include such a requirement in a community rehabilitation order unless it is satisfied—

(a) that arrangements can be made for the offender's attendance at a centre; and

(b) that the person in charge of the centre consents to the inclusion of the requirement.

(4) A requirement under sub-paragraph (1) above shall operate to require the offender—

(a) in accordance with instructions given by his responsible officer, to attend on not more than 60 days at the centre specified in the order; and

(b) while attending there to comply with instructions given by, or under the authority of, the person in charge of the centre.

(5) Instructions given by the offender's responsible officer under sub-paragraph (4) above shall, as far as practicable, be such as to avoid—

(a) any conflict with the offender's religious beliefs or with the requirements of any other community order to which he may be subject; and

(b) any interference with the times, if any, at which he normally works or attends school or any other educational establishment.

4. *Extension of requirements for sexual offenders*

If the court so directs in the case of an offender who has been convicted of a sexual offence—

(a) sub-paragraphs (4) and (6) of paragraph 2 above, and

(b) sub-paragraph (4) of paragraph 3 above,

shall each have effect as if for the reference to 60 days there were substituted a reference to such greater number of days as may be specified in the direction.

5. *Requirements as to treatment for mental condition etc.*

(1) This paragraph applies where a court proposing to make a community rehabilitation order is satisfied, on the evidence of a registered medical practitioner approved for the purposes of section 12 of the Mental Health Act 1983, that the mental condition of the offender—

(a) is such as requires and may be susceptible to treatment; but

(b) is not such as to warrant the making of a hospital order or guardianship order within the meaning of that Act.

(2) Subject to sub-paragraph (4) below, the community rehabilitation order may include a requirement that the offender shall submit, during the whole of the community rehabilitation period or during such part or parts of that period as may be specified in the order, to treatment by or under the direction of a registered medical practitioner or a chartered psychologist (or both, for different parts) with a view to the improvement of the offender's mental condition.

(3) The treatment required by any such order shall be such one of the following kinds of treatment as may be specified in the order, that is to say—

(a) treatment as a resident patient in a hospital or mental nursing home within the meaning of the Mental Health Act 1983, but not hospital premises at which high security psychiatric services within the meaning of that Act are provided;

(b) treatment as a non-resident patient at such institution or place as may be specified in the order;

(c) treatment by or under the direction of such registered medical practitioner or chartered psychologist (or both) as may be so specified;

but the nature of the treatment shall not be specified in the order except as mentioned in paragraph (a), (b) or (c) above.

(4) A court shall not by virtue of this paragraph include in a community rehabilitation order a requirement that the offender shall submit to treatment for his mental condition unless–

    (a) it is satisfied that arrangements have been or can be made for the treatment intended to be specified in the order (including arrangements for the reception of the offender where he is to be required to submit to treatment as a resident patient); and

    (b) the offender has expressed his willingness to comply with such a requirement.

(5) While the offender is under treatment as a resident patient in pursuance of a requirement of the community rehabilitation order, his responsible officer shall carry out the supervision of the offender to such extent only as may be necessary for the purpose of the revocation or amendment of the order.

(6) Where the medical practitioner or chartered psychologist by whom or under whose direction an offender is being treated for his mental condition in pursuance of a community rehabilitation order is of the opinion that part of the treatment can be better or more conveniently given in or at an institution or place which—

    (a) is not specified in the order, and

    (b) is one in or at which the treatment of the offender will be given by or under the direction of a registered medical practitioner or chartered psychologist,

he may, with the consent of the offender, make arrangements for him to be treated accordingly.

(7) Such arrangements as are mentioned in sub-paragraph (6) above may provide for the offender to receive part of his treatment as a resident patient in an institution or place notwithstanding that the institution or place is not one which could have been specified for that purpose in the community rehabilitation order.

(8) Where any such arrangements as are mentioned in sub-paragraph (6) above are made for the treatment of an offender—

    (a) the medical practitioner or chartered psychologist by whom the arrangements are made shall give notice in writing to the offender's responsible officer, specifying the institution or place in or at which the treatment is to be carried out; and

    (b) the treatment provided for by the arrangements shall be deemed to be treatment to which he is required to submit in pursuance of the community rehabilitation order.

6.   *Requirements as to treatment for drug or alcohol dependency*

(1) Subject to sub-paragraph (2) below, this paragraph applies where a court proposing to make a community rehabilitation order is satisfied—

    (a) that the offender is dependent on drugs or alcohol;

    (b) that his dependency caused or contributed to the offence in respect of which the order is proposed to be made; and

    (c) that his dependency is such as requires and may be susceptible to treatment.

(2) If the court has been notified by the Secretary of State that arrangements for implementing drug treatment and testing orders are available in the area proposed to be specified in the community rehabilitation order, and the notice has not been withdrawn, this paragraph shall have effect as if the words "drugs or", in each place where they occur, were omitted.

(3) Subject to sub-paragraph (5) below, the community rehabilitation order may include a requirement that the offender shall submit, during the whole of the community rehabilitation period or during such part of that period as may be specified in the order, to treatment by or under the direction of a person having the necessary qualifications or experience with a view to the reduction or elimination of the offender's dependency on drugs or alcohol.

(4) The treatment required by any such order shall be such one of the following kinds of treatment as may be specified in the order, that is to say—

  (a) treatment as a resident in such institution or place as may be specified in the order;

  (b) treatment as a non-resident in or at such institution or place as may be so specified;

  (c) treatment by or under the direction of such person having the necessary qualifications or experience as may be so specified;

but the nature of the treatment shall not be specified in the order except as mentioned in paragraph (a), (b) or (c) above.

(5) A court shall not by virtue of this paragraph include in a community rehabilitation order a requirement that the offender shall submit to treatment for his dependency on drugs or alcohol unless—

  (a) it is satisfied that arrangements have been or can be made for the treatment intended to be specified in the order (including arrangements for the reception of the offender where he is to be required to submit to treatment as a resident); and

  (b) the offender has expressed his willingness to comply with such a requirement.

(6) While the offender is under treatment as a resident in pursuance of a requirement of the community rehabilitation order, his responsible officer shall carry out the offender's supervision to such extent only as may be necessary for the purpose of the revocation or amendment of the order.

(7) Where the person by whom or under whose direction an offender is being treated for dependency on drugs or alcohol in pursuance of a community rehabilitation order is of the opinion that part of the treatment can be better or more conveniently given in or at an institution or place which—

  (a) is not specified in the order, and

  (b) is one in or at which the treatment of the offender will be given by or under the direction of a person having the necessary qualifications or experience,

he may, with the consent of the offender, make arrangements for him to be treated accordingly.

(8) Where any such arrangements as are mentioned in sub-paragraph (7) above are made for the treatment of an offender—

  (a) the person by whom the arrangements are made shall give notice in writing to the offender's responsible officer, specifying the institution or place in or at which the treatment is to be carried out; and

  (b) the treatment provided for by the arrangements shall be deemed to be treatment to which he is required to submit in pursuance of the community rehabilitation order.

7. *Curfew requirements*

(1) Subject to the provisions of this paragraph, a community rehabilitation order may include a requirement that the offender remain, for periods specified in the requirement, at a place so specified.

(2) A requirement under sub-paragraph (1) above may specify different places or different periods for different days, but shall not specify—

  (a) periods which fall outside the period of six months beginning with the day on which the order is made; or

  (b) periods which amount to less than two hours or more than twelve hours in any one day.

(3) A requirement under sub-paragraph (1) above shall, as far as practicable, be such as to avoid—

  (a) any conflict with the offender's religious beliefs or with the requirements of any other community order to which he may be subject; and

  (b) any interference with the times, if any, at which he normally works or attends school or any other educational establishment.

(4) An order which includes a requirement under sub-paragraph (1) above shall include provision for making a person responsible for monitoring the offender's whereabouts during the curfew periods specified in the requirement; and a person who is made so responsible shall be of a description specified in an order made by the Secretary of State.

(5) A court shall not include in a community rehabilitation order such a requirement as is mentioned in sub-paragraph (1) above unless the court has been notified by the Secretary of State that arrangements for monitoring the offender's whereabouts are available in the area in which the place proposed to be specified in the requirement is situated and the notice has not been withdrawn.

(6) A court shall not include in a community rehabilitation order such a requirement as is mentioned in sub-paragraph (1) above if the community sentence includes a curfew order.

(7) Before including in a community rehabilitation order such a requirement as is mentioned in sub-paragraph (1) above, the court shall obtain and consider information about the place proposed to be specified in the requirement (including information as to the attitude of persons likely to be affected by the enforced presence there of the offender).

8. *Exclusion requirements*

(1) Subject to the provisions of this paragraph, a community rehabilitation order may include a requirement prohibiting the offender from entering a place specified in the requirement for a period so specified of not more than two years.

(2) A requirement under sub-paragraph (1) above—

  (a) may provide for the prohibition to operate only during the periods specified in the order;

  (b) may specify different places for different periods or days.

(3) A requirement under sub-paragraph (1) above shall, as far as practicable, be such as to avoid—

  (a) any conflict with the offender's religious beliefs or with the requirements of any other community order to which he may be subject; and

  (b) any interference with the times, if any, at which he normally works or attends school or any other educational establishment.

(4) An order which includes a requirement under sub-paragraph (1) above shall include provision for making a person responsible for monitoring the offender's whereabouts during the periods when the prohibition operates; and a person who is made so responsible shall be of a description specified in an order made by the Secretary of State.

(5) A court shall not include in a community rehabilitation order such a requirement as is mentioned in sub-paragraph (1) above unless the court has been notified by the Secretary of State that arrangements for monitoring the offender's whereabouts are available in the area in which the place proposed to be specified in the order is situated and the notice has not been withdrawn.

(6) A court shall not include in a community rehabilitation order such a requirement as is mentioned in sub-paragraph (1) above if the community sentence includes an exclusion order.

(7) The Secretary of State may make rules for regulating—

  (a) the monitoring of the whereabouts of an offender who is subject to a requirement under sub-paragraph (1) above; and

  (b) without prejudice to the generality of paragraph (a) above, the functions of any person responsible for monitoring the offender's whereabouts during the periods when the prohibition operates.

(8) The Secretary of State may by order direct that sub-paragraph (3) above shall have effect with such additional restrictions as may be specified in the order.

COMMUNITY PUNISHMENT ORDERS

46   Community punishment orders

(1) Where a person aged 16 or over is convicted of an offence punishable with imprisonment, the court by or before which he is convicted may (subject to sections 34 to 36 above) make an order requiring him to perform unpaid work in accordance with section 47 below.

(3) The number of hours which a person may be required to work under a community punishment order shall be specified in the order and shall be in the aggregate—

(a) not less than 40; and

(b) not more than 240.

(4) A court shall not make a community punishment order in respect of an offender unless, after hearing (if the court thinks it necessary) an appropriate officer, the court is satisfied that the offender is a suitable person to perform work under such an order.

(5) In subsection (4) above "an appropriate officer" means—

(a) in the case of an offender aged 18 or over, a probation officer or social worker of a local authority social services department; and

(b) in the case of an offender aged under 18, a probation officer, a social worker of a local authority social services department or a member of a youth offending team.

(6) A court shall not make a community punishment order in respect of an offender unless it is satisfied that provision for him to perform work under such an order can be made under the arrangements for persons to perform work under such orders which exist in the petty sessions area in which he resides or will reside.

(7) Subsection (6) above has effect subject to paragraphs 3 and 4 of Schedule 4 to this Act (transfer of order to Scotland or Northern Ireland).

(8) Where a court makes community punishment orders in respect of two or more offences of which the offender has been convicted by or before the court, the court may direct that the hours of work specified in any of those orders shall be concurrent with or additional to those specified in any other of those orders, but so that the total number of hours which are not concurrent shall not exceed the maximum specified in subsection (3)(b) above.

(9) A community punishment order—

(a) shall specify the petty sessions area in which the offender resides or will reside; and

(b) where the offender is aged under 18 at the time the order is made, may also specify a local authority for the purposes of section 47(5)(b) below (cases where functions are to be discharged by member of a youth offending team);

and if the order specifies a local authority for those purposes, the authority specified must be the local authority within whose area it appears to the court that the offender resides or will reside.

(10) Before making a community punishment order, the court shall explain to the offender in ordinary language—

(a) the purpose and effect of the order (and in particular the requirements of the order as specified in section 47(1) to (3) below);

(b) the consequences which may follow (under Part II of Schedule 3 to this Act) if he fails to comply with any of those requirements; and

(c) that the court has power (under Parts III and IV of that Schedule) to review the order on the application either of the offender or of the responsible officer.

(11) The court by which a community punishment order is made shall forthwith give copies of the order to—

(a) if the offender is aged 18 or over, a probation officer assigned to the court, or

(b) if the offender is aged under 18, a probation officer or member of a youth offending team so assigned,

and he shall give a copy to the offender and to the responsible officer.

(12) The court by which such an order is made shall also, except where it itself acts for the petty sessions area specified in the order, send to the clerk to the justices for that area—

(a) a copy of the order; and

(b) such documents and information relating to the case as it considers likely to be of assistance to a court acting for that area in the exercise of its functions in relation to the order.

(13) In this section and Schedule 3 to this Act "responsible officer", in relation to an offender subject to a community punishment order, means the person mentioned in subsection (4)(a) or (b) or (5)(b) of section 47 below who, as respects the order, is responsible for discharging the functions conferred by that section.

47 Obligations of person subject to community punishment order

(1) An offender in respect of whom a community punishment order is in force shall—

(a) keep in touch with the responsible officer in accordance with such instructions as he may from time to time be given by that officer and notify him of any change of address; and

(b) perform for the number of hours specified in the order such work at such times as he may be instructed by the responsible officer.

(2) The instructions given by the responsible officer under this section shall, as far as practicable, be such as to avoid—

(a) any conflict with the offender's religious beliefs or with the requirements of any other community order to which he may be subject; and

(b) any interference with the times, if any, at which he normally works or attends school or any other educational establishment.

(3) Subject to paragraph 22 of Schedule 3 to this Act (power to extend order), the work required to be performed under a community punishment order shall be performed during the period of twelve months beginning with the date of the order; but, unless revoked, the order shall remain in force until the offender has worked under it for the number of hours specified in it.

(3A) Subject to subsection (3B) below, the community punishment order shall, if the set of conditions in section 42(2B) above is satisfied, include a drug abstinence requirement and may include such a requirement if the set of conditions in section 42(2C) above is satisfied.

(3B) The order may not include a drug abstinence requirement if the community sentence includes a drug treatment and testing order or a drug abstinence order.

(3C) Subsections (2E) and (2F) of section 42 above apply for the purposes of this section as they apply for the purposes of that.

(4) If the offender is aged 18 or over at the time when the order is made, the functions conferred by this section on "the responsible officer" shall be discharged by—

(a) a probation officer appointed for or assigned to the petty sessions area specified in the order; or

(b) a person appointed for the purposes of this section by the probation committee for that area.

(5) If the offender is aged under 18 at that time, those functions shall be discharged by—

(a) a person mentioned in subsection (4)(a) or (b) above; or

(b) a member of a youth offending team established by a local authority specified in the order.

COMMUNITY PUNISHMENT AND REHABILITATION ORDERS

51   Community punishment and rehabilitation orders

(1) Where a person aged 16 or over is convicted of an offence punishable with imprisonment and the court by or before which he is convicted is of the opinion mentioned in subsection (3) below, the court may (subject to sections 34 to 36 above) make an order requiring him both–

    (a) to be under supervision for a period specified in the order, being not less than twelve months nor more than three years; and

    (b) to perform unpaid work for a number of hours so specified, being in the aggregate not less than 40 nor more than 100.

(3) The opinion referred to in subsection (1) above is that the making of a community punishment and rehabilitation order is desirable in the interests of—

    (a) securing the rehabilitation of the offender; or

    (b) protecting the public from harm from him or preventing the commission by him of further offences.

(4) Subject to subsection (1) above, sections 41, 42, 46 and 47 above and Schedule 2 to this Act shall apply in relation to community punishment and rehabilitation orders—

    (a) in so far as those orders impose such a requirement as is mentioned in paragraph (a) of subsection (1) above, as if they were community rehabilitation orders; and

    (b) in so far as they impose such a requirement as is mentioned in paragraph (b) of that subsection, as if they were community punishment orders.

(5) Schedule 3 to this Act (which makes provision for dealing with failures to comply with the requirements of certain community orders, for revoking such orders with or without the substitution of other sentences and for amending such orders) shall have effect so far as relating to community punishment and rehabilitation orders.

DRUG TREATMENT AND TESTING ORDERS

52   Drug treatment and testing orders

(1) Where a person aged 16 or over is convicted of an offence, the court by or before which he is convicted may (subject to sections 34 to 36 above) make an order which—

    (a) has effect for a period specified in the order of not less than six months nor more than three years ("the treatment and testing period"); and

    (b) includes the requirement and provisions mentioned in sections 53 and 54 below;

but this section does not apply in relation to an offence committed before 30th September 1998.

(2) An order under subsection (1) above is in this Act referred to as a "drug treatment and testing order".

(3) A court shall not make a drug treatment and testing order in respect of an offender unless it is satisfied—

    (a) that he is dependent on or has a propensity to misuse drugs; and

    (b) that his dependency or propensity is such as requires and may be susceptible to treatment.

(4) For the purpose of ascertaining for the purposes of subsection (3) above whether the offender has any drug in his body, the court may by order require him to provide samples of such description as it may specify; but the court shall not make such an order unless the offender expresses his willingness to comply with its requirements.

(5) A court shall not make a drug treatment and testing order unless it has been notified by the Secretary of State that arrangements for implementing such orders are available in the area proposed to be specified in the order under section 54(1) below and the notice has not been withdrawn.

(6) Before making a drug treatment and testing order, the court shall explain to the offender in ordinary language—

    (a) the effect of the order and of the requirements proposed to be included in it;

    (b) the consequences which may follow (under Part II of Schedule 3 to this Act) if he fails to comply with any of those requirements;

    (c) that the order will be periodically reviewed at intervals as provided for in the order (by virtue of section 54(6) below); and

    (d) that the order may be reviewed (under Parts III and IV of Schedule 3) on the application either of the offender or of the responsible officer;

and "responsible officer" here has the meaning given by section 54(3) below.

(7) A court shall not make a drug treatment and testing order unless the offender expresses his willingness to comply with its requirements.

53 The treatment and testing requirements

(1) A drug treatment and testing order shall include a requirement ("the treatment requirement") that the offender shall submit, during the whole of the treatment and testing period, to treatment by or under the direction of a specified person having the necessary qualifications or experience ("the treatment provider") with a view to the reduction or elimination of the offender's dependency on or propensity to misuse drugs.

(2) The required treatment for any particular period shall be—

    (a) treatment as a resident in such institution or place as may be specified in the order; or

    (b) treatment as a non-resident in or at such institution or place, and at such intervals, as may be so specified;

but the nature of the treatment shall not be specified in the order except as mentioned in paragraph (a) or (b) above.

(3) A court shall not make a drug treatment and testing order unless it is satisfied that arrangements have been or can be made for the treatment intended to be specified in the order (including arrangements for the reception of the offender where he is to be required to submit to treatment as a resident).

(4) A drug treatment and testing order shall include a requirement ("the testing requirement") that, for the purpose of ascertaining whether he has any drug in his body during the treatment and testing period, the offender shall during that period, at such times or in such circumstances as may (subject to the provisions of the order) be determined by the treatment provider, provide samples of such description as may be so determined.

(5) The testing requirement shall specify for each month the minimum number of occasions on which samples are to be provided.

54 Provisions of order as to supervision and periodic review

(1) A drug treatment and testing order shall include a provision specifying the petty sessions area in which it appears to the court making the order that the offender resides or will reside.

(2) A drug treatment and testing order shall provide that, for the treatment and testing period, the offender shall be under the supervision of a probation officer appointed for or assigned to the petty sessions area specified in the order.

(3) In this Act "responsible officer", in relation to an offender who is subject to a drug treatment and testing order, means the probation officer responsible for his supervision.

(4) A drug treatment and testing order shall—

    (a) require the offender to keep in touch with the responsible officer in accordance with such instructions as he may from time to time be given by that officer, and to notify him of any change of address; and

(b) provide that the results of the tests carried out on the samples provided by the offender in pursuance of the testing requirement shall be communicated to the responsible officer.

(5) Supervision by the responsible officer shall be carried out to such extent only as may be necessary for the purpose of enabling him—

    (a) to report on the offender's progress to the court responsible for the order;

    (b) to report to that court any failure by the offender to comply with the requirements of the order; and

    (c) to determine whether the circumstances are such that he should apply to that court for the revocation or amendment of the order.

(6) A drug treatment and testing order shall—

    (a) provide for the order to be reviewed periodically at intervals of not less than one month;

    (b) provide for each review of the order to be made, subject to section 55(6) below, at a hearing held for the purpose by the court responsible for the order (a "review hearing");

    (c) require the offender to attend each review hearing;

    (d) provide for the responsible officer to make to the court responsible for the order, before each review, a report in writing on the offender's progress under the order; and

    (e) provide for each such report to include the test results communicated to the responsible officer under subsection (4)(b) above and the views of the treatment provider as to the treatment and testing of the offender.

55   Periodic reviews

(1) At a review hearing (within the meaning given by subsection (6) of section 54 above) the court may, after considering the responsible officer's report referred to in that subsection, amend any requirement or provision of the drug treatment and testing order.

(2) The court—

    (a) shall not amend the treatment or testing requirement unless the offender expresses his willingness to comply with the requirement as amended;

    (b) shall not amend any provision of the order so as to reduce the treatment and testing period below the minimum specified in section 52(1) above, or to increase it above the maximum so specified; and

    (c) except with the consent of the offender, shall not amend any requirement or provision of the order while an appeal against the order is pending.

(3) If the offender fails to express his willingness to comply with the treatment or testing requirement as proposed to be amended by the court, the court may—

    (a) revoke the order; and

    (b) deal with him, for the offence in respect of which the order was made, in any way in which it could deal with him if he had just been convicted by the court of the offence.

(4) In dealing with the offender under subsection (3)(b) above, the court—

    (a) shall take into account the extent to which the offender has complied with the requirements of the order; and

    (b) may impose a custodial sentence (where the order was made in respect of an offence punishable with such a sentence) notwithstanding anything in section 79(2) below.

(5) Where the order was made by a magistrates' court in the case of an offender under 18 years of age in respect of an offence triable only on indictment in the case of an adult, any powers exercisable under subsection (3)(b) above in respect of the offender after he attains the age of 18 shall be powers to do either or both of the following—

(a) to impose a fine not exceeding £5,000 for the offence in respect of which the order was made;

(b) to deal with the offender for that offence in any way in which the court could deal with him if it had just convicted him of an offence punishable with imprisonment for a term not exceeding six months.

(6) If at a review hearing the court, after considering the responsible officer's report, is of the opinion that the offender's progress under the order is satisfactory, the court may so amend the order as to provide for each subsequent review to be made by the court without a hearing.

(7) If at a review without a hearing the court, after considering the responsible officer's report, is of the opinion that the offender's progress under the order is no longer satisfactory, the court may require the offender to attend a hearing of the court at a specified time and place.

(8) At that hearing the court, after considering that report, may—

(a) exercise the powers conferred by this section as if the hearing were a review hearing; and

(b) so amend the order as to provide for each subsequent review to be made at a review hearing.

56   Breach, revocation and amendment of drug treatment and testing orders

Schedule 3 to this Act (which makes provision for dealing with failures to comply with the requirements of certain community orders, for revoking such orders with or without the substitution of other sentences and for amending such orders) shall have effect so far as relating to drug treatment and testing orders.

58   Drug treatment and testing orders: supplementary

The Secretary of State may by order amend subsection (1) of section 52 above by substituting a different period for the minimum or maximum period for the time being specified in that subsection.

58A   Drug abstinence orders

(1) Where a person aged 18 or over is convicted of an offence, the court by or before which he is convicted may (subject to sections 34 to 36 above) make an order which requires the offender—

(a) to abstain from misusing specified Class A drugs; and

(b) to provide, when instructed to do so by the responsible officer, any sample mentioned in the instruction for the purpose of ascertaining whether he has any specified Class A drug in his body.

(3) The court shall not make a drug abstinence order in respect of an offender unless—

(a) in the opinion of the court, the offender is dependent on, or has a propensity to misuse, specified Class A drugs; and

(b) the offence in question is a trigger offence or, in the opinion of the court, the misuse by the offender of any specified Class A drug caused or contributed to the offence in question.

(4) A drug abstinence order shall provide that, for the period for which the order has effect, the offender shall be under the supervision of a person, being a person of a description specified in an order made by the Secretary of State.

(7) A drug abstinence order shall have effect for a period specified in the order of not less than six months nor more than three years.

(8) The Secretary of State may make rules for regulating the provision of samples in pursuance of such instructions.

(9) A court shall not make a drug abstinence order unless the court has been notified by the Secretary of State that arrangements for implementing such orders are available in the area

proposed to be specified in the order under section 54(1) above (as applied by section 58B(2) below) and the notice has not been withdrawn.

58B   Drug abstinence orders: supplementary

(1) Before making a drug abstinence order, the court shall explain to the offender in ordinary language—

(a) the effect of the order and of the requirements proposed to be included in it;

(b) the consequences which may follow (under Part II of Schedule 3 to this Act) if he fails to comply with any of those requirements; and

(c) that the order may be reviewed (under Parts III and IV of that Schedule) on the application either of the offender or of the responsible officer.

(2) Section 54 above (except subsections (2), (3) and (6)) and section 57 above (except subsections (2), (3A) and (4)(b)) shall apply for the purposes of section 58A above and this section as if references to drug treatment and testing orders were references to drug abstinence orders.

(3) Schedule 3 to this Act (which makes provision for dealing with failures to comply with the requirements of certain community orders, for revoking such orders with or without the substitution of other sentences and for amending such orders) shall have effect so far as relating to drug abstinence orders.

PERSISTENT PETTY OFFENDERS

59   Curfew orders and community punishment orders for persistent petty offenders

(1) This section applies where—

(a) a person aged 16 or over is convicted of an offence;

(b) the court by or before which he is convicted is satisfied that each of the conditions mentioned in subsection (2) below is fulfilled; and

(c) if it were not so satisfied, the court would be minded to impose a fine in respect of the offence.

(2) The conditions are that—

(a) one or more fines imposed on the offender in respect of one or more previous offences have not been paid; and

(b) if a fine were imposed in an amount which was commensurate with the seriousness of the offence, the offender would not have sufficient means to pay it.

(3) The court may—

(a) subject to subsections (5) and (7) below, make a curfew order under section 37(1) above, or

(b) subject to subsections (6) and (7) below, make a community punishment order under section 46(1) above,

in respect of the offender instead of imposing a fine.

(4) Subsection (3) above applies notwithstanding anything in subsections (1) and (3)(b) of section 35 above (restrictions on imposing community sentences).

(5) Section 37(1) above (curfew orders) shall apply for the purposes of subsection (3)(a) above as if for the words from the beginning to "make" there were substituted "Where section 59 below applies, the court may make in respect of the offender"; and—

(a) section 37(3), (5) to (8) and (10) to (12), and

(b) so far as applicable, the other provisions of this Part relating to curfew orders,

have effect in relation to a curfew order made by virtue of this section as they have effect in relation to any other curfew order.

(6) Section 46(1) above (community punishment orders) shall apply for the purposes of subsection (3)(b) above as if for the words from the beginning to "make" there were substituted "Where section 59 below applies, the court may make in respect of the offender"; and—

(a)   section 46(3) and (4), and

(b)   so far as applicable, the following provisions of section 46 and the other provisions of this Part relating to community punishment orders,

have effect in relation to a community service order made by virtue of this section as they have effect in relation to any other community punishment order.

(7) A court shall not make an order by virtue of subsection (3)(a) or (b) above unless the court has been notified by the Secretary of State that arrangements for implementing orders so made are available in the relevant area and the notice has not been withdrawn.

SCHEDULE 3

BREACH OF REQUIREMENT OF ORDER

3.   *Issue of summons or warrant*

(1) If at any time while a relevant order is in force in respect of an offender it appears on information to a justice of the peace acting for the petty sessions area concerned that the offender has failed to comply with any of the requirements of the order, the justice may—

(a)   issue a summons requiring the offender to appear at the place and time specified in it; or

(b)   if the information is in writing and on oath, issue a warrant for his arrest.

(2) Any summons or warrant issued under this paragraph shall direct the offender to appear or be brought—

(a)   in the case of a drug treatment and testing order, before the court responsible for the order;

(b)   in the case of any other relevant order which was made by the Crown Court and included a direction that any failure to comply with any of the requirements of the order be dealt with by the Crown Court, before the Crown Court; and

(c)   in the case of a relevant order which is neither a drug treatment and testing order nor an order to which paragraph (b) above applies, before a magistrates' court acting for the petty sessions area concerned.

Editors' note: Paragraph 4 of Schedule 3 of the **Powers of Criminal Courts (Sentencing) Act 2000** is being arrested by the Criminal Justice and Court Services Act 2000 and will read as follows. The text in italic is not in force at the time of going to press.

4.   *Powers of magistrates' court*

"(1) This paragraph applies if it is proved to the satisfaction of a magistrates' court before which an offender appears or is brought under paragraph 3 above that he has failed without reasonable excuse to comply with any of the requirements of the relevant order.

(1A) In a case where the offender is aged 18 or over and the order is one to which the warning provisions apply, the magistrates' court shall impose a sentence of imprisonment for the offence in respect of which the order was made unless it is of the opinion—

(a)   that the offender is likely to comply with the requirements of the order during the period for which it remains in force; or

(b)   that the exceptional circumstances of the case justify not imposing a sentence of imprisonment.

(1B) The sentence of imprisonment—

(a)   where the offence was an offence punishable by imprisonment, shall be for the term which, if—

(i)   he had just been convicted of the offence by the court, and

(ii)   section 79(2) of this Act did not apply,

the court would impose on him for that offence; and

> *(b) in any other case, shall be for a term not exceeding three months;*
>
> *taking account of the extent to which he has complied with the requirements of the order.*

(1C) If in a case within sub-paragraph (1A) above the court does not impose a sentence of imprisonment or if the case is not within that sub-paragraph, the magistrates' court may deal with him in respect of the failure in one of the following ways (and must deal with him in one of those ways if the relevant order is in force)—

> *(a) by making a curfew order in respect of him (subject to paragraph 6A below);*
>
> *(b) where the offender is aged 16 or over it may, subject to paragraph 7 below);*
>
> *(c) where the offender is aged under 21, by making an attendance centre order in respect of him (subject to paragraph 8 below); or*
>
> *(d) where the relevant order was made by a magistrates' court, by dealing with him, for the offence in respect of which the order was made, in any way in which the court could deal with him if he had just been convicted by it of the offence.*

(2) In dealing with an offender under sub-paragraph (1)(d) above, a magistrates' court—

> (a) shall take into account the extent to which the offender has complied with the requirements of the relevant order; and
>
> (b) in the case of an offender who has wilfully and persistently failed to comply with those requirements, may impose a custodial sentence (where the relevant order was made in respect of an offence punishable with such a sentence) notwithstanding anything in section 79(2) of this Act.

(3) Where a magistrates' court deals with an offender under sub-paragraph (1)(d) above, it shall revoke the relevant order if it is still in force.

(4) Where a relevant order was made by the Crown Court and a magistrates' court has power to deal with the offender under sub-paragraph (1)(a), (b) or (c) above, it may instead commit him to custody or release him on bail until he can be brought or appear before the Crown Court.

Editors' note: Sub-paragraph (1) appears here as amended by the **Criminal Justice and Court Services Act 2000**, not in force at the time of going to press.

5. *Powers of Crown Court*

(1) This paragraph applies where under paragraph 3 or by virtue of paragraph 4(4) above an offender is brought or appears before the Crown Court and it is proved to the satisfaction of that court that he has failed without reasonable excuse to comply with any of the requirements of the relevant order.

(1A) In a case where the offender is aged 18 or over and the order is one to which the warning provisions apply, the Crown Court shall impose a sentence of imprisonment for the offence in respect of which the order was made unless it is of the opinion—

> *(a) that the offender is likely to comply with the requirements of the order during the period for which it remains in force; or*
>
> *(b) that the exceptional circumstances of the case justify not imposing a sentence of imprisonment.*

(1B) The sentence of imprisonment—

> *(a) where the offence was an offence punishable by imprisonment, shall be for the term which, if—*
>
> > *(i) he had just been convicted of the offence by the court, and*
> >
> > *(ii) section 79(2) of this Act did not apply,*
>
> *the court would impose on him for that offence; and*
>
> *(b) in any other case, shall be for a term not exceeding three months;*
>
> *taking account of the extent to which he has complied with the requirements of the order.*

(1C) If in a case within sub-paragraph (1A) above the court does not impose a sentence of imprisonment or if the case is not within that sub-paragraph, the Crown Court may deal with him in

respect of the failure in one of the following ways (and must deal with him in one of those ways if the relevant order is in force)—

    (a) *by making a curfew order in respect of him (subject to paragraph 6A below);*

    (b) *where the offender is aged 16 or over, by making a community punishment order in respect of him (subject to paragraph 7 below);*

    (c) *where the offender is aged under 21, by making an attendance centre order in respect of him (subject to paragraph 8 below); or*

    (d) *by dealing with him, for the offence in respect of which the order was made, in any way in which the Crown Court could deal with him if he had just been convicted before it of the offence.*

(2) In dealing with an offender under sub-paragraph (1)(d) above, the Crown Court—

    (a) shall take into account the extent to which the offender has complied with the requirements of the relevant order; and

    (b) in the case of an offender who has wilfully and persistently failed to comply with those requirements, may impose a custodial sentence (where the relevant order was made in respect of an offence punishable with such a sentence) notwithstanding anything in section 79(2) of this Act.

(3) Where the Crown Court deals with an offender under sub-paragraph (1)(d) above, it shall revoke the relevant order if it is still in force.

(4) In proceedings before the Crown Court under this paragraph any question whether the offender has failed to comply with the requirements of the relevant order shall be determined by the court and not by the verdict of a jury.

7.   *Community punishment orders imposed for breach of relevant order*

(1) Section 46(1) of this Act (community punishment orders) shall apply for the purposes of paragraphs 4(1)(b) and 5(1)(b) above as if for the words from the beginning to "make" there were substituted "Where a court has power to deal with an offender aged 16 or over under Part II of Schedule 3 to this Act for failure to comply with any of the requirements of a relevant order, the court may make in respect of the offender".

(2) In this paragraph a "secondary order" means a community punishment order made by virtue of paragraph 4(1)(b) or 5(1)(b) above.

(3) The number of hours which an offender may be required to work under a secondary order shall be specified in the order and shall not exceed 60 in the aggregate; and—

    (a) where the relevant order is a community punishment order, the number of hours which the offender may be required to work under the secondary order shall not be such that the total number of hours under both orders exceeds the maximum specified in section 46(3) of this Act; and

    (b) where the relevant order is a community punishment and rehabilitation order, the number of hours which the offender may be required to work under the secondary order shall not be such that the total number of hours under—

        (i) the secondary order, and

        (ii) the community punishment element of the community punishment and rehabilitation order,

exceeds the maximum specified in section 51(1)(b) of this Act.

REVOCATION OF ORDER

10.   *Revocation of order with or without re-sentencing: powers of magistrates' court*

(1) This paragraph applies where a relevant order made by a magistrates' court is in force in respect of any offender and on the application of the offender or the responsible officer it appears to the appropriate magistrates' court that, having regard to circumstances which have arisen since the order was made, it would be in the interests of justice—

    (a) for the order to be revoked; or

    (b) for the offender to be dealt with in some other way for the offence in respect of which the order was made.

  (2) In this paragraph "the appropriate magistrates court" means—

    (a) in the case of a drug treatment and testing order, the magistrates' court responsible for the order;

    (b) in the case of any other relevant order, a magistrates' court acting for the petty sessions area concerned.

  (3) The appropriate magistrates' court may—

    (a) revoke the order; or

    (b) both—

       (i) revoke the order; and

      (ii) deal with the offender, for the offence in respect of which the order was made, in any way in which it could deal with him if he had just been convicted by the court of the offence.

  (4) The circumstances in which a community rehabilitation, community punishment and rehabilitation or drug treatment and testing order may be revoked under sub-paragraph (3)(a) above shall include the offender's making good progress or his responding satisfactorily to supervision or, as the case may be, treatment.

  (5) In dealing with an offender under sub-paragraph (3)(b) above, a magistrates' court shall take into account the extent to which the offender has complied with the requirements of the relevant order.

  (6) A person sentenced under sub-paragraph (3)(b) above for an offence may appeal to the Crown Court against the sentence.

  (7) Where a magistrates' court proposes to exercise its powers under this paragraph otherwise than on the application of the offender, it shall summon him to appear before the court and, if he does not appear in answer to the summons, may issue a warrant for his arrest.

  (8) No application may be made by the offender under sub-paragraph (1) above while an appeal against the relevant order is pending.

11.   *Revocation of order with or without re-sentencing: powers of Crown Court on conviction etc.*

  (1) This paragraph applies where—

    (a) a relevant order made by the Crown Court is in force in respect of an offender and the offender or the responsible officer applies to the Crown Court for the order to be revoked or for the offender to be dealt with in some other way for the offence in respect of which the order was made; or

    (b) an offender in respect of whom a relevant order is in force is convicted of an offence before the Crown Court or, having been committed by a magistrates' court to the Crown Court for sentence, is brought or appears before the Crown Court.

  (2) If it appears to the Crown Court to be in the interests of justice to do so, having regard to circumstances which have arisen since the order was made, the Crown Court may—

    (a) revoke the order; or

    (b) both—

       (i) revoke the order; and

      (ii) deal with the offender, for the offence in respect of which the order was made, in any way in which the court which made the order could deal with him if he had just been convicted of that offence by or before the court which made the order.

  (3) The circumstances in which a community rehabilitation, community punishment

and rehabilitation or drug treatment and testing order may be revoked under sub-paragraph (2)(a) above shall include the offender's making good progress or his responding satisfactorily to supervision or, as the case may be, treatment.

(4) In dealing with an offender under sub-paragraph (2)(b) above, the Crown Court shall take into account the extent to which the offender has complied with the requirements of the relevant order.

12. *Substitution of conditional discharge for community rehabilitation order or community punishment and rehabilitation order*

(1) This paragraph applies where a community rehabilitation order or community punishment and rehabilitation order is in force in respect of any offender and on the application of the offender or the responsible officer to the appropriate court it appears to the court that, having regard to circumstances which have arisen since the order was made, it would be in the interests of justice—

(a) for the order to be revoked; and

(b) for an order to be made under section 12(1)(b) of this Act discharging the offender conditionally for the offence for which the community rehabilitation or community punishment and rehabilitation order was made.

(2) In this paragraph "the appropriate court" means—

(a) where the community rehabilitation or community punishment and rehabilitation order was made by a magistrates' court, a magistrates' court acting for the petty sessions area concerned;

(b) where the community rehabilitation or community punishment and rehabilitation order was made by the Crown Court, the Crown Court.

(3) No application may be made under paragraph 10 or 11 above for a community rehabilitation order or community punishment and rehabilitation order to be revoked and replaced with an order for conditional discharge under section 12(1)(b); but otherwise nothing in this paragraph shall affect the operation of paragraphs 10 and 11 above.

(4) Where this paragraph applies—

(a) the appropriate court may revoke the community rehabilitation or community punishment and rehabilitation order and make an order under section 12(1)(b) of this Act discharging the offender in respect of the offence for which the community rehabilitation or community punishment and rehabilitation order was made, subject to the condition that he commits no offence during the period specified in the order under section 12(1)(b); and

(b) the period specified in the order under section 12(1)(b) shall be the period beginning with the making of that order and ending with the date when the community rehabilitation period specified in the community rehabilitation or community punishment and rehabilitation order would have ended.

(5) For the purposes of sub-paragraph (4) above, subsection (1) of section 12 of this Act shall apply as if—

(a) for the words from the beginning to "may make an order either" there were substituted the words "Where paragraph 12 of Schedule 3 to this Act applies, the appropriate court may (subject to the provisions of sub-paragraph (4) of that paragraph) make an order in respect of the offender"; and

(b) paragraph (a) of that subsection were omitted.

(6) An application under this paragraph may be heard in the offender's absence if—

(a) the application is made by the responsible officer; and

(b) that officer produces to the court a statement by the offender that he understands the effect of an order for conditional discharge and consents to the making of the application;

and where the application is so heard section 12(4) of this Act shall not apply.

(7) No application may be made under this paragraph while an appeal against the community rehabilitation or community punishment and rehabilitation order is pending.

AMENDMENT OF ORDER

18.   *Amendment by reason of change of residence*
(1) This paragraph applies where, at any time while a relevant order (other than a drug treatment and testing order) is in force in respect of an offender, a magistrates' court acting for the petty sessions area concerned is satisfied that the offender proposes to change, or has changed, his residence from that petty sessions area to another petty sessions area.

(2) Subject to sub-paragraphs (3) to (5) below, the court may, and on the application of the responsible officer shall, amend the relevant order by substituting the other petty sessions area for the area specified in the order or, in the case of a curfew order, a place in that other area for the place so specified.

(3) The court shall not amend under this paragraph a community rehabilitation or curfew order which contains requirements which, in the opinion of the court, cannot be complied with unless the offender continues to reside in the petty sessions area concerned unless, in accordance with paragraph 19 below, it either—

(a)   cancels those requirements; or

(b)   substitutes for those requirements other requirements which can be complied with if the offender ceases to reside in that area.

(4) Sub-paragraph (3) above applies also in relation to a community punishment and rehabilitation order whose community rehabilitation element contains requirements such as are mentioned in that sub-paragraph.

(5) The court shall not amend a community punishment order or community punishment and rehabilitation order under this paragraph unless it appears to the court that provision can be made for the offender to perform work under the order under the arrangements which exist for persons who reside in the other petty sessions area to perform work under such orders.

(6) Where—

(a)   the court amends a community rehabilitation, community punishment or community punishment and rehabilitation order under this paragraph,

(b)   a local authority is specified in the order in accordance with section 41(5) or 46(9) of this Act, and

(c)   the change, or proposed change, of residence also is or would be a change of residence from the area of that authority to the area of another such authority,

the court shall further amend the order by substituting the other authority for the authority specified in the order.

19.   *Amendment of requirements of community rehabilitation, community punishment and rehabilitation or curfew order*
(1) Without prejudice to the provisions of paragraph 18 above but subject to sub-paragraphs (2) and (3) below, a magistrates' court acting for the petty sessions area concerned may, on the application of the offender or the responsible officer, by order amend a community rehabilitation or curfew order or the community rehabilitation element of a community punishment and rehabilitation order—

(a)   by cancelling any of the requirements of the community rehabilitation or curfew order or of the community rehabilitation element of the community punishment and rehabilitation order; or

(b)   by inserting in the community rehabilitation or curfew order or community rehabilitation element of the community punishment and rehabilitation order (either in addition to or in substitution for any of its requirements) any requirement which the court could include if it were then making the order.

(2) A magistrates' court shall not under sub-paragraph (1) above amend a community rehabilitation order or the community rehabilitation element of a community punishment and rehabilitation order—

(a) by reducing the community rehabilitation period, or by extending that period beyond the end of three years from the date of the original order; or

(b) by inserting in it a requirement that the offender shall submit to treatment for his mental condition, or his dependency on or propensity to misuse drugs or alcohol, unless—

(i) the offender has expressed his willingness to comply with such a requirement; and

(ii) the amending order is made within three months after the date of the original order.

(3) A magistrates' court shall not under sub-paragraph (1) above amend a curfew order by extending the curfew periods beyond the end of six months from the date of the original order.

20. *Amendment of treatment requirements of community rehabilitation or community punishment and rehabilitation order on report of practitioner*

(1) Where the medical practitioner or other person by whom or under whose direction an offender is, in pursuance of any requirement of a community rehabilitation or community punishment and rehabilitation order, being treated for his mental condition or his dependency on or propensity to misuse drugs or alcohol—

(a) is of the opinion mentioned in sub-paragraph (2) below, or

(b) is for any reason unwilling to continue to treat or direct the treatment of the offender,

he shall make a report in writing to that effect to the responsible officer and that officer shall apply under paragraph 19 above to a magistrates' court acting for the petty sessions area concerned for the variation or cancellation of the requirement.

(2) The opinion referred to in sub-paragraph (1) above is—

(a) that the treatment of the offender should be continued beyond the period specified in that behalf in the order;

(b) that the offender needs different treatment;

(c) that the offender is not susceptible to treatment; or

(d) that the offender does not require further treatment.

21. *Amendment of drug treatment and testing order*

(1) Without prejudice to the provisions of section 55(1), (6) and (8) of this Act, the court responsible for a drug treatment and testing order may by order—

(a) vary or cancel any of the requirements or provisions of the order on an application by the responsible officer under sub-paragraph (2) or (3)(a) or (b) below; or

(b) amend the order on an application by that officer under sub-paragraph (3)(c) below.

(2) Where the treatment provider is of the opinion that the treatment or testing requirement of the order should be varied or cancelled—

(a) he shall make a report in writing to that effect to the responsible officer; and

(b) that officer shall apply to the court for the variation or cancellation of the requirement.

(3) Where the responsible officer is of the opinion—

(a) that the treatment or testing requirement of the order should be so varied as to specify a different treatment provider,

(b) that any other requirement of the order, or a provision of the order, should be varied or cancelled, or

(c) that the order should be so amended as to provide for each subsequent periodic review (required by section 54(6)(a) of this Act) to be made without a hearing instead of at a review hearing, or vice versa,

he shall apply to the court for the variation or cancellation of the requirement or provision or the amendment of the order.

(4) The court—

(a) shall not amend the treatment or testing requirement unless the offender expresses his willingness to comply with the requirement as amended; and

(b) shall not amend any provision of the order so as to reduce the treatment and testing period below the minimum specified in section 52(1) of this Act, or to increase it above the maximum so specified.

(5) If the offender fails to express his willingness to comply with the treatment or testing requirement as proposed to be amended by the court, the court may—

(a) revoke the order; and

(b) deal with him, for the offence in respect of which the order was made, in any way in which it could deal with him if he had just been convicted by or before the court of the offence.

(6) In dealing with the offender under sub-paragraph (5)(b) above, the court—

(a) shall take into account the extent to which the offender has complied with the requirements of the order; and

(b) may impose a custodial sentence (where the order was made in respect of an offence punishable with such a sentence) notwithstanding anything in section 79(2) of this Act.

22.   *Extension of community punishment or community punishment and rehabilitation order*

Where—

(a) a community punishment order or community punishment and rehabilitation order is in force in respect of any offender, and

(b) on the application of the offender or the responsible officer, it appears to a magistrates' court acting for the petty sessions area concerned that it would be in the interests of justice to do so having regard to circumstances which have arisen since the order was made,

the court may, in relation to the order, extend the period of twelve months specified in section 47(3) of this Act.

ATTENDANCE CENTRE ORDERS

60   **Attendance centre orders**

(1) Where—

(a) (subject to sections 34 to 36 above) a person aged under 21 is convicted by or before a court of an offence punishable with imprisonment, or

(b) a court would have power, but for section 89 below (restrictions on imprisonment of young offenders and defaulters), to commit a person aged under 21 to prison in default of payment of any sum of money or for failing to do or abstain from doing anything required to be done or left undone, or

(c) a court has power to commit a person aged at least 21 but under 25 to prison in default of payment of any sum of money,

the court may, if it has been notified by the Secretary of State that an attendance centre is available for the reception of persons of his description, order him to attend at such a centre, to be specified in the order, for such number of hours as may be so specified.

(3) The aggregate number of hours for which an attendance centre order may require a person to attend at an attendance centre shall not be less than 12 except where—

(a) he is aged under 14; and

(b) the court is of the opinion that 12 hours would be excessive, having regard to his age or any other circumstances.

(4) The aggregate number of hours shall not exceed 12 except where the court is of the opinion, having regard to all the circumstances, that 12 hours would be inadequate, and in that case—

(a) shall not exceed 24 where the person is aged under 16; and

(b) shall not exceed 36 where the person is aged 16 or over but under 21 or (where subsection (1)(c) above applies) under 25.

(5) A court may make an attendance centre order in respect of a person before a previous attendance centre order made in respect of him has ceased to have effect, and may determine the number of hours to be specified in the order without regard—

(a) to the number specified in the previous order; or

(b) to the fact that that order is still in effect.

(6) An attendance centre order shall not be made unless the court is satisfied that the attendance centre to be specified in it is reasonably accessible to the person concerned, having regard to his age, the means of access available to him and any other circumstances.

(7) The times at which a person is required to attend at an attendance centre shall, as far as practicable, be such as to avoid—

(a) any conflict with his religious beliefs or with the requirements of any other community order to which he may be subject; and

(b) any interference with the times, if any, at which he normally works or attends school or any other educational establishment.

(10) A person shall not be required under this section to attend at an attendance centre on more than one occasion on any day, or for more than three hours on any occasion.

(12) Where a person ("the defaulter") has been ordered to attend at an attendance centre in default of the payment of any sum of money—

(a) on payment of the whole sum to any person authorised to receive it, the attendance centre order shall cease to have effect;

(b) on payment of a part of the sum to any such person, the total number of hours for which the defaulter is required to attend at the centre shall be reduced proportionately, that is to say by such number of complete hours as bears to the total number the proportion most nearly approximating to, without exceeding, the proportion which the part bears to the whole sum.

62   Provision, regulation and management of attendance centres

(2) In this Act "attendance centre" means a place at which offenders aged under 21 may be required to attend and be given under supervision appropriate occupation or instruction in pursuance of attendance centre orders.

SCHEDULE 5

BREACH, REVOCATION AND AMENDMENT OF ATTENDANCE CENTRE ORDERS

1.   *Breach of order or attendance centre rules*

(1) Where an attendance centre order is in force and it appears on information to a justice acting for a relevant petty sessions area that the offender—

(a) has failed to attend in accordance with the order, or

(b) while attending has committed a breach of rules made under section 62(3) of this Act which cannot be adequately dealt with under those rules, the justice may issue a summons requiring the offender to appear at the place and time specified in the summons before a magistrates' court acting for the area or, if the information is in writing and on oath, may issue a warrant for the offender's arrest requiring him to be brought before such a court.

2—(1) If it is proved to the satisfaction of the magistrates' court before which an offender appears or is brought under paragraph 1 above that he has failed without reasonable excuse to attend as mentioned in sub-paragraph (1)(a) of that paragraph or has committed such a breach of rules as is mentioned in sub-paragraph (1)(b) of that paragraph, that court may deal with him in any one of the following ways—

(a) it may impose on him a fine not exceeding £1,000;

(b) where the attendance centre order was made by a magistrates' court, it may deal with him, for the offence in respect of which the order was made, in any way in which he could have been dealt with for that offence by the court which made the order if the order had not been made; or

(c) where the order was made by the Crown Court, it may commit him to custody or release him on bail until he can be brought or appear before the Crown Court.

(3) A fine imposed under sub-paragraph (1)(a) above shall be deemed, for the purposes of any enactment, to be a sum adjudged to be paid by a conviction.

(4) Where a magistrates' court deals with an offender under sub-paragraph (1)(b) above, it shall revoke the attendance centre order if it is still in force.

(5) In dealing with an offender under sub-paragraph (1)(b) above, a magistrates' court—

(a) shall take into account the extent to which the offender has complied with the requirements of the attendance centre order; and

(b) in the case of an offender who has wilfully and persistently failed to comply with those requirements, may impose a custodial sentence notwithstanding anything in section 79(2) of this Act.

3—(1) Where by virtue of paragraph 2(1)(c) above the offender is brought or appears before the Crown Court and it is proved to the satisfaction of the court—

(a) that he has failed without reasonable excuse to attend as mentioned in paragraph 1(1)(a) above, or

(b) that he has committed such a breach of rules as is mentioned in paragraph 1(1)(b) above,

that court may deal with him, for the offence in respect of which the order was made, in any way in which it could have dealt with him for that offence if it had not made the order.

(2) Where the Crown Court deals with an offender under sub-paragraph (1) above, it shall revoke the attendance centre order if it is still in force.

(3) In dealing with an offender under sub-paragraph (1) above, the Crown Court—

(a) shall take into account the extent to which the offender has complied with the requirements of the attendance centre order; and

(b) in the case of an offender who has wilfully and persistently failed to comply with those requirements, may impose a custodial sentence notwithstanding anything in section 79(2) of this Act.

4. *Revocation of order with or without re-sentencing*

(1) Where an attendance centre order is in force in respect of an offender, an appropriate court may, on an application made by the offender or by the officer in charge of the relevant attendance centre, revoke the order.

(2) In sub-paragraph (1) above "an appropriate court" means—

(a) where the court which made the order was the Crown Court and there is included in the order a direction that the power to revoke the order is reserved to that court, the Crown Court;

(b) in any other case, either of the following—

    (i) a magistrates' court acting for the petty sessions area in which the relevant attendance centre is situated;

    (ii) the court which made the order.

(3) Any power conferred by this paragraph—

    (a) on a magistrates' court to revoke an attendance centre order made by such a court, or

    (b) on the Crown Court to revoke an attendance centre order made by the Crown Court,

includes power to deal with the offender, for the offence in respect of which the order was made, in any way in which he could have been dealt with for that offence by the court which made the order if the order had not been made.

5. *Amendment of order*

(1) Where an attendance centre order is in force in respect of an offender, an appropriate magistrates' court may, on an application made by the offender or by the officer in charge of the relevant attendance centre, by order—

    (a) vary the day or hour specified in the order for the offender's first attendance at the relevant attendance centre; or

    (b) substitute for the relevant attendance centre an attendance centre which the court is satisfied is reasonably accessible to the offender, having regard to his age, the means of access available to him and any other circumstances.

SUPERVISION ORDERS

63 Supervision orders

(1) Where a child or young person (that is to say, any person aged under 18) is convicted of an offence, the court by or before which he is convicted may (subject to sections 34 to 36 above) make an order placing him under the supervision of—

    (a) a local authority designated by the order;

    (b) a probation officer; or

    (c) a member of a youth offending team.

(5) A court shall not make a supervision order unless it is satisfied that the offender resides or will reside in the area of a local authority; and a court shall be entitled to be satisfied that the offender will so reside if he is to be required so to reside by a provision to be included in the order in pursuance of paragraph 1 of Schedule 6 to this Act.

(6) A supervision order—

    (a) shall name the area of the local authority and the petty sessions area in which it appears to the court making the order (or to the court amending under Schedule 7 to this Act any provision included in the order in pursuance of this paragraph) that the offender resides or will reside; and

    (b) may contain such prescribed provisions as the court making the order (or amending it under that Schedule) considers appropriate for facilitating the performance by the supervisor of his functions under section 64(4) below, including any prescribed provisions for requiring visits to be made by the offender to the supervisor;

and in paragraph (b) above "prescribed" means prescribed by rules under section 144 of the Magistrates' Courts Act 1980.

(7) A supervision order shall, unless it has previously been revoked, cease to have effect at the end of the period of three years, or such shorter period as may be specified in the order, beginning with the date on which the order was originally made.

64 Selection and duty of supervisor and certain expenditure of his

(1) A court shall not designate a local authority as the supervisor by a provision of a supervision order unless—

(a) the authority agree; or

(b) it appears to the court that the offender resides or will reside in the area of the authority.

(2) Where a provision of a supervision order places the offender under the supervision of a probation officer, the supervisor shall be a probation officer appointed for or assigned to the petty sessions area named in the order in pursuance of section 63(6) above and selected under arrangements made under section 4(1)(d) of the Probation Service Act 1993 (arrangements made by probation committee).

(3) Where a provision of a supervision order places the offender under the supervision of a member of a youth offending team, the supervisor shall be a member of a team established by the local authority within whose area it appears to the court that the offender resides or will reside.

(4) While a supervision order is in force, the supervisor shall advise, assist and befriend the offender.

SCHEDULE 6

REQUIREMENTS WHICH MAY BE INCLUDED IN SUPERVISION ORDERS

1. *Requirement to reside with named individual*

A supervision order may require the offender to reside with an individual named in the order who agrees to the requirement, but a requirement imposed by a supervision order in pursuance of this paragraph shall be subject to any such requirement of the order as is authorised by paragraph 2, 3, 6 or 7 below.

2. *Requirement to comply with directions of supervisor*

(1) Subject to sub-paragraph (2) below, a supervision order may require the offender to comply with any directions given from time to time by the supervisor and requiring him to do all or any of the following things—

(a) to live at a place or places specified in the directions for a period or periods so specified;

(b) to present himself to a person or persons specified in the directions at a place or places and on a day or days so specified;

(c) to participate in activities specified in the directions on a day or days so specified.

(2) A supervision order shall not require compliance with directions given by virtue of sub-paragraph (1) above unless the court making it is satisfied that a scheme under section 66 of this Act (local authority schemes) is in force for the area where the offender resides or will reside; and no such directions may involve the use of facilities which are not for the time being specified in a scheme in force under that section for that area.

(3) A requirement imposed by a supervision order in pursuance of sub-paragraph (1) above shall be subject to any such requirement of the order as is authorised by paragraph 6 below (treatment for offender's mental condition).

(4) It shall be for the supervisor to decide—

(a) whether and to what extent he exercises any power to give directions conferred on him by virtue of sub-paragraph (1) above; and

(b) the form of any directions.

(5) The total number of days in respect of which an offender may be required to comply with directions given by virtue of paragraph (a), (b) or (c) of sub-paragraph (1) above shall not exceed 90 or such lesser number, if any, as the order may specify for the purposes of this sub-paragraph.

(6) For the purpose of calculating the total number of days in respect of which such directions may be given, the supervisor shall be entitled to disregard any day in respect of

which directions were previously given in pursuance of the order and on which the directions were not complied with.

(7) Directions given by the supervisor by virtue of sub-paragraph (1)(b) or (c) above shall, as far as practicable, be such as to avoid—

(a) any conflict with the offender's religious beliefs or with the requirements of any other community order to which he may be subject; and

(b) any interference with the times, if any, at which he normally works or attends school or any other educational establishment.

3. *Requirements as to activities, reparation, night restrictions etc.*

(1) This paragraph applies to a supervision order unless the order requires the offender to comply with directions given by the supervisor under paragraph 2(1) above.

(2) Subject to the following provisions of this paragraph and paragraph 4 below, a supervision order to which this paragraph applies may require the offender—

(a) to live at a place or places specified in the order for a period or periods so specified;

(b) to present himself to a person or persons specified in the order at a place or places and on a day or days so specified;

(c) to participate in activities specified in the order on a day or days so specified;

(d) to make reparation specified in the order to a person or persons so specified or to the community at large;

(e) to remain for specified periods between 6 p.m. and 6 a.m.—

(i) at a place specified in the order; or

(ii) at one of several places so specified;

(f) to refrain from participating in activities specified in the order—

(i) on a specified day or days during the period for which the supervision order is in force; or

(ii) during the whole of that period or a specified portion of it;

and in this paragraph "make reparation" means make reparation for the offence otherwise than by the payment of compensation.

(3) The total number of days in respect of which an offender may be subject to requirements imposed by virtue of paragraph (a), (b), (c), (d) or (e) of sub-paragraph (2) above shall not exceed 90.

(4) The court may not include requirements under sub-paragraph (2) above in a supervision order unless—

(a) it has first consulted the supervisor as to—

(i) the offender's circumstances, and

(ii) the feasibility of securing compliance with the requirements,

and is satisfied, having regard to the supervisor's report, that it is feasible to secure compliance with them;

(b) having regard to the circumstances of the case, it considers the requirements necessary for securing the good conduct of the offender or for preventing a repetition by him of the same offence or the commission of other offences; and

(c) if the offender is aged under 16, it has obtained and considered information about his family circumstances and the likely effect of the requirements on those circumstances.

(5) The court shall not by virtue of sub-paragraph (2) above include in a supervision order—

(a) any requirement that would involve the co-operation of a person other than the supervisor and the offender, unless that other person consents to its inclusion;

(b) any requirement to make reparation to any person unless that person—

    (i) is identified by the court as a victim of the offence or a person otherwise affected by it; and

    (ii) consents to the inclusion of the requirement;

(c) any requirement requiring the offender to reside with a specified individual; or

(d) any such requirement as is mentioned in paragraph 6(2) below (treatment for offender's mental condition).

(6) Requirements included in a supervision order by virtue of sub-paragraph (2)(b) or (c) above shall, as far as practicable, be such as to avoid—

(a) any conflict with the offender's religious beliefs or with the requirements of any other community order to which he may be subject; and

(b) any interference with the times, if any, at which he normally works or attends school or any other educational establishment;

and sub-paragraph (7) and (8) below are without prejudice to this sub-paragraph.

(7) Subject to sub-paragraph (8) below, a supervision order may not by virtue of sub-paragraph (2) above include—

(a) any requirement that would involve the offender in absence from home—

    (i) for more than two consecutive nights, or

    (ii) for more than two nights in any one week, or

(b) if the offender is of compulsory school age, any requirement to participate in activities during normal school hours,

unless the court making the order is satisfied that the facilities whose use would be involved are for the time being specified in a scheme in force under section 66 of this Act for the area in which the offender resides or will reside.

(8) Sub-paragraph (7)(b) above does not apply to activities carried out in accordance with arrangements made or approved by the local education authority in whose area the offender resides or will reside.

4.

(1) The place, or one of the places, specified in a requirement under paragraph 3(2)(e) above ("a night restriction") shall be the place where the offender lives.

(2) A night restriction shall not require the offender to remain at a place for longer than ten hours on any one night.

(3) A night restriction shall not be imposed in respect of any day which falls outside the period of three months beginning with the date when the supervision order is made.

(4) A night restriction shall not be imposed in respect of more than 30 days in all.

(6) An offender who is required by a night restriction to remain at a place may leave it if he is accompanied—

(a) by his parent or guardian;

(b) by his supervisor; or

(c) by some other person specified in the supervision order.

5. *Requirement to live for specified period in local authority accommodation*

(1) Where the conditions mentioned in sub-paragraph (2) below are satisfied, a supervision order may impose a requirement ("a local authority residence requirement") that the offender shall live for a specified period in local authority accommodation (as defined by section 163 of this Act).

(2) The conditions are that—

(a) a supervision order has previously been made in respect of the offender;

(b) that order imposed—

    (i) a requirement under paragraph 1, 2, 3 or 7 of this Schedule; or

    (ii) a local authority residence requirement;

(c) the offender fails to comply with that requirement, or is convicted of an offence committed while that order was in force; and

(d) the court is satisfied that—
  (i) the failure to comply with the requirement, or the behaviour which con-
       stituted the offence, was due to a significant extent to the circumstances in
       which the offender was living; and
  (ii) the imposition of a local authority residence requirement will assist in his
       rehabilitation;

except that sub-paragraph (i) of paragraph (d) above does not apply where the condition in
paragraph (b)(ii) above is satisfied.

(3) A local authority residence requirement shall designate the local authority who are to
receive the offender, and that authority shall be the authority in whose area the offender
resides.

(4) The court shall not impose a local authority residence requirement without first
consulting the designated authority.

(5) A local authority residence requirement may stipulate that the offender shall not live
with a named person.

(6) The maximum period which may be specified in a local authority residence
requirement is six months.

6. *Requirements as to treatment for mental condition*

(1) This paragraph applies where a court which proposes to make a supervision order is
satisfied, on the evidence of a registered medical practitioner approved for the purposes of
section 12 of the Mental Health Act 1983, that the mental condition of the offender—
  (a) is such as requires and may be susceptible to treatment; but
  (b) is not such as to warrant the making of a hospital order or guardianship order
       within the meaning of that Act.

(2) Where this paragraph applies, the court may include in the supervision order a
requirement that the offender shall, for a period specified in the order, submit to treatment of
one of the following descriptions so specified, that is to say—
  (a) treatment as a resident patient in a hospital or mental nursing home within the
       meaning of the Mental Health Act 1983, but not a hospital at which high security
       psychiatric services within the meaning of that Act are provided;
  (b) treatment as a non-resident patient at an institution or place specified in the
       order;
  (c) treatment by or under the direction of a registered medical practitioner specified
       in the order; or
  (d) treatment by or under the direction of a chartered psychologist specified in the
       order.

(3) A requirement shall not be included in a supervision order by virtue of sub-paragraph
(2) above—
  (a) in any case, unless the court is satisfied that arrangements have been or can be
       made for the treatment in question and, in the case of treatment as a resident
       patient, for the reception of the patient;
  (b) in the case of an order made or to be made in respect of a person aged 14 or over,
       unless he consents to its inclusion;

and a requirement so included shall not in any case continue in force after the offender attains
the age of 18.

7. *Requirements as to education*

(1) This paragraph applies to a supervision order unless the order requires the offender to
comply with directions given by the supervisor under paragraph 2(1) above.

(2) Subject to the following provisions of this paragraph, a supervision order to which
this paragraph applies may require the offender, if he is of compulsory school age, to comply,
for as long as he is of that age and the order remains in force, with such arrangements for his

education as may from time to time be made by his parent, being arrangements for the time being approved by the local education authority.

(3) The court shall not include such a requirement in a supervision order unless—

(a) it has consulted the local education authority with regard to its proposal to include the requirement; and

(b) it is satisfied that in the view of the local education authority arrangements exist for the offender to receive efficient full-time education suitable to his age, ability and aptitude and to any special educational need he may have.

(5) The court may not include a requirement under sub-paragraph (2) above unless it has first consulted the supervisor as to the offender's circumstances and, having regard to the circumstances of the case, it considers the requirement necessary for securing the good conduct of the offender or for preventing a repetition by him of the same offence or the commission of other offences.

SCHEDULE 7

BREACH, REVOCATION AND AMENDMENT OF SUPERVISION ORDERS

2. *Breach of requirement of supervision order*

(1) This paragraph applies if while a supervision order is in force in respect of an offender it is proved to the satisfaction of a relevant court, on the application of the supervisor, that the offender has failed to comply with any requirement included in the supervision order in pursuance of paragraph 1, 2, 3, 5 or 7 of Schedule 6 to this Act or section 63(6)(b) of this Act.

(2) Where this paragraph applies, the court—

(a) whether or not it also makes an order under paragraph 5(1) below (revocation or amendment of supervision order)—

(i)   may order the offender to pay a fine of an amount not exceeding £1,000; or

(ii) subject to paragraph 3 below, may make a curfew order in respect of him; or

(iii) subject to paragraph 4 below, may make an attendance centre order in respect of him; or

(b) if the supervision order was made by a magistrates' court, may revoke the supervision order and deal with the offender, for the offence in respect of which the order was made, in any way in which he could have been dealt with for that offence by the court which made the order if the order had not been made; or

(c) if the supervision order was made by the Crown Court, may commit him in custody or release him on bail until he can be brought or appear before the Crown Court.

(3) Where a court deals with an offender under sub-paragraph (2)(c) above, it shall send to the Crown Court a certificate signed by a justice of the peace giving—

(a) particulars of the offender's failure to comply with the requirement in question; and

(b) such other particulars of the case as may be desirable;

and a certificate purporting to be so signed shall be admissible as evidence of the failure before the Crown Court.

(4) Where—

(a) by virtue of sub-paragraph (2)(c) above the offender is brought or appears before the Crown Court, and

(b) it is proved to the satisfaction of the court that he has failed to comply with the requirement in question,

that court may deal with him, for the offence in respect of which the supervision order was made, in any way in which it could have dealt with him for that offence if it had not made the order.

(5) Where the Crown Court deals with an offender under sub-paragraph (4) above, it shall revoke the supervision order if it is still in force.

(6) A fine imposed under this paragraph shall be deemed, for the purposes of any enactment, to be a sum adjudged to be paid by a conviction.

(7) In dealing with an offender under this paragraph, a court shall take into account the extent to which he has complied with the requirements of the supervision order.

5. *Revocation and amendment of supervision order*

(1) If while a supervision order is in force in respect of an offender it appears to a relevant court, on the application of the supervisor or the offender, that it is appropriate to make an order under this sub-paragraph, the court may—

    (a) make an order revoking the supervision order; or

    (b) make an order amending it—

        (i) by cancelling any requirement included in it in pursuance of Schedule 6 to, or section 63(6)(b) of, this Act; or

        (ii) by inserting in it (either in addition to or in substitution for any of its provisions) any provision which could have been included in the order if the court had then had power to make it and were exercising the power.

(3) The powers of amendment conferred by sub-paragraph (1) above do not include power—

    (a) to insert in the supervision order, after the end of three months beginning with the date when the order was originally made, a requirement in pursuance of paragraph 6 of Schedule 6 to this Act (treatment for mental condition), unless it is in substitution for such a requirement already included in the order; or

    (b) to insert in the supervision order a requirement in pursuance of paragraph 3(2)(e) of that Schedule (night restrictions) in respect of any day which falls outside the period of three months beginning with the date when the order was originally made.

6. *Amendment of order on report of medical practitioner*

(1) If a medical practitioner by whom or under whose direction an offender is being treated for his mental condition in pursuance of a requirement included in a supervision order by virtue of paragraph 6 of Schedule 6 to this Act—

    (a) is unwilling to continue to treat or direct the treatment of the offender, or

    (b) is of the opinion mentioned in sub-paragraph (2) below, the practitioner shall make a report in writing to that effect to the supervisor.

(2) The opinion referred to in sub-paragraph (1) above is—

    (a) that the treatment of the offender should be continued beyond the period specified in that behalf in the order;

    (b) that the offender needs different treatment;

    (c) that the offender is not susceptible to treatment; or

    (d) that the offender does not require further treatment.

ACTION PLAN ORDERS

69 Action plan orders

(1) Where a child or young person (that is to say, any person aged under 18) is convicted of an offence and the court by or before which he is convicted is of the opinion mentioned in subsection (3) below, the court may (subject to sections 34 to 36 above) make an order which—

    (a) requires the offender, for a period of three months beginning with the date of the order, to comply with an action plan, that is to say, a series of requirements with respect to his actions and whereabouts during that period;

(b) places the offender for that period under the supervision of the responsible officer; and

(c) requires the offender to comply with any directions given by the responsible officer with a view to the implementation of that plan;

and the requirements included in the order, and any directions given by the responsible officer, may include requirements authorised by section 70 below.

(3) The opinion referred to in subsection (1) above is that the making of an action plan order is desirable in the interests of—

(a) securing the rehabilitation of the offender; or

(b) preventing the commission by him of further offences.

(4) In this Act "responsible officer", in relation to an offender subject to an action plan order, means one of the following who is specified in the order, namely—

(a) a probation officer;

(b) a social worker of a local authority social services department;

(c) a member of a youth offending team.

(5) The court shall not make an action plan order in respect of the offender if—

(a) he is already the subject of such an order; or

(b) the court proposes to pass on him a custodial sentence or to make in respect of him a community rehabilitation order, a community punishment order, a community punishment and rehabilitation order, an attendance centre order, a supervision order or a referral order.

(6) Before making an action plan order, the court shall obtain and consider—

(a) a written report by a probation officer, a social worker of a local authority social services department or a member of a youth offending team indicating—

(i) the requirements proposed by that person to be included in the order;

(ii) the benefits to the offender that the proposed requirements are designed to achieve; and

(iii) the attitude of a parent or guardian of the offender to the proposed requirements; and

(b) where the offender is aged under 16, information about the offender's family circumstances and the likely effect of the order on those circumstances.

(7) The court shall not make an action plan order unless it has been notified by the Secretary of State that arrangements for implementing such orders are available in the area proposed to be named in the order under subsection (8) below and the notice has not been withdrawn.

(10) Where an action plan order specifies under that subsection—

(a) a social worker of a local authority social services department, or

(b) a member of a youth offending team,

the social worker or member specified must be a social worker of, or a member of a youth offending team established by, the local authority within whose area it appears to the court that the offender resides or will reside.

(11) Before making an action plan order, the court shall explain to the offender in ordinary language—

(a) the effect of the order and of the requirements proposed to be included in it;

(b) the consequences which may follow (under Schedule 8 to this Act) if he fails to comply with any of those requirements; and

(c) that the court has power (under that Schedule) to review the order on the application either of the offender or of the responsible officer.

70 Requirements which may be included in action plan orders and directions

(1) Requirements included in an action plan order, or directions given by a responsible officer, may require the offender to do all or any of the following things, namely—

(a) to participate in activities specified in the requirements or directions at a time or times so specified;

(b) to present himself to a person or persons specified in the requirements or directions at a place or places and at a time or times so specified;

(c) subject to subsection (2) below, to attend at an attendance centre specified in the requirements or directions for a number of hours so specified;

(d) to stay away from a place or places specified in the requirements or directions;

(e) to comply with any arrangements for his education specified in the requirements or directions;

(f) to make reparation specified in the requirements or directions to a person or persons so specified or to the community at large; and

(g) to attend any hearing fixed by the court under section 71 below.

(2) Subsection (1)(c) above applies only where the offence committed by the offender is an offence punishable with imprisonment.

(3) In subsection (1)(f) above "make reparation", in relation to an offender, means make reparation for the offence otherwise than by the payment of compensation.

(5) Requirements included in an action plan order and directions given by a responsible officer shall, as far as practicable, be such as to avoid—

(a) any conflict with the offender's religious beliefs or with the requirements of any other community order to which he may be subject; and

(b) any interference with the times, if any, at which he normally works or attends school or any other educational establishment.

71 Action plan orders: power to fix further hearings

(1) Immediately after making an action plan order, a court may—

(a) fix a further hearing for a date not more than 21 days after the making of the order; and

(b) direct the responsible officer to make, at that hearing, a report as to the effectiveness of the order and the extent to which it has been implemented.

(2) At a hearing fixed under subsection (1) above, the court—

(a) shall consider the responsible officer's report; and

(b) may, on the application of the responsible officer or the offender, amend the order—

(i) by cancelling any provision included in it; or

(ii) by inserting in it (either in addition to or in substitution for any of its provisions) any provision that the court could originally have included in it.

(e) FINANCIAL PENALTIES AND ORDERS

Powers of Criminal Courts (Sentencing) Act 2000

FINANCIAL CIRCUMSTANCES

126 Powers to order statement as to offender's financial circumstances

(1) Where an individual has been convicted of an offence, the court may, before sentencing him, make a financial circumstances order with respect to him.

(2) Where a magistrates' court has been notified in accordance with section 12(4) of the Magistrates' Courts Act 1980 that an individual desires to plead guilty without appearing before the court, the court may make a financial circumstances order with respect to him.

(3) In this section "a financial circumstances order" means, in relation to any individual, an order requiring him to give to the court, within such period as may be specified in the order, such a statement of his financial circumstances as the court may require.

(4) An individual who without reasonable excuse fails to comply with a financial circumstances order shall be liable on summary conviction to a fine not exceeding level 3 on the standard scale.

(5) If an individual, in furnishing any statement in pursuance of a financial circumstances order—

    (a) makes a statement which he knows to be false in a material particular,

    (b) recklessly furnishes a statement which is false in a material particular, or

    (c) knowingly fails to disclose any material fact,

he shall be liable on summary conviction to imprisonment for a term not exceeding three months or a fine not exceeding level 4 on the standard scale or both.

FINES

127   General power of Crown Court to fine offender convicted on indictment

Where a person is convicted on indictment of any offence, other than an offence for which the sentence is fixed by law or falls to be imposed under section 109(2), 110(2) or 111(2) above, the court, if not precluded from sentencing the offender by its exercise of some other power, may impose a fine instead of or in addition to dealing with him in any other way in which the court has power to deal with him, subject however to any enactment requiring the offender to be dealt with in a particular way.

128   Fixing of fines

(1) Before fixing the amount of any fine to be imposed on an offender who is an individual, a court shall inquire into his financial circumstances.

(2) The amount of any fine fixed by a court shall be such as, in the opinion of the court, reflects the seriousness of the offence.

(3) In fixing the amount of any fine to be imposed on an offender (whether an individual or other person), a court shall take into account the circumstances of the case including, among other things, the financial circumstances of the offender so far as they are known, or appear, to the court.

(5) Where—

    (a) an offender has been convicted in his absence in pursuance of section 11 or 12 of the Magistrates' Courts Act 1980 (non-appearance of accused), or

    (b) an offender—

        (i) has failed to comply with an order under section 126(1) above, or

        (ii) has otherwise failed to co-operate with the court in its inquiry into his financial circumstances,

and the court considers that it has insufficient information to make a proper determination of the financial circumstances of the offender, it may make such determination as it thinks fit.

129   Remission of fines

(1) This section applies where a court has, in fixing the amount of a fine, determined the offender's financial circumstances under section 128(5) above.

(2) If, on subsequently inquiring into the offender's financial circumstances, the court is satisfied that had it had the results of that inquiry when sentencing the offender it would—

    (a) have fixed a smaller amount, or

    (b) not have fined him,

it may remit the whole or any part of the fine.

COMPENSATION ORDERS

130   Compensation orders against convicted persons

(1) A court by or before which a person is convicted of an offence, instead of or in addition to dealing with him in any other way, may, on application or otherwise, make an order (in this Act referred to as a "compensation order") requiring him—

    (a) to pay compensation for any personal injury, loss or damage resulting from that offence or any other offence which is taken into consideration by the court in determining sentence; or

    (b) to make payments for funeral expenses or bereavement in respect of a death resulting from any such offence, other than a death due to an accident arising out of the presence of a motor vehicle on a road;

but this is subject to the following provisions of this section and to section 131 below.

(3) A court shall give reasons, on passing sentence, if it does not make a compensation order in a case where this section empowers it to do so.

(4) Compensation under subsection (1) above shall be of such amount as the court considers appropriate, having regard to any evidence and to any representations that are made by or on behalf of the accused or the prosecutor.

(5) In the case of an offence under the Theft Act 1968, where the property in question is recovered, any damage to the property occurring while it was out of the owner's possession shall be treated for the purposes of subsection (1) above as having resulted from the offence, however and by whomever the damage was caused.

(6) A compensation order may only be made in respect of injury, loss or damage (other than loss suffered by a person's dependants in consequence of his death) which was due to an accident arising out of the presence of a motor vehicle on a road, if—

    (a) it is in respect of damage which is treated by subsection (5) above as resulting from an offence under the Theft Act 1968; or

    (b) it is in respect of injury, loss or damage as respects which—

        (i)   the offender is uninsured in relation to the use of the vehicle; and

        (ii) compensation is not payable under any arrangements to which the Secretary of State is a party.

(7) Where a compensation order is made in respect of injury, loss or damage due to an accident arising out of the presence of a motor vehicle on a road, the amount to be paid may include an amount representing the whole or part of any loss of or reduction in preferential rates of insurance attributable to the accident.

(11) In determining whether to make a compensation order against any person, and in determining the amount to be paid by any person under such an order, the court shall have regard to his means so far as they appear or are known to the court.

(12) Where the court considers—

    (a) that it would be appropriate both to impose a fine and to make a compensation order, but

    (b) that the offender has insufficient means to pay both an appropriate fine and appropriate compensation,

the court shall give preference to compensation (though it may impose a fine as well).

131   Limit on amount payable under compensation order of magistrates' court

(1) The compensation to be paid under a compensation order made by a magistrates' court in respect of any offence of which the court has convicted the offender shall not exceed £5,000.

(2) The compensation or total compensation to be paid under a compensation order or compensation orders made by a magistrates' court in respect of any offence or offences taken into consideration in determining sentence shall not exceed the difference (if any) between—

(a) the amount or total amount which under subsection (1) above is the maximum for the offence or offences of which the offender has been convicted; and

(b) the amount or total amounts (if any) which are in fact ordered to be paid in respect of that offence or those offences.

133   Review of compensation orders

(1) The magistrates' court for the time being having functions in relation to the enforcement of a compensation order (in this section referred to as "the appropriate court") may, on the application of the person against whom the compensation order was made, discharge the order or reduce the amount which remains to be paid; but this is subject to subsections (2) to (4) below.

(2) The appropriate court may exercise a power conferred by subsection (1) above only—

(a) at a time when (disregarding any power of a court to grant leave to appeal out of time) there is no further possibility of an appeal on which the compensation order could be varied or set aside; and

(b) at a time before the person against whom the compensation order was made has paid into court the whole of the compensation which the order requires him to pay.

(3) The appropriate court may exercise a power conferred by subsection (1) above only if it appears to the court—

(a) that the injury, loss or damage in respect of which the compensation order was made has been held in civil proceedings to be less than it was taken to be for the purposes of the order; or

(b) in the case of a compensation order in respect of the loss of any property, that the property has been recovered by the person in whose favour the order was made; or

(c) that the means of the person against whom the compensation order was made are insufficient to satisfy in full both the order and a confiscation order under Part VI of the Criminal Justice Act 1988 made against him in the same proceedings; or

(d) that the person against whom the compensation order was made has suffered a substantial reduction in his means which was unexpected at the time when the order was made, and that his means seem unlikely to increase for a considerable period.

YOUNG OFFENDERS

135   Limit on fines imposed by magistrates' courts in respect of young offenders

(1) Where a person aged under 18 is found guilty by a magistrates' court of an offence for which, apart from this section, the court would have power to impose a fine of an amount exceeding £1,000, the amount of any fine imposed by the court shall not exceed £1,000.

(2) In relation to a person aged under 14, subsection (1) above shall have effect as if for "£1,000", in both places where it occurs, there were substituted "£250".

136   Power to order statement as to financial circumstances of parent or guardian

(1) Before exercising its powers under section 137 below (power to order parent or guardian to pay fine, costs or compensation) against the parent or guardian of an individual who has been convicted of an offence, the court may make a financial circumstances order with respect to the parent or (as the case may be) guardian.

(2) In this section "financial circumstances order" has the meaning given by subsection (3) of section 126 above, and subsections (4) to (6) of that section shall apply in relation to a financial circumstances order made under this section as they apply in relation to such an order made under that section.

137   Power to order parent or guardian to pay fine, costs or compensation

(1) Where–

(a) a child or young person (that is to say, any person aged under 18) is convicted of any offence for the commission of which a fine or costs may be imposed or a compensation order may be made, and

(b) the court is of the opinion that the case would best be met by the imposition of a fine or costs or the making of such an order, whether with or without any other punishment,

the court shall order that the fine, compensation or costs awarded be paid by the parent or guardian of the child or young person instead of by the child or young person himself, unless the court is satisfied—

(i) that the parent or guardian cannot be found; or

(ii) that it would be unreasonable to make an order for payment, having regard to the circumstances of the case.

(2) Where but for this subsection a court would impose a fine on a child or young person under—

(a) paragraph 4(1)(a) or 5(1)(a) of Schedule 3 to this Act (breach of curfew, community rehabilitation, community punishment, community punishment and rehabilitation or drug treatment and testing order),

(b) paragraph 2(1)(a) of Schedule 5 to this Act (breach of attendance centre order or attendance centre rules),

(c) paragraph 2(2)(a) of Schedule 7 to this Act (breach of supervision order),

(d) paragraph 2(2)(a) of Schedule 8 to this Act (breach of action plan order or reparation order),

(e) section 104(3)(b) above (breach of requirements of supervision under a detention and training order), or

(f) section 4(3)(b) of the Criminal Justice and Public Order Act 1994 (breach of requirements of supervision under a secure training order),

the court shall order that the fine be paid by the parent or guardian of the child or young person instead of by the child or young person himself, unless the court is satisfied—

(i) that the parent or guardian cannot be found; or

(ii) that it would be unreasonable to make an order for payment, having regard to the circumstances of the case.

138   Fixing of fine or compensation to be paid by parent or guardian

(1) For the purposes of any order under section 137 above made against the parent or guardian of a child or young person—

(a) section 128 above (fixing of fines) shall have effect as if any reference in subsections (1) to (4) to the financial circumstances of the offender were a reference to the financial circumstances of the parent or guardian, and as if subsection (5) were omitted;

(b) section 130(11) above (determination of compensation order) shall have effect as if any reference to the means of the person against whom the compensation order is made were a reference to the financial circumstances of the parent or guardian; and

(c) section 130(12) above (preference to be given to compensation if insufficient means to pay both compensation and a fine) shall have effect as if the reference to the offender were a reference to the parent or guardian;

but in relation to an order under section 137 made against a local authority this subsection has effect subject to subsection (2) below.

(2) For the purposes of any order under section 137 above made against a local authority, sections 128(1) (duty to inquire into financial circumstances) and 130(11) above shall not apply.

(3) For the purposes of any order under section 137 above, where the parent or guardian of an offender who is a child or young person–

(a) has failed to comply with an order under section 136 above, or

(b) has otherwise failed to co-operate with the court in its inquiry into his financial circumstances,

and the court considers that it has insufficient information to make a proper determination of the parent's or guardian's financial circumstances, it may make such determination as it thinks fit.

MISCELLANEOUS POWERS

139 Powers and duties of Crown Court in relation to fines and forfeited recognizances

(1) Subject to the provisions of this section, if the Crown Court imposes a fine on any person or forfeits his recognizance, the court may make an order—

(a) allowing time for the payment of the amount of the fine or the amount due under the recognizance;

(b) directing payment of that amount by instalments of such amounts and on such dates as may be specified in the order;

(c) in the case of a recognizance, discharging the recognizance or reducing the amount due under it.

(2) Subject to the provisions of this section, if the Crown Court imposes a fine on any person or forfeits his recognizance, the court shall make an order fixing a term of imprisonment or of detention under section 108 above (detention of persons aged 18 to 20 for default) which he is to undergo if any sum which he is liable to pay is not duly paid or recovered.

(3) No person shall on the occasion when a fine is imposed on him or his recognizance is forfeited by the Crown Court be committed to prison or detained in pursuance of an order under subsection (2) above unless—

(a) in the case of an offence punishable with imprisonment, he appears to the court to have sufficient means to pay the sum forthwith;

(b) it appears to the court that he is unlikely to remain long enough at a place of abode in the United Kingdom to enable payment of the sum to be enforced by other methods; or

(c) on the occasion when the order is made the court sentences him to immediate imprisonment, custody for life or detention in a young offender institution for that or another offence, or so sentences him for an offence in addition to forfeiting his recognizance, or he is already serving a sentence of custody for life or a term—

(i) of imprisonment;

(ii) of detention in a young offender institution; or

(iii) of detention under section 108 above.

(4) The periods set out in the second column of the following Table (see p. 231) shall be the maximum periods of imprisonment or detention under subsection (2) above applicable respectively to the amounts set out opposite them.

(5) Where any person liable for the payment of a fine or a sum due under a recognizance to which this section applies is sentenced by the court to, or is serving or otherwise liable to serve, a term of imprisonment or detention in a young offender institution or a term of detention under section 108 above, the court may order that any term of imprisonment or detention fixed under subsection (2) above shall not begin to run until after the end of the first-mentioned term.

(7) Subject to subsection (8) below, the powers conferred by this section shall not be taken as restricted by any enactment which authorises the Crown Court to deal with an offender in any way in which a magistrates' court might have dealt with him or could deal with him.

Table

An amount not exceeding £200	7 days
An amount exceeding £200 but not exceeding £500	14 days
An amount exceeding £500 but not exceeding £1,000	28 days
An amount exceeding £1,000 but not exceeding £2,500	45 days
An amount exceeding £2,500 but not exceeding £5,000	3 months
An amount exceeding £5,000 but not exceeding £10,000	6 months
An amount exceeding £10,000 but not exceeding £20,000	12 months
An amount exceeding £20,000 but not exceeding £50,000	18 months
An amount exceeding £50,000 but not exceeding £100,000	2 years
An amount exceeding £100,000 but not exceeding £250,000	3 years
An amount exceeding £250,000 but not exceeding £1 million	5 years
An amount exceeding £1 million	10 years

(8) Any term fixed under subsection (2) above as respects a fine imposed in pursuance of such an enactment, that is to say a fine which the magistrates' court could have imposed, shall not exceed the period applicable to that fine (if imposed by the magistrates' court) under section 149(1) of the Customs and Excise Management Act 1979 (maximum periods of imprisonment in default of payment of certain fines).

140   Enforcement of fines imposed and recognizances forfeited by Crown Court
    (1) Subject to subsection (5) below, a fine imposed or a recognizance forfeited by the Crown Court shall be treated for the purposes of collection, enforcement and remission of the fine or other sum as having been imposed or forfeited—
    (a) by a magistrates' court specified in an order made by the Crown Court, or
    (b) if no such order is made, by the magistrates' court by which the offender was committed to the Crown Court to be tried or dealt with or by which he was sent to the Crown Court for trial under section 51 of the Crime and Disorder Act 1998,
and, in the case of a fine, as having been so imposed on conviction by the magistrates' court in question.
    (2) Subsection (3) below applies where a magistrates' court issues a warrant of commitment on a default in the payment of—
    (a) a fine imposed by the Crown Court; or
    (b) a sum due under a recognizance forfeited by the Crown Court.
    (3) In such a case, the term of imprisonment or detention under section 108 above specified in the warrant of commitment as the term which the offender is liable to serve shall be—
    (a) the term fixed by the Crown Court under section 139(2) above, or
    (b) if that term has been reduced under section 79(2) of the Magistrates' Courts Act 1980 (part payment) or section 85(2) of that Act (remission), that term as so reduced,
notwithstanding that that term exceeds the period applicable to the case under section 149(1) of the Customs and Excise Management Act 1979 (maximum periods of imprisonment in default of payment of certain fines).
    (5) A magistrates' court shall not, under section 85(1) or 120 of the Magistrates' Courts Act 1980 as applied by subsection (1) above, remit the whole or any part of a fine imposed by, or sum due under a recognizance forfeited by—
    (a) the Crown Court,
    (b) the criminal division of the Court of Appeal, or
    (c) the House of Lords on appeal from that division,
without the consent of the Crown Court.

141   Power of Crown Court to allow time for payment, or payment by instalments, of costs and compensation
Where the Crown Court makes any such order as is mentioned in Part I of Schedule 9 to the Administration of Justice Act 1970 (orders against accused for the payment of costs or compensation), the court may—
>   (a)   allow time for the payment of the sum due under the order;
>   (b)   direct payment of that sum by instalments of such amounts and on such dates as the court may specify.

Deprivation orders

Powers of Criminal Courts (Sentencing) Act 2000

143   Powers to deprive offender of property used etc for purposes of crime
(1) Where a person is convicted of an offence and the court by or before which he is convicted is satisfied that any property which has been lawfully seized from him, or which was in his possession or under his control at the time when he was apprehended for the offence or when a summons in respect of it was issued—
>   (a)   has been used for the purpose of committing, or facilitating the commission of, any offence, or
>   (b)   was intended by him to be used for that purpose,

the court may (subject to subsection (5) below) make an order under this section in respect of that property.

(2) Where a person is convicted of an offence and the offence, or an offence which the court has taken into consideration in determining his sentence, consists of unlawful possession of property which—
>   (a)   has been lawfully seized from him, or
>   (b)   was in his possession or under his control at the time when he was apprehended for the offence of which he has been convicted or when a summons in respect of that offence was issued,

the court may (subject to subsection (5) below) make an order under this section in respect of that property.

(3) An order under this section shall operate to deprive the offender of his rights, if any, in the property to which it relates, and the property shall (if not already in their possession) be taken into the possession of the police.

(4) Any power conferred on a court by subsection (1) or (2) above may be exercised—
>   (a)   whether or not the court also deals with the offender in any other way in respect of the offence of which he has been convicted; and
>   (b)   without regard to any restrictions on forfeiture in any enactment contained in an Act passed before 29th July 1988.

(5) In considering whether to make an order under this section in respect of any property, a court shall have regard—
>   (a)   to the value of the property; and
>   (b)   to the likely financial and other effects on the offender of the making of the order (taken together with any other order that the court contemplates making).

144   Property which is in possession of police by virtue of section 143
(1) The Police (Property) Act 1897 shall apply, with the following modifications, to property which is in the possession of the police by virtue of section 143 above—

(a) no application shall be made under section 1(1) of that Act by any claimant of the property after the end of six months from the date on which the order in respect of the property was made under section 143 above; and

(b) no such application shall succeed unless the claimant satisfies the court either—

   (i)   that he had not consented to the offender having possession of the property; or

   (ii) where an order is made under subsection (1) of section 143 above, that he did not know, and had no reason to suspect, that the property was likely to be used for the purpose mentioned in that subsection.

145   Application of proceeds of forfeited property

(1) Where a court makes an order under section 143 above in a case where—

(a) the offender has been convicted of an offence which has resulted in a person suffering personal injury, loss or damage, or

(b) any such offence is taken into consideration by the court in determining sentence,

the court may also make an order that any proceeds which arise from the disposal of the property and which do not exceed a sum specified by the court shall be paid to that person.

(2) The court may make an order under this section only if it is satisfied that but for the inadequacy of the offender's means it would have made a compensation order under which the offender would have been required to pay compensation of an amount not less than the specified amount.

Misuse of Drugs Act 1971

27   Forfeiture

(1) Subject to subsection (2) below, the court by or before which a person is convicted of an offence under this Act may order anything shown to the satisfaction of the court to relate to the offence, to be forfeited and either destroyed or dealt with in such other manner as the court may order.

(2) The court shall not order anything to be forfeited under this section, where a person claiming to be the owner of or otherwise interested in it applies to be heard by the court, unless an opportunity has been given to him to show cause why the order should not be made.

Firearms Act 1968

52   Forfeiture and disposal of firearms; cancellation of certificate by convicting court

(1) Where a person—

(a) is convicted of an offence under this Act (other than an offence under section 22 (3) or an offence relating specifically to air weapons) or is convicted of a crime for which he is sentenced to imprisonment, preventive detention, corrective training, borstal training or detention in a detention centre or in a young offenders' institution in Scotland; or

(b) has been ordered to enter into a recognizance to keep the peace or to be of good behaviour, a condition of which is that he shall not possess, use or carry a firearm; or

(c) is subject to a probation order containing a requirement that he shall not possess, use or carry a firearm; or

(d) has, in Scotland, been ordained to find caution a condition of which is that he shall not possess, use or carry a firearm,

the court by or before which he is convicted, or by which the order is made, may make such order as to the forfeiture or disposal of any firearm or ammunition found in his possession as the court thinks fit and may cancel any firearm certificate or shot gun certificate held by him.

Prevention of Crime Act 1953

1 Prohibition of the carrying of offensive weapons without lawful authority or reasonable excuse

(1) Any person who without lawful authority or reasonable excuse, the proof whereof shall lie on him, has with him in any public place any offensive weapon shall be guilty of an offence, and shall be liable—

    (a) on summary conviction, to imprisonment for a term not exceeding three months or a fine not exceeding fifty pounds, or both;

    (b) on conviction on indictment, to imprisonment for a term not exceeding two years or a fine not exceeding one hundred pounds, or both.

(2) Where any person is convicted of an offence under subsection (1) of this section the court may make an order for the forfeiture or disposal of any weapon in respect of which the offence was committed.

(f) RESTITUTION ORDERS

Powers of Criminal Courts (Sentencing) Act 2000

148 Restitution orders

(1) This section applies where goods have been stolen, and either—

    (a) a person is convicted of any offence with reference to the theft (whether or not the stealing is the gist of his offence); or

    (b) a person is convicted of any other offence, but such an offence as is mentioned in paragraph (a) above is taken into consideration in determining his sentence.

(2) Where this section applies, the court by or before which the offender is convicted may on the conviction (whether or not the passing of sentence is in other respects deferred) exercise any of the following powers—

    (a) the court may order anyone having possession or control of the stolen goods to restore them to any person entitled to recover them from him; or

    (b) on the application of a person entitled to recover from the person convicted any other goods directly or indirectly representing the stolen goods (as being the proceeds of any disposal or realisation of the whole or part of them or of goods so representing them), the court may order those other goods to be delivered or transferred to the applicant; or

    (c) the court may order that a sum not exceeding the value of the stolen goods shall be paid, out of any money of the person convicted which was taken out of his possession on his apprehension, to any person who, if those goods were in the possession of the person convicted, would be entitled to recover them from him;

and in this subsection "the stolen goods" means the goods referred to in subsection (1) above.

(3) Where the court has power on a person's conviction to make an order against him both under paragraph (b) and under paragraph (c) of subsection (2) above with reference to the stealing of the same goods, the court may make orders under both paragraphs provided that the person in whose favour the orders are made does not thereby recover more than the value of those goods.

(4) Where the court on a person's conviction makes an order under subsection (2)(a) above for the restoration of any goods, and it appears to the court that the person convicted—

(a) has sold the goods to a person acting in good faith, or

(b) has borrowed money on the security of them from a person so acting,

the court may order that there shall be paid to the purchaser or lender, out of any money of the person convicted which was taken out of his possession on his apprehension, a sum not exceeding the amount paid for the purchase by the purchaser or, as the case may be, the amount owed to the lender in respect of the loan.

(5) The court shall not exercise the powers conferred by this section unless in the opinion of the court the relevant facts sufficiently appear from evidence given at the trial or the available documents, together with admissions made by or on behalf of any person in connection with any proposed exercise of the powers.

(6) In subsection (5) above "the available documents" means—

(a) any written statements or admissions which were made for use, and would have been admissible, as evidence at the trial; and

(b) such written statements, depositions and other documents as were tendered by or on behalf of the prosecutor at any committal proceedings.

149   Restitution orders: supplementary

(1) The following provisions of this section shall have effect with respect to section 148 above.

(2) The powers conferred by subsections (2)(c) and (4) of that section shall be exercisable without any application being made in that behalf or on the application of any person appearing to the court to be interested in the property concerned.

(3) Where an order is made under that section against any person in respect of an offence taken into consideration in determining his sentence—

(a) the order shall cease to have effect if he successfully appeals against his conviction of the offence or, if more than one, all the offences, of which he was convicted in the proceedings in which the order was made;

(b) he may appeal against the order as if it were part of the sentence imposed in respect of the offence or, if more than one, any of the offences, of which he was so convicted.

(4) Any order under that section made by a magistrates' court shall be suspended—

(a) in any case until the end of the period for the time being prescribed by law for the giving of notice of appeal against a decision of a magistrates' court;

(b) where notice of appeal is given within the period so prescribed, until the determination of the appeal;

but this subsection shall not apply where the order is made under section 148(2)(a) or (b) and the court so directs, being of the opinion that the title to the goods to be restored or, as the case may be, delivered or transferred under the order is not in dispute.

(g) REPARATION ORDERS ETC.

Reparation orders

Powers of Criminal Courts (Sentencing) Act 2000

73 Reparation orders

(1) Where a child or young person (that is to say, any person aged under 18) is convicted of an offence other than one for which the sentence is fixed by law, the court by or before which he is convicted may make an order requiring him to make reparation specified in the order—

    (a) to a person or persons so specified; or

    (b) to the community at large;

and any person so specified must be a person identified by the court as a victim of the offence or a person otherwise affected by it.

(3) In this section and section 74 below "make reparation", in relation to an offender, means make reparation for the offence otherwise than by the payment of compensation; and the requirements that may be specified in a reparation order are subject to section 74(1) to (3).

(4) The court shall not make a reparation order in respect of the offender if it proposes—

    (a) to pass on him a custodial sentence; or

    (b) to make in respect of him a community punishment order, a community punishment and rehabilitation order, a supervision order which includes requirements authorised by Schedule 6 to this Act, an action plan order or a referral order.

(5) Before making a reparation order, a court shall obtain and consider a written report by a probation officer, a social worker of a local authority social services department or a member of a youth offending team indicating—

    (a) the type of work that is suitable for the offender; and

    (b) the attitude of the victim or victims to the requirements proposed to be included in the order.

(6) The court shall not make a reparation order unless it has been notified by the Secretary of State that arrangements for implementing such orders are available in the area proposed to be named in the order under section 74(4) below and the notice has not been withdrawn.

(7) Before making a reparation order, the court shall explain to the offender in ordinary language—

    (a) the effect of the order and of the requirements proposed to be included in it;

    (b) the consequences which may follow (under Schedule 8 to this Act) if he fails to comply with any of those requirements; and

    (c) that the court has power (under that Schedule) to review the order on the application either of the offender or of the responsible officer;

and "responsible officer" here has the meaning given by section 74(5) below.

74 Requirements and provisions of reparation order, and obligations of person subject to it

(1) A reparation order shall not require the offender—

    (a) to work for more than 24 hours in aggregate; or

    (b) to make reparation to any person without the consent of that person.

(2) Subject to subsection (1) above, requirements specified in a reparation order shall be such as in the opinion of the court are commensurate with the seriousness of the offence, or the combination of the offence and one or more offences associated with it.

(3) Requirements so specified shall, as far as practicable, be such as to avoid—

- (a) any conflict with the offender's religious beliefs or with the requirements of any community order to which he may be subject; and
- (b) any interference with the times, if any, at which he normally works or attends school or any other educational establishment.

SCHEDULE 8

BREACH, REVOCATION AND AMENDMENT OF ACTION PLAN ORDERS AND REPARATION ORDERS

2. *Breach of requirement of action plan order or reparation order*

(1) This paragraph applies if while an action plan order or reparation order is in force in respect of an offender it is proved to the satisfaction of the appropriate court, on the application of the responsible officer, that the offender has failed to comply with any requirement included in the order.

(2) Where this paragraph applies, the court—

- (a) whether or not it also makes an order under paragraph 5(1) below (revocation or amendment of order)—
  - (i) may order the offender to pay a fine of an amount not exceeding £1,000; or
  - (ii) subject to paragraph 3 below, may make a curfew order in respect of him; or
  - (iii) subject to paragraph 4 below, may make an attendance centre order in respect of him; or
- (b) if the action plan order or reparation order was made by a magistrates' court, may revoke the order and deal with the offender, for the offence in respect of which the order was made, in any way in which he could have been dealt with for that offence by the court which made the order if the order had not been made; or
- (c) if the action plan order or reparation order was made by the Crown Court, may commit him in custody or release him on bail until he can be brought or appear before the Crown Court

(4) Where—

- (a) by virtue of sub-paragraph (2)(c) above the offender is brought or appears before the Crown Court, and
- (b) it is proved to the satisfaction of the court that he has failed to comply with the requirement in question,

that court may deal with him, for the offence in respect of which the order was made, in any way in which it could have dealt with him for that offence if it had not made the order.

(5) Where the Crown Court deals with an offender under sub-paragraph (4) above, it shall revoke the action plan order or reparation order if it is still in force.

(6) A fine imposed under this paragraph shall be deemed, for the purposes of any enactment, to be a sum adjudged to be paid by a conviction.

(7) In dealing with an offender under this paragraph, a court shall take into account the extent to which he has complied with the requirements of the action plan order or reparation order.

5. *Revocation and amendment of action plan order or reparation order*

(1) If while an action plan order or reparation order is in force in respect of an offender it appears to the appropriate court, on the application of the responsible officer or the offender, that it is appropriate to make an order under this sub-paragraph, the court may—

- (a) make an order revoking the action plan order or reparation order; or
- (b) make an order amending it—

      (i) by cancelling any provision included in it; or
     (ii) by inserting in it (either in addition to or in substitution for any of its provisions) any provision which could have been included in the order if the court had then had power to make it and were exercising the power.

6. *Presence of offender in court, remands etc.*
   (9) A court may make an order under paragraph 5(1) above in the absence of the offender if the effect of the order is confined to one or more of the following, that is to say—
    (a) revoking the action plan order or reparation order;
    (b) cancelling a requirement included in the action plan order or reparation order;
    (c) altering in the action plan order or reparation order the name of any area;
    (d) changing the responsible officer.

Referral of young offenders

Powers of Criminal Courts (Sentencing) Act 2000

16 Duty and power to refer certain young offenders to youth offender panels
   (1) This section applies where a youth court or other magistrates' court is dealing with a person aged under 18 for an offence and—
    (a) neither the offence nor any connected offence is one for which the sentence is fixed by law;
    (b) the court is not, in respect of the offence or any connected offence, proposing to impose a custodial sentence on the offender or make a hospital order (within the meaning of the Mental Health Act 1983) in his case; and
    (c) the court is not proposing to discharge him absolutely in respect of the offence.
   (2) If—
    (a) the compulsory referral conditions are satisfied in accordance with section 17 below, and
    (b) referral is available to the court,
the court shall sentence the offender for the offence by ordering him to be referred to a youth offender panel.
   (3) If—
    (a) the discretionary referral conditions are satisfied in accordance with section 17 below, and
    (b) referral is available to the court,
the court may sentence the offender for the offence by ordering him to be referred to a youth offender panel.
   (4) For the purposes of this Part an offence is connected with another if the offender falls to be dealt with for it at the same time as he is dealt with for the other offence (whether or not he is convicted of the offences at the same time or by or before the same court).
   (5) For the purposes of this section referral is available to a court if—
    (a) the court has been notified by the Secretary of State that arrangements for the implementation of referral orders are available in the area in which it appears to the court that the offender resides or will reside; and
    (b) the notice has not been withdrawn.
   (7) No referral order may be made in respect of any offence committed before the commencement of section 1 of the Youth Justice and Criminal Evidence Act 1999.

17 The referral conditions

(1) For the purposes of section 16(2) above the compulsory referral conditions are satisfied in relation to an offence if the offender—

(a) pleaded guilty to the offence and to any connected offence;

(b) has never been convicted by or before a court in the United Kingdom of any offence other than the offence and any connected offence; and

(c) has never been bound over in criminal proceedings in England and Wales or Northern Ireland to keep the peace or to be of good behaviour.

(2) For the purposes of section 16(3) above the discretionary referral conditions are satisfied in relation to an offence if—

(a) the offender is being dealt with by the court for the offence and one or more connected offences;

(b) although he pleaded guilty to at least one of the offences mentioned in paragraph (a) above, he also pleaded not guilty to at least one of them;

(c) he has never been convicted by or before a court in the United Kingdom of any offence other than the offences mentioned in paragraph (a) above; and

(d) he has never been bound over in criminal proceedings in England and Wales or Northern Ireland to keep the peace or to be of good behaviour.

(3) The Secretary of State may by regulations make such amendments of this section as he considers appropriate for altering in any way the descriptions of offenders in the case of which the compulsory referral conditions or the discretionary referral conditions fall to be satisfied for the purposes of section 16(2) or (3) above (as the case may be).

(4) Any description of offender having effect for those purposes by virtue of such regulations may be framed by reference to such matters as the Secretary of State considers appropriate, including (in particular) one or more of the following—

(a) the offender's age;

(b) how the offender has pleaded;

(c) the offence (or offences) of which the offender has been convicted;

(d) the offender's previous convictions (if any);

(e) how (if at all) the offender has been previously punished or otherwise dealt with by any court; and

(f) any characteristics or behaviour of, or circumstances relating to, any person who has at any time been charged in the same proceedings as the offender (whether or not in respect of the same offence).

(5) For the purposes of this section an offender who has been convicted of an offence in respect of which he was conditionally discharged (whether by a court in England and Wales or in Northern Ireland) shall be treated, despite—

(a) section 14(1) above (conviction of offence for which offender so discharged deemed not a conviction), or

(b) Article 6(1) of the Criminal Justice (Northern Ireland) Order 1996 (corresponding provision for Northern Ireland),

as having been convicted of that offence.

18 Making of referral orders: general

(1) A referral order shall—

(a) specify the youth offending team responsible for implementing the order;

(b) require the offender to attend each of the meetings of a youth offender panel to be established by the team for the offender; and

(c) specify the period for which any youth offender contract taking effect between the offender and the panel under section 23 below is to have effect (which must not be less than three nor more than twelve months).

(2) The youth offending team specified under subsection (1)(a) above shall be the team

having the function of implementing referral orders in the area in which it appears to the court that the offender resides or will reside.

(3) On making a referral order the court shall explain to the offender in ordinary language—

    (a) the effect of the order; and

    (b) the consequences which may follow—

        (i) if no youth offender contract takes effect between the offender and the panel under section 23 below; or

        (ii) if the offender breaches any of the terms of any such contract.

(4) Subsections (5) to (7) below apply where, in dealing with an offender for two or more connected offences, a court makes a referral order in respect of each, or each of two or more, of the offences.

(5) The orders shall have the effect of referring the offender to a single youth offender panel; and the provision made by them under subsection (1) above shall accordingly be the same in each case, except that the periods specified under subsection (1)(c) may be different.

(6) The court may direct that the period so specified in either or any of the orders is to run concurrently with or be additional to that specified in the other or any of the others; but in exercising its power under this subsection the court must ensure that the total period for which such a contract as is mentioned in subsection (1)(c) above is to have effect does not exceed twelve months.

(7) Each of the orders mentioned in subsection (4) above shall, for the purposes of this Part, be treated as associated with the other or each of the others.

19   Making of referral orders: effect on court's other sentencing powers

(1) Subsections (2) to (5) below apply where a court makes a referral order in respect of an offence.

(2) The court may not deal with the offender for the offence in any of the prohibited ways.

(3) The court—

    (a) shall, in respect of any connected offence, either sentence the offender by making a referral order or make an order discharging him absolutely; and

    (b) may not deal with the offender for any such offence in any of the prohibited ways.

(4) For the purposes of subsections (2) and (3) above the prohibited ways are—

    (a) imposing a community sentence on the offender;

    (b) ordering him to pay a fine;

    (c) making a reparation order in respect of him; and

    (d) making an order discharging him conditionally.

(5) The court may not make, in connection with the conviction of the offender for the offence or any connected offence—

    (a) an order binding him over to keep the peace or to be of good behaviour;

    (b) an order under section 150 below (binding over of parent or guardian); or

    (c) a parenting order under section 8 of the Crime and Disorder Act 1998.

20   Making of referral orders: attendance of parents etc

(1) A court making a referral order may make an order requiring—

    (a) the appropriate person, or

    (b) in a case where there are two or more appropriate persons, any one or more of them,

to attend the meetings of the youth offender panel.

(2) Where an offender is aged under 16 when a court makes a referral order in his case—

    (a) the court shall exercise its power under subsection (1) above so as to require at least one appropriate person to attend meetings of the youth offender panel; and

(b) if the offender falls within subsection (6) below, the person or persons so required to attend those meetings shall be or include a representative of the local authority mentioned in that subsection.

(3) The court shall not under this section make an order requiring a person to attend meetings of the youth offender panel—

(a) if the court is satisfied that it would be unreasonable to do so; or

(b) to an extent which the court is satisfied would be unreasonable.

(5) Where the offender falls within subsection (6) below, each of the following is an "appropriate person" for the purposes of this section—

(a) a representative of the local authority mentioned in that subsection; and

(b) each person who is a parent or guardian of the offender with whom the offender is allowed to live.

(7) If, at the time when a court makes an order under this section—

(a) a person who is required by the order to attend meetings of a youth offender panel is not present in court, or

(b) a local authority whose representative is so required to attend such meetings is not represented in court,

the court must send him or (as the case may be) the authority a copy of the order forthwith.

Youth offender panels

21   Establishment of panels

(1) Where a referral order has been made in respect of an offender (or two or more associated referral orders have been so made), it is the duty of the youth offending team specified in the order (or orders)—

(a) to establish a youth offender panel for the offender;

(b) to arrange for the first meeting of the panel to be held for the purposes of section 23 below; and

(c) subsequently to arrange for the holding of any further meetings of the panel required by virtue of section 25 below (in addition to those required by virtue of any other provision of this Part).

(2) A youth offender panel shall—

(a) be constituted,

(b) conduct its proceedings, and

(c) discharge its functions under this Part (and in particular those arising under section 23 below),

in accordance with guidance given from time to time by the Secretary of State.

(3) At each of its meetings a panel shall, however, consist of at least—

(a) one member appointed by the youth offending team from among its members; and

(b) two members so appointed who are not members of the team.

22   Attendance at panel meetings

(1) The specified team shall, in the case of each meeting of the panel established for the offender, notify—

(a) the offender, and

(b) any person to whom an order under section 20 above applies,

of the time and place at which he is required to attend that meeting.

(2) If the offender fails to attend any part of such a meeting the panel may—

(a) adjourn the meeting to such time and place as it may specify; or

(b) end the meeting and refer the offender back to the appropriate court;

and subsection (1) above shall apply in relation to any such adjourned meeting.

(3) One person aged 18 or over chosen by the offender, with the agreement of the panel, shall be entitled to accompany the offender to any meeting of the panel (and it need not be the same person who accompanies him to every meeting).

(4) The panel may allow to attend any such meeting—

    (a) any person who appears to the panel to be a victim of, or otherwise affected by, the offence, or any of the offences, in respect of which the offender was referred to the panel;

    (b) any person who appears to the panel to be someone capable of having a good influence on the offender.

(5) Where the panel allows any such person as is mentioned in subsection (4)(a) above ("the victim") to attend a meeting of the panel, the panel may allow the victim to be accompanied to the meeting by one person chosen by the victim with the agreement of the panel.

Youth offender contracts

23   First meeting: agreement of contract with offender

(1) At the first meeting of the youth offender panel established for an offender the panel shall seek to reach agreement with the offender on a programme of behaviour the aim (or principal aim) of which is the prevention of re-offending by the offender.

(2) The terms of the programme may, in particular, include provision for any of the following—

    (a) the offender to make financial or other reparation to any person who appears to the panel to be a victim of, or otherwise affected by, the offence, or any of the offences, for which the offender was referred to the panel;

    (b) the offender to attend mediation sessions with any such victim or other person;

    (c) the offender to carry out unpaid work or service in or for the community;

    (d) the offender to be at home at times specified in or determined under the programme;

    (e) attendance by the offender at a school or other educational establishment or at a place of work;

    (f) the offender to participate in specified activities (such as those designed to address offending behaviour, those offering education or training or those assisting with the rehabilitation of persons dependent on, or having a propensity to misuse, alcohol or drugs);

    (g) the offender to present himself to specified persons at times and places specified in or determined under the programme;

    (h) the offender to stay away from specified places or persons (or both);

    (i) enabling the offender's compliance with the programme to be supervised and recorded.

(3) The programme may not, however, provide—

    (a) for the electronic monitoring of the offender's whereabouts; or

    (b) for the offender to have imposed on him any physical restriction on his movements.

(4) No term which provides for anything to be done to or with any such victim or other affected person as is mentioned in subsection (2)(a) above may be included in the programme without the consent of that person.

24   First meeting: duration of contract

(1) This section applies where a youth offender contract has taken effect under section 23 above between an offender and a youth offender panel.

(2) The day on which the contract so takes effect shall be the first day of the period for which it has effect.

25   First meeting: failure to agree contract

(1) Where it appears to a youth offender panel to be appropriate to do so, the panel may—

(a) end the first meeting (or any further meeting held in pursuance of paragraph (b) below) without having reached agreement with the offender on a programme of behaviour of the kind mentioned in section 23(1) above; and

(b) resume consideration of the offender's case at a further meeting of the panel.

(2) If, however, it appears to the panel at the first meeting or any such further meeting that there is no prospect of agreement being reached with the offender within a reasonable period after the making of the referral order (or orders)—

(a) subsection (1)(b) above shall not apply; and

(b) instead the panel shall refer the offender back to the appropriate court.

(3) If at a meeting of the panel—

(a) agreement is reached with the offender but he does not sign the record produced in pursuance of section 23(5) above, and

(b) his failure to do so appears to the panel to be unreasonable,

the panel shall end the meeting and refer the offender back to the appropriate court.

26   Progress meetings

(1) At any time—

(a) after a youth offender contract has taken effect under section 23 above, but

(b) before the end of the period for which the contract has effect,

the specified team shall, if so requested by the panel, arrange for the holding of a meeting of the panel under this section ("a progress meeting").

(2) The panel may make a request under subsection (1) above if it appears to the panel to be expedient to review—

(a) the offender's progress in implementing the programme of behaviour contained in the contract; or

(b) any other matter arising in connection with the contract.

(3) The panel shall make such a request if—

(a) the offender has notified the panel that—

(i) he wishes to seek the panel's agreement to a variation in the terms of the contract; or

(ii) he wishes the panel to refer him back to the appropriate court with a view to the referral order (or orders) being revoked on account of a significant change in his circumstances (such as his being taken to live abroad) making compliance with any youth offender contract impractical; or

(b) it appears to the panel that the offender is in breach of any of the terms of the contract.

(4) At a progress meeting the panel shall do such one or more of the following things as it considers appropriate in the circumstances, namely—

(a) review the offender's progress or any such other matter as is mentioned in subsection (2) above;

(b) discuss with the offender any breach of the terms of the contract which it appears to the panel that he has committed;

(c) consider any variation in the terms of the contract sought by the offender or which it appears to the panel to be expedient to make in the light of any such review or discussion;

(d) consider whether to accede to any request by the offender that he be referred back to the appropriate court.

(5) Where the panel has discussed with the offender such a breach as is mentioned in subsection (4)(b) above—

    (a) the panel and the offender may agree that the offender is to continue to be required to comply with the contract (either in its original form or with any agreed variation in its terms) without being referred back to the appropriate court; or

    (b) the panel may decide to end the meeting and refer the offender back to that court.

(6) Where a variation in the terms of the contract is agreed between the offender and the panel, the panel shall cause a written record of the variation to be produced forthwith—

    (a) in language capable of being readily understood by, or explained to, the offender; and

    (b) for signature by him.

(7) Any such variation shall take effect once the record has been signed—

    (a) by the offender; and

    (b) by a member of the panel on behalf of the panel;

and the panel shall cause a copy of the record to be given or sent to the offender.

(8) If at a progress meeting—

    (a) any such variation is agreed but the offender does not sign the record produced in pursuance of subsection (6) above, and

    (b) his failure to do so appears to the panel to be unreasonable,

the panel may end the meeting and refer the offender back to the appropriate court.

27 Final meeting

(1) Where the compliance period in the case of a youth offender contract is due to expire, the specified team shall arrange for the holding, before the end of that period, of a meeting of the panel under this section ("the final meeting").

(2) At the final meeting the panel shall—

    (a) review the extent of the offender's compliance to date with the terms of the contract; and

    (b) decide, in the light of that review, whether his compliance with those terms has been such as to justify the conclusion that, by the time the compliance period expires, he will have satisfactorily completed the contract;

and the panel shall give the offender written confirmation of its decision.

(3) Where the panel decides that the offender's compliance with the terms of the contract has been such as to justify that conclusion, the panel's decision shall have the effect of discharging the referral order (or orders) as from the end of the compliance period.

(4) Otherwise the panel shall refer the offender back to the appropriate court.

Supplementary

29 Functions of youth offending teams

(1) The functions of a youth offending team responsible for implementing a referral order include, in particular, arranging for the provision of such administrative staff, accommodation or other facilities as are required by the youth offender panel established in pursuance of the order.

(2) During the period for which a youth offender contract between a youth offender panel and an offender has effect—

    (a) the specified team shall make arrangements for supervising the offender's compliance with the terms of the contract; and

    (b) the person who is the member of the panel referred to in section 21(3)(a) above shall ensure that records are kept of the offender's compliance (or non-compliance) with those terms.

SCHEDULE 1

PART I   REFERRAL BACK TO APPROPRIATE COURT

1. *Introductory*
    (2) For the purposes of this Part of this Schedule and the provisions mentioned in sub-paragraph (1) above the appropriate court is—

    (a) in the case of an offender aged under 18 at the time when (in pursuance of the referral back) he first appears before the court, a youth court acting for the petty sessions area in which it appears to the youth offender panel that the offender resides or will reside; and

    (b) otherwise, a magistrates' court (other than a youth court) acting for that area.

2. *Mode of referral back to court*
The panel shall make the referral by sending a report to the appropriate court explaining why the offender is being referred back to it.

4. *Detention and remand of arrested offender*
    (1) Where the offender is arrested in pursuance of a warrant under paragraph 3(2) above and cannot be brought immediately before the appropriate court—

    (a) the person in whose custody he is may make arrangements for his detention in a place of safety (within the meaning given by section 107(1) of the Children and Young Persons Act 1933) for a period of not more than 72 hours from the time of the arrest (and it shall be lawful for him to be detained in pursuance of the arrangements); and

    (b) that person shall within that period bring him before a court which—

    (i) if he is under the age of 18 when he is brought before the court, shall be a youth court; and

    (ii) if he has then attained that age, shall be a magistrates' court other than a youth court.

5. *Power of court where it upholds panel's decision*
    (1) If it is proved to the satisfaction of the appropriate court as regards any decision of the panel which resulted in the offender being referred back to the court—

    (a) that, so far as the decision relied on any finding of fact by the panel, the panel was entitled to make that finding in the circumstances, and

    (b) that, so far as the decision involved any exercise of discretion by the panel, the panel reasonably exercised that discretion in the circumstances,

the court may exercise the power conferred by sub-paragraph (2) below.

    (2) That power is a power to revoke the referral order (or each of the referral orders).

    (3) The revocation under sub-paragraph (2) above of a referral order has the effect of revoking any related order under paragraph 11 or 12 below.

    (4) Where any order is revoked under sub-paragraph (2) above or by virtue of sub-paragraph (3) above, the appropriate court may deal with the offender in accordance with sub-paragraph (5) below for the offence in respect of which the revoked order was made.

    (5) In so dealing with the offender for such an offence, the appropriate court—

    (a) may deal with him in any way in which (assuming section 16 of this Act had not applied) he could have been dealt with for that offence by the court which made the order; and

    (b) shall have regard to—

    (i) the circumstances of his referral back to the court; and

    (ii) where a contract has taken effect under section 23 of this Act between the offender and the panel, the extent of his compliance with the terms of the contract.

PART II   FURTHER CONVICTIONS DURING REFERRAL

10.   *Extension of referral for further offences*
(1) Paragraphs 11 and 12 below apply where, at a time when an offender aged under 18 is subject to referral, a youth court or other magistrates' court ("the relevant court") is dealing with him for an offence in relation to which paragraphs (a) to (c) of section 16(1) of this Act are applicable.
(2) But paragraphs 11 and 12 do not apply unless the offender's compliance period is less than twelve months.

11.   *Extension where further offences committed pre-referral*
If—
  (a) the occasion on which the offender was referred to the panel is the only other occasion on which it has fallen to a court in the United Kingdom to deal with the offender for any offence or offences, and
  (b) the offender committed the offence mentioned in paragraph 10 above, and any connected offence, before he was referred to the panel,
the relevant court may sentence the offender for the offence by making an order extending his compliance period.

12.   *Extension where further offence committed after referral*
(1) If—
  (a) paragraph 11(a) above applies, but
  (b) the offender committed the offence mentioned in paragraph 10 above, or any connected offence, after he was referred to the panel,
the relevant court may sentence the offender for the offence by making an order extending his compliance period, but only if the requirements of sub-paragraph (2) below are complied with.
(2) Those requirements are that the court must—
  (a) be satisfied, on the basis of a report made to it by the relevant body, that there are exceptional circumstances which indicate that, even though the offender has re-offended since being referred to the panel, extending his compliance period is likely to help prevent further re-offending by him; and
  (b) state in open court that it is so satisfied and why it is.
(3) In sub-paragraph (2) above "the relevant body" means the panel to which the offender has been referred or, if no contract has yet taken effect between the offender and the panel under section 23 of this Act, the specified team.

13.   *Provisions supplementary to paragraphs 11 and 12*
(1) An order under paragraph 11 or 12 above, or two or more orders under one or other of those paragraphs made in respect of connected offences, must not so extend the offender's compliance period as to cause it to exceed twelve months.

14.   *Further convictions which lead to revocation of referral*
(1) This paragraph applies where, at a time when an offender is subject to referral, a court in England and Wales deals with him for an offence (whether committed before or after he was referred to the panel) by making an order other than—
  (a) an order under paragraph 11 or 12 above; or
  (b) an order discharging him absolutely.
(2) In such a case the order of the court shall have the effect of revoking—
  (a) the referral order (or orders); and
  (b) any related order or orders under paragraph 11 or 12 above.
(3) Where any order is revoked by virtue of sub-paragraph (2) above, the court may, if appears to the court that it would be in the interests of justice to do so, deal with the offender

for the offence in respect of which the revoked order was made in any way in which (assuming section 16 of this Act had not applied) he could have been dealt with for that offence by the court which made the order.

(4) When dealing with the offender under sub-paragraph (3) above the court shall, where a contract has taken effect between the offender and the panel under section 23 of this Act, have regard to the extent of his compliance with the terms of the contract.

Parenting orders

Crime and Disorder Act 1998

8   Crime and Disorder Act 1998
(1) This section applies where, in any court proceedings—
  (a) a child safety order is made in respect of a child;
  (b) an anti-social behaviour order or sex offender order is made in respect of a child or young person;
  (c) a child or young person is convicted of an offence; or
  (d) a person is convicted of an offence under section 443 (failure to comply with school attendance order) or section 444 (failure to secure regular attendance at school of registered pupil) of the Education Act 1996.

(2) Subject to subsection (3) and section 9(1) below, if in the proceedings the court is satisfied that the relevant condition is fulfilled, it may make a parenting order in respect of a person who is a parent or guardian of the child or young person or, as the case may be, the person convicted of the offence under section 443 or 444 ("the parent").

(3) A court shall not make a parenting order unless it has been notified by the Secretary of State that arrangements for implementing such orders are available in the area in which it appears to the court that the parent resides or will reside and the notice has not been withdrawn.

(4) A parenting order is an order which requires the parent—
  (a) to comply, for a period not exceeding twelve months, with such requirements as are specified in the order; and
  (b) subject to subsection (5) below, to attend, for a concurrent period not exceeding three months and not more than once in any week, such counselling or guidance sessions as may be specified in directions given by the responsible officer;
and in this subsection "week" means a period of seven days beginning with a Sunday.

(5) A parenting order may, but need not, include such a requirement as is mentioned in subsection (4)(b) above in any case where such an order has been made in respect of the parent on a previous occasion.

(6) The relevant condition is that the parenting order would be desirable in the interests of preventing—
  (a) in a case falling within paragraph (a) or (b) of subsection (1) above, any repetition of the kind of behaviour which led to the child safety order, anti-social behaviour order or sex offender order being made;
  (b) in a case falling within paragraph (c) of that subsection, the commission of any further offence by the child or young person;
  (c) in a case falling within paragraph (d) of that subsection, the commission of any further offence under section 443 or 444 of the Education Act 1996.

(7) The requirements that may be specified under subsection (4)(a) above are those which

the court considers desirable in the interests of preventing any such repetition or, as the case may be, the commission of any such further offence.

9 Parenting orders: supplemental

(1) Where a person under the age of 16 is convicted of an offence, the court by or before which he is so convicted—

> (a) if it is satisfied that the relevant condition is fulfilled, shall make a parenting order; and
>
> (b) if it is not so satisfied, shall state in open court that it is not and why it is not.

(2) Before making a parenting order—

> (a) in a case falling within paragraph (a) of subsection (1) of section 8 above;
>
> (b) in a case falling within paragraph (b) or (c) of that subsection, where the person concerned is under the age of 16; or
>
> (c) in a case falling within paragraph (d) of that subsection, where the person to whom the offence related is under that age,

a court shall obtain and consider information about the person's family circumstances and the likely effect of the order on those circumstances.

(3) Before making a parenting order, a court shall explain to the parent in ordinary language—

> (a) the effect of the order and of the requirements proposed to be included in it;
>
> (b) the consequences which may follow (under subsection (7) below) if he fails to comply with any of those requirements; and
>
> (c) that the court has power (under subsection (5) below) to review the order on the application either of the parent or of the responsible officer.

(4) Requirements specified in, and directions given under, a parenting order shall, as far as practicable, be such as to avoid—

> (a) any conflict with the parent's religious beliefs; and
>
> (b) any interference with the times, if any, at which he normally works or attends an educational establishment.

(5) If while a parenting order is in force it appears to the court which made it, on the application of the responsible officer or the parent, that it is appropriate to make an order under this subsection, the court may make an order discharging the parenting order or varying it—

> (a) by cancelling any provision included in it; or
>
> (b) by inserting in it (either in addition to or in substitution for any of its provisions) any provision that could have been included in the order if the court had then had power to make it and were exercising the power.

(7) If while a parenting order is in force the parent without reasonable excuse fails to comply with any requirement included in the order, or specified in directions given by the responsible officer, he shall be liable on summary conviction to a fine not exceeding level 3 on the standard scale.

Binding over to keep the peace

Justices of the Peace Act 1968

1 Appointment of justices, oaths of office, etc

(7) It is hereby declared that any court of record having a criminal jurisdiction has, as ancillary to that jurisdiction, the power to bind over to keep the peace, and power to bind over

to be of good behaviour, a person who or whose case is before the court, by requiring him to enter into his own recognizances or to find sureties or both, and committing him to prison if he does not comply; but there is hereby abolished any power to commit to prison, or to issue warrants of arrest or search warrants, which may have been exercisable at common law by the Sovereign in person, or by the Privy Council, members of the Privy Council or the Secretary of State, whether on their or his own authority or on the special direction of the Sovereign.

Magistrates' Courts Act 1980

115   Binding over to keep the peace or be of good behaviour

(1) The power of a magistrates' court on the complaint of any person to adjudge any other person to enter into a recognizance, with or without sureties, to keep the peace or to be of good behaviour towards the complainant shall be exercised by order on complaint.

(2) Where a complaint is made under this section, the power of the court to remand the defendant under subsection (5) of section 55 above shall not be subject to the restrictions imposed by subsection (6) of that section.

(3) If any person ordered by a magistrates' court under subsection (1) above to enter into a recognizance, with or without sureties, to keep the peace or to be of good behaviour fails to comply with the order, the court may commit him to custody for a period not exceeding 6 months or until he sooner complies with the order.

Binding over of parent or guardian

Powers of Criminal Courts (Sentencing) Act 2000

150   Binding over of parent or guardian

(1) Where a child or young person (that is to say, any person aged under 18) is convicted of an offence, the powers conferred by this section shall be exercisable by the court by which he is sentenced for that offence, and where the offender is aged under 16 when sentenced it shall be the duty of that court—

(a) to exercise those powers if it is satisfied, having regard to the circumstances of the case, that their exercise would be desirable in the interests of preventing the commission by him of further offences; and

(b) if it does not exercise them, to state in open court that it is not satisfied as mentioned in paragraph (a) above and why it is not so satisfied;

but this subsection has effect subject to section 19(5) above and paragraph 13(5) of Schedule 1 to this Act (cases where referral orders made or extended).

(2) The powers conferred by this section are as follows—

(a) with the consent of the offender's parent or guardian, to order the parent or guardian to enter into a recognizance to take proper care of him and exercise proper control over him; and

(b) if the parent or guardian refuses consent and the court considers the refusal unreasonable, to order the parent or guardian to pay a fine not exceeding £1,000;

and where the court has passed a community sentence on the offender, it may include in the recognizance a provision that the offender's parent or guardian ensure that the offender complies with the requirements of that sentence.

(3) An order under this section shall not require the parent or guardian to enter into a recognizance for an amount exceeding £1,000.

(4) An order under this section shall not require the parent or guardian to enter into a recognizance—

(a) for a period exceeding three years; or

(b) where the offender will attain the age of 18 in a period shorter than three years, for a period exceeding that shorter period.

(7) In fixing the amount of a recognizance under this section, the court shall take into account among other things the means of the parent or guardian so far as they appear or are known to the court; and this subsection applies whether taking into account the means of the parent or guardian has the effect of increasing or reducing the amount of the recognizance.

Discharge

Powers of Criminal Courts (Sentencing) Act 2000

12 Absolute and conditional discharge

(1) Where a court by or before which a person is convicted of an offence (not being an offence the sentence for which is fixed by law or falls to be imposed under section 109(2), 110(2) or 111(2) below) is of the opinion, having regard to the circumstances including the nature of the offence and the character of the offender, that it is inexpedient to inflict punishment, the court may make an order either—

(a) discharging him absolutely; or

(b) if the court thinks fit, discharging him subject to the condition that he commits no offence during such period, not exceeding three years from the date of the order, as may be specified in the order.

(2) Subsection (1)(b) above has effect subject to section 66(4) of the Crime and Disorder Act 1998 (as amended by Sch. 9, para 198 Powers of Criminal Courts (Sentencing) Act 2000) (effect of reprimands and warnings).

(3) An order discharging a person subject to such a condition as is mentioned in subsection (1)(b) above is in this Act referred to as an "order for conditional discharge"; and the period specified in any such order is in this Act referred to as "the period of conditional discharge".

(4) Before making an order for conditional discharge, the court shall explain to the offender in ordinary language that if he commits another offence during the period of conditional discharge he will be liable to be sentenced for the original offence.

(5) If (by virtue of section 13 below) a person conditionally discharged under this section is sentenced for the offence in respect of which the order for conditional discharge was made, that order shall cease to have effect.

(6) On making an order for conditional discharge, the court may, if it thinks it expedient for the purpose of the offender's reformation, allow any person who consents to do so to give security for the good behaviour of the offender.

(7) Nothing in this section shall be construed as preventing a court, on discharging an offender absolutely or conditionally in respect of any offence, from making an order for costs against the offender or imposing any disqualification on him or from making in respect of the offence an order under section 130, 143 or 148 below (compensation orders, deprivation orders and restitution orders).

13 Commission of further offence by person conditionally discharged

(1) If it appears to the Crown Court, where that court has jurisdiction in accordance with subsection (2) below, or to a justice of the peace having jurisdiction in accordance with that subsection, that a person in whose case an order for conditional discharge has been made—

(a) has been convicted by a court in Great Britain of an offence committed during the period of conditional discharge, and

(b) has been dealt with in respect of that offence,

that court or justice may, subject to subsection (3) below, issue a summons requiring that person to appear at the place and time specified in it or a warrant for his arrest.

(2) Jurisdiction for the purposes of subsection (1) above may be exercised—

(a) if the order for conditional discharge was made by the Crown Court, by that court;

(b) if the order was made by a magistrates' court, by a justice acting for the petty sessions area for which that court acts.

(5) If a person in whose case an order for conditional discharge has been made by the Crown Court is convicted by a magistrates' court of an offence committed during the period of conditional discharge, the magistrates' court—

(a) may commit him to custody or release him on bail until he can be brought or appear before the Crown Court; and

(b) if it does so, shall send to the Crown Court a copy of the minute or memorandum of the conviction entered in the register, signed by the justices' chief executive by whom the register is kept.

(6) Where it is proved to the satisfaction of the court by which an order for conditional discharge was made that the person in whose case the order was made has been convicted of an offence committed during the period of conditional discharge, the court may deal with him, for the offence for which the order was made, in any way in which it could deal with him if he had just been convicted by or before that court of that offence.

(7) If a person in whose case an order for conditional discharge has been made by a magistrates' court—

(a) is convicted before the Crown Court of an offence committed during the period of conditional discharge, or

(b) is dealt with by the Crown Court for any such offence in respect of which he was committed for sentence to the Crown Court,

the Crown Court may deal with him, for the offence for which the order was made, in any way in which the magistrates' court could deal with him if it had just convicted him of that offence.

(8) If a person in whose case an order for conditional discharge has been made by a magistrates' court is convicted by another magistrates' court of any offence committed during the period of conditional discharge, that other court may, with the consent of the court which made the order, deal with him, for the offence for which the order was made, in any way in which the court could deal with him if it had just convicted him of that offence.

(9) Where an order for conditional discharge has been made by a magistrates' court in the case of an offender under 18 years of age in respect of an offence triable only on indictment in the case of an adult, any powers exercisable under subsection (6), (7) or (8) above by that or any other court in respect of the offender after he attains the age of 18 shall be powers to do either or both of the following—

(a) to impose a fine not exceeding £5,000 for the offence in respect of which the order was made;

(b) to deal with the offender for that offence in any way in which a magistrates' court could deal with him if it had just convicted him of an offence punishable with imprisonment for a term not exceeding six months.

(10) The reference in subsection (6) above to a person's having been convicted of an offence committed during the period of conditional discharge is a reference to his having been so convicted by a court in Great Britain.

14   Effect of discharge

(1) Subject to subsection (2) below, a conviction of an offence for which an order is made under section 12 above discharging the offender absolutely or conditionally shall be deemed not to be a conviction for any purpose other than the purposes of the proceedings in which the order is made and of any subsequent proceedings which may be taken against the offender under section 13 above.

(2) Where the offender was aged 18 or over at the time of his conviction of the offence in question and is subsequently sentenced (under section 13 above) for that offence, subsection (1) above shall cease to apply to the conviction.

(3) Without prejudice to subsections (1) and (2) above, the conviction of an offender who is discharged absolutely or conditionally under section 12 above shall in any event be disregarded for the purposes of any enactment or instrument which—

(a) imposes any disqualification or disability upon convicted persons; or

(b) authorises or requires the imposition of any such disqualification or disability.

(4) Subsections (1) to (3) above shall not affect—

(a) any right of an offender discharged absolutely or conditionally under section 12 above to rely on his conviction in bar of any subsequent proceedings for the same offence;

(b) the restoration of any property in consequence of the conviction of any such offender; or

(c) the operation, in relation to any such offender, of any enactment or instrument in force on 1st July 1974 which is expressed to extend to persons dealt with under section 1(1) of the Probation of Offenders Act 1907 as well as to convicted persons.

(5) In subsections (3) and (4) above—

"enactment" includes an enactment contained in a local Act; and

"instrument" means an instrument having effect by virtue of an Act.

15   Discharge: supplementary

(1) The Secretary of State may by order direct that subsection (1) of section 12 above shall be amended by substituting, for the maximum period specified in that subsection as originally enacted or as previously amended under this subsection, such period as may be specified in the order.

(2) Where an order for conditional discharge has been made on appeal, for the purposes of section 13 above it shall be deemed—

(a) if it was made on an appeal brought from a magistrates' court, to have been made by that magistrates' court;

(b) if it was made on an appeal brought from the Crown Court or from the criminal division of the Court of Appeal, to have been made by the Crown Court.

(h) CONFISCATION ORDERS

Drug Trafficking Act 1994

2   Confiscation orders

(1) Subject to subsection (7) below, where a defendant appears before the Crown Court to be sentenced in respect of one or more drug trafficking offences (and has not previously been

sentenced or otherwise dealt with in respect of his conviction for the offence or, as the case may be, any of the offences concerned), then—

    (a) if the prosecutor asks the court to proceed under this section, or

    (b) if the court considers that, even though the prosecutor has not asked it to do so, it is appropriate for it to proceed under this section,

it shall act as follows.

(2) The court shall first determine whether the defendant has benefited from drug trafficking.

(3) For the purposes of this Act, a person has benefited from drug trafficking if he has at any time (whether before or after the commencement of this Act) received any payment or other reward in connection with drug trafficking carried on by him or another person.

(4) If the court determines that the defendant has so benefited, the court shall, before sentencing or otherwise dealing with him in respect of the offence or, as the case may be, any of the offences concerned, determine in accordance with section 5 of this Act the amount to be recovered in his case by virtue of this section.

(5) The court shall then, in respect of the offence or offences concerned—

    (a) order the defendant to pay that amount;

    (b) take account of the order before—

        (i) imposing any fine on him;

        (ii) making any order involving any payment by him; or

        (iii) making any order under section 27 of the Misuse of Drugs Act 1971 (forfeiture orders) or section 143 of the Powers of Criminal Courts (Sentencing) Act 2000 (deprivation orders); and

(c) subject to paragraph (b) above, leave the order out of account in determining the appropriate sentence or other manner of dealing with him.

3 Postponed determinations

(1) Where the Crown Court is acting under section 2 of this Act but considers that it requires further information before—

    (a) determining whether the defendant has benefited from drug trafficking, or

    (b) determining the amount to be recovered in his case by virtue of that section,

it may, for the purpose of enabling that information to be obtained, postpone making the determination for such period as it may specify.

(2) More than one postponement may be made under subsection (1) above in relation to the same case.

(3) Unless it is satisfied that there are exceptional circumstances, the court shall not specify a period under subsection (1) above which—

    (a) by itself, or

    (b) where there have been one or more previous postponements under subsection (1) above or (4) below, when taken together with the earlier specified period or periods,

exceeds six months beginning with the date of conviction.

4 Assessing the proceeds of drug trafficking

(1) For the purposes of this Act—

    (a) any payments or other rewards received by a person at any time (whether before or after the commencement of this Act) in connection with drug trafficking carried on by him or another person are his proceeds of drug trafficking; and

    (b) the value of his proceeds of drug trafficking is the aggregate of the values of the payments or other rewards.

(2) Subject to subsections (4) and (5) below, the Crown Court shall, for the purpose—

    (a) of determining whether the defendant has benefited from drug trafficking, and

    (b) if he has, of assessing the value of his proceeds of drug trafficking, make the required assumptions.

(3) The required assumptions are—
- (a) that any property appearing to the court—
  - (i) to have been held by the defendant at any time since his conviction, or
  - (ii) to have been transferred to him at any time since the beginning of the period of six years ending when the proceedings were instituted against him,

was received by him, at the earliest time at which he appears to the court to have held it, as a payment or reward in connection with drug trafficking carried on by him;
- (b) that any expenditure of his since the beginning of that period was met out of payments received by him in connection with drug trafficking carried on by him; and
- (c) that, for the purpose of valuing any property received or assumed to have been received by him at any time as such a reward, he received the property free of any other interests in it.

(4) The court shall not make any required assumption in relation to any particular property or expenditure if—
- (a) that assumption is shown to be incorrect in the defendant's case; or
- (b) the court is satisfied that there would be a serious risk of injustice in the defendant's case if the assumption were to be made;

and where, by virtue of this subsection, the court does not make one or more of the required assumptions, it shall state its reasons.

(5) Subsection (2) above does not apply if the only drug trafficking offence in respect of which the defendant appears before the court to be sentenced is an offence under section 49, 50 or 51 of this Act.

(6) For the purpose of assessing the value of the defendant's proceeds of drug trafficking in a case where a confiscation order has previously been made against him, the court shall leave out of account any of his proceeds of drug trafficking that are shown to the court to have been taken into account in determining the amount to be recovered under that order.

5   Amount to be recovered under confiscation order

(1) Subject to subsection (3) below, the amount to be recovered in the defendant's case under the confiscation order shall be the amount the Crown Court assesses to be the value of the defendant's proceeds of drug trafficking.

(2) If the court is satisfied as to any matter relevant for determining the amount that might be realised at the time the confiscation order is made (whether by reason of the acceptance of an allegation made in a statement given under section 11 of this Act or made in the giving of information under section 12 of this Act, or otherwise) the court may issue a certificate giving the court's opinion as to the matters concerned, and shall do so if satisfied as mentioned in subsection (3) below.

(3) If the court is satisfied that the amount that might be realised at the time the confiscation order is made is less than the amount the court assesses to be the value of his proceeds of drug trafficking, the amount to be recovered in the defendant's case under the confiscation order shall be—
- (a) the amount appearing to the court to be the amount that might be so realised; or
- (b) a nominal amount, where it appears to the court (on the information available to it at the time) that the amount that might be so realised is nil.

6   Meaning of "amount that might be realised" and "realisable property"

(1) For the purposes of this Act the amount that might be realised at the time a confiscation order is made against the defendant is—
- (a) the total of the values at that time of all the realisable property held by the defendant, less

  (b) where there are obligations having priority at that time, the total amount payable in pursuance of such obligations,

together with the total of the values at that time of all gifts caught by this Act.

  (2) In this Act "realisable property" means, subject to subsection (3) below—
  (a) any property held by the defendant; and
  (b) any property held by a person to whom the defendant has directly or indirectly made a gift caught by this Act.

7 Value of property etc.

  (1) Subject to the following provisions of this section and to section 8 of this Act, for the purposes of this Act the value of property (other than cash) in relation to any person holding the property is the market value of the property, except that, where any other person holds an interest in the property, the value is—
  (a) the market value of the first-mentioned person's beneficial interest in the property, less
  (b) the amount required to discharge any incumbrance (other than a charging order) on that interest.

8 Gifts caught by this Act

  (1) A gift (including a gift made before the commencement of this Act) is caught by this Act if—
  (a) it was made by the defendant at any time since the beginning of the period of six years ending when the proceedings were instituted against him; or
  (b) it was made by the defendant at any time and was a gift of property—
  (i) received by the defendant in connection with drug trafficking carried on by him or another person; or
  (ii) which in whole or in part directly or indirectly represented in the defendant's hands property received by him in that connection.

Criminal Justice Act 1988 (as amended)

71 Confiscation orders

  (1) Where an offender is convicted, in any proceedings before the Crown Court or a magistrates' court, of an offence of a relevant description, it shall be the duty of the court—
  (a) if the prosecutor has given written notice to the court that he considers that it would be appropriate for the court to proceed under this section, or
  (b) if the court considers, even though it has not been given such notice, that it would be appropriate for it so to proceed,

to act as follows before sentencing or otherwise dealing with the offender in respect of that offence or any other relevant criminal conduct.

  (1A) The court shall first determine whether the offender has benefited from any relevant criminal conduct.

  (1B) Subject to subsection (1C) below, if the court determines that the offender has benefited from any relevant criminal conduct, it shall then—
  (a) determine in accordance with subsection(6) below the amount to be recovered in his case by virtue of this section, and
  (b) make an order under this section ordering the offender to pay that amount.

  (1C) If, in a case falling within subsection (1B) above, the court is satisfied that a victim of any relevant criminal conduct has instituted, or intends to institute, civil proceedings against the defendant in respect of loss, injury or damage sustained in connection with that conduct—

(a) the court shall have a power, instead of a duty, to make an order under this section;

(b) subsection (6) below shall not apply for determining the amount to be recovered in that case by virtue of this section; and

(c) where the court makes an order in exercise of that power, the sum required to be paid under that order shall be of such amount, not exceeding the amount which (but for paragraph (b) above) would apply by virtue of subsection (6) below, as the court thinks fit.

(1D) In this Part of this Act "relevant criminal conduct", in relation to a person convicted of an offence in any proceedings before a court, means (subject to section 72AA(6) below) that offence taken together with any other offences of a relevant description which are either—

(a) offences of which he is convicted in the same proceedings, or

(b) offences which the court will be taking into consideration in determining his sentence for the offence in question.

(1E) For the purposes of this Part of this Act an offence is an offence of a relevant description—

(a) in the case of an offence of which a person is convicted in any proceedings before the Crown Court or which is or will be taken into consideration by the Crown Court in determining any sentence, if it is an offence to which this Part of this Act applies; and

(b) in the case of an offence of which a person is convicted in any proceedings before a magistrates' court or which is or will be taken into consideration by a magistrates' court in determining any sentence, if it is an offence listed in Schedule 4 to this Act.

(4) For the purposes of this Part of this Act a person benefits from an offence if he obtains property as a result of or in connection with its commission and his benefit is the value of the property so obtained.

(5) Where a person derives a pecuniary advantage as a result of or in connection with the commission of an offence, he is to be treated for the purposes of this Part of this Act as if he had obtained as a result of or in connection with the commission of the offence a sum of money equal to the value of the pecuniary advantage.

(6) Subject to subsection (1C) above the sum which an order made by a court under this section requires an offender to pay shall be equal to—

(a) the benefit in respect of which it is made; or

(b) the amount appearing to the court to be the amount that might be realised at the time the order is made,

whichever is the less.

72   Making of confiscation orders

(1) A court shall not make a confiscation order unless the prosecutor has given written notice to the court to the effect that it appears to him that, were the court to consider that it ought to make such an order, it would be able to make an order requiring the offender to pay at least the minimum amount.

(2) If the prosecutor gives the court such a notice, the court shall determine whether it ought to make a confiscation order.

(3) When considering whether to make a confiscation order the court may take into account any information that has been placed before it showing that a victim of an offence to which the proceedings relate has instituted, or intends to institute, civil proceedings against the defendant in respect of loss, injury or damage sustained in connection with the offence.

(4) If the court determines that it ought to make such an order, the court shall, before

sentencing or otherwise dealing with the offender in respect of the offence or, as the case may be, any of the offences concerned, determine the amount to be recovered in his case by virtue of this section and make a confiscation order for that amount specifying the offence or offences.

(5) Where a court makes a confiscation order against a defendant in any proceedings, it shall be its duty, in respect of any offence of which he is convicted in those proceedings, to take account of the order before—

(a) imposing any fine on him;

(b) making any order involving any payment by him, other than an order under section 130 of the Powers of Criminal Courts (Sentencing) Act 2000 (compensation orders); or

(c) making any order under—

(i) section 27 of the Misuse of Drugs Act 1971 (forfeiture orders); or

(ii) section 143 of the Powers of Criminal Courts (Sentencing) Act 2000 (deprivation orders),

but subject to that shall leave the order out of account in determining the appropriate sentence or other manner of dealing with him.

72A   Postponed determinations

(1) Where a court is acting under section 71 above but considers that it requires further information before—

(a) determining whether the defendant has benefited from any relevant criminal conduct; or

(c) determining the amount to be recovered in his case,

it may, for the purpose of enabling that information to be obtained, postpone making that determination for such period as it may specify.

(2) More than one postponement may be made under subsection (1) above in relation to the same case.

(3) Unless it is satisfied that there are exceptional circumstances, the court shall not specify a period under subsection (1) above which—

(a) by itself; or

(b) where there have been one or more previous postponements under subsection (1) above or (4) below, when taken together with the earlier specified period or periods,

exceeds six months beginning with the date of conviction.

72AA   Confiscation relating to a course of criminal conduct

(1) This section applies in a case where an offender is convicted, in any proceedings before the Crown Court or a magistrates' court, of a qualifying offence which is an offence of a relevant description, if—

(a) the prosecutor gives written notice for the purposes of subsection(1)(a) of section 71 above;

(b) that notice contains a declaration that it is the prosecutor's opinion that the case is one in which it is appropriate for the provisions of this section to be applied; and

(c) the offender—

(i) is convicted in those proceedings of at least two qualifying offences (including the offence in question); or

(ii) has been convicted of a qualifying offence on at least one previous occasion during the relevant period.

(2) In this section "qualifying offence", in relation to proceedings before the Crown Court or a magistrates' court, means any offence in relation to which all the following conditions are satisfied, that is to say—

(a) it is an offence to which this Part of this Act applies;

(b) it is an offence which was committed after the commencement of section 2 of the Proceeds of Crime Act 1995; and

(c) that court is satisfied that it is an offence from which the defendant has benefited.

(3) When proceeding under section 71 above in pursuance of the notice mentioned in subsection (1)(a) above, the court may, if it thinks fit, determine that(subject to subsection (5) below) the assumptions specified in subsection (4) below are to be made for the purpose—

(a) of determining whether the defendant has benefited from relevant criminal conduct; and

(b) if he has, of assessing the value of the defendant's benefit from such conduct.

(4) Those assumptions are—

(a) that any property appearing to the court—

(i) to be held by the defendant at the date of conviction or at any time in the period between that date and the determination in question, or

(ii) to have been transferred to him at any time since the beginning of the relevant period,

was received by him, at the earliest time when he appears to the court to have held it, as a result of or in connection with the commission of offences to which this Part of this Act applies;

(b) that any expenditure of his since the beginning of the relevant period was met out of payments received by him as a result of or in connection with the commission of offences to which this Part of this Act applies; and

(c) that, for the purposes of valuing any benefit which he had or which he is assumed to have had at any time, he received the benefit free of any other interests in it.

(5) Where the court has determined that the assumptions specified in subsection (4) above are to be made in any case it shall not in that case make any such assumption in relation to any particular property or expenditure if—

(a) that assumption, so far as it relates to that property or expenditure, is shown to be incorrect in the defendant's case;

(b) that assumption, so far as it so relates, is shown to be correct in relation to an offence the defendant's benefit from which has been the subject of a previous confiscation order; or

(c) the court is satisfied that there would (for any other reason) be a serious risk of injustice in the defendant's case if the assumption were to be made in relation to that property or expenditure.

73   Statements, etc. relevant to making confiscation orders

(1) Subsection (1A) below applies in a case where a person has been convicted of an offence of a relevant description if—

(a) the prosecutor has given written notice to the court for the purposes of subsection (1)(a) of section 71 above; or

(b) the court is proceeding in pursuance of subsection (1)(b) of that section and requires a statement under this section from the prosecutor.

(1A) Where this subsection applies, the prosecutor shall, within such period as the court may direct, tender to the court a statement as to any matters relevant—

(a) to determining whether the defendant has benefited from any relevant criminal conduct; or

(b) to an assessment of the value of the defendant's benefit from that conduct;

and, where such a statement is tendered in a case in which a declaration has been made for the purposes of subsection (1)(b) of section 72AA above, that statement shall also set out all such information available to the prosecutor as may be relevant for the purposes of subsections (4) and (5)(b) or (c) of that section.

(1B) Where a statement is tendered to the court under this section—

  (a) the prosecutor may at any time tender to the court a further statement as to the matters mentioned in subsection (1A) above; and

  (b) the court may at any time require the prosecutor to tender a further such statement within such period as it may direct.

(1C) Where—

  (a) any statement has been tendered to any court by the prosecutor under this section, and

  (b) the defendant accepts to any extent any allegation in the statement,

the court may, for the purpose of determining whether the defendant has benefited from any relevant criminal conduct or of assessing the value of the defendant's benefit from such conduct, treat his acceptance as conclusive of the matters to which it relates.

(2) In subsection (2)(a) of that section (power of court to require defendant to indicate extent of acceptance of allegations), for "under subsection (1)(a) above" there shall be substituted "by the prosecutor under this section".

73A   Provision of information by defendant

(1) This section applies in a case where a person has been convicted of an offence of a relevant description if—

  (a) the prosecutor has given written notice to the court for the purposes of subsection (1)(a) of section 71 above; or

  (b) the court is proceeding in pursuance of subsection(1)(b) of that section or is considering whether so to proceed.

(2) For the purpose of obtaining information to assist it in carrying out its functions under this Part of this Act, the court may at any time order the defendant to give it such information as may be specified in the order.

(3) An order under subsection (2) above may require all, or any specified part, of the required information to be given to the court in such manner, and before such date, as may be specified in the order.

(4) Rules of court may make provision as to the maximum or minimum period that may be allowed under subsection (3) above.

(i) DISQUALIFICATION AND EXCLUSION ETC.

Recommendation for deportation

Immigration Act 1971

6   Recommendations by court for deportation

(1) Where under section 3(6) above a person convicted of an offence is liable to deportation on the recommendation of a court, he may be recommended for deportation by any court having power to sentence him for the offence unless the court commits him to be sentenced or further dealt with for that offence by another court:

Provided that in Scotland the power to recommend a person for deportation shall be exercisable only by the sheriff or the High Court of Justiciary, and shall not be exercisable by the latter on an appeal unless the appeal is against a conviction on indictment or against a sentence upon such a conviction.

(2) A court shall not recommend a person for deportation unless he has been given not less than seven days' notice in writing stating that a person is not liable to deportation if he is partial, describing the persons who are partial and stating (so far as material) the effect of section 3(8) above and section 7 below; but the powers of adjournment conferred by section 14 (3) of the Magistrates' Courts Act 1952, section 26 of the Criminal Justice (Scotland) Act 1949 or any corresponding enactment for the time being in force in Northern Ireland shall include power to adjourn, after convicting an offender, for the purpose of enabling a notice to be given to him under this subsection or, if a notice was so given to him less than seven days previously, for the purpose of enabling the necessary seven days to elapse.

7   Exemption from deportation for certain existing residents

(1) Notwithstanding anything in section 3(5) or (6) above but subject to the provisions of this section, a Commonwealth citizen or citizen of the Republic of Ireland who was such a citizen at the coming into force of this Act and was then ordinarily resident in the United Kingdom—

  (a) shall not be liable to deportation under section 3(5)(b) if at the time of the Secretary of State's decision he had at all times since the coming into force of this Act been ordinarily resident in the United Kingdom and Islands; and

  (b) shall not be liable to deportation under section 3(5)(a), (b) or (c) if at the time of the Secretary of State's decision he had for the last five years been ordinarily resident in the United Kingdom and Islands; and

  (c) shall not on conviction of an offence be recommended for deportation under section 3 (6) if at the time of the conviction he had for the last five years been ordinarily resident in the United Kingdom and Islands.

(2) A person who has at any time become ordinarily resident in the United Kingdom or in any of the Islands shall not be treated for the purposes of this section as having ceased to be so by reason only of his having remained there in breach of the immigration laws.

(3) The "last five years" before the material time under subsection (1)(b) or (c) above is to be taken as a period amounting in total to five years exclusive of any time during which the person claiming exemption under this section was undergoing imprisonment or detention by virtue of a sentence passed for an offence on a conviction in the United Kingdom and Islands, and the period for which he was imprisoned or detained by virtue of the sentence amounted to six months or more.

SCHEDULE 3

SUPPLEMENTARY PROVISIONS AS TO DEPORTATION

1.   *Removal of persons liable to deportation*

(1) Where a deportation order is in force against any person, the Secretary of State may give directions for his removal to a country or territory specified in the directions being either—

  (a) a country of which he is a national or citizen; or

  (b) a country or territory to which there is reason to believe that he will be admitted.

2.   *Detention or control pending deportation*

(1) Where a recommendation for deportation made by a court is in force in respect of any person, and that person is neither detained in pursuance of the sentence or order of any court nor for the time being released on bail by any court having power so to release him, he shall, unless the court by which the recommendation is made otherwise directs, be detained pending the making of a deportation order in pursuance of the recommendation, unless the Secretary of State directs him to be released pending further consideration of his case.

Exclusion from licensed premises

Licensed Premises (Exclusion of Certain Persons) Act 1980

1   Exclusion orders
(1) Where a court by or before which a person is convicted of an offence committed on licensed premises is satisfied that in committing that offence he resorted to violence or offered or threatened to resort to violence, the court may, subject to subsection (2) below, make an order (in this Act referred to as an "exclusion order") prohibiting him from entering those premises or any other specified premises, without the express consent of the licensee of the premises or his servant or agent.

(2) An exclusion order may be made either—
  (a) in addition to any sentence which is imposed in respect of the offence of which the person is convicted; or
  (b) where the offence was committed in England or Wales, notwithstanding the provisions of sections 12, 14 and 41 of the Powers of Criminal Courts (Sentencing) Act 2000 (cases in which community rehabilitation orders and absolute and conditional discharges may be made, and their effect), in addition to a community rehabilitation order or an order discharging him absolutely or conditionally; or
  (c) where the offence was committed in Scotland, notwithstanding the provisions of sections 228 to 234, 246, 247 of the Criminal Procedure (Scotland) Act 1995 (cases in which community rehabilitation orders and absolute discharges may be made, and their effect), in addition to a community rehabilitation order or an order discharging him absolutely;
but not otherwise.

(3) An exclusion order shall have effect for such period, not less than three months or more than two years, as is specified in the order, unless it is terminated under section 2 (2) below.

2   Penalty for non-compliance with exclusion order
(1) A person who enters any premises in breach of an exclusion order shall be guilty of an offence and shall be liable on summary conviction or, in Scotland, on conviction in a court of summary jurisdiction to a fine not exceeding £200 or to imprisonment for a term not exceeding one month or both.

(2) The court by which a person is convicted of an offence under subsection (1) above shall consider whether or not the exclusion order should continue in force, and may, if it thinks fit, by order terminate the exclusion order or vary it by deleting the name of any specified premises, but an exclusion order shall not otherwise be affected by a person's conviction for such an offence.

Football banning orders

Football Spectators Act 1989 (as amended)

14   Main definitions
(1) This section applies for the purposes of this Part.

(2) "Regulated football match" means an association football match (whether in England and Wales or elsewhere) which is a prescribed match or a match of a prescribed description.

(3) "External tournament" means a football competition which includes regulated football matches outside England and Wales.

(4) "Banning order" means an order made by the court under this Part which—

    (a) in relation to regulated football matches in England and Wales, prohibits the person who is subject to the order from entering any premises for the purpose of attending such matches, and

    (b) in relation to regulated football matches outside England and Wales, requires that person to report at a police station in accordance with this Part.

(5) "Control period", in relation to a regulated football match outside England and Wales, means the period—

    (a) beginning five days before the day of the match, and

    (b) ending when the match is finished or cancelled.

(6) "Control period", in relation to an external tournament, means any period described in an order made by the Secretary of State—

    (a) beginning five days before the day of the first football match outside England and Wales which is included in the tournament, and

    (b) ending when the last football match outside England and Wales which is included in the tournament is finished or cancelled,

but, for the purposes of paragraph (a), any football match included in the qualifying or pre-qualifying stages of the tournament is to be left out of account.

14A Banning orders made on conviction of an offence

(1) This section applies where a person (the "offender") is convicted of a relevant offence.

(2) If the court is satisfied that there are reasonable grounds to believe that making a banning order would help to prevent violence or disorder at or in connection with any regulated football matches, it must make such an order in respect of the offender.

(3) If the court is not so satisfied, it must in open court state that fact and give its reasons.

(4) A banning order may only be made under this section—

    (a) in addition to a sentence imposed in respect of the relevant offence, or

    (b) in addition to an order discharging him conditionally.

(5) A banning order may be made as mentioned in subsection (4)(b) above in spite of anything in sections 12 and 14 of the Powers of Criminal Courts (Sentencing) Act 2000 (which relate to orders discharging a person absolutely or conditionally and their effect).

(6) In this section, "the court" in relation to an offender means—

    (a) the court by or before which he is convicted of the relevant offence, or

    (b) if he is committed to the Crown Court to be dealt with for that offence, the Crown Court.

14B Banning orders made on a complaint

(1) An application for a banning order in respect of any person may be made by the chief officer of police for the area in which the person resides or appears to reside, if it appears to the officer that the condition in subsection (2) below is met.

(2) That condition is that the respondent has at any time caused or contributed to any violence or disorder in the United Kingdom or elsewhere.

(3) The application is to be made by complaint to a magistrates' court.

(4) If—

    (a) it is proved on the application that the condition in subsection (2) above is met, and

(b) the court is satisfied that there are reasonable grounds to believe that making a banning order would help to prevent violence or disorder at or in connection with any regulated football matches,

the court must make a banning order in respect of the respondent.

14C Banning orders: supplementary

(1) In this Part, "violence" means violence against persons or property and includes threatening violence and doing anything which endangers the life of any person.

(2) In this Part, "disorder" includes—

(a) stirring up hatred against a group of persons defined by reference to colour, race, nationality (including citizenship) or ethnic or national origins, or against an individual as a member of such a group,

(b) using threatening, abusive or insulting words or behaviour or disorderly behaviour,

(c) displaying any writing or other thing which is threatening, abusive or insulting.

(3) In this Part, "violence" and "disorder" are not limited to violence or disorder in connection with football.

(4) The magistrates' court may take into account the following matters (among others), so far as they consider it appropriate to do so, in determining whether to make an order under section 14B above—

(a) any decision of a court or tribunal outside the United Kingdom,

(b) deportation or exclusion from a country outside the United Kingdom,

(c) removal or exclusion from premises used for playing football matches, whether in the United Kingdom or elsewhere,

(d) conduct recorded on video or by any other means.

(5) In determining whether to make such an order—

(a) the magistrates' court may not take into account anything done by the respondent before the beginning of the period of ten years ending with the application under section 14B(1) above, except circumstances ancillary to a conviction,

(b) before taking into account any conviction for a relevant offence, where a court made a statement under section 14A(3) above (or section 15(2A) below or section 30(3) of the Public Order Act 1986), the magistrates' court must consider the reasons given in the statement,

and in this subsection "circumstances ancillary to a conviction" has the same meaning as it has for the purposes of section 4 of the Rehabilitation of Offenders Act 1974 (effect of rehabilitation).

(6) Subsection (5) does not prejudice anything in the Rehabilitation of Offenders Act 1974.

14E Banning orders: general

(1) On making a banning order, a court must in ordinary language explain its effect to the person subject to the order.

(2) A banning order must require the person subject to the order to report initially at a police station in England and Wales specified in the order within the period of five days beginning with the day on which the order is made.

(3) A banning order must, unless it appears to the court that there are exceptional circumstances, impose a requirement as to the surrender in accordance with this Part, in connection with regulated football matches outside the United Kingdom, of the passport of the person subject to the order.

(4) If it appears to the court that there are such circumstances, it must in open court state what they are.

(5) In the case of a person detained in legal custody—

(a) the requirement under this section to report at a police station, and

(b) any requirement imposed under section 19 below,

is suspended until his release from custody.

(6) If—

(a) he is released from custody more than five days before the expiry of the period for which the order has effect, and

(b) he was precluded by his being in custody from reporting initially,

the order is to have effect as if it required him to report initially at the police station specified in the order within the period of five days beginning with the date of his release.

14F   Period of banning orders

(1) Subject to the following provisions of this Part, a banning order has effect for a period beginning with the day on which the order is made.

(2) The period must not be longer than the maximum or shorter than the minimum.

(3) Where the order is made under section 14A above in addition to a sentence of imprisonment taking immediate effect, the maximum is ten years and the minimum is six years; and in this subsection "imprisonment" includes any form of detention.

(4) In any other case where the order is made under section 14A above, the maximum is five years and the minimum is three years.

(5) Where the order is made under section 14B above, the maximum is three years and the minimum is two years.

14G   Additional requirements of orders

(1) A banning order may, if the court making the order thinks fit, impose additional requirements on the person subject to the order in relation to any regulated football matches.

(2) The court by which a banning order was made may, on an application made by—

(a) the person subject to the order, or

(b) the person who applied for the order or who was the prosecutor in relation to the order,

vary the order so as to impose, replace or omit any such requirements.

(3) In the case of a banning order made by a magistrates' court, the reference in subsection (2) above to the court by which it was made includes a reference to any magistrates' court acting for the same petty sessions area as that court.

14H   Termination of orders

(1) If a banning order has had effect for at least two-thirds of the period determined under section 14F above, the person subject to the order may apply to the court by which it was made to terminate it.

(2) On the application, the court may by order terminate the banning order as from a specified date or refuse the application.

(3) In exercising its powers under subsection (2) above, the court must have regard to the person's character, his conduct since the banning order was made, the nature of the offence or conduct which led to it and any other circumstances which appear to it to be relevant.

(4) Where an application under subsection (1) above in respect of a banning order is refused, no further application in respect of the order may be made within the period of six months beginning with the day of the refusal.

(5) The court may order the applicant to pay all or any part of the costs of an application under this section.

(6) In the case of a banning order made by a magistrates' court, the reference in subsection (1) above to the court by which it was made includes a reference to any magistrates' court acting for the same petty sessions area as that court.

14J   Offences

(1) A person subject to a banning order who fails to comply with—

(a) any requirement imposed by the order, or

(b) any requirement imposed under section 19(2B) or (2C) below,

is guilty of an offence.

(2) A person guilty of an offence under this section is liable on summary conviction to imprisonment for a term not exceeding six months, or a fine not exceeding level 5 on the standard scale, or both.

Disqualification of company directors

Company Directors Disqualification Act 1986

1   Disqualification orders: general

(1) In the circumstances specified below in this Act a court may, and under section 6 shall, make against a person a disqualification order, that is to say an order that he shall not, without leave of the court—

(a) be a director of a company, or

(b) be a liquidator or administrator of a company, or

(c) be a receiver or manager of a company's property, or

(d) in any way, whether directly or indirectly, be concerned or take part in the promotion, formation or management of a company,

for a specified period beginning with the date of the order.

(2) In each section of this Act which gives to a court power or, as the case may be, imposes on it the duty to make a disqualification order there is specified the maximum (and, in section 6, the minimum) period of disqualification which may or (as the case may be) must be imposed by means of the order.

(3) Where a disqualification order is made against a person who is already subject to such an order, the periods specified in those orders shall run concurrently.

(4) A disqualification order may be made on grounds which are or include matters other than criminal convictions, notwithstanding that the person in respect of whom it is to be made may be criminally liable in respect of those matters.

2   Disqualification on conviction of indictable offence

(1) The court may make a disqualification order against a person where he is convicted of an indictable offence (whether on indictment or summarily) in connection with the promotion, formation, management or liquidation of a company, or with the receivership or management of a company's property.

(2) "The court" for this purpose means—

(a) any court having jurisdiction to wind up the company in relation to which the offence was committed, or

(b) the court by or before which the person is convicted of the offence, or

(c) in the case of a summary conviction in England and Wales, any other magistrates' court acting for the same petty sessions area;

and for the purposes of this section the definition of "indictable offence" in Schedule 1 to the Interpretation Act 1978 applies for Scotland as it does for England and Wales.

(3) The maximum period of disqualification under this section is—

(a) where the disqualification order is made by a court of summary jurisdiction, 5 years, and

(b) in any other case, 15 years.

13   Criminal penalties

(1) If a person acts in contravention of a disqualification order or of section 12(2), or is guilty of an offence under section 11, he is liable—

(a) on conviction on indictment, to imprisonment for not more than 2 years or a fine, or both; and

(b) on summary conviction, to imprisonment for not more than 6 months or a fine not exceeding the statutory maximum, or both.

Disqualification from driving

Road Traffic Offenders Act 1988

34   Disqualification for certain offences

(1) Where a person is convicted of an offence involving obligatory disqualification, the court must order him to be disqualified for such period not less than twelve months as the court thinks fit unless the court for special reasons thinks fit to order him to be disqualified for a shorter period or not to order him to be disqualified.

(2) Where a person is convicted of an offence involving discretionary disqualification, the court may order him to be disqualified for such period as the court thinks fit.

(3) Where a person convicted of an offence under any of the following provisions of the Road Traffic Act 1988, that is—

(a) section 4(1) (driving or attempting to drive while unfit),

(b) section 5(1)(a) (driving or attempting to drive with excess alcohol), and

(c) section 7(6) (failing to provide a specimen) where that is an offence involving obligatory disqualification,

has within the ten years immediately preceding the commission of the offence been convicted of any such offence, subsection (1) above shall apply in relation to him as if the reference to twelve months were a reference to three years.

(4) Where a person is convicted of an offence under section 1 of the Road Traffic Act 1988 (causing death by reckless driving), subsection (1) above shall apply in relation to him as if the reference to twelve months were a reference to two years.

(5) The preceding provisions of this section shall apply in relation to a conviction of an offence committed by aiding, abetting, counselling or procuring, or inciting to the commission of, an offence involving obligatory disqualification as if the offence were an offence involving discretionary disqualification.

35   Disqualification for repeated offences

(1) Where—

(a) a person is convicted of an offence involving obligatory or discretionary disqualification, and

(b) the penalty points to be taken into account on that occasion number twelve or more,

the court must order him to be disqualified for not less than the minimum period unless the court is satisfied, having regard to all the circumstances, that there are grounds for mitigating the normal consequences of the conviction and thinks fit to order him to be disqualified for a shorter period or not to order him to be disqualified.

(2) The minimum period referred to in subsection (1) above is—

(a) six months if no previous disqualification imposed on the offender is to be taken into account, and

(b) one year if one, and two years if more than one, such disqualification is to be taken into account;

and a previous disqualification imposed on an offender is to be taken into account if it was imposed within the three years immediately preceding the commission of the latest offence in respect of which penalty points are taken into account under section 29 of this Act.

(3) Where an offender is convicted on the same occasion of more than one offence involving obligatory or discretionary disqualification—

(a) not more than one disqualification shall be imposed on him under subsection (1) above,

(b) in determining the period of the disqualification the court must take into account all the offences, and

(c) for the purposes of any appeal any disqualification imposed under subsection (1) above shall be treated as an order made on the conviction of each of the offences.

(4) No account is to be taken under subsection (1) above of any of the following circumstances—

(a) any circumstances that are alleged to make the offence or any of the offences not a serious one,

(b) hardship, other than exceptional hardship, or

(c) any circumstances which, within the three years immediately preceding the conviction, have been taken into account under that subsection in ordering the offender to be disqualified for a shorter period or not ordering him to be disqualified.

36   Disqualification until test is passed

(1) Where a person is convicted of an offence involving obligatory or discretionary disqualification, the court may order him to be disqualified until he passes the test of competence to drive prescribed by virtue of section 89(3) of the Road Traffic Act 1988.

39   Suspension of disqualification pending appeal

(1) Any court in England and Wales (whether a magistrates' court or another) which makes an order disqualifying a person may, if it thinks fit, suspend the disqualification pending an appeal against the order.

(2) The court by or before which a person disqualified by an order of a court in Scotland was convicted may, if it thinks fit, suspend the disqualification pending an appeal against the order.

40   Power of appellate courts in England and Wales to suspend disqualification

(1) This section applies where a person has been convicted by or before a court in England and Wales of an offence involving obligatory or discretionary disqualification and has been ordered to be disqualified; and in the following provisions of this section—

(a) any reference to a person ordered to be disqualified is to be construed as a reference to a person so convicted and so ordered to be disqualified, and

(b) any reference to his sentence includes a reference to the order of disqualification and to any other order made on his conviction and, accordingly, any reference to an appeal against his sentence includes a reference to an appeal against any order forming part of his sentence.

(2) Where a person ordered to be disqualified—

(a) appeals to the Crown Court, or

(b) appeals or applies for leave to appeal to the Court of Appeal,

against his conviction or his sentence, the Crown Court or, as the case may require, the Court of Appeal may, if it thinks fit, suspend the disqualification.

(3) Where a person ordered to be disqualified has appealed or applied for leave to appeal to the House of Lords—

(a) under section 1 of the Administration of Justice Act 1960 from any decision of a Divisional Court of the Queen's Bench Division which is material to his conviction or sentence, or

(b) under section 33 of the Criminal Appeal Act 1968 from any decision of the Court of Appeal which is material to his conviction or sentence,

the Divisional Court or, as the case may require, the Court of Appeal may, if it thinks fit, suspend the disqualification.

(4) Where a person ordered to be disqualified makes an application in respect of the decision of the court in question under section 111 of the Magistrates' Courts Act 1980 (statement of case by magistrates' court) or section 28 of the Supreme Court Act 1981 (statement of case by Crown Court) the High Court may, if it thinks fit, suspend the disqualification.

(5) Where a person ordered to be disqualified—

(a) applies to the High Court for an order of certiorari to remove into the High Court any proceedings of a magistrates' court or of the Crown Court, being proceedings in or in consequence of which he was convicted or his sentence was passed, or

(b) applies to the High Court for leave to make such an application,

the High Court may, if it thinks fit, suspend the disqualification.

(6) Any power of a court under the preceding provisions of this section to suspend the disqualification of any person is a power to do so on such terms as the court thinks fit.

42   Removal of disqualification

(1) Subject to the provisions of this section, a person who by an order of a court is disqualified may apply to the court by which the order was made to remove the disqualification.

(2) On any such application the court may, as it thinks proper having regard to—

(a) the character of the person disqualified and his conduct subsequent to the order,

(b) the nature of the offence, and

(c) any other circumstances of the case,

either by order remove the disqualification as from such date as may be specified in the order or refuse the application.

(3) No application shall be made under subsection (1) above for the removal of a disqualification before the expiration of whichever is relevant of the following periods from the date of the order by which the disqualification was imposed, that is—

(a) two years, if the disqualification is for less than four years,

(b) one half of the period of disqualification, if it is for less than ten years but not less than four years,

(c) five years in any other case;

and in determining the expiration of the period after which under this subsection a person may apply for the removal of a disqualification, any time after the conviction during which the disqualification was suspended or he was not disqualified shall be disregarded.

43   Rule for determining end of period of disqualification

In determining the expiration of the period for which a person is disqualified by an order of a court made in consequence of a conviction, any time after the conviction during which the disqualification was suspended or he was not disqualified shall be disregarded.

Powers of Criminal Courts (Sentencing) Act 2000

146   Driving disqualification for any offence

(1) The court by or before which a person is convicted of an offence committed after 31st December 1997 may, instead of or in addition to dealing with him in any other way,

order him to be disqualified, for such period as it thinks fit, for holding or obtaining a driving licence.

(3) A court shall not make an order under subsection (1) above unless the court has been notified by the Secretary of State that the power to make such orders is exercisable by the court and the notice has not been withdrawn.

(4) A court which makes an order under this section disqualifying a person for holding or obtaining a driving licence shall require him to produce—

    (a) any such licence held by him together with its counterpart; or

    (b) in the case where he holds a Community licence (within the meaning of Part III of the Road Traffic Act 1988), his Community licence and its counterpart (if any).

147 Driving disqualification where vehicle used for purposes of crime

(1) This section applies where a person—

    (a) is convicted before the Crown Court of an offence punishable on indictment with imprisonment for a term of two years or more; or

    (b) having been convicted by a magistrates' court of such an offence, is committed under section 3 above to the Crown Court for sentence.

(2) This section also applies where a person is convicted by or before any court of common assault or of any other offence involving an assault (including an offence of aiding, abetting, counselling or procuring, or inciting to the commission of, an offence).

(3) If, in a case to which this section applies by virtue of subsection (1) above, the Crown Court is satisfied that a motor vehicle was used (by the person convicted or by anyone else) for the purpose of committing, or facilitating the commission of, the offence in question, the court may order the person convicted to be disqualified, for such period as the court thinks fit, for holding or obtaining a driving licence.

(4) If, in a case to which this section applies by virtue of subsection (2) above, the court is satisfied that the assault was committed by driving a motor vehicle, the court may order the person convicted to be disqualified, for such period as the court thinks fit, for holding or obtaining a driving licence.

(5) A court which makes an order under this section disqualifying a person for holding or obtaining a driving licence shall require him to produce—

    (a) any such licence held by him together with its counterpart; or

    (b) in the case where he holds a Community licence (within the meaning of Part III of the Road Traffic Act 1988), his Community licence and its counterpart (if any).

(6) Facilitating the commission of an offence shall be taken for the purposes of this section to include the taking of any steps after it has been committed for the purpose of disposing of any property to which it relates or of avoiding apprehension or detection.

(j) MENTALLY DISORDERED OFFENDERS

Powers of Criminal Courts (Sentencing) Act 2000

82 Additional requirements in case of mentally disordered offender

(1) Subject to subsection (2) below, in any case where the offender is or appears to be mentally disordered, the court shall obtain and consider a medical report before passing a custodial sentence other than one fixed by law or falling to be imposed under section 109(2) below.

(2) Subsection (1) above does not apply if, in the circumstances of the case, the court is of the opinion that it is unnecessary to obtain a medical report.

(3) Before passing a custodial sentence, other than one fixed by law or falling to be imposed under section 109(2) below, on an offender who is or appears to be mentally disordered, a court shall consider—

(a) any information before it which relates to his mental condition (whether given in a medical report, a pre-sentence report or otherwise); and

(b) the likely effect of such a sentence on that condition and on any treatment which may be available for it.

(4) No custodial sentence which is passed in a case to which subsection (1) above applies shall be invalidated by the failure of a court to comply with that subsection, but any court on an appeal against such a sentence—

(a) shall obtain a medical report if none was obtained by the court below; and

(b) shall consider any such report obtained by it or by that court.

(5) In this section, "mentally disordered", in relation to any person, means suffering from a mental disorder within the meaning of the Mental Health Act 1983.

COMMUNITY REHABILITATION ORDERS
SCHEDULE 2

5. *Requirements as to treatment for mental condition etc.*

(1) This paragraph applies where a court proposing to make a community rehabilitation order is satisfied, on the evidence of a registered medical practitioner approved for the purposes of section 12 of the Mental Health Act 1983, that the mental condition of the offender—

(a) is such as requires and may be susceptible to treatment: but

(b) is not such as to warrant the making of a hospital order or guardianship order within the meaning of that Act.

(2) Subject to sub-paragraph (4) below, the community rehabilitation order may include a requirement that the offender shall submit, during the whole of the probation period or during such part or parts of that period as may be specified in the order, to treatment by or under the direction of a registered medical practitioner or a chartered psychologist (or both, for different parts) with a view to the improvement of the offender's mental condition.

(3) The treatment required by any such order shall be such one of the following kinds of treatment as may be specified in the order, that is to say—

(a) treatment as a resident patient in a hospital or mental nursing home within the meaning of the Mental Health Act 1983, but not hospital premises at which high security psychiatric services within the meaning of that Act are provided;

(b) treatment as a non-resident patient at such institution or place as may be specified in the order;

(c) treatment by or under the direction of such registered medical practitioner or chartered psychologist (or both) as may be so specified;

but the nature of the treatment shall not be specified in the order except as mentioned in paragraph (a), (b) or (c) above.

(4) A court shall not by virtue of this paragraph include in a community rehabilitation order a requirement that the offender shall submit to treatment for his mental condition unless—

(a) it is satisfied that arrangements have been or can be made for the treatment intended to be specified in the order (including arrangements for the reception of the offender where he is to be required to submit to treatment as a resident patient); and

(b) the offender has expressed his willingness to comply with such a requirement.

(5) While the offender is under treatment as a resident patient in pursuance of a requirement of the community rehabilitation order, his responsible officer shall carry out the supervision of the offender to such extent only as may be necessary for the purpose of the revocation or amendment of the order.

(6) Where the medical practitioner or chartered psychologist by whom or under whose direction an offender is being treated for his mental condition in pursuance of a community rehabilitation order is of the opinion that part of the treatment can be better or more conveniently given in or at an institution or place which—

(a) is not specified in the order, and

(b) is one in or at which the treatment of the offender will be given by or under the direction of a registered medical practitioner or chartered psychologist,

he may, with the consent of the offender, make arrangements for him to be treated accordingly.

(7) Such arrangements as are mentioned in sub-paragraph (6) above may provide for the offender to receive part of his treatment as a resident patient in an institution or place notwithstanding that the institution or place is not one which could have been specified for that purpose in the probation order.

(8) Where any such arrangements as are mentioned in sub-paragraph (6) above are made for the treatment of an offender—

(a) the medical practitioner or chartered psychologist by whom the arrangements are made shall give notice in writing to the offender's responsible officer, specifying the institution or place in or at which the treatment is to be carried out; and

(b) the treatment provided for by the arrangements shall be deemed to be treatment to which he is required to submit in pursuance of the community rehabilitation order.

SCHEDULE 3

20.   *Amendment of treatment requirements of community rehabilitation or community punishment and rehabilitation order on report of practitioner*

(1) Where the medical practitioner or other person by whom or under whose direction an offender is, in pursuance of any requirement of a community rehabilitation or community punishment and rehabilitation order, being treated for his mental condition or his dependency on or propensity to misuse drugs or alcohol—

(a) is of the opinion mentioned in sub-paragraph (2) below, or

(b) is for any reason unwilling to continue to treat or direct the treatment of the offender,

he shall make a report in writing to that effect to the responsible officer and that officer shall apply under paragraph 19 above to a magistrates' court acting for the petty sessions area concerned for the variation or cancellation of the requirement.

(2) The opinion referred to in sub-paragraph (1) above is—

(a) that the treatment of the offender should be continued beyond the period specified in that behalf in the order;

(b) that the offender needs different treatment;

(c) that the offender is not susceptible to treatment; or

(d) that the offender does not require further treatment.

SUPERVISION ORDERS

SCHEDULE 6

6. *Requirements as to treatment for mental condition*
    (1) This paragraph applies where a court which proposes to make a supervision order is satisfied, on the evidence of a registered medical practitioner approved for the purposes of section 12 of the Mental Health Act 1983, that the mental condition of the offender—
    (a) is such as requires and may be susceptible to treatment; but
    (b) is not such as to warrant the making of a hospital order or guardianship order within the meaning of that Act.
    (2) Where this paragraph applies, the court may include in the supervision order a requirement that the offender shall, for a period specified in the order, submit to treatment of one of the following descriptions so specified, that is to say—
    (a) treatment as a resident patient in a hospital or mental nursing home within the meaning of the Mental Health Act 1983, but not a hospital at which high security psychiatric services within the meaning of that Act are provided;
    (b) treatment as a non-resident patient at an institution or place specified in the order;
    (c) treatment by or under the direction of a registered medical practitioner specified in the order; or
    (d) treatment by or under the direction of a chartered psychologist specified in the order.
    (3) A requirement shall not be included in a supervision order by virtue of sub-paragraph (2) above—
    (a) in any case, unless the court is satisfied that arrangements have been or can be made for the treatment in question and, in the case of treatment as a resident patient, for the reception of the patient;
    (b) in the case of an order made or to be made in respect of a person aged 14 or over, unless he consents to its inclusion;
and a requirement so included shall not in any case continue in force after the offender attains the age of 18.

Mental Health Act 1983 (as amended)

HOSPITAL AND GUARDIANSHIP ORDERS

37   Powers of courts to order hospital admission or guardianship
(1) Where a person is convicted before the Crown Court of an offence punishable with imprisonment other than an offence the sentence for which is fixed by law, or is convicted by a magistrates' court of an offence punishable on summary conviction with imprisonment, and the conditions mentioned in subsection (2) below are satisfied, the court may by order authorise his admission to and detention in such hospital as may be specified in the order or, as the case may be, place him under the guardianship of a local social services authority or of such other person approved by a local social services authority as may be so specified.
(2) The conditions referred to in subsection (1) above are that—
    (a) the court is satisfied, on the written or oral evidence of two registered medical practitioners, that the offender is suffering from mental illness, psychopathic disorder, severe mental impairment or mental impairment and that either—

   (i) the mental disorder from which the offender is suffering is of a nature or degree which makes it appropriate for him to be detained in a hospital for medical treatment and, in the case of psychopathic disorder or mental impairment, that such treatment is likely to alleviate or prevent a deterioration of his condition; or

   (ii) in the case of an offender who has attained the age of 16 years, the mental disorder is of a nature or degree which warrants his reception into guardianship under this Act; and

  (b) the court is of the opinion, having regard to all the circumstances including the nature of the offence and the character and antecedents of the offender, and to the other available methods of dealing with him, that the most suitable method of disposing of the case is by means of an order under this section.

(3) Where a person is charged before a magistrates' court with any act or omission as an offence and the court would have power, on convicting him of that offence, to make an order under subsection (1) above in his case as being a person suffering from mental illness or severe mental impairment, then, if the court is satisfied that the accused did the act or made the omission charged, the court may, if it thinks fit, make such an order without convicting him.

(4) An order for the admission of an offender to a hospital (in this Act referred to as "a hospital order") shall not be made under this section unless the court is satisfied on the written or oral evidence of the registered medical practitioner who would be in charge of his treatment or of some other person representing the managers of the hospital that arrangements have been made for his admission to that hospital in the event of such an order being made by the court, and for his admission to it within the period of 28 days beginning with the date of the making of such an order; and the court may, pending his admission within that period, give such directions as it thinks fit for his conveyance to and detention in a place of safety.

(5) If within the said period of 28 days it appears to the Secretary of State that by reason of an emergency or other special circumstances it is not practicable for the patient to be received into the hospital specified in the order, he may give directions for the admission of the patient to such other hospital as appears to be appropriate instead of the hospital so specified; and where such directions are given—

  (a) the Secretary of State shall cause the person having the custody of the patient to be informed, and

  (b) the hospital order shall have effect as if the hospital specified in the directions were substituted for the hospital specified in the order.

(6) An order placing an offender under the guardianship of a local social services authority or of any other person (in this Act referred to as "a guardianship order") shall not be made under this section unless the court is satisfied that that authority or person is willing to receive the offender into guardianship.

(7) A hospital order or guardianship order shall specify the form or forms of mental disorder referred to in subsection (2)(a) above from which, upon the evidence taken into account under that subsection, the offender is found by the court to be suffering; and no such order shall be made unless the offender is described by each of the practitioners whose evidence is taken into account under that subsection as suffering from the same one of those forms of mental disorder, whether or not he is also described by either of them as suffering from another of them.

(8) Where an order is made under this section, the court shall not pass sentence of imprisonment or impose a fine or make a probation order in respect of the offence or make any such order as is mentioned in paragraph (b) or (c) of section 7(7) of the Children and Young Persons Act 1969 in respect of the offender, but may make any other order which the court has power to make apart from this section; and for the purposes of this subsection "sentence of imprisonment" includes any sentence or order for detention.

38   Interim hospital orders

(1) Where a person is convicted before the Crown Court of an offence punishable with imprisonment (other than an offence the sentence for which is fixed by law) or is convicted by a magistrates' court of an offence punishable on summary conviction with imprisonment and the court before or by which he is convicted is satisfied, on the written or oral evidence of two registered medical practitioners—

    (a) that the offender is suffering from mental illness, psychopathic disorder, severe mental impairment or mental impairment; and

    (b) that there is reason to suppose that the mental disorder from which the offender is suffering is such that it may be appropriate for a hospital order to be made in his case,

the court may, before making a hospital order or dealing with him in some other way, make an order (in this Act referred to as "an interim hospital order") authorising his admission to such hospital as may be specified in the order and his detention there in accordance with this section.

(2) In the case of an offender who is subject to an interim hospital order the court may make a hospital order without his being brought before the court if he is represented by counsel or a solicitor and his counsel or solicitor is given an opportunity of being heard.

(3) At least one of the registered medical practitioners whose evidence is taken into account under subsection (1) above shall be employed at the hospital which is to be specified in the order.

(4) An interim hospital order shall not be made for admission of an offender to a hospital unless the court is satisfied, on the written or oral evidence of the registered medical practitioner who would be in charge of his treatment or of some other person representing the managers of the hospital, that arrangements have been made for his admission to that hospital and for his admission to it within the period of 28 days beginning with the date of the order; and if the court is so satisfied the court may, pending his admission, give directions for his conveyance to and detention in a place of safety.

(5) An interim hospital order—

    (a) shall be in force for such period, not exceeding 12 weeks, as the court may specify when making the order; but

    (b) may be renewed for further periods of not more than 28 days at a time if it appears to the court, on the written or oral evidence of the responsible medical officer, that the continuation of the order is warranted;

but no such order shall continue in force for more than six months in all and the court shall terminate the order if it makes a hospital order in respect of the offender or decides after considering the written or oral evidence of the responsible medical officer to deal with the offender in some other way.

(6) The power of renewing an interim hospital order may be exercised without the offender being brought before the court if he is represented by counsel or a solicitor and his counsel or solicitor is given an opportunity of being heard.

(7) If an offender absconds from a hospital in which he is detained in pursuance of an interim hospital order, or while being conveyed to or from such a hospital, he may be arrested without warrant by a constable and shall, after being arrested, be brought as soon as practicable before the court that made the order; and the court may thereupon terminate the order and deal with him in any way in which it could have dealt with him if no such order had been made.

39   Information as to hospitals

(1) Where a court is minded to make a hospital order or interim hospital order in respect of any person it may request—

(a) the Regional Health Authority for the region in which that person resides or last resided; or

(b) any other Regional Health Authority that appears to the court to be appropriate,

to furnish the court with such information as that Authority has or can reasonably obtain with respect to the hospital or hospitals (if any) in its region or elsewhere at which arrangements could be made for the admission of that person in pursuance of the order, and that Authority shall comply with any such request.

(2) In its application to Wales subsection (1) above shall have effect as if for any reference to any such Authority as is mentioned in paragraph (a) or (b) of that subsection there were substituted a reference to the Secretary of State, and as if for the words "in its region or elsewhere" there were substituted the words "in Wales".

39A   Information to facilitate guardianship orders

Where a court is minded to make a guardianship order in respect of any offender, it may request the local social services authority for the area in which the offender resides or last resided, or any other local social services authority that appears to the court to be appropriate—

(a) to inform the court whether it or any other person approved by it is willing to receive the offender into guardianship; and

(b) if so, to give such information as it reasonably can about how it or the other person could be expected to exercise in relation to the offender the powers conferred by section 40(2) below;

and that authority shall comply with any such request.

40   Effect of hospital orders, guardianship orders and interim hospital orders

(1) A hospital order shall be sufficient authority—

(a) for a constable, an approved social worker or any other person directed to do so by the court to convey the patient to the hospital specified in the order within a period of 28 days; and

(b) for the managers of the hospital to admit him at any time within that period and thereafter detain him in accordance with the provisions of this Act.

(2) A guardianship order shall confer on the authority or person named in the order as guardian the same powers as a guardianship application made and accepted under Part II of this Act.

(3) Where an interim hospital order is made in respect of an offender—

(a) a constable or any other person directed to do so by the court shall convey the offender to the hospital specified in the order within the period mentioned in section 38(4) above; and

(b) the managers of the hospital shall admit him within that period and thereafter detain him in accordance with the provisions of section 38 above.

(4) A patient who is admitted to a hospital in pursuance of a hospital order, or placed under guardianship by a guardianship order, shall, subject to the provisions of this subsection, be treated for the purposes of the provisions of this Act mentioned in Part I of Schedule 1 to this Act as if he had been so admitted or placed on the date of the order in pursuance of an application for admission for treatment or a guardianship application, as the case may be, duly made under Part II of this Act, but subject to any modifications of those provisions specified in that Part of that Schedule.

(5) Where a patient is admitted to a hospital in pursuance of a hospital order, or placed under guardianship by a guardianship order, any previous application, hospital order or guardianship order by virtue of which he was liable to be detained in a hospital or subject to guardianship shall cease to have effect; but if the first-mentioned order, or the conviction on which it was made, is quashed on appeal, this subsection shall not apply and section 22 above shall have effect as if during any period for which the patient was liable to be detained or

subject to guardianship under the order, he had been detained in custody as mentioned in that section.

RESTRICTION ORDERS

41 Power of higher courts to restrict discharge from hospital

(1) Where a hospital order is made in respect of an offender by the Crown Court, and it appears to the court, having regard to the nature of the offence, the antecedents of the offender and the risk of his committing further offences if set at large, that it is necessary for the protection of the public from serious harm so to do, the court may, subject to the provisions of this section, further order that the offender shall be subject to the special restrictions set out in this section, either without limit of time or during such period as may be specified in the order; and an order under this section shall be known as "a restriction order".

(2) A restriction order shall not be made in the case of any person unless at least one of the registered medical practitioners whose evidence is taken into account by the court under section 37(2)(a) above has given evidence orally before the court.

(3) The special restrictions applicable to a patient in respect of whom a restriction order is in force are as follows—

    (a) none of the provisions of Part II of this Act relating to the duration, renewal and expiration of authority for the detention of patients shall apply, and the patient shall continue to be liable to be detained by virtue of the relevant hospital order until he is duly discharged under the said Part II or absolutely discharged under section 42, 73, 74 or 75 below;

    (b) no application shall be made to a Mental Health Review Tribunal in respect of a patient under section 66 or 69(1) below;

    (c) the following powers shall be exercisable only with the consent of the Secretary of State, namely—

        (i) power to grant leave of absence to the patient under section 17 above;

        (ii) power to transfer the patient in pursuance of regulations under section 19 above; and

        (iii) power to order the discharge of the patient under section 23 above;

and if leave of absence is granted under the said section 17 power to recall the patient under that section shall vest in the Secretary of State as well as the responsible medical officer; and

    (d) the power of the Secretary of State to recall the patient under the said section 17 and power to take the patient into custody and return him under section 18 above may be exercised at any time;

and in relation to any such patient section 40(4) above shall have effect as if it referred to Part II of Schedule 1 to this Act instead of Part I of that Schedule.

(4) A hospital order shall not cease to have effect under section 40(5) above if a restriction order in respect of the patient is in force at the material time.

(5) Where a restriction order in respect of a patient ceases to have effect while the relevant hospital order continues in force, the provisions of section 40 above and Part I of Schedule 1 to this Act shall apply to the patient as if he had been admitted to the hospital in pursuance of a hospital order (without a restriction order) made on the date on which the restriction order ceased to have effect.

42 Powers of Secretary of State in respect of patients subject to restriction orders

(1) If the Secretary of State is satisfied that in the case of any patient a restriction order is no longer required for the protection of the public from serious harm, he may direct that the patient shall cease to be subject to the special restrictions set out in section 41(3) above; and where the Secretary of State so directs, the restriction order shall cease to have effect, and section 41(5) above shall apply accordingly.

(2) At any time while a restriction order is in force in respect of a patient, the Secretary of State may, if he thinks fit, by warrant discharge the patient from hospital, either absolutely or subject to conditions; and where a person is absolutely discharged under this subsection, he shall thereupon cease to be liable to be detained by virtue of the relevant hospital order, and the restriction order shall cease to have effect accordingly.

(3) The Secretary of State may at any time during the continuance in force of a restriction order in respect of a patient who has been conditionally discharged under subsection (2) above by warrant recall the patient to such hospital as may be specified in the warrant.

(4) Where a patient is recalled as mentioned in subsection (3) above—

    (a) if the hospital specified in the warrant is not the hospital from which the patient was conditionally discharged, the hospital order and the restriction order shall have effect as if the hospital specified in the warrant were substituted for the hospital specified in the hospital order;

    (b) in any case, the patient shall be treated for the purposes of section 18 above as if he had absented himself without leave from the hospital specified in the warrant, and, if the restriction order was made for a specified period, that period shall not in any event expire until the patient returns to the hospital or is returned to the hospital under that section.

(5) If a restriction order in respect of a patient ceases to have effect after the patient has been conditionally discharged under this section, the patient shall, unless previously recalled under subsection (3) above, be deemed to be absolutely discharged on the date when the order ceases to have effect, and shall cease to be liable to be detained by virtue of the relevant hospital order accordingly.

(6) The Secretary of State may, if satisfied that the attendance at any place in Great Britain of a patient who is subject to a restriction order is desirable in the interests of justice or for the purposes of any public inquiry, direct him to be taken to that place; and where a patient is directed under this subsection to be taken to any place he shall, unless the Secretary of State otherwise directs, be kept in custody while being so taken, while at that place and while being taken back to the hospital in which he is liable to be detained.

43 Power of magistrates' courts to commit for restriction order

(1) If in the case of a person of or over the age of 14 years who is convicted by a magistrates' court of an offence punishable on summary conviction with imprisonment—

    (a) the conditions which under section 37(1) above are required to be satisfied for the making of a hospital order are satisfied in respect of the offender; but

    (b) it appears to the court, having regard to the nature of the offence, the antecedents of the offender and the risk of his committing further offences if set at large, that if a hospital order is made a restriction order should also be made,

the court may, instead of making a hospital order or dealing with him in any other manner, commit him in custody to the Crown Court to be dealt with in respect of the offence.

(2) Where an offender is committed to the Crown Court under this section, the Crown Court shall inquire into the circumstances of the case and may—

    (a) if that court would have power so to do under the foregoing provisions of this Part of this Act upon the conviction of the offender before that court of such an offence as is described in section 37(1) above, make a hospital order in his case, with or without a restriction order;

    (b) if the court does not make such an order, deal with the offender in any other manner in which the magistrates' court might have dealt with him.

(3) The Crown Court shall have the same power to make orders under sections 35, 36 and 38 above in the case of a person committed to the court under this section as the Crown Court has under those sections in the case of an accused person within the meaning of section 35 or 36 above or of a person convicted before that court as mentioned in section 38 above.

(4) The power of a magistrates' court under section 38 of the Magistrates' Courts Act 1980 (which enables such a court to commit an offender to the Crown Court where the court is of the opinion that greater punishment should be inflicted for the offence than the court has power to inflict) shall also be exercisable by a magistrates' court where it is of the opinion that greater punishment should be inflicted as aforesaid on the offender unless a hospital order is made in his case with a restriction order.

(5) The power of the Crown Court to make a hospital order, with or without a restriction order, in the case of a person convicted before that court of an offence may, in the same circumstances and subject to the same conditions, be exercised by such a court in the case of a person committed to the court under section 5 of the Vagrancy Act 1824 (which provides for the committal to the Crown Court of persons who are incorrigible rogues within the meaning of that section).

45 Appeals from magistrates' courts

(1) Where on the trial of an information charging a person with an offence a magistrates' court makes a hospital order or guardianship order in respect of him without convicting him, he shall have the same right of appeal against the order as if it had been made on his conviction; and on any such appeal the Crown Court shall have the same powers as if the appeal had been against both conviction and sentence.

(2) An appeal by a child or young person with respect to whom any such order has been made, whether the appeal is against the order or against the finding upon which the order was made, may be brought by him or by his parent or guardian on his behalf.

45A Power of higher courts to direct hospital admission

(1) This section applies where, in the case of a person convicted before the Crown Court of an offence the sentence for which is not fixed by law—
  (a) the conditions mentioned in subsection (2) below are fulfilled; and
  (b) except where the offence is one the sentence for which falls to be imposed under section 109 of the Powers of Criminal Courts (Sentencing) Act 2000, the court considers making a hospital order in respect of him before deciding to impose a sentence of imprisonment ("the relevant sentence") in respect of the offence.

(2) The conditions referred to in subsection (1) above are that the court is satisfied, on the written or oral evidence of two registered medical practitioners—
  (a) that the offender is suffering from psychopathic disorder;
  (b) that the mental disorder from which the offender is suffering is of a nature or degree which makes it appropriate for him to be detained in a hospital for medical treatment; and
  (c) that such treatment is likely to alleviate or prevent a deterioration of his condition.

(3) The court may give both of the following directions, namely—
  (a) a direction that, instead of being removed to and detained in a prison, the offender be removed to and detained in such hospital as may be specified in the direction (in this Act referred to as a "hospital direction"); and
  (b) a direction that the offender be subject to the special restrictions set out in section 41 above (in this Act referred to as a "limitation direction").

(4) A hospital direction and a limitation direction shall not be given in relation to an offender unless at least one of the medical practitioners whose evidence is taken into account by the court under subsection (2) above has given evidence orally before the court.

(5) A hospital direction and a limitation direction shall not be given in relation to an offender unless the court is satisfied on the written or oral evidence of the registered medical practitioner who would be in charge of his treatment, or of some other person representing the managers of the hospital that arrangements have been made—

(a) for his admission to that hospital; and

(b) for his admission to it within the period of 28 days beginning with the day of the giving of such directions;

and the court may, pending his admission within that period, give such directions as it thinks fit for his conveyance to and detention in a place of safety.

(6) If within the said period of 28 days it appears to the Secretary of State that by reason of an emergency or other special circumstances it is not practicable for the patient to be received into the hospital specified in the hospital direction, he may give instructions for the admission of the patient to such other hospital as appears to be appropriate instead of the hospital so specified.

(7) Where such instructions are given—

(a) the Secretary of State shall cause the person having the custody of the patient to be informed, and

(b) the hospital direction shall have effect as if the hospital specified in the instructions were substituted for the hospital specified in the hospital direction.

45B Effect of hospital and limitation directions

(1) A hospital direction and a limitation direction shall be sufficient authority—

(a) for a constable or any other person directed to do so by the court to convey the patient to the hospital specified in the hospital direction within a period of 28 days; and

(b) for the managers of the hospital to admit him at any time within that period and thereafter detain him in accordance with the provisions of this Act.

(2) With respect to any person—

(a) a hospital direction shall have effect as a transfer direction; and

(b) a limitation direction shall have effect as a restriction direction.

(3) While a person is subject to a hospital direction and a limitation direction the responsible medical officer shall at such intervals (not exceeding one year) as the Secretary of State may direct examine and report to the Secretary of State on that person; and every report shall contain such particulars as the Secretary of State may require.

47 Removal to hospital of persons serving sentences of imprisonment, etc

(1) If in the case of a person serving a sentence of imprisonment the Secretary of State is satisfied, by reports from at least two registered medical practitioners—

(a) that the said person is suffering from mental illness, psychopathic disorder, severe mental impairment or mental impairment; and

(b) that the mental disorder from which that person is suffering is of a nature or degree which makes it appropriate for him to be detained in a hospital for medical treatment and, in the case of psychopathic disorder or mental impairment, that such treatment is likely to alleviate or prevent a deterioration of his condition;

the Secretary of State may, if he is of the opinion having regard to the public interest and all the circumstances that it is expedient so to do, by warrant direct that that person be removed to and detained in such hospital (not being a mental nursing home) as may be specified in the direction; and a direction under this section shall be known as "a transfer direction".

(2) A transfer direction shall cease to have effect at the expiration of the period of 14 days beginning with the date on which it is given unless within that period the person with respect to whom it was given has been received into the hospital specified in the direction.

(3) A transfer direction with respect to any person shall have the same effect as a hospital order made in his case.

(4) A transfer direction shall specify the form or forms of mental disorder referred to in paragraph (a) of subsection (1) above from which, upon the reports taken into account under that subsection, the patient is found by the Secretary of State to be suffering; and no such direction shall be given unless the patient is described in each of those reports as suffering

from the same form of disorder, whether or not he is also described in either of them as suffering from another form.

54 Requirements as to medical evidence

(1) The registered medical practitioner whose evidence is taken into account under section 35(3)(a) above and at least one of the registered medical practitioners whose evidence is taken into account under sections 36(1), 37(2)(a), 38(1) and 51(6)(a) above and whose reports are taken into account under sections 47(1) and 48(1) above shall be a practitioner approved for the purposes of section 12 above by the Secretary of State as having special experience in the diagnosis or treatment of mental disorder.

(2) For the purposes of any provision of this Part of this Act under which a court may act on the written evidence of—

    (a) a registered medical practitioner or a registered medical practitioner of any description; or

    (b) a person representing the managers of a hospital,

a report in writing purporting to be signed by a registered medical practitioner or a registered medical practitioner of such a description or by a person representing the managers of a hospital may, subject to the provisions of this section, be received in evidence without proof of the signature of the practitioner or that person and without proof that he has the requisite qualifications or authority or is of the requisite description: but the court may require the signatory of any such report to be called to give oral evidence.

Criminal Procedure (Insanity) Act 1964 (as amended)

5 Powers to deal with persons not guilty by reason of insanity or unfit to plead etc

(1) This section applies where—

    (a) a special verdict is returned that the accused is not guilty by reason of insanity; or

    (b) findings are recorded that the accused is under a disability and that he did the act or made the omission charged against him.

(2) Subject to subsection (3) below, the court shall either—

    (a) make an order that the accused be admitted, in accordance with the provisions of Schedule 1 to the Criminal Procedure (Insanity and Unfitness to Plead) Act 1991, to such hospital as may be specified by the Secretary of State; or

    (b) where they have the power to do so by virtue of section 5 of that Act, make in respect of the accused such one of the following orders as they think most suitable in all the circumstances of the case, namely—

       (i)   a guardianship order within the meaning of the Mental Health Act 1983;

       (ii) a supervision and treatment order within the meaning of Schedule 2 to the said Act of 1991; and

       (iii) an order for his absolute discharge.

(3) Paragraph (b) of subsection (2) above shall not apply where the offence to which the special verdict or findings relate is an offence the sentence for which is fixed by law.

SCHEDULE 1

EFFECT OF ORDERS FOR ADMISSION TO HOSPITAL

1.—(1) An order for admission to hospital under subsection (1) or (2) of section 5 of this Act shall be sufficient authority for any person acting under the authority of the Secretary of

State to take the person to whom the order relates and convey him at any time within the period of two months, in the case of an order under the said subsection (1), or seven days, in the case of an order under the said subsection (2), beginning with the date on which the order was made to the hospital specified by the Secretary of State.

(2) The court by which any such order as aforesaid is made may give such directions as it thinks fit for the conveyance of the person to whom the order relates to a place of safety and his detention therein pending his admission to the hospital within the relevant period mentioned in the foregoing sub-paragraph.

(3) Where a person is admitted within the said period to the hospital specified by the Secretary of State, any such order as aforesaid shall be sufficient authority for the managers to detain him in the hospital in accordance with the provisions of the Mental Health Act, 1959, as applied by the next following paragraph in the case of an order under the said subsection (1) or paragraph 3 of this Schedule in the case of an order under the said subsection (2).

2.—(1) A person who is admitted to a hospital in pursuance of an order under subsection (1) of section 5 of this Act shall be treated for the purposes of the said Act of 1959 as if he had been so admitted in pursuance of a hospital order made, on the date of the first-mentioned order, under section 60 of that Act, together with an order restricting discharge made under section 65 of that Act without limitation of time.

(2) For the purposes of subsection (4) of section 5 of this Act a person shall not be treated as detained in pursuance of an order at any time after the Secretary of State has directed (under section 66 of the said Act of 1959) that the said person shall cease to be subject to the special restrictions set out in the said section 65.

(k) HUMAN RIGHTS

Human Rights Act 1998

Introduction

1 The Convention Rights

(1) In this Act "the Convention rights" means the rights and fundamental freedoms set out in—

(a) Articles 2 to 12 and 14 of the Convention,
(b) Articles 1 to 3 of the First Protocol, and
(c) Articles 1 and 2 of the Sixth Protocol,

as read with Articles 16 to 18 of the Convention.

(2) Those Articles are to have effect for the purposes of this Act subject to any designated derogation or reservation(as to which see sections 14 and 15).

(3) The Articles are set out in Schedule 1.

(4) The Secretary of State may by order make such amendments to this Act as he considers appropriate to reflect the effect, in relation to the United Kingdom, of a protocol.

(5) In subsection(4) "protocol" means a protocol to the Convention—

(a) which the United Kingdom has ratified; or
(b) which the United Kingdom has signed with a view to ratification.

(6) No amendment may be made by an order under subsection(4) so as to come into force before the protocol concerned is in force in relation to the United Kingdom.

2 Interpretation of Convention rights

(1) A court or tribunal determining a question which has arisen in connection with a Convention right must take into account any—

(a) judgment, decision, declaration or advisory opinion of the European Court of Human Rights,

(b) opinion of the Commission given in a report adopted under Article 31 of the Convention,

(c) decision of the Commission in connection with Article 26 or 27(2) of the Convention, or

(d) decision of the Committee of Ministers taken under Article 46 of the Convention,

whenever made or given, so far as, in the opinion of the court or tribunal, it is relevant to the proceedings in which that question has arisen.

(2) Evidence of any judgment, decision, declaration or opinion of which account may have to be taken under this section is to be given in proceedings before any court or tribunal in such manner as may be provided by rules.

(3) In this section "rules" means rules of court or, in the case of proceedings before a tribunal, rules made for the purposes of this section—

(a) by the Lord Chancellor or the Secretary of State, in relation to any proceedings outside Scotland;

(b) by the Secretary of State, in relation to proceedings in Scotland; or

(c) by a Northern Ireland department, in relation to proceedings before a tribunal in Northern Ireland—

(i) which deals with transferred matters; and

(ii) for which no rules made under paragraph(a) are in force.

3 Interpretation of legislation

(1) So far as it is possible to do so, primary legislation and subordinate legislation must be read and given effect in a way which is compatible with the Convention rights.

(2) This section—

(a) applies to primary legislation and subordinate legislation whenever enacted;

(b) does not affect the validity, continuing operation or enforcement of any incompatible primary legislation; and

(c) does not affect the validity, continuing operation or enforcement of any incompatible subordinate legislation if(disregarding any possibility of revocation) primary legislation prevents removal of the incompatibility.

4 Declaration of incompatibility

(1) Subsection (2) applies in any proceedings in which a court determines whether a provision of primary legislation is compatible with a Convention right.

(2) If the court is satisfied that the provision is incompatible with a Convention right, it may make a declaration of that incompatibility.

(3) Subsection(4) applies in any proceedings in which a court determines whether a provision of subordinate legislation, made in the exercise of a power conferred by primary legislation, is compatible with a Convention right.

(4) If the court is satisfied—

(a) that the provision is incompatible with a Convention right, and

(b) that(disregarding any possibility of revocation) the primary legislation concerned prevents removal of the incompatibility,

it may make a declaration of that incompatibility.

(5) In this section "court" means—

(a) the House of Lords;

(b) the Judicial Committee of the Privy Council;

(c) the Courts-Martial Appeal Court;

(d) in Scotland, the High Court of Justiciary sitting otherwise than as a trial court or the Court of Session;

(e) in England and Wales or Northern Ireland, the High Court or the Court of Appeal.

(6) A declaration under this section ("a declaration of

    (a) does not affect the validity, continuing operation or enforcement of the provision in respect of which it is given; and

    (b) is not binding on the parties to the proceedings in which it is made.

5 Right of Crown to intervene

(1) Where a court is considering whether to make a declaration of incompatibility, the Crown is entitled to notice in accordance with rules of court.

(2) In any case to which subsection (1) applies—

    (a) a Minister of the Crown(or a person nominated by him),

    (b) a member of the Scottish Executive,

    (c) a Northern Ireland Minister,

    (d) a Northern Ireland department,

is entitled, on giving notice in accordance with rules of court, to be joined as a party to the proceedings.

(3) Notice under subsection (2) may be given at any time during the proceedings.

(4) A person who has been made a party to criminal proceedings(other than in Scotland) as the result of a notice under subsection (2) may, with leave, appeal to the House of Lords against any declaration of incompatibility made in the proceedings.

(5) In subsection (4)—

"criminal proceedings" includes all proceedings before the Courts-Martial Appeal Court; and

"leave" means leave granted by the court making the declaration of incompatibility or by the House of Lords.

6 Acts of public authorities

(1) It is unlawful for a public authority to act in a way which is incompatible with a Convention right.

(2) Subsection (1) does not apply to an act if—

    (a) as the result of one or more provisions of primary legislation, the authority could not have acted differently; or

    (b) in the case of one or more provisions of, or made under, primary legislation which cannot be read or given effect in a way which is compatible with the Convention rights, the authority was acting so as to give effect to or enforce those provisions.

(3) In this section "public authority" includes—

    (a) a court or tribunal, and

    (b) any person certain of whose functions are functions of a public nature,

but does not include either House of Parliament or a person exercising functions in connection with proceedings in Parliament.

(4) In subsection (3) "Parliament" does not include the House of Lords in its judicial capacity.

(5) In relation to a particular act, a person is not a public authority by virtue only of subsection (3)(b) if the nature of the act is private.

(6) "An act" includes a failure to act but does not include a failure to—

    (a) introduce in, or lay before, Parliament a proposal for legislation; or

    (b) make any primary legislation or remedial order.

7 Proceedings

(1) A person who claims that a public authority has acted(or proposes to act) in a way which is made unlawful by section 6(1) may—

(a) bring proceedings against the authority under this Act in the appropriate court or tribunal, or

(b) rely on the Convention right or rights concerned in any legal proceedings,

but only if he is (or would be) a victim of the unlawful act.

(2) In subsection (1)(a) "appropriate court or tribunal" means such court or tribunal as may be determined in accordance with rules; and proceedings against an authority include a counterclaim or similar proceeding.

(3) If the proceedings are brought on an application for judicial review, the applicant is to be taken to have a sufficient interest in relation to the unlawful act only if he is, or would be, a victim of that act.

(4) If the proceedings are made by way of a petition for judicial review in Scotland, the applicant shall be taken to have title and interest to sue in relation to the unlawful act only if he is, or would be, a victim of that act.

(5) Proceedings under subsection (1)(a) must be brought before the end of—

(a) the period of one year beginning with the date on which the act complained of took place; or

(b) such longer period as the court or tribunal considers equitable having regard to all the circumstances,

but that is subject to any rule imposing a stricter time limit in relation to the procedure in question.

(6) In subsection (1)(b) "legal proceedings" includes—

(a) proceedings brought by or at the instigation of a public authority; and

(b) an appeal against the decision of a court or tribunal.

(7) For the purposes of this section, a person is a victim of an unlawful act only if he would be a victim for the purposes of Article 34 of the Convention if proceedings were brought in the European Court of Human Rights in respect of that act.

(8) Nothing in this Act creates a criminal offence.

(9) In this section "rules" means—

(a) in relation to proceedings before a court or tribunal outside Scotland, rules made by the Lord Chancellor or the Secretary of State for the purposes of this section or rules of court,

(b) in relation to proceedings before a court or tribunal in Scotland, rules made by the Secretary of State for those purposes,

(c) in relation to proceedings before a tribunal in Northern Ireland—

(i)   which deals with transferred matters; and

(ii) for which no rules made under paragraph(a) are in force,

rules made by a Northern Ireland department for those purposes,

and includes provision made by order under section 1 of the Courts and Legal Services Act 1990.

(10) In making rules, regard must be had to section 9.

(11) The Minister who has power to make rules in relation to a particular tribunal may, to the extent he considers it necessary to ensure that the tribunal can provide an appropriate remedy in relation to an act (or proposed act) of a public authority which is(or would be) unlawful as a result of section 6(i), by order add to—

(a) the relief or remedies which the tribunal may grant; or

(b) the grounds on which it may grant any of them.

(12) An order made under subsection(11) may contain such incidental, supplemental, consequential or transitional provision as the Minister making it considers appropriate.

(13) "The Minister" includes the Northern Ireland department concerned.

8 Judicial remedies

(1) In relation to any act (or proposed act) of a public authority which the court finds

is (or would be) unlawful, it may grant such relief or remedy, or make such order, within its powers as it considers just and appropriate.

(2) But damages may be awarded only by a court which has power to award damages, or to order the payment of compensation, in civil proceedings.

(3) No award of damages is to be made unless, taking account of all the circumstances of the case, including—

      (a) any other relief or remedy granted, or order made, in relation to the act in question(by that or any other court), and

      (b) the consequences of any decision (of that or any other court) in respect of that act,

the court is satisfied that the award is necessary to afford just satisfaction to the person in whose favour it is made.

(4) In determining—

      (a) whether to award damages, or

      (b) the amount of an award,

the court must take into account the principles applied by the European Court of Human Rights in relation to the award of

(5) A public authority against which damages are awarded is to be treated—

      (a) in Scotland, for the purposes of section 3 of the Law Reform(Miscellaneous Provisions)(Scotland) Act 1940 as if the award were made in an action of damages in which the authority has been found liable in respect of loss or damage to the person to whom the award is made;

      (b) for the purposes of the Civil Liability(Contribution) Act 1978 as liable in respect of damage suffered by the person to whom the award is made.

(6) In this section—

"court" includes a tribunal;

"damages" means damages for an unlawful act of a public authority; and

"unlawful" means unlawful under section 6(1).

SCHEDULE 1   THE ARTICLES

PART 1   THE CONVENTION

Article 3   Prohibition of torture

No one shall be subjected to torture or to inhuman or degrading treatment or punishment.

Article 5   Right to liberty and security

1.   Everyone has the right to liberty and security of person. No one shall be deprived of his liberty save in the following cases and in accordance with a procedure prescribed by law:

      (a) the lawful detention of a person after conviction by a competent court;

      (b) the lawful arrest or detention of a person for non-compliance with the lawful order of a court or in order to secure the fulfilment of any obligation prescribed by law;

      (c) the lawful arrest or detention of a person effected for the purpose of bringing him before the competent legal authority on reasonable suspicion of having committed an offence or when it is reasonably considered necessary to prevent his committing an offence or fleeing after having done so;

      (d) the detention of a minor by lawful order for the purpose of educational supervision or his lawful detention for the purpose of bringing him before the competent legal authority;

      (e) the lawful detention of persons for the prevention of the spreading of infectious diseases, of persons of unsound mind, alcoholics or drug addicts or vagrants;

(f) the lawful arrest or detention of a person to prevent his effecting an unauthorised entry into the country or of a person against whom action is being taken with a view to deportation or extradition.

2. Everyone who is arrested shall be informed promptly, in a language which he understands, of the reasons for his arrest and of any charge against him.

3. Everyone arrested or detained in accordance with the provisions of paragraph 1(c) of this Article shall be brought promptly before a judge or other officer authorised by law to exercise judicial power and shall be entitled to trial within a reasonable time or to release pending trial. Release may be conditioned by guarantees to appear for trial.

4. Everyone who is deprived of his liberty by arrest or detention shall be entitled to take proceedings by which the lawfulness of his detention shall be decided speedily by a court and his release ordered if the detention is not lawful.

5. Everyone who has been the victim of arrest or detention in contravention of the provisions of this Article shall have an enforceable right to compensation.

Article 7   No punishment without law

1. No one shall be held guilty of any criminal offence on account of any act or omission which did not constitute a criminal offence under national or international law at the time when it was committed. Nor shall a heavier penalty be imposed than the one that was applicable at the time the criminal offence was committed.

2. This Article shall not prejudice the trial and punishment of any person for any act or omission which, at the time when it was committed, was criminal according to the general principles of law recognised by civilised nations.

(I) REHABILITATION

Rehabilitation of Offenders Act 1974 (as amended)

1   Rehabilitated persons and spent convictions

(1) Subject to subsection (2) below, where an individual has been convicted, whether before or after the commencement of this Act, of any offence or offences, and the following conditions are satisfied, that is to say—

(a) he did not have imposed on him in respect of that conviction a sentence which is excluded from rehabilitation under this Act; and

(b) he has not had imposed on him in respect of a subsequent conviction during the rehabilitation period applicable to the first-mentioned conviction in accordance with section 6 below a sentence which is excluded from rehabilitation under this Act;

then, after the end of the rehabilitation period so applicable (including, where appropriate, any extension under section 6 (4) below of the period originally applicable to the first-mentioned conviction) or, where that rehabilitation period ended before the commencement of this Act, after the commencement of this Act, that individual shall for the purposes of this Act be treated as a rehabilitated person in respect of the first-mentioned conviction and that conviction shall for those purposes be treated as spent.

(2) A person shall not become a rehabilitated person for the purposes of this Act in respect of a conviction unless he has served or otherwise undergone or complied with any sentence imposed on him in respect of that conviction; but the following shall not, by virtue of this subsection, prevent a person from becoming a rehabilitated person for those purposes—

(a) failure to pay a fine or other sum adjudged to be paid by or imposed on a conviction, or breach of a condition of a recognizance or of a bond of caution to keep the peace or be of good behaviour;

(b) breach of any condition or requirement applicable in relation to a sentence which renders the person to whom it applies liable to be dealt with for the offence for which the sentence was imposed, or, where the sentence was a suspended sentence of imprisonment, liable to be dealt with in respect of that sentence (whether or not, in any case, he is in fact so dealt with);

(c) failure to comply with any requirement of a suspended sentence supervision order.

(3) In this Act "sentence" includes any order made by a court in dealing with a person in respect of his conviction of any offence or offences, other than—

(a) an order for committal or any other order made in default of payment of any fine or other sum adjudged to be paid by or imposed on a conviction, or for want of sufficient distress to satisfy any such fine or other sum;

(b) an order dealing with a person in respect of a suspended sentence of imprisonment.

(4) In this Act, references to a conviction, however expressed, include references—

(a) to a conviction by or before a court outside Great Britain; and

(b) to any finding (other than a finding linked with a finding of insanity) in any criminal proceedings or in care proceedings under section 1 of the Children and Young Persons Act 1969 that a person has committed an offence or done the act or made the omission charged;

and notwithstanding anything in section 9 of the Criminal Justice (Scotland) Act 1949 or section 14 of the Powers of Criminal Courts (Sentencing) Act 2000 (conviction of a person discharged to be deemed not to be a conviction) a conviction in respect of which an order is made discharging him absolutely or conditionally shall be treated as a conviction for the purposes of this Act and the person in question may become a rehabilitated person in respect of that conviction and the conviction a spent conviction for those purposes accordingly.

4   Effect of rehabilitation

(1) Subject to sections 7 and 8 below, a person who has become a rehabilitated person for the purposes of this Act in respect of a conviction shall be treated for all purposes in law as a person who has not committed or been charged with or prosecuted for or convicted of or sentenced for the offence or offences which were the subject of that conviction; and, notwithstanding the provisions of any other enactment or rule of law to the contrary, but subject as aforesaid—

(a) no evidence shall be admissible in any proceedings before a judicial authority exercising its jurisdiction or functions in Great Britain to prove that any such person has committed or been charged with or prosecuted for or convicted of or sentenced for any offence which was the subject of a spent conviction; and

(b) a person shall not, in any such proceedings, be asked, and, if asked, shall not be required to answer, any question relating to his past which cannot be answered without acknowledging or referring to a spent conviction or spent convictions or any circumstances ancillary thereto.

(2) Subject to the provisions of any order made under subsection (4) below, where a question seeking information with respect to a person's previous convictions, offences, conduct or circumstances is put to him or to any other person otherwise than in proceedings before a judicial authority—

(a) the question shall be treated as not relating to spent convictions or to any circumstances ancillary to spent convictions, and the answer thereto may be framed accordingly; and

(b) the person questioned shall not be subjected to any liability or otherwise prejudiced in law by reason of any failure to acknowledge or disclose a spent conviction or any circumstances ancilary to a spent conviction in his answer to the question.

(5) For the purposes of this section and section 7 below any of the following are circumstances ancillary to a conviction, that is to say—

(a) the offence or offences which were the subject of that conviction;

(b) the conduct constituting that offence or those offences; and

(c) any process or proceedings preliminary to that conviction, any sentence imposed in respect of that conviction, any proceedings (whether by way of appeal or otherwise) for reviewing that conviction or any such sentence, and anything done in pursuance of or undergone in compliance with any such sentence.

(6) For the purposes of this section and section 7 below "proceedings before a judicial authority" includes, in addition to proceedings before any of the ordinary courts of law, proceedings before any tribunal, body or person having power—

(a) by virtue of any enactment, law, custom or practice;

(b) under the rules governing any association, institution, profession, occupation or employment; or

(c) under any provision of any agreement providing for arbitration with respect to questions arising thereunder;

to determine any question affecting the rights, privileges, obligations or liabilities of any person, or to receive evidence affecting the determination of any such question.

5 Rehabilitation periods for particular sentences

(1) The sentences excluded from rehabilitation under this Act are—

(a) a sentence of Imprisonment for life;

(b) a sentence of imprisonment, youth custody detention in a young offender institution or corrective training for a term exceeding thirty months;

(c) a sentence of preventive detention;

(d) a sentence of detention during Her Majesty's pleasure or for life, under section 90 or 91 of the Powers of Criminal Courts (Sentencing) Act 2000, or under section 205(2) or (3) of the Criminal Procedure (Scotland) Act 1975 or a sentence of detention for a term exceeding thirty months passed under section 91 of the said Act of 2000 (young offenders convicted of grave crimes) or under section 206 of the said Act of 1975 (detention of children convicted on indictment), or a corresponding court-martial punishment, and

(e) a sentence of custody for life.

and any other sentence is a sentence subject to rehabilitation under this Act.

(1A) In subsection (1)(d) above "corresponding court-martial punishment" means a punishment awarded under section 71A(3) or (4) of the Army Act 1955, section 71A(9) or (4) of the Air Force Act 1955 or section 43A(3) or (4) of the Naval Discipline Act 1957.

(2) For the purposes of this Act—

(a) the rehabilitation period applicable to a sentence specified in the first column of Table A below is the period specified in the second column of that Table in relation to that sentence, or, where the sentence was imposed on a person who was under eighteen years of age at the date of his conviction, half that period; and

(b) the rehabilitation period applicable to a sentence specified in the first column of Table B below is the period specified in the second column of that Table in relation to that sentence;

reckoned in either case from the date of the conviction in respect of which the sentence was imposed.

(3) The rehabilitation period applicable—

(a) to an order discharging a person absolutely for an offence; and

(b) to the discharge by a children's hearing under section 69(1)(b) and (12) of the
Children (Scotland) Act 1995 of the referral of a child's case;
shall be six months from the date of conviction.

(4) Where in respect of a conviction a person was conditionally discharged, bound over
to keep the peace or he of good behaviour . . . the rehabilitation period applicable to the
sentence shall be one year from the date of conviction or a period beginning with that
date and ending when the order for conditional discharge . . . or (as the case may be) the
recognizance or bond of caution to keep the peace or be of good behaviour ceases or ceased to
have effect, whichever is the longer.

(4A) Where in respect of a conviction a person was placed on probation, the rehabilitation period applicable to the sentence shall be—

(a) in the case of a person aged eighteen years or over at the date of his conviction.
five years from the date of his conviction.
(b) in the case of a person aged under the age of eighteen years at the date of his
conviction, two and a half years from the date of conviction or a period beginning
with the date of conviction and ending when the probation order ceases or ceased
to have effect whichever is the longer.

(4B) Where is respect of a conviction a referral order (within the meaning of the Powers
of Criminal Courts (Sentencing) Act 2000) is made in respect of the person convicted, the
rehabilitation period applicable to the sentence shall be—

(a) if a youth offender contract takes effect under section 23 of that Act between him
and a youth offender panel, the period beginning with the date of conviction and
ending on the date when (in accordance with section 24 of the Act) the contract
ceases to have effect;
(b) if no such contract so takes effect, the period beginning with the date of conviction and having the same length as the period for which such a contract would
ignoring any order under paragraph 11 or 12 of Schedule 1 to that Act have had
effect had one so taken effect.

(4C) Where in respect of a conviction an order is made in respect of the person convicted
under paragraph 11 or 12 of Schedule 1 to the Powers of Criminal Court (Sentencing) Act 2000

Table A Rehabilitation periods subject to reduction by half for persons under18

Sentence	Rehabilitation period
A sentence of imprisonment, detention in a young offender institution or youth custody or corrective training for a term exceeding six months but not exceeding thirty months.	Ten years
A sentence of cashiering, discharge with ignominy or dismissal with disgrace from Her Majesty's service.	Ten years
A sentence of imprisonment, detention in a young offender institution or youth custody for a term not exceeding six months.	Seven years
A sentence of dismissal from Her Majesty's service.	Seven years
Any sentence of detention in respect of a conviction in service disciplinary proceedings.	Five years
A fine or any other sentence subject to rehabilitation under this Act, not being a sentence to which Table B below or any of subsections (3) to (8) below applies.	Five years

Table B Rehabilitation periods for certain sentences confined to young offenders

Sentence	Rehabilitation period
A sentence of Borstal training.	Seven years
A custodial order under Schedule 5A to the Army Act 1955 or the Air Force Act 1955, or under Schedule 4A to the Naval Discipline Act 1957, where the maximum period of detention specified in the order is more than six months.	Seven years
A custodial order under section 71AA of the Army Act 1955 or the Air Force Act 1955, or under section 43AA of the Naval Discipline Act 1957, where the maximum period of detention specified in the order is more than six months.	Seven years
A sentence of detention for a term exceeding six months but not exceeding thirty months passed under section 91 of the Powers of Criminal Courts (Sentencing) Act 2000 or under section 206 of the Criminal Procedure (Scotland) Act 1975.	Five years
Any sentence of detention for a term not exceeding six months passed under either of those provisions.	Three years
An order for detention in a detention centre made under section 4 of the Criminal Justice Act 1982 or section 4 of the Criminal Justice Act 1961.	Three years
A custodial order under any of the Schedules to the said Acts of 1955 and 1957 mentioned above, where the maximum period of detention specified in the order is six months or less.	Three years
A custodial order under section 71AA of the said Acts of 1955, or section 43AA of the said Act of 1957, where the maximum period of detention specified in the order is six months or less.	Three years

(extension of period for which youth offender contract has effects the rehabilitation period applicable to the sentence shall be—

    (a) if a youth offender contract takes effect under section 23 of that Act between the offender and a youth offender panel, the period beginning with the date of conviction and ending on the date when (in accordance with section 24 of that Act) the contract ceases to have effect

    (b) if no such contract so takes effect, the period beginning with the date of conviction and having the same length as the period for which, in accordance with the order, such a contract would have had effect had one no taken effect.

6   The rehabilitation period applicable to a conviction

(1) Where only one sentence is imposed in respect of a conviction (not being a sentence excluded from rehabilitation under this Act) the rehabilitation period applicable to the conviction is, subject to the following provisions of this section, the period applicable to the sentence in accordance with section 5 above.

(2) Where more than one sentence is imposed in respect of a conviction (whether or not in the same proceedings) and none of the sentences imposed is excluded from rehabilitation under this Act, then, subject to the following provisions of this section, if the periods applicable to those sentences in accordance with section 5 above differ, the rehabilitation period applicable to the conviction shall be the longer or the longest (as the case may be) of those periods.

(4) Subject to subsection (5) below, where during the rehabilitation period applicable to a conviction—

    (a) the person convicted is convicted of a further offence; and

(b) no sentence excluded from rehabilitation under this Act is imposed on him in respect of the later conviction;

if the rehabilitation period applicable in accordance with this section to either of the convictions would end earlier than the period so applicable in relation to the other, the rehabilitation period which would (apart from this subsection) end the earlier shall be extended so as to end at the same time as the other rehabilitation period.

(5) Where the rehabilitation period applicable to a conviction is the rehabilitation period applicable in accordance with section 5 (8) above to an order imposing on a person any disqualification, disability, prohibition or other penalty, the rehabilitation period applicable to another conviction shall not by virtue of subsection (4) above be extended by reference to that period; but if any other sentence is imposed in respect of the first-mentioned conviction for which a rehabilitation period is prescribed by any other provision of section 5 above, the rehabilitation period applicable to another conviction shall, where appropriate, be extended under subsection (4) above by reference to the rehabilitation period applicable in accordance with that section to that sentence or, where more than one such sentence is imposed, by reference to the longer or longest of the periods so applicable to those sentences, as if the period in question were the rehabilitation period applicable to the first-mentioned conviction.

7 Limitations on rehabilitation under this Act, etc.

(1) Nothing in section 4 (1) above shall affect—

(a) any right of Her Majesty, by virtue of Her Royal prerogative or otherwise, to grant a free pardon, to quash any conviction or sentence, or to commute any sentence;

(b) the enforcement by any process or proceedings of any fine or other sum adjudged to be paid by or imposed on a spent conviction;

(c) the issue of any process for the purpose of proceedings in respect of any breach of a condition or requirement applicable to a sentence imposed in respect of a spent conviction; or

(d) the operation of any enactment by virtue of which, in consequence of any conviction, a person is subject, otherwise than by way of sentence, to any disqualification, disability, prohibition or other penalty the period of which extends beyond the rehabilitation period applicable in accordance with section 6 above to the conviction.

(2) Nothing in section 4 (1) above shall affect the determination of any issue, or prevent the admission or requirement of any evidence, relating to a person's previous convictions or to circumstances ancillary thereto—

(a) in any criminal proceedings before a court in Great Britain (including any appeal or reference in a criminal matter);

(b) in any service disciplinary proceedings or in any proceedings on appeal from any service disciplinary proceedings;

(bb) in any proceedings on an application for a sex offender under section 2 or, as the case may be, 20 of the Crime and Disorder Act 1998 or in any appeal against the making of such an order;

(c) in any proceedings relating to adoption or to the guardianship, wardship, marriage, custody, care or control of, or access to, any minor, or to the provision by any person of accommodation, care or schooling for minors;

(cc) in any proceedings under Part II of the Children (Scotland) Act 1995;

(d) in any care proceedings under the Powers of Criminal Courts (Sentencing) Act 2000 or on appeal from any such proceedings, or in any proceedings relating to the variation or discharge of a care order or supervision order under that Act;

(e) in any proceedings before a children's hearing under the Social Work (Scotland) Act 1968 or on appeal from any such hearing; or

(f) in any proceedings in which he is a party or a witness, provided that, on the occasion when the issue or the admission or requirement of the evidence falls to be determined, he consents to the determination of the issue or, as the case may be, the admission or requirement of the evidence notwithstanding the provisions of section 4 (1).

In the application of this subsection to Scotland, "minor" means a child under the age of eighteen, including a pupil child.

INDEX